THE SPORTS AFIELD
TREASURY OF FLY FISHING

Delta Books of Interest:

NIGHT FISHING FOR TROUT
Jim Bashline

OPEN SEASON: Sporting Adventures
William Humphrey

THE

TREASURY OF
FLY FISHING

EDITED BY TOM PAUGH

Delta

A Delta Book
Published by
Dell Publishing
a division of
Bantam Doubleday Dell Publishing Group, Inc.
666 Fifth Avenue
New York, New York 10103

ISBN: 0-385-30246-0

Reprinted by arrangement with Lyons & Burford, Publishers

Manufactured in the United States of America

Published simultaneously in Canada

April 1992

10 9 8 7 6 5 4 3 2 1

RRH

ACKNOWLEDGMENT

"I am the editor of this book," I said, "It will say so on the cover and on the inside. That means that I am the one who decides which stories will be in and which out!"

"Yes, but," the other person said, "that story is boring, boring, boring and this one I like."

"Okay, okay," I said, "I'll read it."

The other person, of course, was Anne Paugh, my wife of 35 years and counting. I had long ago learned to take her advice seriously. She is a puzzle person—crossword, jigsaw, you name it—and therefore a person of patience. I am a restless decision maker. Right or wrong I am not afraid to choose. It was Anne's job to dig out all the flyfishing material run in *Sports Afield* over the past century-plus so that I could read and select. Of course, Anne, a voracious reader, could not resist giving me little hints as to what I should choose and what I should leave out; little penciled subtleties such as "lousy" or "a winner."

So I hereby thank Anne for her hard work collecting all that flyfishing verbiage from past issues, her back-straining hours over the copier, her weekends spent cutting and pasting to create order from chaos. Without her dedication and enthusiasm this book would be considerably less than it is.

CONTENTS

INTRODUCTION

Flyfishing is very much a sport of the times. As far as *Sports Afield* is concerned it always has been. The following poem was written especially for the magazine in 1889 during its third year of publication in Denver, Colorado.

THE WHOLE STORY

by Dan De Foe

The fluttering fly
Is tossed on high,
And lightly on the pool descends.
In shade of ash,
A flash, a splash
The reel responds, the bamboo bends.

With twitch and twirl,
And swish and swirl,
The ripples wide and wider whirl—
Speeding, receding,
The line scarcely heeding;
'Mid boulders and eddies,
A frantic chase leading—
The prize contends,
Retreats, defends—

Aha—he's done—he scarcely bends
  The yielding cane;
  His struggles wane—
The net! and lo, the conflict ends.

Well, maybe not Shakespeare, but a lyric tribute nonetheless to this particular area of fishing expertise. Whoever wrote a poem about spincasting?

From that same issue published more than a century ago comes flyfishing advice from a reluctant expert who suggests that information gained "through long months, aye, years of toil" perhaps should not easily be passed on "to Tom, Dick and Harry." Of course he then proceeds to pontificate anyway, mostly, I think, so that he can relate the tale of how he caught the largest "river trout" of his life on Maine's Mad River using a fly rod that was "made out of cedar from butt to tip, did not exceed nine ounces, and was the most lively, quick, light casting treasure I ever used."

Flyfishing is still flyfishing and so we can relate to that time. Presenting the fly, experiencing the strike, fighting the fish on hook, line, rod, and reel, netting the quarry, are the eternals of the sport that we can share with all anglers back to Izaak Walton. So much remains the same . . . but so very much has changed. What would our friend with the cedar rod think of the action of a modern-quality graphite nine-footer weighing less than four ounces? Wouldn't you love to show him a nylon tapered leader tied to a weight-forward plastic-coated bright orange fly line, or watch his face as you revealed the contents of your own over-stuffed fishing vest item by item?

It is the essential spirit of flyfishing that remains the constant, the tools of the trade that mark the times. And now we have this book, which reveals the sport and its practitioners over the years as *Sports Afield* contributors, then and now, wrote fondly, with wit and depth, about this subject so dear to their hearts—and ours.

"There is certainly something in angling that tends to produce a gentleness of spirit and a pure serenity of mind."

WASHINGTON IRVING

BATTLING WITH
A SALMON

Lawrence Wilson

*Alternately sulking and surging, a "big" Irish
salmon proves to be both a problem and a surprise.
(July 1889)*

I WAS enjoying my after-breakfast pipe on the piazza of one of the most hospitable of Irish manor houses one lovely morning in autumn—just as the leaves were donning their variegated dresses of red and yellow—when, looking up, I chanced to notice the keeper coming across the grass plot which lies between the river and the house. He looked the very picture of stalwart manhood as he strolled along with his usual lazy gait. On seeing me he stopped, and we each bade each other the time of day. "Ah, but it's the river as what you should see, sir," he said, "sure an' it's in splendid trim, and a finer morning to try for a salmon I've not seen this many a day." I suppose, in his case at least, the wish was father to the thought. Be that as it may, I "rose" at the idea, in much the same manner as a lazy old trout rises to the fly which he has no intention of taking. But my host arriving on the scene, advises me to be off, regretting at the same time his inability to accompany me. Thus admonished, I stroll over to the game keeper's lodge, in the direction of the park gates, where I don the fisher's garb. I almost envy my good-natured guide the consummate skill with which he selects me a rod from some ten or a dozen standing in a rack in the gun-room. "This heavy one is Sir Hugh's" he says, showing me an old and much used rod; "ah, but its the fine sight to see him play a big 'un!"

The flies are next selected, a gaff picked up, and, the keeper having slipped a stout brown flask into one of his capacious pockets, we are off for the river.

I had whipped the water a number of times with no visible result, when, about my tenth cast, as the fly was floating down to the end of a swirl, I saw a sudden movement in the water and struck. Alas! I had struck too soon. The keeper scolds me with evident good humor as he puts on a new fly, remarking, "Perhaps you'll be more to the gentleman's liking" (meaning Mr. Salmon). And now, wading out about ten yards, I cast again and begin working down gradually to the place where I had first risen the fish. About the seventh cast covered the place where he had been lying. No sign of him. I tried two more; still all was quiet. The next cast, however, resulted very differently—there was another glimmer of light, another rush, and another strike. The rod bends and quivers, and I have him fast.

"Keep the point of your rod up, sir." "Give him more line." "Tighten up now, sir!" "Ease him a little, Mr. Lawrence." And similar expressions salute my ears every minute.

"Little, I can feel him now; he's a big one," I exclaim, as the line begins to spin out—Mr. Salmon rushing up-stream the meanwhile. Still he keeps on, and my line is nearly all run out. I work my way to the bank, hoping to check him; but I cannot. There is no other course left me but to run with the fish, which I do for about 200 yards along the bank, until he reaches the pool next above the one I had hooked him in. And there he doggedly sulks. We now try stones, sticks, strong language, everything, to move him; but all is of no avail. At last Little leaves me, to soon reappear round a bend in the river, paddling a light skiff. He has a punting pole with him, with which he soon commences "prodding" in the direction of our fish. Suddenly—of course, at the most unexpected moment—whirr, whirr, whirr! the line sings out and he is off again down-stream—I running helter-skelter after him. And now we come to a place where the river makes a sharp turn, and I must either cross it or lose my fish. Whilst I was debating which to do, Little rushes up, quite out of breath, and tells me to cross, saying I could get through without letting in the water. I tried—the second

step sending me in about five feet. The splash I made seemed to lend Mr. Salmon renewed force, and off he went like mad. My waders were full, and so heavy as to render me useless. (I had only about twenty yards of line left).

"Hold on a bit," says Little, slipping off his heavy shoes; and then, with a "Give me the rod, sir," he slipped into the water and half swam and half walked to the opposite bank. The picture he presented—half drowned as he was, yet still gamely playing a very game fish—is one I shall never forget. Emptying my waders, I dashed along to a ford some distance further down, and crossing over, joined my guide, philosopher and friend.

"Keep a cool head, sir," says Little, handing me the rod, "and you've got him safe."

I wound up slowly, drawing my fish nearer and nearer. At last we saw him, and the same remark burst from both of us simultaneously: "My! What a small one!" But the end was not yet—an ill-advised gesture of mine sending him off again like a flash. These tactics he repeated once more; but it was plain that he was giving up.

Little makes one or two imaginary passes with the gaff (a deadly weapon in his hands); and I commence to reel in. The keeper by this time is kneeling close to the water's edge, as rigid as a statue; but as the now thoroughly exhausted fish approaches the bank there is a swift movement and uprising on his part, and the next minute a 12¾-pound salmon lands with a thump on the sward directly back of us. When it was all over I realized how tired I was. I had hooked Mr. Salmon in the tail, and it had taken me a little less than three and one-half hours to land him. We lay and rested for a brief period after the battle—Little mixing me a mild bracer and taking a very liberal one himself from the bottle of "Mountain Dew" in his pocket. And so ends the greatest fight with a fish I ever had.

THE DEMON OF THE FOAM

H. Prescott Beach

*Split bamboo and a Silver Doctor: "Many a
seemingly incurable case thy power has overcome."
(June 1894)*

IT IS A wild, swirling river that opens when you leave the placid Lake
St. John, dark and restless, full of rifts and eddies. The path of this torrent
is far from smooth, blocked as it is by jagged ledges and polished, water-
worn boulders that push back and fret the eager stream. Round and round
the hollowed basins scooped out of living rock by the struggles of the
waters pent up like caged beasts, the currents whirl like giant mills. The
wheels of these mills are never idle. Years as numberless as the creases cut
by the tide in the hard, black stone have passed since first the flood felt the
rough barriers thrown across its way, driving its drops back into this weary
bondage, where to-day they are still slaving, grinding the blackness into
bubbles that rise and drift and shine. An outstretched arm of the reef
gathers in these gleaming jewels as they come and piles them in a mass,
an island of floating foam. These islands are the gleaming spots that flash

upon you when first the birch-bark feels the throbbing, the heaving of the river and leaps forward like a living thing. Strange, startling is the effect of these creamy mounds that lie here and there upon the sullen swirls like ivory set in ebony. They are too like old ivory, stained and discolored, for with them are gathered in all the chips and saw-dust and dead boughs and stumps that have come down from the woods.

Queer moths and millers hover all day around the yellow islands. They dance and flit untiringly over the drift, seeking their tiny prey— miniature sea terns skirting little shores. Brown, drab, buff and black flecked with scarlet, twinkle in the sunshine and skim over the surface in airy play. Now and again there is a ripple on the water, a crease, a wrinkle, a dimple in the foam; sometimes it is a heavy splash and one or more of the dancers disappears. As the sun gets higher the dance grows livelier; thousands of wings are beating time in the warmth and glow, and as the revels swell the revellers one by one drop and are lost. What is this little flurry, this stir upon the froth that brings such sudden end to these innocent moths? Only is a dark form visible for an instant; a waving toss of a glistening tail, a plunge and the thing is gone. This is a very dance of death! And this spectre, this destroyer—half seen and half imagined—swift, cunning and relentless; who and what is it? It is the Demon of the Foam. It is the Ouananiche.

Through the mists of early morning that hang over the rapids is gliding a bark canoe. Three men are in the craft; one gray-haired and old who peers through the fog, and two—long-armed they are and dark of skin— are keeping the course with strong strokes of their paddles. These are bold spirits who hold their way amid this rush of water—who do not jump when the bark grazes an ugly rock—or quivering, slides over a hidden ledge to dash her mouth into a caldron below. They only smile when she careens against a floating timber and drinks—yes, stoops and drinks—a bucket-full of green water, though he of the gray hair clutches the thwart more tightly and leans lower to the far side. Too many times have these weather-painted Chippewas felt their way down this same path of whirl-pools to feel uneasy when the bright fringe of a wave curls over the edge and the swash sprinkles their skins. They were boys upon this same stream, swimming its maddest freshets and knowing its every turn and trick. The one at the bow is On-ik-mah (the kingfisher) and the stout fellow at the stern is Mon-ah-quic (the paddle-lover) both trusty and two of Patterson's best guides. The elder man amidships—still young in his love for ways in the woods, the streams and the open sky; too full of wonder; too wrapped in watching this unquiet scene to feel afraid—is my old self, and we are shooting Le Grande Décharge.

Into calm and still water at last we slip; calm and still only as compared with yon wild mill-race above, for does it not boil and seethe all around us who drift along the foam? It is here I put together my well-tried split-bamboo and, with feverish fingers, thread the eyelets with the filmy gray silk. The slender thing shakes like an aspen in my hands as I feel for my fly-book, hardly able in my panic of anticipations to unfasten the leathern strap. Then a moment of indecision. My eye runs over the gorgeous bits of feather and is led from blue to crimson, from crimson to green, from green to gold, from gold to black and from black to white, each seeming more alluring—more beautiful—than the last. Then I forsake them all and, turning to the last leaf, my finger plays among a few flies of quiet tones. Here are the Hackles, brown, red and gray; here is the Dun Midge and the Montreal; and here, half-hidden by less worthy wings, is nestled the tempter of them all—the Silver Doctor.

"A famous medicine-man thou art, too, old friend," I murmur as I bend

it fluttering to the leader, "and many a seemingly incurable case thy power has overcome. Would that the human leech of to-day had so little of show and pretense as thou in thy modest cloak, and but a half of thy unfailing skill. Here stretch thy wings again!"

The guides, with paddles stayed, leaned forward to watch as the invisible line followed the speck of gray that shot out toward the nearest patch of foam. Among a band of brown millers it alighted gayest of all the dancers, and fell as with tired pinions, helpless to the water, there to struggle for life. Its small tumult does not disturb the others, who skip on as aimlessly and as lightly as before, but down below, in the shadow of that reef of bubbles, fierce eyes are watching—eyes that see every speck that floats and even the reflections of things in the air. Instantly and without warning, there comes a tumbling leap of foam, and from the island rises a sharp fin that plunges in again. It has tried for the Doctor and it missed him. Another cast and the M. D. flickers away over beyond the outside of the eddy. Barely does he strike, when—splash! again the rise and the silvery moth has gone. The pliant rod curls to a round letter O when I draw back and find that the hook has gone home. The Demon has caught this latest dancer and has carried him down to his cave. Now the water swirls again, broken by an angry leap, and the Demon thrashes out into the mid-tide. It feels the goad now and knows this victim has a sting. Gladly, Ouananiche of the Foam, wouldst cast forth this bitter morsel, but it clings; it grapples thy cruel jaw with a strength that never yields to thine!

Back, back to its old haunt it returns, diving deep into the green gulf, striving hard to drag loose the unfeeling line, shaking its strong head in madness, rushing fast and hard. Turn from the tangled float of logs beyond, good fish! What! You will not? Oh, how that stout reed bends and writhes when I give this mighty fish the butt! It is a struggle, and for an instant I feared; then felt the pull lessen and the furious fellow lunged past the canoe in full flight up-stream. Nothing can check him for thirty yards or more, when he flashes to the top and vaults high into air; then his strength ebbing, he turns with the tide and, fighting out toward the centre, hangs sullen and lies still. A sharp shaking sends him on—this time weak but still game—and taking advantage of the eddies, he whirls off around a low boulder. Was he free? No! the line had followed over the top, not twisted around the rock where it would surely have parted, and the Demon is not yet free. No charm for him now in the swarm of gay flies; he settles deeper in the basin and digs for the bottom. Persistently I urge him upward—rebelling, sulking, but slowly giving way. His dark mottled back gleams for a moment beside the bark when I raise him and Kingfisher, with a ready net, lifts him into the boat.

I take a long breath of triumph. This is a good fish—a four-pound catch—and I rise in the bark and point out another pool below where a heavy plunge has just sent the spray flying. Thither we go and, letting the canoe drift against a big snag, I send the Doctor flying out over the foam. For a time he pirouettes and prances all in vain. Nothing heeds his antics and yet beyond, every moment or two, a rise tells the death of some real, living harlequin. Kingfisher yawns and I glare at him. What does the man want? Does he think I am a magician that I should land four-pound fish every other minute? He avoids my glance and says something in Chippewa to the other. They look off at the clouds and smile. I demand to know what he said and do not believe it when he calmly replies, "That day was got warm 'fore noon." There is no time to scold, for—whiz! my reel calls me back to fishing. A demon has hooked himself during the discussion and now he is carrying my good line down stream at a furious rate. No giving this chap the butt! We follow in the birch-bark, keeping clear of the thick brush and dead debris that is jammed among the rocks, and corner him in a narrow hole. Here he gives battle for the first and last time; here he smashes my favorite tip, and here at the end I bring him to net—savage to the very finish—a giant Ouananiche of seven pounds.

Kingfisher unbent himself so far as to smile a dignified approval on the great flapping fish; then relapsed into his ordinary graven image condition.

"Brother mine catch one fish long tam go mos' twice big sam's that!" he ventured, running the canoe out into the current again. Once more we found a temporary harbor in a rocky cove behind a high point of hemlocks half a mile below the Grande Décharge. Here the flecks or spots of foam were small, not more than a yard across, and slowly floated around with the eddy. In some places one could see as many as four Ouananiche feeding beneath and around one mass of bubbles, their sharp dorsal fins cutting the surface in every direction. Surely, this was a promising lair.

"Too much feesh; no bite any!" was Kingfisher's comment, but it was not until I had exhausted my stock of flies and had sent flitting over the pool, Scarlet Ibises, Coachmen, Parmachene Belles and Seth Greens without even a passing nibble, that I had faith in his diagnosis. Why it was so I could not discover. Here were the fish, and big ones, too; they were feeding, too, as was testified by their long leaps and flashing springs after the live moths. At last I hit upon an expedient. I had often heard of trolling for the Ouananiche but had never believed it possible to accomplish any good results in that way. In my breast-pocket was a tin case filled with miscellaneous traps and among them a brass pickerel-spoon which I had made after a peculiar design of my own. It had slain its scores of pickerel and many bass and, as results showed, was ready to conquer new foes.

I bent it on a stout braided line and, biting over the line a split buckshot just above the spoon, insured its sinking to a depth of six inches or so, even when the canoe moved at a rapid rate. The guides sent us spinning across the pool and behind gleamed the new bait which I have named the "Golden Death." Scarcely had we gone a dozen paddle-strokes when a smashing tug made me brace myself for a struggle. It was a monster; but with a tearing plunge he freed himself and was gone in a shower of spray. Another snatched as he let go and that one, too, managed to shake out the grapple of hooks at the first jump. The third—a smaller fish—took the whole thing fairly and, badly struck, bolted for the shore. Of course, with a heavy linen line I "snubbed" him easily and, though he finned it furiously, dragged him in after a few minutes of resistance.

Barely did that bit of whirling brass touch the water again ere a mighty fellow attacked and captured it, throwing himself a full yard out of water when he felt the barb. Wildly he dove and tugged below; eagerly he worked the line out toward the river; swiftly he headed for his deep hole below and, oh! how he withstood my remorseless twitches and heavy pulls, reaching out with every ounce of muscle (and he was all muscle) for his old den. Despite my every effort he gained his stronghold—down oh! so far —and there he lay unmoving. No device could start or stir him from his hiding place now; see-sawing the line, jerking it, sagging back till I feared it would part, were of no avail. Then suddenly, of his own accord, he tore up to the very edge of the canoe, skating past our very eyes with slack enough to free himself ten times over if he had not been frightfully hooked. Three or four times he dashed into the air, turning complete somersaults, then made six or more short, mad rushes like a bull, once charging the canoe and scraping its side as he went under the bottom. When at last he came, breathless and beaten, to the net he bit and snapped at the meshes as if he would tear all to bits. In the bottom of the birch-bark he lay, angrily clashing his jaws till he died. Though not so large as my second fish, he was more powerful. Five more of these beautiful captives we took with the spoon in this placid cove under the overhanging hemlocks, and then, no more appearing, we gave up a little before noon and put ashore for lunch.

There on a bank of soft moss, with those great trees leaning over me and the broad, curling, petulant river before me, I lay and smoked after our simple meal. On broad, green leaves lay the noble, handsome fish. Bravely had they fought and bravely died, and it was with almost a reverent touch, when we headed home for the Island House now two miles away, that I laid them in the basket. It was my first day of many, many happy ones among the grandest fish in all the Canadas—the king of the whirl-pools, the Ouananiche, Demon of the Foam.

THE BIG TROUT OF THE HOG-BACK

O.W. Smith

The parson, the game warden, and the merchant go atrouting on the West Branch of the Wolf with unpredictable results. (March 1906)

HOW A fisherman loves his favorite streams! There is no love like a first love, after all. Many years ago—I don't care to remember how many—I first fished for trout in the Pine River, Waushara County, Wisconsin, and since then I have visited that stream every year with one exception—that year was lost. Now, when the birds are nesting, I long to worship at the shrine of the Red Gods. I smell the smoke of the camp-fire; I hear the entrancing murmur of the musical Pine and the splash of the leaping trout; I see the foam-flecked pool at the foot of the Dane's Meadow, and so well acquainted am I with it that I almost feel as though I could cast a fly blindfolded. When the Red Gods thus call in the springtime it is hard to remain at desk or counter. This getting acquainted with a stream is an advantage; for you learn every fall, current and hole, and can cast almost without looking. Then, too, some big fish—usually THE big fish—gets away and you dream all winter long that he is waiting for you at the foot of the rapid or beneath the great cedar log where he broke away—waiting just for you! Why he is waiting for you, why some other fellow may not have caught him, you can't explain, but you believe he is waiting for you—now, don't you? Of course there are certain advantages in fishing a new stream: you see new country and solve new problems, but there is nothing quite like fishing the old stream. It's the first love; it's getting back home again—that's what it is.

I first visited the West Branch of Wolf River up in Shawano County, Wisconsin, on the 21st day of May, '03, and twice during the year 1904 I made that long, weary journey; then I said I'd go no more; but when the 15th of April, 1905, rolled around and the buds began to swell, while the yellow-throats shouted, Wichety! wichety! wichety! from every willow copse, I found myself longingly looking north-westward, while I listened for something—the music of Hemlock Falls. We experienced no trouble in making up a party. The Merchant stood ready to go and for a 3d man the Game Warden filled the place admirably; the Butcher was to have made a 4th but at the last moment business gripped him and we three were compelled to go on alone. To my mind three is not an ideal party—too one-sided like a jug handle. Neither do I like a large party; to my mind, even four are too many. Of course with four you can fish two and two, but when you have an odd number you have—well, an odd man. I think two the ideal party. A small tent, a few supplies, good fishing and a congenial companion—what more can mortal want here below?

Our first camp was on a little creek some 6 or 8 miles northwest of Cecil. I find by referring to my notes that we did not reach the creek until after sundown and the lateness of the hour compelled a hasty camp—therefore, an uncomfortable one. I, for one, was glad to get up. The night was very cold and as soon as it was light enough to get about I built a fire and soon three shivering figures were huddled about it. A heavy frost lay white and cold upon the ground and the little creek was frozen over, as I found when I went to get water for coffee. O! but that coffee was good!

"Say, Parson!" said the Merchant, as he scraped up a handful of frost with which to cool his coffee, "you said we'd have nice warm weather, but if that's not frost, dum me if it ain't frozen dew!" "Blamed if I don't believe it's snow," grumbled the Game Warden in turn. "No, it's not snow," I replied, "for it was too cold to snow; if you don't believe me, just go down and look at the hole I chopped in the ice when I got the water." "You don't mean that the creek was frozen over?" exclaimed the Game Warden; "well, if that is so, it accounts for my cold feet." "Hope they didn't get cold clean through," remarked the Merchant, "for if they did we'll have frosts until July." "And you can sell some more of your all cotton woolsocks," retorted the Game Warden. "Yes, on time," returned the Merchant. O! but they were good men, those two fellows; the frost did not effect their spirits in the least but seemed to have a contrary effect.

We did not linger long after breakfast but were soon upon the road and bowling along between giant red pine (wrongly called Norway pine), whose smooth reddish trunks marked with pike-like reticulations towered from 80 to 120 ft. above us. If I were a poet I would sing the praises of the red pine as Longfellow did of the Hemlock—so immaculate, sturdy and independent, I know no tree possessing more character. Reaching Keshena, we tarried only long enough to replenish our larder; then on, over sand beaten hard by much rain. From Keshena Falls, where we crossed the Wolf River, on we were continually crossing little trout streams— streams fragrant with precious memories—and I must have tired the boys with my stories of the large trout I caught in bygone years and the larger ones that got away. Just let me mention three of those clear, purling brooks: Oshkosh, Stockbridge, Chickininny. Now can't you hear them laugh as the red and gold trout leap and splash and play? If Shakespeare had known the music of Indian names he never would have caused a character to ask "What's in a name?"

Taking two trout fresh from the water—one from the West Branch and the other from the Chickininny—the observer would find it hard to believe that they were of the same species. The fish from the first-named stream is short and chunky, its back is a greenish black with prominent vermiculations, the belly is a bright orange red, while the red spots upon the side are prominent. The fish is a typical Eastern brook trout as described by Jordan and Evermann. The fish from the latter stream is long and slim, of a silvery, washed out color, with no prominent markings; often the red spots are entirely absent. The West Branch fish is more active as becomes so clipper-built a body—leaping clear from the water time after time in its efforts to reach the fly and upon occasion taking it in mid-air. Indeed, the fish seems to delight in acrobatic feats and leaps just for the fun of the thing. Now the fish of the Chickininny are logy, lack gusto and enthusiasm, will come to the landing net almost without protest. When one remembers that the two streams are not more than 10 miles apart and both empty into the same stream the wonder grows. I have caught a few dark trout in the West Branch but I have never taken a light fish from the Chickininny and the Indians told me that they were not to be found in the stream. Commend me to the clipper-built fighter of the West Branch every time.

We reached our old camp-ground just above Hemlock Falls at 12:30 and after a hasty lunch set about building a permanent camp, for we were to remain until the last of the week. Hemlock browse was cut and laid "just so" to form our bed. A stone fire-place was built with crane all complete. Fire-wood enough to last the week was cut. A dining table was built and a tarpaulin which we carried for that purpose stretched above it. At 4 o'clock all was completed and we shouldered our rods and set out to get enough fish for supper; it did not take us long and we were back at the tent before dark with a pan of dressed fish just the right size for frying. Fish, potatoes, bread and butter and coffee made a meal to remember. I will not soon forget that night around the campfire. The little glade in which our tents were pitched was surrounded upon all sides by tall hemlocks, which reached up and up until they seemed to touch the stars, forming a splendid background for the flashing firelight. It was pleasant to lie wrapped in my fur coat, listening to the Game Warden's yarns; for he has had interesting experiences and a few close shaves, and the Merchant could spin good yarns, for in his younger days he had been a log-driver and a noted one too; then when the conversation would flag I would tell of my adventures with the Sioux Indians, for once in my life I was a missionary among them. So that evening and others passed in pleasant conversation.

The next day I suggested to the Merchant that we visit the Hog-back—a locally famous spot some 3 miles down the river of which the Indians had often told me but which I had never visited. He was nothing loath; for anything in the way of a new experience is always welcome to him; so we set out, following a trail which Nolan, an agéd Indian friend, told me led to the Hog-back. The Merchant led off, setting a stiffish pace, and I soon tumbled to his game; he was trying to wind me, but daily walks of 4 and 5 miles had rendered my leg muscles like iron and I was not worried; when I noticed the perspiration standing out on his neck I suggested that he walk a little faster and he let out another notch, though it required an effort to do so. When we reached the Hog-back he was steaming but game, and never squealed, though he has never led off since. The Hog-back is one of the strangest rock formations it has ever been my good fortune to behold. Let the Reader imagine a dam, with rounded top 10 ft. high and 5 rods long, carved out of solid granite with one end broken down, through which water rushes with great force and noise and he will have a mental picture of the Hog-back. The photograph was taken from the south bank, therefore the ledge is in the distance and appears smaller than it really is. Let the Reader remember that it is about a rod from the Merchant to the end of the ledge and about 4 rods from the end of the ledge to the further shore. The rock upon which the Merchant is standing bears witness to the fact that at one time the dam was complete. What an upheaval there must have been when Mother Earth built that great dam! What could have been the cause? How long ago was it built? Nolan, my Indian friend, told me that the river men had destroyed the beauty of the place and I can well believe it. What must it have been like before dynamite destroyed the south end? One glance at the picture is enough to convince a trout fisher that a large trout had its home in the hole just below the rock. A trout *did*, and in as few words as possible I will tell you the story of his capture.

I reached the Hog-back alone, the Merchant having stopped to fish a likely looking hole a few rods above, where the trail hits the river. Experience has taught me that the deepest hole is a little below the fall and that the proper way to reach it is if possible to cast from above the fall—not into the moil of water but upon the comparatively quiet water farther down. So, just above the rock on which the Merchant is standing in the picture, I paused and examined my tackle, finding everything O. K. I sent my fly, a Royal Coachman, out on the wings of the wind. It was a good place for a cast and it was a good cast. For an instant my line hung in the air—a graceful curve; then quickly changed to a double curve or letter S; then straightened out and the fly poised light as thistle down above the foam-pitted water, as though in doubt whether to descend or to fly on in mid-air forever, but, feeling the restraining line, it settled upon the water. At once without any preliminary skirmishing as is so often the case, a great pair of jaws opened and my fly disappeared—without any fuss or furore but calmly, dispassionately, inevitably as Fate. I had caught a glimpse of the great head and wide open jaws and waited with beating heart for the rush, but to my surprise it did not come. The seconds, hour long in duration, dragged by, and nothing was doing. There was something uncanny about the whole proceeding. When it was impossible to wait another second, I began to reel in slowly, and the fish—an inert dead-weight followed. I never experienced anything just like it and I began to think that I would land my quarry without a struggle. But when the fish reached the boiling water below the rock it awoke from its sleep, trance, bewilderment or whatever it was, and did things a-plenty. The way it dashed about that little rock-bound pool more than made up for its former inertness. I could only say in helpless impotence, as did the Dutchman the other day when his team ran away: "You son-vun-guns vent den." In my eagerness to do something I stepped out upon a wet rock, slipped and went into the water, which fortunately was only shoulder-deep but O! so cold! when I say that ice and snow yet remained in unexposed-places, the reader can imagine how cold that water was. Striking outside the swiftest current, I was able to keep my feet, but the trout spied my legs as it rushed by in one of its great circles and promptly dashed between them, over the Hog-back, up into the quiet water above; happily the line did not foul and my reel was soon madly shrieking as the rushing fish ate up the reserve line. As quickly as possible I passed the rod between my legs and faced about, pressing my burning thumb upon the madly flying spool, and when the reader remembers that my hands were beneath the water he will see that I was seriously handicapped. I shouted for the Merchant, but the hemlock and cedar threw back my shout with mocking laughter. Would no one come? Suddenly a shadow darkened the water and I looked shoreward, to see the grinning face of my Indian friend Nolan. Talk about angels! As though finding a man in ice-cold water was an ordinary thing, he asked imperturbably, "What do in there? water blame cold yet." "Big fish going up there!" I chattered —"stop him!" A gleam of intelligence shot across his swarthy face, while the lust of battle lighted his eye and he sped away up the bank in a manner to belie his 70 odd summers, while I waded to the shore, my reel still spinning and the reserve line diminishing rapidly as the spool grew smaller. When Nolan got above the trout, he promptly jumped into the water, which was waist-deep, and by dint of splashing turned the trout, and I breathed once more. At this juncture the Merchant appeared upon the bank, and, seeing the Indian in the water, shouted, "Here! you old fool! you'll catch your death of cold!' "Fool yourself," returned Nolan, "blame big trout on Parson's line—go and help land!" Realizing that something extraordinary was taking place, the Merchant dropped his rod and came to my aid, but the battle was about over and the trout easily brought to net. Shivering, chattering, Nolan and I shook hands, while the Merchant built a fire. "Nolan," said I, "you take the trout, for without you it would have got away." "No, no," he replied, "you take um home to squaw and papoose." "Parson," said the Merchant, as we stood about the welcome fire, "you are the confoundedest fellow to get into scrapes when you go fishing that I ever knew. Do you remember the fight at Hemlock Falls?" As though I ever could forget! I experienced no ill effects from my wetting and have had many a hearty laugh over the battle at the Hog-back.

I might tell you of each day's adventures and I flatter myself that they would prove interesting, but space forbids. Thursday night, our last night on the stream, was warm and before morning we experienced a thunder-storm—the first of the season; it was impossible to sleep; the vivid lightning played among the hemlock tops, while heavy thunder boomed and crashed. As I lay awake watching the fiery serpents crawling about upon the canvas roof, I found myself repeating:

> *"You sulphurous and thought-executing fires—*
> *Vaunt couriers to oak-cleaving thunderbolts!—*
> *Singe my white head! And thou, all-shaking thunder,*
> *Strike flat the thick rotundity o' the world!*
> *Rumble thy—"*

But just then a great hand was clapped over my mouth and I perforce kept silent.

The next morning we were early on the road; for we planned to spend one night on the Chickininny and have a try at the red-bellied trout. We reached the stream a little after noon, set up our tent and got everything ready for the night; then we went fishing. We fished the stream carefully, yet not a fish did we get. At 5 o'clock we were back at the tent—wet, hungry and disgusted, but after a hearty supper of bacon and eggs we felt better and held a consultation. As it was necessary that I reach home the next day, I suggested that we start out and drive all night; the other boys were nothing loath, so at 6 we started. At Keshena we refilled our lantern and made ready for our long journey. While our rig stood in front of the store there was a muttering of distant thunder in the west. "Do you hear that, boys?" said the store-keeper. "You'd better put out your team and stay with me, for we're going to have a wild night—black too—for there is no moon and you'll miss your way among the trails on the east end of the Reservation." But the lust of travel was upon us and we bade him a gay Goodby, jumped into our rig and drove out of town. It *was* a black night, and it *did* rain all night long, and we *did* have trouble keeping the road. At midnight we stopped on the shores of Mud Lake, to feed our horses and make coffee; we had trouble when we attempted to start a fire, but when the coffee was made how good it tasted. What a picture we must have made, standing about the little fire in the dense woods, while the rain pelted us unmercifully. Well, it was disagreeable, but one of the pleasantest things to look back upon; for the disagreeable is pleasant in perspective. We reached home the next day, tired and sleepy, but satisfied with our trip and I more than satisfied with the battle at the Hog-back.

TWO POUNDS OF
LIGHTNING

Joe Godfrey, Jr.

*SPORTS AFIELD's second editor in chief during
the late 20s and early 30s, was also a writer and
sportsman. Here he pays his respects to the
cutthroat. (March 1928)*

NO place in the world can offer such enticing trout fishing and so much
of it as the Triangle area in British Columbia. In the uncounted lakes, rivers
and smaller streams adjacent to the triangle made on the map of British
Columbia by its lines which join Prince Rupert, Jasper and Vancouver there
is a pack of wonderful trout.

Men who travel the world in search of good trout fishing are each
year coming back to their favorite parts of this triangle because they find
that nowhere else on the globe can they be assured of the sport these
waters offer. From March until late November along some part of the
Triangle they find trout eager to take the fly.

Flashing little fighters like the cutthroat and rainbow ranging from
three-quarters to five pounds; steelhead, those five to fifteen pound sturdy

monarchs of the swift water, plunging, dashing Kamloops trout up to forty pounds. And every ounce of every pound of them ready to give battle. To appreciate the vastness of this heritage one should take a large scale map of the territory mentioned and note the water systems the railroad touches, where it follows rivers, crosses creeks, skirts the wooded shores of lakes. But even that affords only a suggestion of the possibilities for in that new country hundreds of the smaller streams and many of the lesser lakes are nameless and not shown on the maps.

The six hundred miles of coast along the Inside Passage is sprinkled with lakes, some not more than a quarter of mile inland, sheltered in the folds of the timber clad mountains. How many of these smaller lakes do you find shown on the map? A lifetime would not be long enough for an angler to cast a fly on all the waters along the Triangle Tour. Should he decide to devote his life to such pleasant work he would, in more cases than one, be the first white man to see, let alone fish, some of the hidden angling heavens. One needs only to have fished a few of these waters to appreciate the magnitude of the whole. When one tries to picture the quantities of sporting fish all these waters rear and feed for generation after generation he finds himself pondering on what seems to be infinity.

Then think of the fish! No pampered degenerates these, artificially reared and nurtured, gorged each day on liver and the other poor substitutes for natural, elusive food, but everyone a fighter who has learned nature's lesson that only the aggressive survives and that the weakling must go down.

Hard-hitting flashing fellows these, bred and reared in no protected pond, but in the cold crystal mountain waters. Any angler who has matched his skill with one of Nature's trout and then with the pampered stall-fed darlings of the intensively stocked preserve, need not be told the difference between the two.

Today I saw an Eastern sportsman—that word is used in its best sense—kill a cutthroat trout. Just one trout. We dropped downstream from the cabin in the high-prowed dugout canoe and anchored about thirty feet above where the clear water curved and swept over a riffle. Cedars, like drowsing giants, lined the banks, and upstream was a white patch of snow-topped mountain range showing through the dark green branches. Beneath us, on the clean gravel bottom the ripples caught the sunlight and twisted it, in long streamers of mellow light, across the mosaic of the river's floor. My sportsman stood on the poling platform in the downstream end of the canoe and rolled out the long lash of line from his eleven foot, six ounce casting rod. The fly, a brown hackle, sank in the foam-dotted broken water just below the sheen of the riffle, was lifted and laid down again a little farther to the left. There came a surging lunge, a flash of new silver. The trout came short. He was interested—but wary. Something did not look quite right to him. The sportsman reeled in and changed to a smaller dressing of the same fly. Then carefully he laid the fly down within a foot of where the feeding trout had risen. It settled and seemed to dissolve in the dancing water, so craftily was it cast. And then the water was shattered—a little silver flash showed—the trout was hooked.

He threw himself two feet out of the water, he plunged, leaped, plunged and leaped again, weaving a crescent of curving leaps that carried him twenty feet or more to the right.

It was sublime to see that fish and that sportsman battle. The reel shrilled its vibrant song, the song that sets your nerves a-tingling, and the line hummed as it cut the water above the rushing trout as he made for the foot of the pool. He checked, plunged madly then angled upward again. His opponent reeled in while he came upstream to where the broken water began and as he followed it to the right, past where he had been hooked until he was directly downstream from us. Then he leaped again. This time not in his first swinging leaps but straight up. He seemed to hang as he shook viciously at the fly that held him. The sportsman dipped the point of his rod, let the line sag so the trout had no resistance to work against and so could not wrench the point loose.

Then the trout went deep, curving and dodging. But he was not a sulker. The cutthroat lives and fights near the surface. As he swung and rushed, the light rod kept up the steady pull that seemed so gentle but which was wearing him down and gradually lessening his resistance. It curved gracefully from tip to butt. The leaps were not so lusty now. The fish was tiring but would not quit. He had never quit before and he did not know its meaning. The reel was slowly drawing him in.

But not yet. Another round began. All the old moves of combat and strategy were repeated. Ten tense minutes had passed. The trout came to where the riffle broke and swimming broadside to the fast water used the current to win a good ten feet for him. But he was not allowed to repeat the trick. He was brought above the riffle to where the river did not flow so swiftly.

He passed astern, saw the canoe and fled headlong. The reel sang again. Then seeing his chance the man pointed the tip of his rod upstream and brought the trout skittering over the surface and into the waiting landing net. He weighed two pounds and one ounce.

The sportsman dispatched him at once and laid down his rod. "That will do," he said. I lifted the anchor and poled upstream to the cabin. Covertly I watched the figure in the bow. He sat looking at his trout and there was a respect and something akin to reverence in his eyes. All other anglers know why he felt like that.

A while back we associated infinity with the supply of trout in the Triangle area of British Columbia. That was a figure of speech only, because anglers and fish culturists know that abundantly stocked waters can be, and have been, fished out. And they know how difficult it is to re-stock those waters. The best trout waters of British Columbia can be depleted but the story of our sportsman and the thousands of his kind seem to indicate that these virgin streams will not meet this fate. People have learned either by study or by bitter experience that no waters will stand unreasonable fishing for year after year. The supply may and does stand up wonderfully well, but eventually the danger point is reached and eventually the piper must be paid. Moderate fishing uses only the interest of our inheritance; too heavy fishing eats up the capital until one day Nature, the banker, says "N. S. F." Our birthright has been squandered. We used to talk largely of our "limitless" natural resources; now we know there is a limit to them all. We know and we are warned. Anglers always have known that but most of us earlier in our lives, used to think differently. We simply did not know. We did not know that a trout must survive for three years before it reproduces the first time; we did not know that the percentage of survival of the eight or so hundred eggs is small and seems to be calculated not to increase the supply greatly but merely to take care of a moderate loss only; we did not know the many hazards a fish must meet before it reaches the age of reproduction.

Nowadays people in general do not waste trout like a few used to do. There have been instances of immense catches of trout being made, photographed, the fish discarded and the picture proudly kept to prove the prowess of the so-called fisherman. But such things are becoming rarer. We are finding out that the quantity of game killed is not the proof of sportsmanship and that the method of getting them is.

Some die-hards may still be found who snort at the elaborate care taken by the modern angler. They profess to see no sense in light tackle and what we call sportsmanlike methods. They cite instances of great catches being made with any old bit of gear from a spear and pit lamp to a headline. Really fly fishing and other skilled ways of angling are comparable to golf. Our same critics could easily tell us we could go round the eighteen holes in a lot fewer strokes than we do if we'd not bother about following the rules. It's not so hard to sink a ball if you throw away the clubs and merely drop or kick the ball in. But that is not the game. In angling, merely catching fish is not the game. And the more expert we become the stiffer handicap we impose on ourselves.

This increasing interest in expert angling is a good sign, a sign that the end does not always justify the means. Long after we have laid away our rods for the last time those who follow us in the divine old art will be able to go to those British Columbia waters and find the stock of sporting fish there as abundant as when we knew them. For we are going to keep our trust with future generations of our fellow anglers and pass on to them our natural heritage unhampered and unharmed—a country of glorious fishing for every coming man and woman. It can be done. It will be done.

NORTH UMPQUA STEELHEADS

Zane Grey

This world-renowned author and angler fished around the globe, pioneering new areas and techniques. It was the steelhead, though, that captured his heart. (September 1935)

FIFTY miles or so above its junction with Steamboat Creek the Umpqua has its source in the high ranges and probably receives most of its ice-cold water from an underground outlet in Diamond Lake. For many miles down this rushing river seldom feels the sun. Great fir trees and canyon walls shade it halfway down. Numerous small brooks and creeks augment its flow. There are two big waterfalls and innumerable rapids. Ten miles above Steamboat cut-throat and rainbow trout up to five pounds are abundant. We know that steelhead run up at least that far. There is a good trail up the river, and two homesteaders. Not until you reach Steamboat on the way down does the Umpqua know anything about fishermen, or automobiles. It is virgin. It has unsurpassed beauty. Deer and bear and cougar, wolves and coyotes are abundant.

From Steamboat an auto road makes the Umpqua accessible to anglers. That is to say it is easy to *see* the river from the road. But there are only a few places where you can get down to the river without great exertion and a risking of your neck, and a very decided chance of your being hit by a rattler. There is a succession of long channels, cut in solid granite, and white rapids. We call many places pools. But they certainly are not eddies.

The Umpqua is the most dangerous river to wade, and therefore to fish, that I know this side of Canada. In June it is high, swift, heavy, and cold. It would be bad for any fisherman to slip in. And the rocks are slipperier than slippery-elm. July it begins to drop, half an inch a day and by August you can reach most of the water. This summer was hot and dry, making the Umpqua lower than ever known before, so it was possible for some young and vigorous fishermen, like my boys, to wade it without waders. At that I have seen them come back to camp, blue in the face, shivering as if with the ague, and yelping for the fire. I would not advise wading the Umpqua very much without waders.

It is not a good river for spoon and bait fishermen. I watched upwards of several dozen hardware fishermen this summer and very few of them caught steelhead. Some of them got good bags of small trout. I am not one of the many who advocate closing the Umpqua to spoon-fishermen. That is arbitrary, and would be inclined to affront many Oregonians who live near the river. My idea has been to educate spoon-fishermen, and I have succeeded with several. There are two reasons why this should be easy; first, a spoon-fishermen, by a few casts in any stretch of water, spoils the fishing in that particular place for fly-fishermen all the rest of that day. A good angler with the fly, especially the dry fly, can spend all day in a hundred-yard stretch of water. It is obvious that only a fish-hog, or an unthinking fisherman, will go on down the river, spoiling all the water for others who start in behind him. The second reason has no ethical or sporting side. It is merely that even a novice can, as soon as he learns a little about casting, get more rises, hook more steelhead and have infinitely more sport than the spooner. Only the expert spoon-fisherman can contend with an expert fly fisherman, and even the very best ones would get nowhere in a contest with my son Romer. The question of tackle is negligible. You can buy usable fly tackle almost as cheap as spoon tackle.

But if the spooner waives this and tells me where to get off I come back at him thusly. If you must fish with a spoon, O.K. But don't flog all the river, and be a sport enough to give the fly fisherman a wide berth.

*

I have had many requests by letter and otherwise to tell what kind of tackle we use and how we fish. Romer is partial to light tackle. This summer, as usual, he started with 5½ ounce Leonards and Grangers, Ashaway lines, and 357 Hardy leaders. These English leaders are tapered, nine foot in length, and they cost plenty. In spite of his skill, and delicate handling of big fish, and his wonderful daring in wading, and in a pinch swimming the Umpqua, Romer began right at the outset to lose many steelhead. He broke two tips, and many leaders. He graduated down to 6 oz. rods and 345 leaders. And when he quit on Sept. 21, his last fish a 11¾-pound steelhead, about which I will tell later, he was using my favorite leader, 341.

Romer fishes fine and far away. He can cast a hundred feet with ease. But he begins on a pool by keeping out of sight and fishing close. He is like an Indian in his wary approach. He never scares any trout. He preferred always, until this summer, small flies No. 6 and 8, and he used a good many English flies.

As is well known, the Parmachene Belle and Hair Coachman are the best flies on the Umpqua, during June and July. But toward the middle of this month they let up a good deal rising to these patterns. The old Turkey and Red failed to raise fish, and the Turkey and Gold, that Joe Wharton had made for me, soon lost its effectiveness. I had Wharton make a pattern after the New Zealand Gold Demon, adding hair and jungle cock. It was good for a while. Then that too slowed up, and we were hard put to it to find flies that would raise fish.

I had always been partial to larger flies, No. 4, and No. 3. And I had Loren and Joe Debernardi get busy with the fly-tying kits. It was my idea, but Loren hit upon a fly that beat any I ever used, and it was quite different in pattern and color from all the others. With that fly, and others almost similar, we had the most magnificent sport that I ever heard of on a steelhead river. We really made the Umpqua steelhead fishing no less than salmon fishing. And I mean Atlantic salmon fishing.

My bag of steelhead was impressive. Sixty-four in all, including three over 11, five of 9, a dozen around 8, and so on down to 5 pounds. Of course, I let a good many fish go. We never kept any we could not use, except a big one that we wanted to photograph. And these we smoked. Steelhead properly smoked, and salted correctly, are most delectable.

But that number 64 does not say anything. It was the steelhead I raised and could not hook, and those that I hooked and could not land, which counted. My favorite rod was a Hardy, 7 ounces, with an extension butt

I used after I hooked a fish. It was a wonderful rod. I do not see how it stood all the fights I had. Some of the steelhead I caught took over an hour to subdue. One that I did not catch and never even saw in all the 2½-hour battle took me half a mile down the river where I would certainly have drowned but for Joe.

Curious to relate this fish and the two largest I got fast to were all hooked in the same place—a pool we called Island Pool. It was a channel in a bend with rocky islands here and there. The water was swift. Below was a rapid, then a long succession of small islands, and then a series of white rapids. The one I caught out of this hole weighed 11¼. I was one hour and five minutes on this bird. At that I never got him fairly, for he ran down the river so fast I could not follow. He took 160 yards of the 192 yards I had on my reel—this was the Crandall new camouflage salmon line, G.B.H. with 150 yards of the strongest and finest silk backing—the most wonderful line I have ever used.

Joe ran down river and wading out to the islets below he succeeded in catching hold of my line. He held the steelhead for a while in the swift current, then carefully handlined him up river, until the fish took a notion to run again. This happened three times, and the last time he got the steelhead close up to him, or even with him, then he had to let go.

"Big pink buck!" yelled Joe. "He's tired. Put the wood on him!"

I was over a hundred yards above Joe. How I ever pumped that steelhead up to me, inch by inch, I cannot tell. But eventually I did, and led him ashore and beached him on a flat rock. Then breathless and wet and exhausted by excitement and exertion I sat down to gaze spellbound at this magnificent steelhead. He was over thirty inches long, deep and thick, with a tail spread of eight inches, and a blending of silver and rose exquisitely beautiful.

Joe and I, naturally, overestimated his weight. We said surely 13 pounds. But I was happy, no matter what his weight.

The second whale I hooked in that hole I did not see rise. I felt a heavy drag and thought my fly had caught. It had, as a galvanizing vibrant pull proved. I saw a long white fish wiggle and jerk in the shadow of the green water. Then he came up stream slowly. He swam all the way up the Island Pool to where it was shallow. And there in scarcely three feet of water he fooled around in plain sight. Joe nearly fell off the rocks in his frenzy to get that fish. I nearly collapsed. For we could *see* him, and he was forty inches long, ten deep, a pink fresh-run steelhead that must have been lifted over the salmon racks by the netters at the hatchery. Sometimes they dip out a few steelhead and release them up river. Gus, my driver, saw them lift out six, all over 20 pounds, and one they said would go 28. No other way could those giant steelhead get above the racks. Well, this one was so big that I could not do anything but keep the rod up and let him bend it. To make a long and agonizing story short this monster swam there in plain sight for over a half hour, until the hook pulled out. I have lost 1,000-pound swordfish with less misery! Joe swore he would get drunk.

The third one I hooked there, of these huge steelhead, must have been even larger. We never saw him once. The first one, I forgot to tell, had leaped prodigiously and often. This third one made my reel shriek and smoke as no Newfoundland salmon had done. He ran a hundred yards, then stopped in the current. We ran, fell, waded, climbed, all but swam. At times Joe had to hold me up. I got half or more of that line back, then the son-of-a-gun ran again. This happened five times during that half mile. At last down at the head of a fall above what we call the Divide Pool he hung for half an hour more, then took his hardest run. I was glad he got off, but Joe was sick. I shall never forget what thrills and pangs that steelhead packed into the two-and-a-half-hour battle.

Loren put up a remarkable and enviable record of 100 steelhead for the three months of our stay. A third of these, at least all the small ones, he carefully unhooked and let go.

During July I used to sit in camp with my glass and watch him fish the Z. G. Pool. Out of this water he caught 43 steelhead, and here he learned the fine points of the game. He developed.

But Loren's best work came in August in the pools down the river. He would leave early in the afternoon and come back at dark, wet, tired, but with shining eyes. And once only do I recall that he came without fish. For that single exception he had a story that even I dare not tell. Allowing for the exaggeration and inaccuracy of a youngster it still was the most remarkable fish yarn I ever heard. Some days he would climb down the almost unscalable mountain, kick rattlers off the rocks, raise from ten to twenty steelhead, hook some, fight them, and catch one or two, or more.

One night—the night—he came back with Gus packing a huge red steelhead that weighed in camp, hours after it had dried out, a little over 12 pounds.

"Here he is, fellows," he flashed with vibrant voice. "Look him over.

Thirty-two and one-half inches! Look at that spread of tail. . . . Look at me! Soakin' wet. An' look at this skinned place on my shin! An' look at Gus!—He swam out above that bad rapid—you know, the hole, *my* hole, where I have hooked an' lost so many—Gus swam out to save the line. I thought he would go over the falls. But he didn't. An' this darn fish then swam up stream again. He'd done that a dozen times. Jump? Oh, it was terrible. Right in our faces! He splashed water right on me. He shook himself—tussled, like a dog. All silver an' red—jaws like a wolf!. . . . Oh, boy, I'm tellin' you, it was great!"

I did not need to be told that. It was. And not all the greatness was in the sport, the luck, the fish itself. It is the spirit that counts. The boy or man who can be true to an ideal, stick to a hard task, carry on in the face of failure, exhaustion, seeming hopelessness—he is the one who earns the great reward.

As for Romer, dynamic drama always attended his fishing activities. He could not keep out of trouble with fish. One day he spent the whole long day trying to raise a big steelhead that lay dark against a green rock in the Z. G. Pool. This fish was so big he could be seen from automobiles on the road, high above the river. Romer must have tried a hundred flies over that fish. He must have rested him almost as many times. He did not come in for supper. We yelled and waved. No use! Finally I sent Joe out to drag him in. But Joe forgot that—forgot all in the passion to raise this steelhead. I interpreted Joe's wild wave to us to mean that Romer had, sometime or other that day, raised this fish.

I sat in my camp chair with my glass trained on Romer. And I was watching when he at last persuaded or drove this steelhead to rise. I saw the great boil on the water, then the angry upcurl of white. Romer's piercing yell of triumph and Joe's hoarse yell of exultation came to our ears above the roar of the falls.

I yelled like a maniac, and then all of us lined up on the cliff to watch in intense excitement. That steelhead ran up the river. The channel was tortuous and impossible to wade in a straight line. But Romer and Joe followed as best they could. Once a great splash far upstream warned me that this steelhead was going places. He did not show again. He ploughed through two rapids before he broke off. Romer stood as one dazed, looking up the river. Then he turned and waded back toward camp.

We were all sympathy. Romer was pale and grim. His big dark eyes burned. "Eighteen pounds!" he said. "I raised him at noon on a New Zealand fly And tonight he took a Turkey and Gold—after all that time. I think he got sore, like an Eastern salmon does when you cast a lot over him."

Another evening I was just getting back to camp when I heard yelling. I ran. When I got out where I could see, the crowd was lined up on the cliff, greatly excited. They yelled and pointed. Then I saw Romer pile into the deep swift channel above the big falls. Long ago I had ceased to be scared when he pulled some stunt like this. He is a champion swimmer. He waded out on the other side, his bent rod held high. He could not stop the fish. It went over the falls. Romer plunged in to swim back to the point he had started from. And then straight down the middle of this wide reach in the Umpqua he ran with great strides. We knew, of course, he had hooked another of the bad fighters. There was a ledge of rock extending across the river, with the heavy fall at the far side, and a lesser one on our side. Romer piled right off this ledge to swim the few yards to the head of an island. There he ran again, winding his reel like a madman. Evidently the demon of a fish kept on. At the foot of this island Romer waded a bad rapid that he had never attempted before. He reached another island, where we thought he would be marooned. We hurried along the cliff, kept even with him, climbed down to the bank, yelling encouragement. There was a white mill race between Romer and the shore on our side. He leaped in with bent rod, and swam. We saw the rod wag with his powerful strokes. He came out safely, crossed the shallow rocky place, ran to the gravel bar below, and at length clear round the bend he stopped that fish in a deep eddy.

And there, for twenty minutes longer, by my watch, Romer pumped and worked on that steelhead before he could lift him. We were all dumbfounded to see the fish which had put up that fight. It was one of the smallest size. In fact it weighed 4½ pounds. But what a rare, colorful, quivering, magnificently built steelhead!

I happened to be with Romer when he got fast to a big steelhead that like this little one was almost unbeatable.

It happened at the Takahashi Pool, near sunset, on our last day of fishing. We had been far down the river. No luck! I had not even had a rise. Romer whipped the lower reaches in Takahashi while I watched. The sun set. The river sped by, shimmering in amber-green light. The mountain slope was bathed in gold. Insects had begun to chirp. The air had grown cold.

At last Romer climbed a high rock at the head of this Takahashi Pool and cast from there. This is at the foot of a heavy rapid. The waves were white-crested and big, the current fast. Few trout fishermen would ever try such a place. But we raised steelhead out of such water. When your fly dances over these waves steelhead will rise straight from the bottom in a rush, and come clear out. Sometimes they miss the fly; seldom do they hook themselves; but when they get fast—what a wonderful experience!

I was watching the fly when a vicious splash flew up and Romer's yell pealed out. I ran to a more advantageous point. This steelhead ran up stream against that current so that the line seethed cuttingly, audible to the ears. Romer stood high with a long line out. He reeled fast, but there was no need, for the bag in the line was as tight as a wire. I ran on up beside him, and got there in time to see this steelhead leap fully six feet out of that white water. He looked enormous and he caught all the gold of the setting sun.

Turning he made down river with extraordinary speed. I could not keep pace with Romer. At the foot of that long stretch there is a ledge where all hooked steelhead foul the line. This one did. We had a moment of despair. Then the reel sang again. The line was around the ledge but not fouled. Romer got out on the platform of poles Joe had built there for the purpose of releasing our lines when caught. Romer worked there carefully to get free. He reached out so far with his rod that I feared he would fall in. With sunset the canyon had begun to fill with shadow and soon the line was hard to see. But we could hear the reel clear enough. Jerk by jerk it warned us that the line was nearing the spool. Presently it ceased.

"There!—All—out," cried Romer, tragically.

"What? Not all your line!"

"Yes. What'll I do now?"

The old poignant query in moments of baffled effort!

"My heavens. All that 190 yards!" Then I bethought myself of the long forked pole Joe and I had used before we built the platform. Finding that, I waded as far as I dared and reached out. The pole was heavy. When I got it extended it sank of its own weight. Another desperate try while Romer called huskily: "Hurry, Dad!"

I released the line. It sang like a telephone wire. Romer plunged off the platform and made the water fly. I followed. We came out upon the flat ledge round the corner to a long deep stretch of river. Here had always been the ideal place to have it out with a big steelhead. Dusk had mantled the gap between the wooded slopes.

"He's stopped. But I can't get—any line," panted Romer.

"You've got to. It's now or never. What kind of leader and hook have you on?"

"That short salmon leader you gave me—and a big hook. I put them on—to try in that rough water."

"What a break! Lam it into him before he takes a notion to run again."

"Hook'll tear out. . . . Oh, he's heavy."

"No it won't. Not this time. Put the wood on him, Romer."

The moment was one of severe strain for more than the tackle and steelhead. But nothing broke. Romer got him headed up stream. Little by little he recovered line. What an endless task it seemed! I believe he was half an hour on that fish before he got to the enameled end. Forty-two yards from the steelhead! I begged Romer not to be afraid to pull him. In a long fight the hook wears out of the jaw!

The moon came up over the mountain—a full moon, bright as silver, and it made a vast difference. We could see. But another quarter of an hour passed before we saw the first white flash of the big trout. He was far from whipped, at least as badly whipped as Romer wanted.

"Don't let him have an inch! Hold him!" I remonstrated. "Romer, that steelhead is as tired as he will ever get."

"Oh—Lord!" was all my son replied.

Moments dragged by. And we saw the steelhead on each turn. In that black water, when he flashed in the moonlight, he looked monstrous. Everything was magnified. I never saw such delicate handling of a big fish. Afterward I acknowledged Romer's incredible patience and judgment. But I could not have done it. And I began to sag under the strain. Fifty-five minutes on that ledge! I had not noted the hour when the fish was hooked. However it was at sunset. Finally I could not endure any longer.

"My God—son! Pull him in."

"Not ready—yet," panted Romer.

"Romer, you *know* some of these steelhead *never* get dead tired. Take that 4½ pounder of yours the other afternoon."

"All right, Dad. I'll horse him," replied Romer, and tightened up a little. "Never—did this—before. . . . God help you—if I lose him!"

Romer worked the steelhead up on the ledge and approached the shore. I could see the fish and I would have yelled to Romer if I had not been panic-stricken. Why is it a big fish always has this effect upon a fisherman? I believe it is a regurgitation back to boyhood.

I kept wading in behind the steelhead, determined to fall on him if he got his head turned out again. Presently he lodged on a hollow place to turn on his side. Gaping with wide jaws, his broad side shining like silver, he galvanized me into action. With a plunge I scooped him out on the bank, where he flopped once, then lay still, a grand specimen if I ever saw one.

"How—much?" whispered Romer, relaxing limp as a rag.

"Fourteen—thirteen pounds!" I pealed out. "Oh, what a fish! Am I glad you got him!"

"Whew!—Is he that big?. . . . Gosh, what'll Loren say?"

"It'll be tough on the kid. He's so proud of his record. And that twelve-pounder! But Loren can take it."

"Dad, don't weigh this one. We'll say 11¾!"

6

THAT RIVER . . . THE BRULE

Gorden MacQuarrie

*One of SPORTS AFIELD's most popular writers
of the 30s and 40s rhapsodizes about his favorite
river. (May 1935)*

THAT RIVER —that Brule—sweeping for 66 miles from the heart of Douglas county, Wisconsin, to Lake Superior. I've already said too much about it. Those who didn't know it before are finding it out. I must be cautious, but it is hard to even think of it without accompanying rhapsody. But maybe it's not a bad thing to fall in love with a river.

If this most famous of Wisconsin trout streams is to have a biographer I ask no better job than to be that biographer. Let's see, now. I've been fishing it for 25 years. Part of it's running through me most of the time, like a well-remembered old song. Its loveliness, its trout, its perfect wildness even though millions have gone into homes along its bank, constitute a modern-day miracle. Thirty miles from Superior-Duluth, with 150,000 people, this ancient highway of the fur traders today is a piece of the splendid heritage which has fallen into the laps of this generation. It should be guarded well.

But there is a story and it must be told. It is about Old Mountain, a legendary rainbow that lives in the Brule. He and his brother, the far-famed Mule, worked in harness for several winters for Paul Bunyan when he was logging out of Lake Nebagamon, with headquarters in George Babb's barber shop in Nebagamon. George, one of this country's finest dry-fly fishermen, can tell you more. If you ever meet him—and you will if you are a fisherman—you will hear many, many things.

Now, about Old Mountain and the Mule. Paul Bunyan employed them on various jobs. During a log jam they'd hitch up to it and pull the key logs apart. That saved money on dynamite. They were also useful in placing themselves at the mouths of feeder creeks and backing up water. Then, when they had quite a lake, Bunyan would give the signal. They'd swim out of the way and the full tide of water would come down, bringing the timber into the main stream. That eliminated the need for expensive dams. To this day there have never been more than four logging dams the full length of the creek. The four or five tons of table scraps they consumed daily, was a mere nothing. The Gillagilee birds would have eaten them anyway.

Well, sir, these two fish got along splendidly until they got into an argument over some trollop of a trout that came up from Lake Superior one spring to spawn. The resulting battle continued for several days and so great was the disturbance that Big Lake was formed, giving the otherwise narrow stream its one wide stretch of still water. After that battle Old Mountain pre-empted the upper part of the stream and the Mule took up his dwelling down below.

They haven't spoken since, excepting the day President Coolidge arrived to spend the summer on the Brule. That day the Mule came up-stream and the river rose two feet. Coolidge was sore about it because the fishing was bad for three days. No one has invited the Mule back since.

"George," said I to the famous one who was called into the hallowed precincts of the Pierce estate to teach the President the intricacies of the dry fly, "we ought to run out some day and have a look at Old Mountain. His whiskers must be a mile long by now."

"Young man," retorted George, "his whiskers are no such thing. I trimmed them for him the other day and sold the clippin's to a mattress factory. But if you want to go name the day and Uncle George will lead the way."

You who have stood on the bank of your favorite river at dawn, know about the exhilarating thrill. We were three, George, myself, and Paul (not Bunyan) who said he just came for the ride and finished the day in a blaze of glory by hooking Old Mountain himself. We started from Stone's bridge on the upper river, a bridge that's launched a thousand anglers in any two years you want to name. It was built by a Chicago attorney who came to the Brule years and years ago to build a fine summer home and invite his soul. Our objective was Winnebijou, a station on the Brule 17 miles down-stream, by river.

George and I were rigged up and went to it while Paul, who had never before used a fly-rod, bided his time. We got several small strikes, mostly from native brook trout which are numerous up-stream. It was evident they were hitting freely. George is one of those rare Brule experts who can handle a boat with one hand and fish with the other. Try it sometime. We kept a number of the 9- and 10-inchers for the noon snack.

"I'm waiting for the big ones," quoth Paul, the uninitiated. "I propose to bring home some meat. You chaps can play around."

After awhile he went to sleep, which stamps him as of the true phil-osophic breed of which fishermen are made. I halted to watch George in action.

George Babb is a fisherman. That morning he was swinging an eight-foot, four-ounce rod and was dry-fly-fishing in a boat going down-stream. And after you see it done don't let anyone ever tell you dry flies can't be fished down-stream. Maybe it cannot be done when you are wading, but in a boat, drifting with the current, it is managed very well by all the upper Brule fishermen. His No. 10 Coachman, which he uses more than half the time, fell like thistledown.

Babb for a short time once held the world's record for brown trout. His was a 14-pounder, taken at night. After that they began getting bigger ones in western streams but so far as I know George's 14-pounder from the Brule has never been equaled in that stream. His ability to hook rising fish is uncanny. Years of training have sharpened his eye.

"Bend your wrist when you see 'em," cried George to me after I had lost one.

"But how do you see 'em?"

"Watch for 'em."

Thus endeth the lesson.

I drank in the morning air and watched, with supreme contentment, the piscatorial perfection which George Babb has attained through 35 years of angling and guiding on the Brule. He places a fly where you or I would never essay a try. His is a vigorous style, with plenty of power in the back cast and worlds of finesse in the forward cast. He found the trout feeding inshore, under tangled, overhanging branches and went right in after them. Every cast, almost, was accompanied by the risk of becoming hung up but this happened seldom and when it did he usually freed the fly by a freakish roll of the line which snapped the fly back and free. He seemed to know by instinct how much room he had behind him. I never saw him look back. Perhaps he knows all the spots on the Brule by heart. His fishing he accompanies by a constant and interesting flow of trout lore. It seems as though all his mental faculties are engaged in making conversation the while he fishes automatically. It does seem a fact that all good fishermen spend a lot of time fishing. They keep their lines wet.

George kept plying his paddle and rod while I set about to emulate him. The results were anything but successful. Trying to send out a fly with a man like George around is a bit difficult. One may be a fair performer at any branch of sport but when placed side by side with a real expert, morale and style often suffer. The Hon. Babb, however, is very kindly under ordinary circumstances and resorts only to his milder methods of oral castigation when fishing with amateurs, like myself. When he has a real pupil, however, in whom he thinks there is a possibility of producing results, he really oils up his vocabulary and gets down to work. When he was teaching President Coolidge the mysteries of the dry fly it is said he achieved some genuinely remarkable flights of oratory. Enough anecdotes about George and the President are told in the Brule country to fill this magazine. I decided to prod him into telling one I had heard before through other sources.

"George," said I, "is it a fact that you wouldn't let the President use his own line dubbing?"

"Yep," said George. "The President had some dope someone had foisted on him. It was all right but nothing like my dope. You know that. Why, man alive, the virtues of my line grease are such as to cause a demand for it in all quarters of the globe. Once used you'll use no other and many an angler I've taken down the Brule can testify to that. Made from the marrowbone of three-year-old bucks with just a dash of fish oil in it to bring a familiar odor to the fish when the line lays on the water. I've seen lines with that stuff on—"

"I know you have, George," I interposed. "I believe anything you say, but it is a fact that the President didn't want to use it. Isn't that so?"

"Yes, guess you're right—and he didn't use it either—after he decided he wasn't going to."

"Out with it."

It's a story I love to hear, for it illustrates well the whimsical humor of the former President and his complete understanding of the vociferous guide. George's pride about that line dressing is tremendous. He defends it with might and main, and woe unto the angler who discounts its usefulness. It took the genial wit of the vacationing President to assert his right to use any doggone line dressing he chose. So far as I know he is the only angler who ever fished with George and got away with anything but the private ointment of which he is so proud.

"Well, it was like this," said George, continuing to fish assiduously. "He was dry-fly-fishin' and I was sittin' in the boat, paddlin' easy and making a helpful remark from time to time. Every once in a while I'd remind him I ought to fatten up the line a bit. You know that dope of mine comes off easy but it's great while it lasts. President Coolidge asked me, in a matter-of-fact tone, to use his own line dressing. Said he thought it'd stay on better or something. I heard him all right but wasn't plannin' on having him spoil his fishin' by oiling up the water all around the boat. I kept putting on my own dope, when it was needed. Finally, the President must have got wise. He handed back the rod to get the line buttered up again. He never turned around to face me but kept looking straight ahead. I opened my own little box and went to work on that line. The President never turned his head, but chuckled a little bit. All he said was, 'You're a stubborn fellow, aren't you, George?' I never peeped. After that we used his own dope. And no wonder he made a good fisherman. Anyone who can see in back of him without turning around can certainly see a trout when it makes for a fly!"

I went on with my casting. Paul slept until I awakened him and offered him my place in the bow. He peeped into the creel. A dozen or so small fish were caught by that time.

"Ho hum," he yawned. "Calling on old Paul to come to the rescue. Never cast a fly in his life but he brings home the bacon. Gimme 'at 'ere pole, son."

"Now you'll see some fishing," cried George. "I'm pulling in my outfit to teach that fellow a few rudiments."

I retired to the stern to run the boat so that George could come up amidship and conduct another class in icthyological pursuit. Everything in his long years of angling went into the sincere discourse which he poured into Paul's ear with an earnest constancy which would do credit to a machine gun. The whole expressive arsenal of the veteran angler's vocabulary exploded with delightful detonations on Paul's unheeding ear drums. And, don't think that George Babb cannot teach one how to handle a fly-rod. If he can't, no one can. With him it is an art and the success of a pupil is his greatest pleasure. Paul was rigged with two wet flies, a Western Bee and a Black Gnat, but paid not the slightest attention to the implorings of his adept teacher. That man had the audacity to persist in fishing with reckless amateurishness before the eyes of the old master of the Brule. Another would have been consigned to the river but these two were old friends of the wars.

"Just watch my smoke, George," said Paul, "Maybe I don't know anything about handling this little curtain rod, but if there's a fish in this river, I'll get him. Don't bother about my style. I ain't got no style."

"Fine grammar for the business manager of a newspaper to be using," quoth George. " 'Ain't' ain't language. You'll never learn to cast a fly. Next time you and I go fishing it'll be over to the Eau Claire lakes. I know where there's some good croppie beds there. We'll take a couple of kids along. They enjoy it so."

"Croppies, eh?" exclaimed Paul with a grunt. His line tightened as there was a rush in the water inshore, where the flies had alighted. In another instant a tremendous trout surged above the surface. He didn't leap but writhed for a moment partly out of water. The big ones sometimes do that.

"Keep your rod up and let him take it! Let him go with it," screamed George.

"He's going places all right," said Paul. "And he doesn't like running in harness."

I watched the battle from the rear seat, holding the boat well out in midstream. Paul really did valiant work for a few moments. He snubbed the trout when it came to the end of a run and instinctively kept the line taut. I thought he was doing remarkably well for one who had never before handled a fly-rod. George thought otherwise, and maybe he was right. The trout broke water but once, in that first thrashing, vicious surge. I guessed him to be a large rainbow, although large ones up-stream at that season are not the usual thing. It may have been a brown, or even a native, although I doubt it could have been the latter because of the furiousness of its fight.

The fish was actually tiring and George was getting a little tired, too. He was so busy giving directions my throat got sore listening. Paul was the calmest of the three.

"Now, listen, Paul," shouted George for the last time. "I'm your friend and brother man and I love every blond hair in your head, but you're going to lose that fish if you keep applying so much pressure. You're roughing him. The leader on that line will test just exactly three pounds, tensile strength. The rod weighs less than your fountain pen and that fish is using the current like nobody's business. It may be Old Mountain himself!"

"Just get the frying pan ready," responded the phlegmatic Paul.

Then Paul conceived a brilliant idea. Turning to George he handed him the vibrant rod.

"You take it then," said he. "I've tamed him. Now you go in for the kill!"

George seized the extended rod in his expert hand, played it for perhaps 10 seconds—and then reeled in an empty line. The gut had given way near the tail fly. A maniacal light came into Paul's eye and he whistled "Nearer My God to Thee," while George surveyed the end of the tackle.

"It's a frame-up," said George.

Paul began the second movement of the grand old hymn.

"That was my fish, George," he declared. "I'm the dub fisherman that doesn't know anything about fly-casting and when I get a real one on you lose him for me. Rather would I be guilty of treason to my country than dish a friend in such fashion. George Babb, thou who hast ministered unto me and who has been ministered unto by me, thou has spilled the beans of friendship. I weep for thee and thine."

"Should have let you keep the rod," said George. "Gut was probably ready to bust when you handed it to me. Show's what I get for being a big-hearted sap. Well, anyway, by the time we get back to Nebagamon we can chalk up another win for Old Mountain. That was him all right. Did you see his eyes pop out when he saw me? Scared. Knew he hadn't a chance. But he got a break."

"Shame on you, George."

Paul clung to his seat in the bow and actually made considerable progress, under George's tutelage. He was doing well when we stopped at the mouth of a small creek at George's command.

"Stay here, I'll be right back," said George as he vanished in the cedars.

In a few minutes he was back with a couple handsful of watercress.

"That's for our Brule salad," he explained.

We proceeded. The trout were still on the feed. George himself admitted they were "taking well" although we hooked no more large ones. None of those brought to net were over 11 or 12 inches but all possessed the fierce doggedness that comes to trout living in the frigid Brule. In the hottest summers the river is entirely unfit for swimming. A ducking while wading is more than a wetting. The cold goes right to the marrow.

We came to a place where the river made a fairly sharp turn to the left, over a mild rapids. A log, perhaps 15 feet long, projected out from the bank at the turn. Along its edge the water curled and eddied. I stopped the boat 50 feet away, up-stream and across from the log.

"There's one in there, George," said I, in the wisdom of my years.

It was beautiful to see him drop his fly six inches from the log. He had judged the flow of the water well for the dry Coachman was carried down-stream almost parallel with the log. It might have fallen off the log into the water, so easily did it come to rest. It bobbed to nearly the end of the log, a fleck of brown and white against the shadowed water beside the log. The trout came from beneath the end of the projection. George struck before I saw the fish and a split second after the strike, the trout broke water in a shimmering curve. It was a Lochleven, weighing about two pounds. In a few moments, due to expert handling, it was creeled.

At noon we stopped for two hours, ate fried trout and Brule river salad, the component parts of which are as mysterious to me as the ingredients of George's line dope. Some day I hope to extract both secrets. On down-stream we continued, through rapids and slow stretches, through the amazing Cedar Island lodge of the Pierce estate where we stopped to pay our respects to Superintendent Lambert, and so on, through an everchanging valley of pines and cedars, trickling creeks, shadowed pools.

Paul caught a number of fairly good fish, to his complete delight. By the time we slid under the high railway trestle at Winnebijou the Brule valley was darkening and the chill of the river was being felt a little. Warm jackets were in order, although I knew in the open the sun was still warm. The Brule has a way of sending forth its chills at sundown. It is not long after that when vaporous mist-wraiths commence their all-night dance over its surface. He who fishes it at night must prepare for that, even in midsummer. But whatever slight discomfort it may bring one may reconcile himself with the knowledge that it is that cold, pure water that makes it one of the country's greatest trout streams.

Up the rollway at Winnebijou we skidded the boat to the waiting trailer, lashed it into place and prepared for departure homeward.

"You'll learn, Paul," said George with paternal accent as he handed over the entire creel, refusing to keep any for himself. "In fact, I'm quite proud of you. For one day you've done well. Next time you'll know a little bit about it."

For answer the new-born angler pursed his lips and whistled with solemn intonation the first strain of "Nearer My God to Thee."

7

BIG FUN WITH LITTLE FISH

Cal Johnson

*This famed SPORTS AFIELD fishing columnist
of the 30s popularized the largemouth bass but
here writes about flyrodding for the more diminutive
panfishes. (January 1939)*

BY NATURE the several species of panfish known to American fresh waters are gamey and they possess a handsome dress which lists them as the "peacocks" of our finny tribe. In this list we find the beautiful orange-throated sunfish, bluegill, crappie, calico bass, rock bass, white bass and yellow perch. All of 'em are worthy foes when taken with flyrod equipment—and don't think it isn't a sport for fully matured anglers. A few years ago we might have looked upon the panfish as something for the kids to play with, but not so in these modern times. Nix! These little scrappers have finally become recognized for their spunk and fighting hearts by the fly-fisherman and as time progresses we feel they will become even more popular with the angling fraternity.

One of the fine things in favor of the panfish is the fact that they are willing strikers throughout the day. Rain or shine they are on their feed and the fisherman can enjoy several hours of good sport when other species of so-called game fish are logy and unwilling to do battle. Sunfish love to nose around among the weeds and water-plants in quest of aquatic insects and small minnows. Even when the bright sun is casting warm rays upon the surface the sunfish will feed and remain lively until sundown. Around old piling and docks, or in among snags and submerged treetops, the "sunny" finds cover as well as a place to feed, so never pass up such locations when angling for these excellent little fish of clear waters.

The crappie is one of the best known species for taking on a fly and when they are feeding the limit can be taken in a short time. In many northern lakes the crappie feeds late in the afternoon and early evening. The fish stay in deep water during the heat of the day and they can be seen swirling near the surface well out from shore about an hour before they commence to work their way into the semi-shallows. Crappies travel in schools and the waters fairly boil when they are feeding heartily upon a new hatch of insects. It is then that these silvery-sided panfish take a fly with zest.

If you wish to enjoy the ultra sport when fly-fishing for panfish it is well to select an outfit that will contribute toward extending the fish more power to fight. I have a split-bamboo fly-rod which tips the scale at only two and one-half ounces, being a trifle over seven feet in length. A size F enameled line of the tapered variety, a nine foot tapered leader of finely drawn gut and an ordinary single-action click type fly-reel constitute the outfit. A selection of wet and dry flies ranging in sizes from twelve to eight will suffice in so far as lures are concerned. However, I have also taken some fine panfish on the very small fly-rod lures manufactured from rubber, wood or metal.

The wet-fly of size ten or twelve is always good. I like a bit of tinsel wrapped around the body of my panfish fly. This added sparkle seems to attract the fish from a greater distance than the more somber fly. However when casting into a school of crappies it makes little difference just so that the fly represents fairly closely the color of the insect seen flitting above the waters. The small size fly will hold just as securely as the larger fly. In fact, it is well to remember that a crappie's lips are extremely tender and frail and it is an easy matter to pull the hook from their lip if the fish is handled carelessly. Always permit the crappie to lead the fight—let him spin and dive to his heart's content before retrieving line. Handle him lightly and you will manage to land most of the fish you hook.

I like a boggy shored lake for sunfish, especially if it is spring fed and deep. Schools of fish can be seen swimming around in the shade of your boat, or underneath the overhanging moss and cranberry plants that fringe the shores. Such lakes are ideal for sunfish and oodles of fun can be had taking them on a fly during mid-day when the sun is well up. The fish are not shy and seem a bit too friendly when the fly is cast among their number within a few feet of the boat.

The bluegill tops the list with many fishermen, due somewhat to its size, excellent flesh and general all around ability to scrap well when hooked. This species of panfish loves to swim around in the cool deep waters of a pool where submerged tree-tops or snags are in evidence. A dry-fly will attract the bluegill when he is feeding near the surface late in the afternoon, but as a general rule it is necessary to resort to the wet-fly and spinner. Cast the fly well out into the open waters and permit it to sink deep, then retrieve slowly. The bluegill strikes hard and fast and has a habit of cupping its body and giving you a very peculiar scrap. The fish will sort of back up on the fly and hold its body saucer fashion against the pull of the line, causing one to believe that a fish twice the size has become hooked.

The white-bass is another small species which gives the fly-fisherman plenty of fun. It is a great food fish, the flesh being firm and flaky and as tasty a dish as any fisherman ever stuck a fork into. The best time to catch white-bass is during the early months of the fishing season, for at that time the fish travels up tributary streams of lakes. Later in the season and during the autumn period the fish are found in deeper waters and the wet-fly is the most successful if fished during later afternoon and early evening.

When fishing for any species of panfish it is well to remember that no fish rise readily to any fly unless they are frequenting semi-shallow to shallow waters. That's one reason why it is sometimes necessary to place a small lead shot on the gut leader to bring the wet-fly near the bottom to attract fish; especially is this so with the white bass after they have left the rivers and descended to the deep holes of the lakes. The white-bass, however, is not the best quarry for the summer fly-rod fisherman as they do not frequent the shallows like other species of panfish do throughout the season. In all waters where a gravel and sandy bottom are in evidence the crappie and sunfish can be located from spring until fall. Small clumps of water-

grasses, reeds, rushes and lily-pads usually serve as cover and feeding grounds for "sunnies" and crappies and a fly cast around such places usually catches panfish.

The rock-bass is one of the most pugnacious members of the panfish group. This fish will rise freely to hackles and almost any trout fly toward evening. However, the rock-bass prefers to take the fly underneath the surface, not upon the surface. Therefore it is best to cast the fly upon the surface and work it momentarily with a few twitches of the rod tip, causing the fly to sink. The fish will stalk the fly as it struggles upon the waters and the moment it commences to sink it will dash forward with a rush and mouth it. The rock-bass is a strong fighter and knows plenty of stunts to perform after becoming hooked. It will cup its dark sides and fight from a side-wise position that strains the rod and gives the angler a thrill.

There is a small bay in a northern lake that I like to fish when the weeds are up and the lily-pads in full growth. The waters are clear and a small river flows from the lake at this point. Plenty of perch, crappies and sunfish are always around the weed beds, and large-mouth black bass also rove among the stems of the water vegetation seeking stray minnows, water-bugs and other forms of food. Here is a real spot for the fly-fisherman, for a cast may bring a perch, crappie or sunfish, and in the event a larger fly or artificial bass-bug is used it is not unlikely to scare up a fighting large-mouth bass.

During the bright of day, however, it is my custom to fish this spot for panfish with a fly. A silver doctor, professor, yellow sally, gray hackle,

Montreal, coachman or gnat attracts the fish, and on certain occasions when the mosquitoes are thick I find a spinner fly or very small evening dun very effective. When using a dropper fly it is not unusual to catch a double—and sometimes it happens to be a crappie on the lead fly and a perch on the trailer fly. The biggest thrill of all is a double of sunfish as these little fellows scrap from the word go, and rarely will they tug in the same direction.

Fly-fishing for rock-bass, sunfish and perch of the flowing stream is much like angling for brook trout. The fish are found in much the same locations in most streams and the identical equipment and methods are practiced. I always carry my panfishing outfit when fishing a river for muskies and wall-eye pike, for in such waters one usually finds some species of panfish, particularly rock-bass. The river perch is not as good a fish as the deep water lake perch when it comes to a good scrap or the campfire meal, but the river sunfish and rock-bass are usually found in fine fettle and can fight just as hard as the panfish taken from the lake.

The beauty of fishing a river lies in the fact that it is usually possible to wade the stream and fish long stretches of varying waters. A stream extends new experiences at every bend, while a lake is much the same regardless of where you fish it. On a river the panfisherman seeks rocky bars, deep eddies and pools, tumble down bridges, shallow rapids and quiet holes that form in small bayous that penetrate back into the woods a short distance from the stream. When fishing a lake the best locations are usually close to camp, around the dock or along the shores where weeds and rocky bottoms harbor the fish. Panfish are never hard to locate in either river or lake, which is another point in their favor.

Perch do not strike as quickly as other species of panfish, so it is advisable to fish slowly and patiently. When a school is located several fish will be taken before they move on. They are an inquisitive fish and when one member of the group snaps up a particle of food other fish will dart to the same spot in hopes of either stealing the food the first perch captured or find more in the neighborhood.

I prefer to use only a single fly when fishing for sunfish, crappies and rock-bass. Any one of these species is capable of giving you all the fun you want, and the chance to cast a more delicate and precise fly is presented. Dropping a fly into the small pockets of clear water between lily-pads calls for accuracy, and when a sunfish gobbles the offering and dives into the thick weeds and lily-stems below the surface it is perhaps a good thing that no extra flies are attached to the leader to get snagged when the fish cuts capers in an effort to get free. If you happen to be using a very lightweight fly rod the strain is too great when added stress must be forced to pull a snagged hook from tough weed stems. It's far more fun to lead the panfish through the tanglement of weeds and into clear waters where he can be viewed as he performs his cork-screw antics near the surface.

On account of the abundance of panfish in a school it is not uncommon to hook many very small fish during the course of a day's fishing. When the fish spies your fly it's a case of a free for all scramble to see who gets it first—and the closest fish might happen to be a small one. For that reason the fish should be handled carefully in view of liberating after landing. A barbless hook is ideal for all forms of panfishing as it permits returning the fish to the waters without any damage to the mouth. I have seen half the lip of a crappie dangling from its mouth after a hard scrap, but there is an excuse for that when crappie fishing as these fellows possess a "paper" mouth. However, other species of panfish are built a bit more sturdy in the bow end and there should be no danger of harm if the fisherman handles the fish lightly.

Fortunately panfish are very prolific and their number should increase in all waters that are free from pollution and where food and cover are provided. These little fish will always prove excellent substitutes for larger and perhaps more gamey species, and we already know that they are wonderful fill-ins when the black bass are off color or when the trout stream is not in condition for fly-fishing. The more we fish for these great little underwater fire-crackers the more we appreciate their worth.

GIANTS OF THE LONG SHADOWS

Ozark Ripley

*SPORTS AFIELD's one-time gun dog editor
knew a trick or two about hooking bronzebacks on
fly that still work. (1939 Sports Afield Fishing
Annual)*

NOT SO many years ago I discovered, while angling with the late
Emerson Hough, that the real things to angling were the occasions when
apparently every condition was against you. A roily river of great swiftness
was considerably above normal stage of water. But I wanted to see the
writer of that great American epic, *The Covered Wagon*, take a fish with a fly
which he had publicly and privately berated, *Jenny Lind*, since I had con-
verted a trout fancy of that designation into a bass pattern which I had
used successfully à la dry fly with small-mouth bass.

When a mountain stream, in which the aristocrats of the bass family
reside, takes on a murky hue, it is next to useless to fish it. But here was
perhaps my only opportunity of ever converting my esteemed friend to
my precious *Jenny Lind*. As will happen occasionally in time of flood, bits of

backwater assume perfect clarity. I waded out with Hough and pointed to a small piece at the end of a gravel bar into which a leaning sweet gum threw a long, graceful shadow. The writer's artistry and aim were perfect. *Jenny Lind* seemed about to settle a few feet away from where I wanted it. An unexpected impulse of wind caught and flung it joyously under the very roots of the tree, floating perfectly, with a slightly saltatory action.

When Emerson started to make the retrieve, his face suddenly became grave as he witnessed the tremendous commotion just where the bug had dropped. He immediately realized he was connected with the largest swift water small-mouth bass he had ever caught, and the first fish he had ever risen with a *Jenny Lind*, and the first time he had, in my presence, admitted that bass have more than ordinary fighting ability!

Since then the long shadows have become an obsession with me. I play them meticulously and continually during these days when both trout and bass in hot, bright weather seem to be nowhere willing to give even the most persistent angler's dependable creations the slightest recognition.

I yield to the influence of long shadows with bass at those lakes and streams especially where visiting anglers declare that it is useless to try for them with anything but live bait. Such fishing grounds are those most affected when the weather is hot and the sky cloudless. Most every artificial offering at such a time fails to bring a rise. The bronze backs appear to be down deep and temporarily too lethargic to feed or move about. It was at Lake Mazinaw, in the North Country, when I made a long trip to meet unfavorable fishing weather of this sort. Anglers I met threw up their hands in despair and told me confidentially that it was useless to fish in this region.

A bluff of tremendous proportions across from camp held my attention. First, I contemplated it with brief cynosure. Looking at it again it had a fascination for me, despite the fact that I was repeatedly informed by local savants that no bass ever harbored there; the water was too deep. All the fish that had been taken near its base were lake trout via the leisurely trolling method. Nevertheless, that huge bluff frowned down at me. The more I looked at it, the more I began to take a hopeful slant on its location, until its potentials for long shadows actually gripped me.

The shadows from it gradually lengthened as the sun dropped slowly in the west; a bronze ball of fire altogether too hot for an angler for the time being to realize he was in the North Country. And such shadows! Big, murky, well defined contrasts of vivid black floating in cerulean blue. *McGinty* is a fly of tremendous popularity on account of its elasticity with anglers insofar that they can imagine it resembles so many things in Nature and, after all, nothing very closely, save a mythical bumble bee. It is good to try out waters, when fishing, with the curiosity idea or natural belligerence of game fish. What better offering for my long shadows?

From the very terminus lakeward of the shadow I shot my big floater from a long distance, taking advantage of a slight breeze at my back, which would float by enticement, after giving it time, to the very foot of the bluff; my objective was farther than I was able to achieve.

The fly dropped lightly and, as I wished, the wind gradually bore it down, dancing slowly on small wavelets to its intended destiny. For a brief space of time, nothing occurred. Then all at once as I thought it opportune to begin to take in slack to make a pick-up for the next cast, I saw a monster rise, smash my bug and create as much disturbance on the lake as if a huge rock had fallen from a height into it.

Fifteen minutes after I landed a five-pound small-mouth bass after a strenuous battle. After that, I rose a fish at almost every cast, which I duly returned to the water. But all of them would have been of keepable size, if my first response in the long shadows had not been all I needed.

The land of the Habitant, especially in the Gatineau valley, repeatedly fulfills my fondness for fishing long shadows. Pat told me of Green Lake and its abundance of fighting, resourceful small-mouthed bass. I wondered afterwards how I had missed it on my first trip there. Pat showed it to me after we had crossed Whitefish Lake, and achieved the short portage to its shores. Pat's Celtic appellation comes from his Irish forbears, who had sought their destiny in the Laurentian mountains and, like a lot of other Irishmen, their names remained with their descendants, but not their language. Pat spoke only the Breton accented French of the province and deported himself with its mannerisms.

Green Lake was a substitute for two promised trout lakes to which we were unable to carry in a canoe. No trails had been cut, the second growth spruce making it impossible. *"Lac pour lachigans!"* Pat said, pointing a brown finger at the spread of rocky-shored water in front of us. If ever a lake was made to order for bass this certainly was one, and needed no such announcement from the sturdy woodsman. Every indentation was impeccably right for bass, the sloping shoals, weed beds and irregular, boulder strewn bottom.

Nevertheless, the elements were against us. The noon hour had just passed; not a hint of a breeze dimpled the surface. Such a hot day as this was rarely experienced in northern Quebec. If I were able to "rise" a fish, it would certainly be through bass bug or big, floating bass fly artistry. A more difficult method of delicate casting than the finest of dry fly trout fishing ever exacts for success. The timing is different and the weight of the fly, as well as not being able to use a tapered leader effectively explain this. Some of my most skilled dry fly fishing companions, though they have tried for years, have never mastered casting a bass bug as it should be done.

A swarm of dragon flies hovering close to a bed of lilies, altogether too close to the water for their safety in a bass lake caused my hopes to fall several degrees.

"*Au jourd'hui* better try live minnows," Pat suggested politely, "or *ecrivisse*, what you call crawfish in English."

The guide, however when I nodded my head without words on my part, realized the reason I demurred. For I assembled my hard action dry fly rod and fingered over my feathered and bucktail dependables, and finally selected a coal black bug with a heavy body fabricated entirely from bucktail hair, save two tiny streamers of hackle feathers.

"Don't expect me to catch anything at this time of day, Pat," I remarked in advance of assured failure. "But I am going to scare any bass that happens to be out in shallow water nearly to death."

"I t'ink so, too, eh!" the Habitant retorted with a doubtful glare at my dark atrocity. "When you want start, I be ready."

What I had in mind Pat could not divine since I made no comment after working carefully a mile of ideal shoreline without a rise from a bass of consequence. True, there were curious, agile little fellows aplenty, corroborative evidence of parents somewhere.

"Mebbe better use live minnows," the Habitant again suggested while I observed with self-contained humor his sole anachronism of locality. This dyed-in-the-wool, capable outdoorsman had yielded to one trend of the times. His hair had been slicked in the effeminate fashion of modern youth. It actually, while glistening in the sun, struck an inharmonious note in the surroundings.

I stared at the contented little man, smiling to myself, as I cast here and there without objective. All the time he paddled silently and slowly. And during the alternate process of gazing at him and directing my fly at potential nooks, unintentionally I looked over his head at the background on the right side of the long, rocky bay and drew immediate hope. A big pocket of water tucked back in this sun-heating rimming of rock, showing here and there sporadic growths of bulrushes.

"What about across the bay, Pat?" I directed my companion's attention.

"Her no d---n good," the Habitant answered deprecatingly and began to explain the reason thereof. "Shallow, very shallow."

I never heard his last words. Even at the distance from which I observed the commotion, I could distinguish the unexpected smash of a large bass at something. Further survey revealed a large circling of wavelike water, the wake of the strike of a big fish darting for concealment through a shoal; and finally its disappearance in a long shadow created by a triumvirate of leaning cedars that defied anyone to tell the reason they did not lose their hold on the cleavages of the rocky embankment and fall into the water.

Pat had not seen what I saw. When I told him of the fish and how I would try for it, he protested against such futility with numerous "too shallows" and "ketch *lachigans* now with live minnows only." But his objections were of no avail. At that moment I wanted to try for that huge bronze back, the outcome of which pro team I relegated to speculating. Nevertheless, I was positive that one bass was secreted in the recess of the long shadows and the potentials of that locality held me spellbound.

When the outcome of an angler's planning results in the capture of a prize fish, he takes great credit unto himself, though old Dame Nature may have been subtly arranging things for him. But I gave no thought to this. I explained my plans to Pat. Soberly he agreed to them after he had rid himself of some of his objections. There was not sufficient depth of water to hold a fish of the size I had mentally approximated, of this he felt sure, and deep water nearby was now its lair from which only with his beloved minnows could it be tempted.

The distance at which a fish, especially a bass, can see its enemies in shallow water no angler knows accurately. At any rate, it is altogether too far. I knew I was in for some long casting, with an objectionable wind at my back suddenly quartering, which possibly would defeat a part of my intentions. The instant I realized this, I sacrificed three feet of a six-foot leader to guard against any possible bellying after I had attached a rather weighty dragon fly of two strange shades of blue bucktail. It was a real enticer but difficult, usually, to pick up off the water easily which always subtracts something from an efficient backcast.

No fish, when on the alert, is so wary as a sophisticated old bass. You can give an old brook trout a glimpse of your presence and often hook him five minutes afterwards. With a mature small-mouth, once one sees you, you had better wait a half hour at least before you resume casting. He will stand for a loud splash occasionally but the vision of his enemy, man, may put him on extra guard against his offerings for some time to come, though he may be the boldest of fish under certain conditions.

When our canoe approached within seventy-five feet of my prospective prize, I called a halt. The Habitant held the light craft still with no extra effort in the shallow water. Closer approach was not good tactics, nor is seventy-five feet an easy distance to cast while seated in the bow of a canoe. Standing up was unpardonable. What a sight of me it would give to the lurking bronze warrior! I noted my position, the extreme shallowness of the water and the long shadows of the leaning cedars merged apparently into one.

Dark, secret water, cutting under the bank, laced with a drooping curtain of ferns. Suddenly I noticed there was a yard long of considerable depth there, and the width of it I had no way of approximating. My eyes were unable to penetrate it. That the huge bass was in it I had not the least doubt, there was no other visible place for concealment. My first glimpse of it, too, had assured me it had not gone to deep water on our side.

Fortunately my fly line was heavy and the light rod possessed a powerful, hard action. I shot high from my seat, as though I was trying to put my fly over a fair sized building to one side of my objective since I had to take some advantage of the way in which a quartering wind had shifted. Eventually, without the slightest disturbance, I dropped my dragon fly close to the base of the leaning cedars.

Though it was but a matter of brief happening seconds, I held my breath with suspense, as I saw an immense small-mouth swim out from the dark crypt and leisurely survey from several feet away my blue bucktail contraption. With indolent gaze he seemed to regard it and then with an ultimate quick scrutiny, as though trying at the last moment to detect something different from the real. Then he circled it appraisingly at the exact moment I made the pick-up and again fortunately negotiated my shoot for the identical spot where it had rested untouched.

To this day I do not know if my fly ever touched the water, so quick and virile was its immediate acceptance. But on one point my memory is clear and that is again I had hooked into one of the truculent warriors of the long shadows.

THE FIRST RISE

C.B.H. Vail

Not ice, nor storm nor sleet nor bitter cold can stay
the enthusiasm of the ardent flyfisher on the brink
of a new season. (May 1940)

STEADYING myself on a smooth stone, I cast my bucktail into a dark eddy formed where the ripping water of the Farmington turned sharply at the broken face of a large boulder. The fly lay for a moment on the little backwater and then was snatched away by the current. As it started to move, there was a flash, and a trout cleared the water in his attempt to nail it. The current was too fast for him, however, and he made a clean miss.

I let the fly drag in the fast water and retrieved it slowly. That fish would need a few minutes rest before he would strike again. I took in the slack line sullenly. I didn't care whether that trout struck again or not. He probably would, and I, forewarned, would probably catch him. What of it? There were already three nice trout in the creel, all taken on that selfsame bucktail. It was a good enough catch, but nevertheless I was cross, rebellious, and petulant.

The weather matched my feelings perfectly. It was cold and raw and dismal, a sort of hiccough in the orderly progress of spring. The sharp gusts of wind picked up flying spray from the fast water, and made sweeping corrugated patches in the still places. Sometimes the unkind gale brought sharp squalls of stinging wet snow with it, and the bare branches of the elms and the maples moaned and whistled as if it were mid-January. Two entirely necessary sweaters bound my arms awkwardly, and no amount of heavy wool socks could prevent the penetration of an icy chill to the very bones of my feet.

These physical discomforts were nothing, however, compared to my state of mind. I was betrayed and bedevilled by the weather. I had come out for a day with the dry fly, and I had confidently expected some great sport. True, it was only the end of April, but I had good reason to expect a better break than this, and I had waited for it patiently . . .

Waited since that day, a week before the season opened, when I had gone up the river to look it over and get a foretaste of the sport to come. That day had been bright and sunny, with no bite in the air. The ice had left the river, and the water was, for the time being, clear. As I scrambled along the edge, observing what changes the winter had made in the bed and the banks, I saw a startled deer, and a little later, a lithe mink slipped silently out of sight up a small feeder stream. The cawing of the crows was almost gay.

And just when I was most strongly feeling the delight of the awakening spring and the brilliant day, I saw a trout rise! For a minute I doubted my senses. A rising trout on April tenth? Impossible! But even as I thought it, the fish rose again. He left no room for doubt this time, showing at least two inches of his broad tail as he turned. And again he rose!

I watched him for several minutes, long enough to see that he was feeding steadily, and that it was not a mere erratic gesture. Then I scrambled upstream to the Island Pool, in whose long still reaches many trout spend the winter. As I approached, I saw dimples on the quiet surface. Sure enough, the trout were rising here, too. It was not just one crazy fish acting unseasonably; it was a general feeding movement.

It continued for half an hour and stopped as suddenly as it had begun. The river was lifeless when the sun began to sink and throw long shadows across the water. The normal chill returned. But I went home happily. If they were rising now, five days before the season opened, what wouldn't they be doing after it had opened? It looked as if we would have dry fly fishing right from the word "Go!"

But the fine weather held only for a few days, and the season opened in cold and rain. The water rose and lost its clarity, and every morning found a film of ice on spray-splashed rocks, and glittering pendants on the bushes which fringed the river. For a week, the entire countryside was drenched in gloom, and thousands of rivulets rushing down the still-frozen hillsides blended their voices in a continuous complaining murmur. There was little fishing to be had, what with the river threatening to top its banks, and the back roads a sea of bottomless mud. The intrepid worm fishermen, seeking the depths and the backwaters, took a few trout, but hardly enough to compensate for the arctic discomfort which attended their efforts.

I betook myself to the brooks and caught a few small thin fish on the reliable Royal Coachman, fished very, very wet. Under the hemlocks of the headwaters there were still banks of hard-packed snow disintegrating into the streams. There was no sign of the fulfillment of the promise given by the earlier weather. I went to look at the river once or twice, but turned away from its roily flood in disappointment.

And then the rain stopped. It remained cold, and down went the water, clearing gradually. Familiar pools again became recognizable, and

the mudholes in the roads dried into deep ruts, awkward and unpleasant, but passable. All that was wanting was a warm sunny day, and the fishing would be good. Surely, if the trout were rising two weeks ago, they would not hesitate to repeat the performance at the first opportunity!

Finally a morning came when the early air was soft, the breezes gentle, and the sun honestly warm. I shed all other considerations as a snake sheds its skin, and started for the river, confident that the day would redeem the entire spring with its benevolent excellence.

The river murmured sweetly in its normal channels, clear and inviting. As if drawn up by the sun, the green spikes of the hellebore were thrusting through the sand, and the thickets were dusted with the greenish-grey of adventurous pussy-willows. Eagerly I strung up my tackle and stepped into the river.

A medium-sized brown bivisible seemed like a good bet. My first cast fell on the water as accurately and as gently as if I had been practising all winter. The fly came dancing down the current, riding high and proudly, straight toward a dependable rock which always harbors a good brown trout. I drew a deep breath of expectation, fingered the handgrasp preparatory to the firm but gentle setting of the hook, and . . .

Nothing happened. The fly bounced past the proper spot and drowned itself, and I lifted it from the water, a little chagrined, but not overly surprised. The days of waiting had worked me up to too high a pitch; it was too much to expect a rise on the very first cast of the season. The second might do it.

The second did not do it, nor the third. Very well, I said to myself, I'll Labranche the beast out of his reluctance; there must be a trout there . . . Again and again the fly travelled down that strip of current unmolested. On the fortieth cast, I changed to a small Pink Lady; on the sixtieth, I tried a Badger, and with the eightieth, I gave up in disgust. Create a hatch! Bah!

I moved on upstream a little, to the place where I had seen that first trout rise weeks earlier. Perhaps he had not yet fallen for the charms of a nightcrawler. Maybe he could be persuaded to rise. At least, I'd have a somewhat more definite assurance that I was actually casting to a fish. But at the end of half an hour, innumerable casts, and several changes of flies, the assurance had dwindled considerably. There was very little left of my morning elation.

Then, suddenly, the color went out of the river. The diamond glittering of the rapids turned to lead, the blues and yellows and reds in the water faded to an even gunmetal, and the tentative green of the trees and bushes shrank back to tired brown and grey. In surprise, I looked over my shoulder and saw that during my pre-occupation with the casting, a swirling bank of dirty grey clouds had crept up out of the northeast and had just now swallowed the sun. Even as I looked, the first evil breath of icy wind hissed across the water and set the bare branches and bushes to tossing in indignant protest. It was a complete return to the weather of the past ten days; the rain would begin any minute.

The rain had not begun when I got back to the car. I found that the unaccustomed strain of wading fast water after a long layoff had tired me, and I relaxed on the seat before taking down the rod. There was a package of sandwiches and a thermos of coffee. I ate and drank and smoked, and I felt better. An occasional snowflake whipped past the car, but no rain . . . Now I was warm and rested. Why not do a little more fishing? The water was not too high, and I might as well bring something home. I donned an extra sweater, changed leaders, put on a big bucktail, and went back to the place I had left when the sun was blotted out.

On my first cast to that spot which I had belabored so long and so carefully before lunch, there was a smashing strike. The fish had been there all the time, ignoring my best and fanciest efforts! I slipped him into the creel with warm satisfaction, tempered with just a little disappointment at the means needed to catch him. I wanted to use the dry fly.

The wind grew stronger and the snow more plentiful, and as I worked downstream, the feeling of well-being was pretty far used up, despite two more easily caught fish. Conditions became steadily worse right up to the time I cast to the eddy back of the rock and missed that strike.

I'll take this fish, I said to myself, and then quit. One more and home.

For five long cold minutes I waited. Then I flicked the fly on to the proper spot, and as the current started to take it away, I tightened my wrist to make an automatic strike of it. But there was no rise. Surely I had rested that trout long enough; it seemed like an hour to me!

I cast twice more without response, and then made myself admit that perhaps I had been hasty. I knew that I had made no other mistake; I was positive that the fish had had no disillusioning taste of the fly, and I was using the same technique throughout which had brought the initial strike. It was ten full minutes by my wrist watch before I cast again, ten minutes of shivering exasperation. I wouldn't have waited ten seconds except that I had incautiously told myself that I would take that fish!

Again I set myself for an instantaneous response, and again it did not come. I changed flies and tried again. No results. The last remnants of my temper were whirled away in a blinding flurry of snow, and I plunked a great four-inch bright orange streamer against the side of the rock. It bounced and fell into the water, lay still a moment, and slithered temptingly away as the current seized the bight of the leader.

With that failure, reason and balance returned. I realized that this fish was not like his gullible brothers, to be taken in by any moving object crossing his line of vision. This worthy creature must be fished for. It was an interesting problem; no longer a matter of catching another fish and going home, but a complicated business requiring that I pit my skill and knowledge against a recalcitrant trout under abominably bad conditions. This was worth doing!

I sat for some time in a miniature blizzard and let the trout recover from the probable effects of that last gaudy streamer before I attacked again. My hands, which had stiffened into mere claws while changing flies, were now warm, and my feet forgot that ice had apparently been forming between my toes. I could still tell when a wet snowflake went down my neck, but otherwise my concentration on the immediate problem was complete.

First I tried several small wet flies, a Royal Coachman, a Cowdung, a March Brown, a Brown Hackle. Then I slowly worked through my supply of bucktails, light, dark, small, large, smooth, fuzzy, sober and outlandish. Then I fooled about with nymphs of various sorts. Then I put on a small spinner, but I did not use it; on my first backcast, a gust of wind snapped it off, and I could find no trace of where it fell. That ended my resources, except for dry flies, and since it was snowing steadily and heavily, and the sky growing ever darker and gloomier as the afternoon waned, I did not give them a thought until I was out of the stream on the way to the car, and the fish lay triumphantly in the river behind me.

That idea halted me. I had not used every resource! I still had the dry flies. Foolish, perhaps, considering the conditions, but that fish deserved everything I had. I stepped back into the river below the rock and put on a Badger bivisible, hoping that no one would happen by to witness my folly. A dry fly in a snowstorm!

The wind was troublesome, since the size of the eddy gave little latitude, and the fly must land accurately. It could only rest an instant before the side current would whip it away. And if it collided with one of those big snowflakes in the air, it would be matted and soaked before it ever reached its destination. But finally I worked it out as I wished, and let it drop on the little backwater.

The response was instantaneous, competent, and satisfactory. I was much too surprised by the trout's enthusiastic leap to think of striking, but the current helpfully seized the leader at the proper moment and drove the barb home.

He put up a battle-royal, that trout, but after a weary time I netted him and waded ashore. He would weigh about a pound, I estimated. That was good enough for me, and I decided not to bother with scales. I slipped him into the creel to join his refrigerated brethren, and started back to the car. I was plastered with wet snow, my feet were again like blocks of ice in my waders, and my joints worked creakingly and with protest. The guides of my rod were half-plugged with ice, and the reel was matted with slush. I had to clip the line to detach it from the leader.

But I whistled a merry tune as I walked back to the car. The dry fly season had begun!

LET'S GO FISHIN'

Herbert Hoover

The 31st President of the United States was a dedicated and enthusiastic angler who here recommends the pastime to salve a war-torn nation's wounds. (June 1944)

RECENTLY I made some suggestions for an economic and social tidying-up of our country in preparation for the return of our boys from overseas. As I wrote, I was depressed by the thousand mournful voices chanting daily of "postwar problems" in such powerful terms as recovery, reconstruction and regeneration.

But in their research efforts in speech and their labors in type, they all concern themselves solely with what we are to do while we are on their promised jobs. Civilization, however, is not going to depend so much on what we do when we are on the job, as what we do in our time off. The moral and spiritual forces do not lose ground while we are pushing "the instrumentalities of production and distribution." Their battle is in our leisure time.

When the guns cease firing, and the gas comes on again, some of us are going fishing. We American men and boys (and some women) are born fishermen—twelve million of us. We have proved it in bygone days by the annual licenses we took out from thrifty state governments.

We have had mostly to postpone the fishing beatitudes for the duration. Many of us are busy at the military front. Some of us on the home front could possibly get a day or a week off, but the fishing holes can only be approached by automobile or motorboats, and a stern government refuses to recognize that fish do not flourish near railway depots.

In the meantime, I suspect that Mother Nature is making the fish bigger and more plentiful by way of preparing to celebrate peace, and our paternal government is doing its duty to solve our post-war problems by running the hatcheries full blast, turning out billions of infant fish and trying to decrease infant mortality.

I have discussed this important subject in years past, but some review and extension of those remarks are not out of place in these days when we are groping for postwar regeneration. Nothing can stop these regenerative forces.

Even the Four Horsemen cannot stop them. War, murrain, famine, pestilence, dictators, the rise and fall of empires or republics may defeat the game fisherman temporarily, but he rises again to invade the streams and the sea. More people have gone fishing over more centuries than for any other human recreation.

Sometimes the uninstructed and the people who have bad "isms" scoff at the game fishermen and demand to know how they get that way. It is very, very simple. These regenerative impulses are physical, spiritual and economic—and they are strong.

The human animal originally came from out-of-doors. When spring begins to move in his bones, he just must get out again. One time, in the spring, our grandmothers used to give us nasty brews from herbs to purify our blood of the winter's corruptions. They knew something was the matter with the boys. They could have saved trouble by giving them a pole, a string and a hook. Some wise ones (among them my own) did just that.

Moreover, as civilization, cement pavements, office buildings, radios have overwhelmed us, the need for regeneration has increased, and the impulses are even stronger. When all the routines and details and the human bores get on our nerves, we just yearn to go away from here to somewhere else. To go fishing is a sound, a valid and an accepted reason for such an escape.

It is the chance to wash one's soul with pure air, with the rush of the brook, or with the shimmer of the sun on blue water. It brings meekness and inspiration from the decency of nature, charity toward tackle-makers, patience toward fish, a mockery of profits and egos, a quieting of hate, a rejoicing that you do not have to decide a darned thing until next week. And it is discipline in the equality of men—for all men are equal before fish.

Necessarily, fishermen are gregarious. Otherwise, the mighty deeds of the day or of a year ago or of ten years ago would go unsung. No one else will listen to them. Also, they are an optimistic class or they would not be fishermen. Therefore, as two or three are gathered together, the spiritual vitamins of faith, hope and charity have constant regeneration. And we need all that in these years of creaking civilization, and especially in the coming years of postwar tribulation.

Nor does this source of spiritual vitamins require any governmental bureau to administer it. All that is required of Congress is to restore our freedom from the fellows who restrict the use of gasoline, and the rugged individualism of the fisherman will do the rest.

His joys are not all confined to the hours near the water. I asserted years ago that one of the elements in the advance of civilization was the progress in the equipment to overcome the mysteries of fish. We have moved upward and onward from the primitive willow pole with a butcher-string line and hooks (ten for a dime) whose compelling lure was one segment of a worm and whose incantation was spitting on the bait. We have arrived at labor-saving devices and increased efficiency in tackle assembled from the bamboo of Burma, the steel of Sweden, the lacquer of China, the tin of Bangkok, the nickel of Madagascar, the silver of Nevada, and the feathers of Brazil—all compounded into mass production at Akron, Ohio.

For magic and incantations, we have moved forward to cosmetics for artificial flies, and wonders in special clothes, and bags with pigeonholes for everything, including mosquito repellents. We no longer call it a "pole," for it is a "rod," and we no longer say that a fish "bites," he now "strikes."

Out of all this progress, a good fisherman can secure many regenerative hours of winter, polishing up the rods and reels, greasing the lines and discussing the relative merits of gay-colored flies and dead-sure lures—thereby recalling that Big One from the pool just below the rapids and the fly he rose to.

Nor is fishing a rich man's regeneration. That boy with the worm and a grin is always a reminder that men are equal before fish. However, that boy misses out in one particular that I hope to see attended to in our next era of national reform. There is regenerative joy in contemplating and fondling adequate tackle, which he cannot get out of a collection of angleworms. And his joys are more seasonal because he cannot put in the winter nights polishing up that tackle with its reminder of that Big One from that pool and thereby the renewed smell of battles to come.

I acknowledge to a prominent official an idea to reform this. All boys should be guaranteed from birth to manhood a quart of polish and a collection of tackle with an assortment of special flies. There has been sad neglect in this question of assuring artificial flies to the youth of our land, for flies proved their inspiring worth perhaps four hundred years ago—long before Izaak Walton.

When I was a boy and lived at the social level of worms, a true fisherman gave me three flies—a coachman, a gray hackle and a professor. I treasured them greatly and used them successfully for two or three years—until the wings were all worn off. But there were more fish in proportion to the water in those times.

There are some class distinctions among fishermen. The dry-fly devotees hold themselves a bit superior to the wet-fly fishermen; the wet-fly fishermen, superior to the spinner fishermen; and the spinners, superior to the bait fishermen. I have noticed, however, that toward the end of the day when there were no strikes each social level sometimes descends down the scale until it gets some fish for supper.

This class distinction may perhaps be ignored in the general reformation, for it is not based on the economic levels. The best dry fisherman I have known is a lady cook at a lumber camp in Montana. She scorned the wet-fly fishermen and rose to indignation at bait.

The swordfish and tarpon fishermen likewise have some social distinctions on the basis of the size of line and reel. The lower-thread line operators are the dukes and earls in that aristocracy. Also, the swordfish and marlin devotees are naturally superior to those who take mere mackerel, amber jacks or flounders. The bonefish fishermen claim a little superiority to the tarpon seekers. But again it is not economic status that counts in such good society so much as knowing what the fish bite.

Someone propounded the question to me: "Why have all Presidents in modern times been fishermen?" It seemed to me a worthy investigation, for the habits of Presidents are likely to influence the nation's youth. Some of us had been fishermen from boyhood and required no explanation. But others only became fishermen after entering the White House. In examining this national phenomenon, I concluded that the pneumatic hammering of demands on the President's mind had increased in frequency with the rising tide of economic and international complexity, and he just had to get away somehow, somewhere, and be alone for a few hours once in a while. But there are only two occasions when Americans respect privacy, especially in Presidents. Those are prayer and fishing. So that some have taken to fishing.

President Cleveland was both a stream and a sea fisherman from youth. His stiff trout rod is still preserved by a devoted fisherman, and it is recorded that his sea-fishing boatman was chosen for silence. Whether President Coolidge fished in his youth is uncertain. He was a good deal of a fundamentalist in economics, government and fishing, so he naturally preferred angleworms. But when the fly fishermen of the nation raised their eyebrows in surprise, he took to artificial flies. However, his backcast was so much a common danger that even the Secret Service men kept at a distance until they were summoned to climb trees to retrieve flies.

But I should return to expanding on postwar regeneration and its moral and spiritual values in a gloomy world. Statistics tell us that the gainfully employed have steadily decreased in hours of work during the whole of thirty years. And in shorter hours and longer week ends and holidays, we have devoted more time to making merry and stirring the caldron of evil. Crime has increased. Yet nobody ever was in jail or plotted a crime when fishing. The increase of crime is among those deprived of those regenerations that impregnate the mind and character of fishermen.

Our standards of material progress include the notion and the hope that we shall still further lessen the daily hours of labor. We also dream of longer annual holidays as scientific discovery and mass production do our production job faster and faster. But when they do the job, they dull the souls of men unless their leisure hours become the period of life's real objective—regeneration by fishing.

Moreover, while we are steadily organizing increased production of leisure time, the production of what to do with it still lags greatly. We do have some great machinery of joy, some of it destructive, some of it synthetic, much of it mass production. We go to chain theaters and movies. We watch somebody else knock a ball over the fence or kick it over the goal post.

I do that and I believe in it. But these forms of organized joy are sadly lacking in the values which surround the fish. We gain none of the lift of soul coming from a return to the solemnity, the calm and inspiration of primitive nature.

Nor is it the fish that we get that counts, for they can be had in the market for mere silver. It is the break of the waves in the sun, the joyous rush of the brook, the contemplation of the eternal flow of the stream, the stretch of forest and mountain in their manifestation of the Maker, that soothes our troubles, shames our wickedness and inspires us to esteem our fellow men—especially other fishermen.

UPSTREAM OR DOWN?

John Alden Knight

*The father of the Solunar Tables® resisted rules
about flyfishing including the one about always
fishing above your position in a stream.
(March 1949)*

WHEN, I wonder, are folks going to learn that it is a dangerous thing to attempt to lay down hard and fast rules about fishing? It's been tried many times, always with embarrassing repercussions. No sooner does a fellow arrive at a nice, neat set of common-sense rules of fishing and, still worse, make these rules a matter of public record, than the fish hold a meeting, conspire, and proceed to upset the applecart. Let's take a quick look at a couple of these dicta. Some of them have been found, rather quickly, to be unsound. Others have persisted down through all too many years. It is contrary to human nature to doubt the veracity of the printed word, especially when it's reprinted over and over, time without end.

In his day and age, Dr. J. A. Henshall was No. 1 man on black bass. His book, *Book of the Black Bass*, published first in 1881, was for many, many years—and still is, for that matter—generally accepted as the standard work on the subject. His famous line, "I consider him, *inch for inch*, and *pound for pound*, the gamest fish that swims," no doubt will live forever. Yet in that very book the good doctor makes this astonishing statement:

"It is folly for the angler to cast his flies upon a smooth surface, if the water is clear enough for fishing."

No hedging there; no side-stepping; there it is, an outright, flat-footed pronouncement. In view of what we know of bass fishing today, it is needless to comment on that rule of fishing, save to remind you of the power of the printed word. To show you its lasting effect, this same sentence was used as the keynote of the instructions on fly-fishing for bass in the *Forest and Stream Sportsmen's Encyclopedia*, published in 1923, 42 years later.

Or consider the admonitions we used to receive on the futility of fishing anything other than fast water in a trout stream, especially if we happened to be using dry flies. Fish the fast water if you really want trout. Leave the pools alone. In fast water a trout must decide quickly to take or reject a fly; in a pool he can look it over and take his own sweet time about making up his mind. Don't waste your time in the pools.

Fortunately for some of us, it took the general run of trout fishermen about 25 years to find the holes in that one. Meanwhile we unbelievers had the pools to ourselves. Today it is apt to be the fast water, not the pools, that is fished by the minority.

There are many other instances of exploded theories, but there is neither space nor need here to explore them. Let's take a look—a good, close look—at one of the *un*-explored ones.

Ever since the introduction of the dry fly, we have been coached in the ritual of its use. Fish always above your position, so that your fly will drift like a natural insect. Let the current carry it without motion imparted to it by the leader. Avoid drag at all costs. Always that bugbear DRAG is held up before us as the constant danger signal. Drag, they tell you, is a sure-fire way to put down your rising trout. Shun it as you would the plague. What they *don't* tell you is why it is common practice to drag a wet fly—and, incidentally, catch plenty of fish by so doing—and not to drag a dry fly. Both wet flies and dry flies simulate, theoretically, natural insects. Why differentiate?

When you come right down to cases, I don't know a better way to put down a big trout than to cast a leader and, still worse, a line over him. Even in a small stream, where the trees and bushes on the bank make it impossible to cast any other way than directly upstream or directly downstream, it is better to approach a large trout from the upstream side. You can say all you wish about curve casts, but the light disturbance that is caused by the fall of a leader and line often will ruin your chances and put down a big fish.

Even though a large fish decides to ignore the leader, an upstream cast often is hazardous. Leaders are hard, resilient things, entirely foreign in "feel" to the sensibilities of a trout. Thus, when a big fellow rises, if his nose happens to touch the leader as he takes your fly the resultant frightened splash will put down every feeding fish in the area.

One June day I was fishing one of the smaller streams in central Pennsylvania. The weather was fine, a solunar period was in progress, and a liberal hatch of big May-fly drakes was coming down from the riffle above the pool. As I rounded the bend at the tail of the pool, moving upstream, I saw that several large trout were feeding actively to the hatch. Wishing to plan my approach before casting to them, I watched them feed for a while, making careful note of their locations as they rose. There were seven of them, all big fish, and I was pleased to note that the one nearest me was the best of the lot.

This pool is a long, narrow affair, quite deep, and flanked by over-hanging trees. It can be fished only from directly below or directly above. I knew that in any event it would be a long cast, as the water was low and gin-clear. The probabilities were that it would be a one-cast job. By de-touring through the woods, I could have approached the pool from the upstream side, but I knew that my fly would then be taken by one of the lesser fish upstream, and I wanted to hook the big fellow. After thinking it over, I decided to risk a wide, right-hand negative curve cast, and see if luck would favor me.

Slowly I made my way as close to the feeding fish as I dared. When I was still 50 feet or so from them I began to work out line by false casting. When I had the range, I let go the final cast. It was a good cast and I could see that it was going where I wanted it to go. Unfortunately, at that moment a puff of wind came up the valley, caught my big fly, and straightened the right curve so that my leader flanked the feeding lane, perhaps two feet to the left of the big fish's location. However, the fly looked edible, so he drifted over to take it. Up came his big nose and the leader lay right across it as he opened his mouth. The frenzied splash he made as he discovered the deception sounded like that of a beaver slapping the water with his tail. And that was that.

I reeled in my line and waded over to the bank. There I sat for more than an hour while the May-fly hatch drifted down past me unmolested. During that full hour's time not another fish fed in the pool. Then the hatch was over and all was quiet. Had I approached the pool from above, I am quite sure that, barring unforeseen misfortune, I would have had at least one large trout to show for my pains, and would have saved a full hour of good fishing time.

In the big rivers it is not always possible to take your position directly above a feeding fish. These streams are too sizable for indiscriminate wading. Thus, the downstream technique often must be elaborated with the use of curve casts. Only occasionally, however, do we find an instance where the fly cannot be brought down to the fish with the leader point extending upstream. In these rare instances we cast to the side of the trout's location and, if we do this often enough, usually we can persuade him to leave his feeding station and move toward us. This, of course, places the leader point in line with his direction of motion, still unobtrusive and out of the way so that he can take the fly without touching the hard gut.

Taking big brown trout on light tackle with what have come to be called "orthodox" methods often is somewhat of a paradox. If your tackle is large enough to hold the fish, he refuses to take; if your tackle is fine enough to interest him, more often than not he will smash your terminal gear as though it were gossamer. By using the downstream technique, you can eliminate at least part of this hazard. With your fly coming to him first and the leader and line out of sight upstream, it is not necessary to use extra-fine leader points. Thus, I never fish anything finer than 3-x points, and in the early season I use 2-x points quite successfully.

Here and there in our big Pennsylvania streams there are long, reasonably shallow "flats." These places almost always hold their full share of big brown trout. During broad daylight, it is impossible to come within casting range of a big fish in such water. No matter how much care is used, he will stop feeding while you are still 70 or 80 feet away, and you can cast your arm off for all the good it will do you. Reasoning that there must be some way to take these fish, we evolved the method of drift-wading.

The procedure is to wade out into the feeding lane at the head of the flat. The location of this feeding lane is usually well marked by the line of riffle foam extending right down through the entire pool. Once in position, we cast downstream as much line as we can. Then we strip off line and perhaps 20 or 30 feet of backing. This done, we wade right down through the flat, our fly, leader, line and backing drifting ahead. If the fly is well oiled and the line and all but two feet of the leader well treated with line dressing, we can fish for 200 or 300 feet before reeling in and recasting. The current in these places always is slow, and it is possible to wade along at the same speed so that the tackle won't be pulled under by current action. When we first tried this method, we were surprised at the number of good fish we were able to take—fish that otherwise would have remained untouched from one season to the next.

Even in the fast water, we no longer fish above our positions. Instead, we use curve casts and fish directly across or slightly below. It is not as easy or pleasant fishing as it is to fish upstream, but we do take more trout that way with a dry fly.

Last spring I had the dubious assignment of doing the fishing scenes for a motion picture that was being made for one of the film rental services. Knowing the approximate date of the annual caddis hatch on our streams, I arranged to have the cameraman here at that time. As we had hoped, the caddis hatch showed up on the appointed day and the weather was sunny—sunny but very windy. The trout fed freely to the drifting insects, but the strong wind was blowing upstream. The water had been chosen for its photographical excellence, and was too deep to permit unhampered wading. We had to fish where we could, not where we wished.

With the upstream wind, it was virtually impossible to throw a downstream curve. Never have I seen so many leadershy trout. Just let one of them catch a glimpse of a leader and he would stop feeding for 15 or 20 minutes.

Though the wind was strong, it was slightly puffy and irregular. We adopted the expedient of waiting for a lull, and then getting a curve cast on the water as quickly as possible. After that it was merely a case of selecting the trout you wanted, waiting for a lull, and then drifting the fly to him with a downstream curve. Not once did one of them refuse a fly that was presented to him in that manner. So long as the trout could not see the leader, he took without hesitation.

Inevitably in downstream fishing there comes a point where drag sets in. What then? If drag does all the horrible things that they tell us about, each trout would resolve itself into a one-cast proposition. After some experimentation I have learned that it is quite practical to utilize drag and convert it from a liability into an asset. I found this out more or less accidentally many years ago. When fishing big water, I would cast across and up (in the correct "orthodox" fashion), and allow my fly to drift down opposite me before picking up to recast. Now and then, in the hope of picking up a fish which had refused my offerings, I would allow the fly to drift down past me. Then when drag set in, I would skip the fly in short jumps across the current in a semicircle until my line was directly downstream. To my surprise, I found that I caught fish that way, but I had heard too many expert instructions to believe that drag could be utilized as an effective method for taking extra-selective trout. Utilize drag! Take fish on a dragging fly! Why, that was nothing short of pure heresy.

One day I was fishing the Brodhead with a friend of mine. We had come to a pool that is a right-angled affair. You know the kind. The current comes in from the side, sweeps across the top of the pool up against the far bank and then down along that bank to the next riffle, leaving a deep backwater eddy to form the center of the pool proper. My friend remarked that he had never caught a trout from that pool.

"Why?" I inquired.

"My fly drifts only about two feet. Then it starts to drag. One cast, and I've put every trout down."

"There are all sorts of drags," I told him. "Why don't you utilize your drag? There must be fish in that pool."

He looked at me as though I were a little mad, and told me to see what I could do. Fortunately, I had on a palmered fly at the time, so I cast it to the edge of the fast water. The line rested on the still water, not moving, so of course the fly began to drag before it had drifted more than a few feet. When drag set in, I raised my rod tip and brought the fly skipping toward me in erratic jumps about eight inches or a foot long. The fly made about three jumps and socko!—up from the bottom of the deep eddy came a nice brownie and took it into camp. A glance at my friend's face showed that a great light had dawned.

For a while, when we were investigating the possibilities of a dragging dry fly, we contented ourselves with fussing around with "skater" or "skitter" flies—big spiders with stiff hackles, sometimes reinforced about the hook shank with an application of clear lacquer. We used these only when we were "bump casting." This highly unorthodox procedure consists of casting in rough water with a fairly short line. The forward cast is aimed so that it terminates at least two or three feet above the water. Then, as the fly drops, the rod tip is raised rather sharply, causing the fly to strike the water at an angle and to bounce once or twice toward the caster before coming to rest.

Bump casting, however, is effective only in rough, broken water. Smooth water requires a longer line, as you can't crowd your trout without scaring them. Thus, the next logical step in this unethical series was the use of a well-greased line and leader, and skittering the big skater flies across perfectly flat water. Strangely enough, this method seems to have unusual appeal to large trout.

Exactly 18 minutes by car from the desk where this is being written is a stretch of trout water that is nearly always surprisingly productive. Year after year it holds its full quota of trout. The area is hard-fished but it is discouraging to the rank and file of the trout fishermen because the trout therein quickly develop a degree of superselectivity that often is difficult, if not impossible, to combat. A great deal of the time these fish feed on midges, of which there seems to be an inexhaustible supply. When they're doing that, you may just as well fold up your tent.

It so happened that I had located an unusually large trout in this water. Not one of the two- or three-pound ones, but a real old buster of a fish. Naturally, I spent much more time in that pool than was compatible with finished manuscripts and publishers' deadlines. One fine June morning I suffered at my desk until I could stand the pressure no longer. A glance at the solunar tables showed me that I could just about make it, so I climbed into my car and set sail.

Sure enough, the solunar period had brought a scattered hatch of flies down from the riffle, and I saw my big fish rise and take one of them. So that I wouldn't disturb the water, I made my way up the bank before wading in quietly to my casting position. There I waited until the big trout fed again.

The hatch was mixed, and I had not been able to see which fly the trout had taken, so I showed him a selection of five imitations of the drifting naturals. Nothing doing. The flies were well tied and they were presented properly, still he wasn't interested. At last, despairing of raising him, I made my way upstream in the hope of picking up a mess of lesser fry. My best efforts failed to raise so much as one single trout.

When I reached the top of the riffle, still fishless, I sat down on the bank to think things over. Then I happened to recall that skittering spiders sometimes took big fish, so I tied on a big brown bivisible spider. At that location, using a long, well-greased line, I heaved this cart wheel diagonally across-current and brought it back again below me in a series of short, well-spaced jerks. On the second cast a two-pound rainbow engulfed it with high gusto.

Having dealt sucessfully with the rainbow, I tied on a fresh spider, oiled it thoroughly, and went down to the home of my big trout. Fearing to crowd him, I cast as long a line as I could, and then started the spider on its erratic journey across the pool. The spider passed over his feeding station without incident and was well out toward the center of the pool when the big boy decided that he wanted it. Over he came, top speed, his dorsal fin cutting the water, and he fell on that spider like a wolf on a rabbit. That he came unhooked after a 10-minute tussle is of little consequence here; what is important is the fact that in water where "orthodox" methods had produced nothing, a skittering fly had hooked two large trout.

Since then, things have been going from bad to worse. We have elaborated the skittering method, combining it quite successfully with the downstream technique. Believe it or not, it really works wonders. This is the system as we now use it.

Suppose, for instance, there is a hatch of insects that look like Gray Quills drifting. Naturally we tie on Gray Quills. These we fish across and down so that the leader stays away from the fish. When the end of the natural drift is reached, we make the fly skitter its way to a point directly below us before picking it up. Should a fish refuse a quietly drifting fly, as a last resort we skitter the fly as it approaches the trout's feeding station. Believe it or not, we have taken more trout on dragging flies than we have on orthodox drifts.

When there is no hatch on the water, we don't resort to the big skaters any more. Instead, we use a palmered version of the hatch which is currently due, and employ the downstream-skittering technique. You'd be surprised how much action we can kick up among a group of nonfeeding trout.

This season it was our pleasure to have as a guest an editor of one of the outdoor magazines. I told him that we had been flying in the face of tradition by taking plenty of trout on dragging dry flies. He regarded me as though I had lost my mind. Despite his obvious reaction, I showed him the method and then stood back to watch him raise 24 trout to dragging dry flies in about an hour's fishing.

In case you do decide to turn pagan and try out this highly irregular procedure, let me give you a word of warning. *Don't* strike a downstream trout. Light gut simply will not stand the strain. When you raise a fish that is below you, merely lift the rod tip and tighten. That way, your days astream will be long and happy ones and your terminal tackle bills reduced by one half.

TROUT LORE FROM THE HOTTEST FISHERMAN I KNOW

Pete Barrett

*This highly regarded outdoor writer has some words
of wisdom handed down from an even higher
source. (February 1951)*

THIS IS for trout fishermen, particularly the newcomers of the season.
What I am about to do, in effect, is to interview an eminent authority on
his methods. I'll not reveal who he is just now, but I will say this: *The
information you are about to read is guaranteed to help you catch more fish.*

But first a thumbnail sketch of the fellow. He is along in years now,
and affects a style of clothing and speech that some would consider old-
fashioned, though if you met him fishing a stream in the Tennessee hill
country I dare say he wouldn't seem out of place. He carries a long-handled
net and a sturdy creel that, while still serviceable, sags at the bottom from
the weight of many fish. A kit bag for flies and such, and a light rod that

wears its set with an air—as fine rods will, so that you sense no ordinary trout strained its polished wood—completes his outfit.

I well remember the first question I put to him. It was just after the war and I had a tough decision to make—whether to buy a three-piece or a two-piece rod. The trend seemed to favor the latter. And should it be stiff or on the limber side? His answer was direct.

"Let your rod be light and very gentle. I think the best are two pieces."

So I bought a two-piecer just under four ounces, a bit on the supple side. Handle well? This rod is a dream! It's so sensitive you can practically feel the nymph bumping over the rocks as it sneaks downstream. But I had a little trouble casting at first. He had the straight dope, of course.

"Be sure not to cumber yourself with too long a line, as most do. Before you begin, have the wind at your back and the sun, if it shines, before you.

"Fish down the stream and carry the tip of the rod downward, by which means the shadow of yourself, and rod, too, will be the least offensive to the fish."

He may not speak in the idiom of Bop City, but gentlemen, he has the low-down on the trout fisherman's curse—shadow.

Perhaps you've noted that men who have spent a lifetime playing chess with trout use live bait when the occasion demands. So it is with this fellow. Moreover, he knows a trick or two. That's why I consulted him one hot August day after worms I had dug that very morning had lost their pep.

"Whatever worms you fish with are better for being long kept before they are used. If you have time, then they are best preserved in an earthen pot with a good store of moss, which is to be fresh every week or eight days, or at least taken from them and washed, and wrung between your hands till it be dry.

"Lobworms are noted to be the best because they are the toughest, and live longest in the water. A dead worm is but a dead bait and like to catch nothing compared to a lively, stirring worm."

This was all very interesting but not, I felt, the whole story. You get to hear rumors of secret baits after you've been fishing a few years. And there are several pastes and lotions on the market, all claimed to be highly effective when properly applied. Well, sir, it took some digging but I finally got something special.

"I have been fishing with old Oliver Henley," he said reflectively, "and have observed that he would usually take three or four worms out of his bag and put them in a little box in his pocket, where he would usually let them continue half an hour or more before he would bait his hook with them.

"He has been observed by others and myself to catch more fish than anybody. I have been told lately that the box in which he put those worms was anointed with a drop or two or three of the oil of ivyberries. And that by the worms' remaining in that box, they had incorporated a kind of smell that was irresistibly attractive—enough to force any fish, within the smell of them, to bite."

A secret potion! Trust an old gaffer to cherish at least one such concoction. Now that he had opened up a little on the matter of bait, perhaps I could draw him out. There was a problem trout that lived under the roots of a willow tree; strictly a surface-bait proposition and one that had had me licked all summer.

Somehow my offerings lacked the conviction of unhooked, struggling insects. No matter how gently I'd cast it, a grasshopper would sink with hardly a surface ripple.

It was evident the old fellow had dealt with such trout before.

"On a hot evening, when you walk by and see or hear him leap at flies," he said, "get a grasshopper, put it on your hook. With your line about two yards long, stand behind a bush or tree where his hole is and make your bait stir up and down on the top of the water.

"You may, if you stand close, be sure of a bite but not sure to catch him"—was that a sly smile?—"and in this manner you may fish for him with almost any kind of fly, but especially with a grasshopper."

P.S.—I caught the trout.

One day I got to wondering about what he carried in that kit bag. Some flies and a few hooks, I suppose, with probably a tin of line dressing. But, in an unusual case like this, one needs to *know*.

"The ingenious angler may walk by the river and mark what fly falls on the water, and catch one of them if he sees trout leap at a fly of this kind. And always having hooks with him . . ."

Of course—fly-tying materials!

"Bear hair, or the hair of a brown heifer, hackles of a cock or capon, several colored silks and crewel (yarn) to make the body of the fly, the feathers of a drake's head, black or brown sheep wool, or hogs' wool or hair"—a deep breath here—"thread of gold and silver, silk of several colors, and other colored feathers."

Any fly fisherman can guess what came next. Here was someone with a knowledge of flies that just shouldn't be kept secret.

"When you fish with a fly, if possible, let no part of the line touch the water, but your fly only. Usually the smallest flies are best. And note also that the light fly usually makes most sport on a dark day; and the darkest fly on a bright or clear day.

"With a short line you may dap behind a tree or in any deep hole, making the fly move on the top of the water as if it were alive. By keeping yourself out of sight, you shall certainly have sport if there are trout," he continued.

The old gentleman never wore rubber boots. All his life he must have been strictly a shore fisherman. But no crude bank runner! I can see him now, sneaking ever so gently and slowly upon a hole.

And the fly he takes from the trout's jaw? In summertime I'm betting it's one of his May flies. Here's how he makes them:

"Make the body with a greenish-colored crewel, or willow-colored, darkening it in most places with waxed thread, or ribbed with a dark hair. Some should be ribbed with silver thread. Make the wings of a color as you see the fly to have at that season—no, that very day."

But despite such talk about flies, I have always had the feeling that my instructor's real love had long been in the use of bait.

He can discourse expertly on the toughening of grubs, how to preserve bait, the reviving of worms and such. I therefore had no hesitancy in consulting him about small problems relating to bait, such as the one that came up one day when my favorite stream was discolored after a rain—a day when the trout took worms ravenously and got hooked deep.

I had heard that in extreme cases—when a small fish is badly hooked—it is safe to snip off the gut at his mouth and leave the hook embedded. But you hear a lot of things. He was emphatically for cutting the leader.

"Unless the hook is fast in his very gorge, he will live, and a little time—with the help of the water—will rust the hook away."

He was also emphatic in his endorsement of night fishing. Ah, there is a way to tangle with big brown trout!

"Pick a quiet place near some swift current, and there draw your bait over the top of the water to and fro. If there is a good trout in the hole, he will take it, especially if the night is dark, for then he lies boldly near the top of the water watching for the motion of any frog or water mouse or rat between him and the sky. These he hunts for if he sees the water but wrinkle.

"You must fish for him with a strong line, and not a little hook, and let him have time to gorge your hook, for he does not usually forsake it as he often will in day fishing. If the night isn't dark, then fish so with an artificial fly of light color.

"He will sometimes rise at a dead mouse or a piece of cloth, or anything that seems to swim across the water or be in motion. This is a choice way but I have not often used it because it is void of the pleasures that such days as these afford an angler."

Well, I'd better stop before this turns from a sampling to a lecture. Earlier I mentioned that the information you'd pick up was guaranteed to help you catch more trout. I hope you don't feel cheated. Believe me, this stuff is the goods. All of it. Some ideas may seem a trifle advanced, I'll admit.

Who is he, this old-fashioned modern angler?

Except for some spelling changes, shortening of sentences, and the substitution of a word here and there, all of the dialogue is exactly as Izaak Walton wrote it in the first edition of *The Compleat Angler*, just about 300 years ago.

A NEW THEORY OF FLIES AND LEADERS

Ted Trueblood

A famous angler has some useful theories worth trying when the trout become a question with no apparent answer. (September 1951)

THE IDEA came while I was sitting on the bank of the Snake River, watching the trout rise. I had waded the heavy current, my line flashing in the sunlight, for six long hours. Now I had to rest. And the notion, like many others, was born of desperation.

From the spot where I sat, legs stretched full length upon the blessed earth, rod lying beside them and 12 feet of tapered gut and nylon trailing in the clear water, I could watch 500 feeding trout. No, there were more than half a thousand. I don't know how many. There were rings everywhere, constantly, and each ring spread from the spot where a steel-blue nose, followed by silvery pink sides and a wide curving tail, broke the glassy flow.

Two insects, both May flies, were on the water. One was the color of faded straw, scarcely larger than a mosquito. The other, equally small, had the indefinable pale blue-gray color of the soft underfur of a kitten. Some of the trout were chasing nymphs to the surface; others were taking the floating insects.

The ephemerids had begun their nuptial dance above the long smooth glide of the river at 8 o'clock, and the trout had moved to the top after them. Now it was 2 in the afternoon. My creel had become no heavier during these six hours. I had spent them vainly adding extra, finer tippets to my leader and hopefully laying a succession of tiny flies as gently as I could upon the water.

True, I had hooked fish. I had even thrilled to the powerful surge of broad-shouldered rainbows when they felt the steel of a tiny hook and the restraint of a gossamer leader. But not for long. The trout that I had mastered and released were striplings, 12-inch juveniles that I was ashamed to keep, while, even as I turned them loose, I could see others five times as heavy rolling an easy cast away.

My difficulties were these: The river here is gorged with moss. Great bunches of it spring from the gravel bottom to sweep and roll and undulate beneath the smooth surface. The big trout would strike only a small fly on a light leader. Once hooked, they slashed away downstream, then swung across. The line came tight around the moss. The tiny hook pulled out or the leader broke. When I used a larger fly and a heavier tippet, only small fish would hit.

Now, as I sat there watching those beautiful, wonderful, totally unattainable trout, it occurred to me that perhaps I was on the wrong track completely. I couldn't hold the big ones on 4X gut and a No. 18 fly. I couldn't make them strike on coarser tackle. Was it possible to devise a heavier leader that would not alarm them, a fly tied on a larger hook that they still would take?

It was worth thinking about. It seemed to me that the development of terminal tackle has been based largely upon the assumption that trout don't see particularly well. We use light leaders in hope that they won't be seen and we tie on bright flies to make sure they will be.

Is the reasoning behind this sound? I doubt it. A trout may take your fly because he doesn't happen to notice the leader, or because he does see it and doesn't become suspicious, but the thought that we conceivably could use gut too fine for trout to see is preposterous.

Sometime when they are rising, but hard to catch, sacrifice a half-dozen flies in an experiment. Drop them into the stream well above the rising trout and let them float down to them. Few flies unattached to a leader will escape being taken. Yet you can cast the same pattern to the same fish and never get a touch. It is the leader that makes the difference.

All of us have seen trout rising to midges, tiny gray flies so small they become invisible to a man at a distance of a few feet. Yet the trout can see them, and on evenings when the rise continues through the dusk the fish feed on them after we can no longer see anything at all.

Even more convincing is the knowledge that trout feed on plankton, usually on such tiny crustaceans as daphnia, which are smaller than the head of a pin and nearly transparent. Of course, all young fish utilize this food, but it is not so commonly known that good-sized trout in some waters feed extensively upon it.

One day while my brother Burtt and I were camped on the shore of a wonderful trout lake near the continental divide, I noticed big fish feeding in the shallow water before our tent. We tried a number of flies, but failed to interest them. Finally, in desperation, I set up a casting rod and took a three-pound cut-throat on a spoon. He was gorged with daphnia.

Experiences such as these—and many others—have led me to the firm conviction that it is impossible to use a leader so fine that trout can't see it. Fine gut is less conspicious, less alarming, but not invisible.

It was Al Klotz, of Boise, Idaho, an expert and thoughtful angler, who gave me the solution. "You know," he said one evening after I had outlined my idea, "most of the good streams that we fish have a lot of moss. Even clear mountain brooks have some.

"Trout aren't afraid of moss. They're used to it. I've seen them take damsel flies that were sitting on it. I don't believe they'd think it unnatural to see an insect—your fly, that is—drifting along clinging to the end of a piece of moss. If the leader were dyed exactly the right color . . ."

"I think it would work!"

He chuckled. "As a matter of fact, I know it will. I've tried it. I've been dyeing my leaders the color of moss for some time."

I bought some ordinary household dye in brown and green. The stringy moss I wanted to imitiate was not a clear bright green, but rather a dull shade, strongly tinged with brown. I dissolved a piece of the green dye and a fourth as much brown in a quart of water, simmering hot.

The first scrap of nylon that I soaked in it came out too green. I added a little more brown. Finally, after coloring innumerable pieces of leader material and adding a pinch of blue dye, one took on the color I wanted. I dyed several leaders and extra tippets and bottled the solution for future use.

A few days later I went to Silver Creek. It is a crystal-clear spring-fed stream with an abundance of moss, countless small hatchery trout, and a few wise old lunkers. I spent most of the day fishing with wet flies and nymphs because only little trout seemed to be rising. Not once did I use a leader finer than 2X. When I walked back to the car after sunset, I was completely satisfied. The moss-dyed leader worked. I had released 21 trout. I had kept one, a three-and-a-half-pound rainbow.

That was three years ago. I have since used the brown-green leaders in a great variety of streams and lakes. Some of them contained a great deal of moss. Others, especially the granite-bottomed, churning mountain rivers, were almost devoid of vegetation, except for algae on the rocks. In most waters I found that I could hook fish on tippets a full size larger, and occasionally two sizes larger, than before.

The results were gratifying, but they led to further experiments. Assuming that trout do have incredibly keen eyesight, which the success of the moss-dyed leaders seemed to confirm, why not apply the same reasoning to flies—especially wet flies, which run to more vivid colors than those that are tied to float?

Why try to make them highly visible? When we fail to get strikes, is it because the trout don't see our flies or because they see them only too well? Why not try making them hard to see?

These questions were not answered so quickly, but I gradually did begin to get the answers to them. As they came, they confirmed the theory that there is nothing too small nor too indistinct for a trout to see. And if it is suggestive of food, he will investigate.

Except during the spawning season, all activity of trout is governed by two overwhelming stimuli: fear and hunger. They are hungry most of the time, the severe cold season excepted.

Scientific tests have proved that fish have five well-developed senses —sight, hearing, taste, smell and touch, the same as mammals. When something that looks like food comes along and they are not frightened, they investigate it, just as a hungry man would walk across the lawn to check a picnic basket left on a table.

The trout is more restricted in the use of his senses than man, however. To investigate a fly, which gives off no odor, he must take it into his mouth. Then he can both taste and feel it. All that is required of an artificial fly is that it be sufficiently suggestive of food so that the trout will take it into his mouth.

A distinct, boldly patterned fly, such as a Coachman or its scarlet-sashed royal offspring, a tinsel-ribbed Professor, a Parmacheene Belle or any other bright fly, does not require this investigation. In my experience, all of them have been poor catchers of trout in waters that are heavily fished. Trout don't strike them simply because they are too easy to see.

On the other hand, dull-colored, indifferent-looking flies, such as the March Brown, Gold-ribbed Hare's Ear and Cahill, always have done well for me. They are hard for the trout to see, yet, being suggestive of food, they are taken into their mouths to taste and feel.

Just at the time I was beginning to experiment along this line, Jack B. Schneider, the San Jose, California rod maker, gave me a fly. He called it the Fledermouse, a fitting name for an utterly fantastic creation. The thing had neither hackles nor tail. It had a sparse wing of gray squirrel tail and a misshapen, ragged, hair body. It was tied on a No. 2 hook!

Art Bailie and I were fishing a lake in Montana. We had been using size 18 flies on long light leaders and, after becoming accustomed to them, the Fledermouse looked as huge as a grizzly bear at a cat show.

But it took trout. Man! how it took trout.

Jack's tying calls for a body of muskrat fur with the guard hairs left in to give it a ragged appearance. I mix muskrat with the long fur from the tail of a coyote for mine. That makes the fly even more nondescript.

Now, you might say, "How does that fit your theory? A No. 2 fly certainly can't be hard to see."

Correct. It isn't hard to see, but it is hard to define, and there is an important difference. In the water, the Fledermouse has a vague, translucent appearance. When you twitch the leader, the hair waves. Maybe it looks a little like a dragonfly nymph.

Actually, I tie very few flies. I can buy better flies and I can buy cheaper flies than I can tie, but I do make up off-breed patterns for experimenting.

The question naturally arises whether the same theory could be applied to dry flies. The answer is that it has been, almost from the beginning. List your best dry flies—Quill Gordon, Light Cahill, Hendrickson, Blue Dun, all the others—most of them are hard to see. When you consider that the finest dry flies ride high, resting on the tips of hackle and tail, with these points making little breaks and light flashes in the surface, it becomes increasingly apparent that the trout in many instances do not see the fly itself clearly.

Thus while dry flies have long been made of natural feathers and fur in dull tones, wet flies, which must undergo a more searching scrutiny by the trout, have run to bold colors. My experiments in making them hard to see called for a wide variety of materials in neutral shades. I obtained

scraps of fur from mink, otter, muskrat, beaver, various squirrels, rabbit, coyote, a few imported kinds from one of the houses that cater to the needs of flytiers, and an unfortunate yellow cat that ventured into my garage one evening.

These gave me various shades of blue, gray, tan, cream, buff and brown. Some of the longer hair was used for wings, although many of the flies were tied as nymphs without either wings or hackle. A few strands of coarse hair made their legs.

Exact imitation, naturally, was unimportant in the testing of this theory. The purpose of flies of this type was merely to suggest food so that the trout would take them to investigate.

For example, I fish a number of streams and lakes in which fresh-water shrimps (scuds) are abundant. Wherever they occur, they are an important item on the bill of fare of the trout. I spent the better part of two seasons trying to create an exact imitation, but none of my attempts were very good, judging both from the reaction of the fish and my own inspection in the water.

One day I tied on a nymph made from cream-colored fur. I was standing on a grassy bank that overhung clear shallow water literally teeming with shrimps. When I dropped the fly at my feet and twitched it along, it was almost impossible to distinguish it from the real thing. Of course, it caught fish.

Last year I took the idea back to the Snake River where it was born. It was late in the season, and when you are more than a mile above the sea, October calls for long wool underwear, a warm jacket and gloves. Burtt and I were afraid the trout would not be rising.

Our fears were groundless, however. The water was low and its clarity rivaled that of the frost-chilled air, but we found a spot where the trout were dimpling and ringing a long sweeping wide run. The same wise wild rainbows that had driven me to despair three years before. They began every morning about 10. They continued until dark. We could see them at the surface and we could see them lying in the water, small trout, fair trout, good trout, and some long, dark, drifting shadows to which a man could not cast without trembling.

There was one difference. This time the fish were not taking little May flies. They were feeding on something worse, midges so small that they could not be copied, even by a few turns of silk and a wisp of hackle on a No. 20 hook.

It was a challenge. We met it, not by attempting to imitate the midges, but by fishing our ragged, hairy, unkempt, suggestive flies on our moss-dyed leaders.

Possibly, for the sake of the story and to prove my point, I should tell you that we turned the river inside out. That would not be true. We fished all day, until we were so tired we could not stand, just as I had done before, but there was this difference: Now we occasionally caught a trout that could honestly be called good, or big, or BIG, depending on the yardstick of comparison. Any rainbow that shades 20 inches may well inspire pride.

We fished three days, and we caught them every day.

Our leaders were never finer than 2X. We used wet flies exclusively. They ranged in size from the No. 2 Fledermouse (which took a few trout!) to vague-looking No. 14 fur nymphs.

Is the theory proved? Will it revolutionize your fishing? The answer to both these questions, of course, is no. The idea has been confirmed as sound, not proved. And it wouldn't revolutionize anybody's fishing, even if it were.

What it definitely will do, however, is this: It will open up an interesting new field for experimentation. It will result in the catching of some trout that would not otherwise be taken. This justification, to any thoughtful angler, should be sufficient.

HOW TO CATCH MORE BASS ON A FLY ROD

Jason Lucas

*Pound for pound the most famous bass writer of
his time, SPORTS AFIELD's angling editor of
the 50s knew all about the special pleasures of
catching them with bugs. (September 1951)*

A BASS IS like a cat in that he prefers to hide and dart out at his prey,
taking it off guard. In fact his shape shows that, unlike the pike, for instance,
he's fitted for a short dart, not a long chase. So generally, in a river—of
which fishing this article will mainly treat—he will be found under long
grass or bushes overhanging the bank, or perhaps behind a log or boulder.
Sometimes he does feed in open water—but even there, close inspection
of the bottom will usually show some boulder close to which he had been
staying. However, since it's harder to find the good spots out there, usually
one will end with a heavier creel by fishing only the easy-to-find spots
along the bank.

(Though this article will deal basically with river bass fishing—fly
rod—and with the use of a single lure type—the bass bug—the general

application to lake fishing and to comparable lure types will be readily apparent.)

The average bass bug angler goes along thrashing the shore line furiously. He slaps his bug down hard, jerks it hard a time or two, and picks it up for another cast. He seems to think that the more water he can cover, the more bass he must catch. And this is about true—when bass are striking madly at anything of edible size they see moving. But no bass fisherman needs to be told how rare these times are.

Then along will come some grizzled old fellow, a pipe in his mouth, dawdling sleepily, seeming not to care whether he gets to that first bend this evening or not. He eases up to place, dobs his bug casually beside the long grass—and stands sleepily puffing his pipe as if he'd forgotten it was there. Presently he gives it a sharp little twitch, moving it perhaps an inch or two. Then he'll let it rest and twitch it two or three times more. Suddenly, possibly while it's lying perfectly still, there's a terrific splash—and there he is, with bending rod, calmly playing a fine bass.

There's no question about it. The rest-and-twitch method is old Meat-in-the-Pot—or Fish-in-the-Pan, if you prefer to call it that. Probably no better retrieve ever will be devised, for times when "they just aren't hitting." It teases a wary old bass, not hungry, into striking.

What if the current is sweeping your bug down, so that it can't be rested and twitched over the bass's nose? All the better, perhaps—cast so far above him that he isn't aware of the splash of the bug falling, and give some very gentle twitches, with good pauses, as it goes along. Then, to a bass that sees it, it's some big live bug that fell in up above and is washing down, struggling, with rests, to swim somewhere.

There lies the whole secret of getting bass on bugs when "they aren't hitting." The bug should act like a live one that fell in, is half stunned and half drowned, but is trying, between rests, to get out of there. Keeping this always in mind, it's extremely easy to give your bug fish-taking action—action natural enough to fool a bass.

A fine method is to cast your bug onto the bank, if it looks as though it's not too likely to tangle there, and then gently twitch it onto the water. Then, since a live bug falling in that short distance wouldn't be stunned, nor yet half drowned, the pauses shouldn't be long. Still, the twitches should be very gentle, not an imitation of Johnny Weismuller in a Tarzan movie.

One of my most productive tricks, a modification of this, is to imagine that it's a small frog that has jumped in—and, since I believe the action that you give a bug is far more important than what it looks like, often I won't bother to change to a frog lure. A bass is extremely likely to see the object coming through the air. And, though a bug may come from any direction, a frog will come only from the bank—and a grassy bank or such, at that, not out of branches.

A little frog starts swimming as soon as he hits—swimming with short, smooth, easy strokes, *never* kicking up a ripple to speak of. And my frog, at least, doesn't make many strokes before he stops on the surface to look around before going on. He acts like a frog at his leisure, not one scared stiff by just having eluded the grasp of a fisherman who wanted to use him for bait. At times, I've got bass so fast by this method that it almost ceased to be fun—too easy.

Yes, it's well to think up new tricks—always remembering that you are attempting to imitate something alive. Not long ago, I knew that there was a lunker bass in some lily pads, but I couldn't do anything with him. He seemed too smart for me.

Then, one evening, I slipped up there, and my first cast happened to land on a lily pad. A new trick, worth trying, suddenly came to me. I let the bug lie still a long time, and then began to twitch the line gently indeed, barely moving the pad but not pulling the bug from it. I could just see faint ripples coming from around the edge of the pad. To a bass lying in watch below, it must have seemed that there was a big live bug up there, walking around and wondering where to go next. And probably that bass was getting more excited every moment he waited, watching.

Then, my bug plopped gently off, and started "swimming" to the next pad. *Zowie!* It looked as if a small depth bomb had exploded among the lily pads—that bug, doggone him, wasn't going to escape! And there I was, hooked onto a beaut of a bass. Catching him was one of the easiest things I ever did—after I had thought of that new trick, to fool him.

The foregoing tells about all I know of how to get the best results with bugs. Make the bug look like something *alive.*

There are exceptions to nearly all rules, and there's one to this: On those few occasions when bass are feeding madly—generally it will be in the very early morning or very late evening—and especially if I am floating the stream in a boat, I work a bank far more rapidly, to cover as much water as possible. One cast and twitch to a spot, and I pick up for another cast farther on. But I do not, as I've seen some do, try to give an imitation of a man angrily whipping a balky mule.

There's no difficulty whatever about knowing when to change to this faster method. I do it whenever I find bass taking my bug immediately after I lay it down, without waiting for me to tease them into striking.

Most who try to set the hook only with the rod seem to miss on an extremely high percentage of their strikes, and get that many fewer fish. One trouble is that a sudden sharp upward movement of the rod sends the tip *down*, wasting a valuable instant during the often lightninglike strike of a bass. Just now, I walked outside and, measuring beside a tree trunk, found that I could make a tip duck, in this way, actually more than three feet.

Another trouble is that, if the tip is well up, it is too flexible to drive the barb home in the hard mouth of a bass. And if the hook does take hold, a forceful sweep of the rod may break the tip—I've seen it happen. Here's my method: After casting, I bring my tip close to the water, pointing directly out the line toward the bug. I work the bug solely with little jerks of my left hand holding the line. Of course the line slides under a finger of my right hand, against the grip. Otherwise I couldn't drop the line to reach out for another pull. If a bass strikes while I'm reaching, I try to set the hook with the rod only.

When you are working the bug in this way, and a bass strikes, it's purely a reflex action to jerk back with the left hand, socking the barb home solidly and instantly. Almost unconsciously, too, you begin to raise the rod, to help matters. But now the pull isn't against the weak tip; it's against the stiff, strong butt, driving the barb in more. Once I feel the fish hooked, I raise the rod to the vertical, to play him, letting line slip out under that finger of my right hand as it comes up.

But if he's a big one, and heading for weeds or snags from which he must be held by force, again I lower the tip, so that there will be little bend in it, the strain coming on the heavier parts of the rod. Thus a broken tip is impossible; let the leader break, if something must—I think it foolish to risk a good rod for any fish, especially since he is almost sure to escape anyhow if the rod is broken.

All the foregoing, of course, can be easily adapted to lake fishing for either largemouths or smallmouths. In most lakes, a fly rod will be found most suitable for largemouths, since smallmouths are more inclined to stay deep, where they can find deep water, except in the early part of the season. When they're far down, deep-running plugs and a casting rod will nearly always be more productive, especially of the big fellows. But there are exceptions. Sometimes they'll come a long way up for streamers, or even surface bugs.

A bed of quite dense weeds is a good place for largemouths—and about the most agreeable way to work it with a fly rod, as well as the way likely to be most productive of big ones, is to slip along quietly in a boat, one man rowing, the other casting, just a nice, comfortable casting distance beyond its outer edge. Then, you can dob your bug into little bays in the weeds, giving it exactly the same little twitches—*and rests*—that you would by a riverbank.

In a lake, smallmouths favor much more open shore lines than do largemouths—generally rocky ones. But it's a great mistake to think that they'll never be found in weeds. Some of the finest catches of lake small-mouths I've ever made have been in spindly, scattering weeds growing to about the surface from deep water.

Sometimes, in such a place, they'll come up to streamers or surface bugs; sometimes you must use plugs fished almost on the bottom.

In lake fishing for bass, almost always I keep both fly and casting rod rigged up under my hand, to use whichever is best at the time, or for a particular spot. And this changing back and forth in itself makes fishing more interesting as well as, of course, more productive.

These are the methods I use in fly-rod fishing for bass. They're so childishly easy and simple that a beginner can be using them successfully in a week—and get plenty of bass.

THE NYMPHING STORY

Ted Janes

*One of the most successful lures for deceiving
stubborn trout is also one of the most under-
employed. (February 1952)*

IT WAS just before sundown, the trout fisherman's finest hour. But the
magic of the spring afternoon was lost upon me as I stood hip-deep in a
dimpling pool, straining my wrist and my credulity. From the deep water
against the far bank a trout rose rhythmically. In mid-pool another roll
sent wide rings spreading across the dark surface and, as I watched, a really
big fish bulged the water within a foot of my Quill Gordon, drifting jauntily
on the current.

This had been going on for 15 minutes; at one time I counted six
separate rises in the pool. I floundered ashore to search my soul and my fly
box for something . . . anything . . . that these hypercritical fish might find
edible. Ten minutes and three flies later I was still feverishly searching while
the trout continued to roll mockingly around my waders. Then Don came
into view around the bend.

"How many?" he called, clambering toward me over the rocks.

"A basketful!" I assured him with a fine irony, just as a foot and a half of gleaming rainbow arced completely over my Coachman.

"I haven't got that many," he said, cheerfully, shoving a cigarette into his face, "but I've got a half-dozen fairly decent fish."

I left a foaming wake behind me. "What on earth did you take 'em on, a grenade?" I demand, staring into his smugly opened creel. "I've tried every fly in the book and they keep rising all around my feet . . ."

"Not rising," he corrected. "They're tailing—feeding on nymphs. Like this." And he held up a wispy deer-hair concoction with two or three scraggly whiskers sticking out here and there. "Try it."

The show was about over by then but the 12-inch rainbow against the far bank dimpled as I waded within range. I cast the nymph upstream and across, as Don told me, and let it drift on a slack line. Suddenly the bellying loop straightened. As I struck sharply, the line tightened and a pink and silver arc somersaulted out of the pool.

That was the end and the beginning—the end of that day's fishing and the beginning of my acquaintance with the nymph, one of the deadliest lures ever invented for putting the whammy on a trout—and one of the most neglected. In a country heavily populated with dry-fly artists, streamer experts and spinning virtuosos, you find few competent hands with the nymph. This is unfortunate, for in passing up this lure anglers are missing out on a lot of good fish, and what is more to the point, a lot of good fishing as well.

The reason for this neglect is not hard to discover. Nymph fishing has somehow come to be surrounded with a great deal of mystery and black magic which long since should have been stripped away. For some reason, entirely competent anglers consider nymphing beyond them, the same as fishermen of a generation ago felt that dry-fly fishing was a complicated business for experts only. Today's anglers generally realize the absurdity of such thinking about the dry fly. Anyone who can cast 20 feet can catch fish on a floating fly—and the same is true of the nymph. Truer, in fact, for with the latter you don't have to worry about such factors as light casting and the prevention of drag, so important in dry-fly work.

I once introduced nymph fishing to a young friend who, until that day, had never used anything but bait. I stationed him at the head of a sweeping run and tried to give him an idea of the rudiments of fly casting, enough at least so that he could separate the nymph from his feet. Line, leader and lure dropped in a splashing coil on the water and the current did the rest, drifting the nymph downstream until the line had straightened. Then the angler retrieved it slowly. After four or five of these performances, as he picked up line for a backcast, the rod arced sharply and he was fast to a good brown. And another nymph fisherman was launched.

As most anglers know, nymphs represent the pupa stage of insects, living at the bottom of streams and other waters. At a certain stage in their development, they float to the surface where the nymphal cases split and the true insects emerge. This is the moment for which the trout have been waiting and they go to work, eagerly sucking in these slowly rising morsels. A dozen luckless nymphs disappear inside their greedy maws for every one which successfully completes its metamorphosis. Then it is that the still pools erupt in a rash of bulges, and dry-fly fishermen mutter hoarsely in their beards.

Nymph fishing, like dry-fly fishing, came to us originally from England where it derived considerable impetus from the writings of the noted angler G.E.M. Skues. The customary method used on the English chalk streams, and to some extent in this country as well, is that of casting upstream and across, with line and leader greased up to the final strand. The floating gut acts as a sort of indicator. When it plunges under, strike! But while the nymph is as effective here as in England, early American exponents of the sport found that techniques which were effective on the Test and Itchen were not always successful on the Beaverkill and Brodheads—and they were quick to adapt their methods to the heavier American waters. That is one of the great advantages of this lure; it can be fished in half a dozen different ways, all of them effective, to meet changing water and weather conditions.

Some form of nymphal life is hatching out in the streams during the greater part of the year; therefore nymphs are always in season. On a cold April day with the swollen Farmington River swirling in a yellow torrent about my waders, I fished a nymph upstream and across. When this proved nonproductive, I tried casting almost directly upstream and letting the nymph drift deep on a slack line. Still nothing happened. But when I got it even deeper by adding a split shot to the leader, I took three good brown trout from the quiet water at the edge of the runs.

At other times nymphs can be skimmed along the surface and retrieved against or even across the current. There is still another method, which I discovered one day by accident. I was hopefully drifting a nymph through a swirling glide on the Deerfield when another angler, who was using dry flies, waded upstream toward me. He fished the lower end of the run and then left the water to walk around me. I lengthened line and let my nymph drift farther downstream. I was about to pick up for another cast when the dry-fly man stopped abreast of me.

"Any business?" he asked, and I shook my head.

"No, I've only . . ." I started to reply, and then a big brownie exploded clear out of water in a furious smash at the dancing nymph.

It was embarrassing because the dry-fly man had just whipped that particular spot thoroughly and expertly. When I had subdued the trout and lifted him in the net, the dry-fly angler had gone away. On several occasions since then I've caught trout by letting a nymph do an animated Charleston at the end of 50 feet of motionless line. It's a sight the trout can't seem to resist.

This method is particularly effective on small, brushy streams where it is impossible to cast a fly. By fishing the nymph almost like a worm, letting it drift under banks and overhanging branches, I have taken many a native brookie. Nymphs will slide easily into places where the larger bait hook would become lodged or stranded on the bottom.

Nymph fishing should bother no American angler for we have been for generations a race of wet-fly fishermen. And the nymph is a very wet fly indeed. In fact, it seems altogether likely that on many occasions when the trout take our wet flies they do so under the impression they are inhaling a nymph. This explains the effectiveness of many a frayed and tattered wet fly, treasured by its owner as a super-duper killer with almost magical properties. For that matter, a very workable nymph can be improvised in moments of need by judiciously clipping the wings and most of the hackle from a traditional wet-fly pattern.

Nymph fishing requires special tackle in order to obtain the best results. It's a good idea to use a tapered line, although the line is not the important factor in nymphing that it is in dry-fly or bass-bug fishing. At all events, stay away from the bug-head or quick-taper line which carries too much weight forward. The essential thing is to have the line match the rod—it should be, if anything, a little on the light side. The leader should taper to about a 3X point. Owing to the nature of the fishing, it is imprudent to go much finer in running water. Nor is it usually necessary, except under conditions of extremely low and clear water. These conditions excepted, a 7½- to 9-foot leader is plenty long enough.

Most important of all is the rod. Nymph fishing, to be successful, requires a rather specialized tool, a soft-action rod of a sort infrequently found in American tackle stores today. For here in this country in the last

10 years we have gone completely off the deep end over stiff-action rods. This was a normal result of the adoption of the dry fly by American anglers. As wet-fly fishermen we were accustomed to long, willowy rods, entirely adequate for the job they were designed to do, but hopelessly inadequate to the task of flinging a dry fly into the teeth of a rushing wind. And, furthermore, early experimenters with English rods found that even these tools were insufficient for our brawling northern waters.

The tendency was toward stiffer action, and like many another reform we have carried it too far. Urged on by the anglers, rod manufacturers built more and more backbone into their products. The modern dry-fly rod, I submit, is better designed for holding up a television aerial than for tossing a No. 16 Leadwing Coachman. Such rods, in my opinion, are bad enough for the dry-fly fishing for which they were designed; for nymph fishing they are hopeless.

Nymphing requires a slow, flexible rod which will impart its own action to the fly. Happily, a few manufacturers have seen the writing on the waters and are turning out such tools—but they are few and far between. If you want to take up nymphing, find the softest rod on the market today. It will still be a little stiff.

Boulder-strewn pocket water is made to order for the nymph. It can be cast into tricky eddies and quiet places around the rocks and turned loose to go into its act. It will dip and dance and swirl about until the current sweeps the line downstream. Sometimes the lure remains in the pocket for only a second or two; but frequently that brief instant is enough.

One day I was wading the spruce-bordered white water of Maine's Sandy River, flicking a nymph into glassy swirls around the rocks. I saw one likely-looking spot, a still pool behind a big granite slab, and I felt sure it would hold a good fish. But the water was too deep to wade nearer and a steep ledge at my back made casting impossible from the bank. At last I clambered up the ledge and stood perched some 15 feet above the stream. With plenty of room for a backcast, I shot a long line to midstream. As the nymph settled to the black surface of the rock pool, what looked like a chunk of the bottom rose deliberately to meet it. I struck and the biggest brown I have ever hooked launched out of water.

He bored for his den under the rock and then decided to hit the rapids. And there I stood high above the stream with the fish rampaging across 40 feet of white water. I couldn't climb down from my perch without using both hands and my teeth so I clung grimly to the slippery ledge, giving line and waiting for the leader to snap.

It must have been 15 minutes later that my companion came along. Finding me in this equivocal situation, he unlimbered his movie camera and started shooting.

"Never mind the Darryl Zanuck act!" I roared at the top of my lungs. "Do something!"

But he couldn't hear me over the rushing water. He nodded and beamed and went on shooting.

Finally, by eloquent pantomime I transferred his attention to the other actor in the drama. The brown now was wearily finning on his side, taking the full weight of the sweeping current. My friend let go of the camera in a hurry and sloshed out to net the fish, which tipped the scales at five and a half pounds.

In the late season when the foaming glides of spring have shrunk to narrow gin-clear trickles, nymphs are still hatching out and trout are still taking them. Last season on a broiling summer day I was fishing a stretch of the Manahan River and not doing very well. The trout were logy, lying in the shade of rocks and around spring holes, and by the time I had fished back to the car I had one smallish brownie.

I had my fly jacket off when my glance wandered to a sweep of broken water chattering over the rocks below the iron bridge. It was a normally unproductive stretch, shunned by anglers in spring; but on a day like this, I thought, trout might be lying in those shallow rapids, where the oxygen supply would be more plentiful. I decided to try it. The stretch was too shallow to float a spinner or even a streamer, too swift for dry flies. I tied on a nymph and waded over the slippery rocks. Casting across and slightly downstream for a better float, I let the nymph drift with the current and swing in a wide arc at the end of the line. Then I retrieved it in short jerks directly against the current.

Working slowly, I moved downstream. I was about to give it up when I felt a fleeting tug as the nymph skipped past a flat rock. I cast again, and this time I saw the silvery flash of a rainbow lancing from behind the rock. This time he was fast. There was nothing logy about this trout. He danced and bored and darted as I drew him slowly toward me through the quick water. At the end of that 200-yard stretch I had four more trout, one of them better than a pound.

I don't say that nymphs will automatically fill your creel when the fish aren't hitting, but I do say that very often they will save you from a fishless day. I'll even go further and say that an angler who fishes with nymphs day in and day out will catch more fish in a season than anglers who use bait, dry flies or spinning lures exclusively. I've sliced open the stomachs of a great many trout in 35 years of persistent fishing and by far the preponderant item of diet has been some form of nymph. It would seem, therefore, that a few of these lures and a knowledge of how to use them are essential to the angler who wishes to be "compleat."

Artificials are numerous and are becoming more so each year but there remain certain tried and true patterns which should be in every fisherman's book—such nymphs as the Stone Creeper, Caddis, Iron Blue and Basset Gray.

There's a pond near my home where the rainbows come big and fighting. You can take an occasional fish trolling streamers or spinners, and early in the season the bank fishermen take a few good trout on worms. If you had never been there before, you might think the pond was fished out, but along toward late afternoon you would change your mind. For suddenly, close to the boat, you would see a dimpling bulge. A second later you would see a broad tail roll ahead of you while rings still spread astern. Another bulge and another and another would break the mirror surface until the pond literally came alive with rainbows rolling and tumbling all around. And you would fling a wide assortment of dry flies, confidently at first and then with growing desperation as two- and three-pound trout dived mockingly over your offerings.

It happened to me several times before I found the answer. The answer is a tiny black nymph on a No. 20 hook, fished on a 5X point. You let it sink and then retrieve it with slow twitches, and the strikes come fast and furious. So furious, in fact, that you lose more fish than you hold. But even one fish out of four or five is better than going crazy staring at a floating fly, waiting for the strike that never comes.

THE MAGIC OF TROUT FISHING

Mike Hudoba

SPORTS AFIELD's one-time Washington, D.C. watchdog, this dedicated outdoorsman had a lifetime love affair with the long rod. (March 1956)

TROUT fishing gives a man time for meditation; a chance to absorb the meaning of a blue sky and pines sighing to the breeze. Tiny mosses on a streamside boulder, just placed right for resting, hold tiny scarlet flags above their soft green; in a cluster of forget-me-nots a shimmering green tiger beetle waves his antennae to a nether world of charm a man needs to know.

Trout fishing is the whirr of a hummingbird probing the columbine; a chipmunk staring curiously from a rock crevass; a phoebe darting from a limb to snatch an insect in mid-air; a small snapping turtle crawling along the bottom.

Trout fishing is trout at their stations, slowly finning, watching the surface where the stream smoothes out into a pool. Trout fishing is a May fly dappling the water. Watch there as the trout turn; one moves to break the surface. Slowly widening ripples mark the spot where the May fly tried to leave its eggs.

Resist the urge to cast as two other May flies touch the water and slowly drift. Perhaps the trout you see show no interest. You wonder why until a large dark shape materializes where nothing was before. It is a trout once again as large as the incautious youngsters. You sit, tree-still, heart throbbing, planning your next move. This, is trout fishing.

There are trout fishermen who never seem to reach the released tempo of effective trouting. One sees them hurrying from pool to pool in a rush to cover as much stream mileage as time will allow. Others may stay at one pool and flail the water for hours without interruption, impatient over the lack of rises. True, there is a magnetic attraction to the stream ahead, the next riffle. There is a hungry desire to round the bend where a bigger trout must be waiting. This is a part, an important part, of trout fishing, this spirit to explore, to seek the new. Just as it is an important part to return to old, treasured spots. But how much of the in-between flavor we miss if we overlook the little things? In fact, a man *is* trout fishing only if each day's success is not measured by the creel alone.

This does not mean that trout should not be caught, or that a day in which no trout are caught is more enjoyable than one with abundant rises. Rather, it means that the sting of disappointment when trout do not readily take can be tempered by the observations of the wonders nature parades for those who will but look and see.

There are streams to which I have returned so many times the trout in each pool have become familar companions. And I have found that a cast placed so and a fly drifted such will renew a pleasant acquaintance. If it doesn't, I wonder if someone else, more creel-conscious than I, has tempted them. I have tagged trout with a device available from the Fish Taggers' Association, and in one season took the same 15-inch rainbow six times. Each time the thrill of catching him was stronger than the last.

There is a stream in the Blue Ridges where I once caught an 18-inch brookie and released it. For several seasons afterwards, I tried for that same fish. Once he rolled short of the fly, but he never struck. I'm glad he didn't. He made me a better fisherman.

A stream I often fished in Colorado contained a particularly beautiful pool that had never produced a trout for me. The water was so deep and turmoiled by a waterfall that I could not see into the pool, even with polaroid glasses.

It became a spot where I liked to rest and study the view of the canyon. I'd fish the pool more out of respect for good-looking water than from any faith in the results. Only once did I raise a fish. My fly had finished its drift, and I paused to watch a deer drinking from the stream below. When I looked back, a trout was turning with my fly in its mouth. As if in slow motion, the trout continued to turn, exposing a rainbow-lined side not less than a foot wide. Finally its tail, as broad as this page, made one twisted flip and disappeared from view. The rod and my arm were in position to set the hook but I was completely unable to move. The trout did not hook itself. I fished that pool many times but never raised the gigantic rainbow again. That fish also made me a better fisherman.

Yet I'm not sure that if the same thing were to happen this season, I might again fail for the same reason. For such is trout fishing that you can fully prepare only for what has happened. Future days hold only the unexpected.

While I have often wondered what would have happened if I had hooked that trout, my life is no less full for failing to do so. In fact the outcome of that surely prodigious battle gives me a special daydream I use when things get dull at Congressional hearings. It also helps me fight harder to save similar places which others cherish.

Although I have caught many trout, it seems the ones I remember best are those I did not catch. There is a delight in recalling the streams and pools. Each one is a world of its own with a particular charm surrounding it. Fishing is real fun . . . all kinds of fishing. But the places where trout live have a special appeal that gives fishing for them the extra plus.

There is a bond between trout fishermen. Like every well-knit family, relations seem strained only to an outsider. It's not only true, but entirely as it should be that an artificial-lure trouter speaks curtly to the live-bait fisherman—if at all. A dry-fly purist may cross the street to avoid being seen with a known wet-fly man. I have known friends to fall out over outspoken preferences between brook and brown trout. I know two members of a trout club who don't like to sit at the same table because one uses a nine-foot instead of a seven-foot rod on a certain brook-trout stream. They, of course, are considered a little extreme. One even has been seen bass fishing.

But let someone make a slur about trout as compared to other fish species, and let him beware. Trout fishermen close ranks like a herd of maddened bison. Only when the infidel is in full rout do they realign in their individual compartments and sneer at all the other compartments.

With the growth of this country and its population, the unspoiled environment for trout is becoming scarcer. Those who appreciate trout fishing and the quiet beauty of the places of trout must unite to help protect those values. It means too that we must appreciate the trout themselves.

There are many kinds of natural beauty, from the expansiveness of a sky showing through a covering of multigreen forest, to the myriad forms of wondrous natural life. But there is a special something, a washing of the spirit, a re-creation of the individual, for those who take to the streamside where trout waters sing.

AMERICA'S COMPLEAT ANGLER

Bill Wolf

During his time he was one of SPORTS AFIELD's most popular and prolific feature writers. Here he interviews Edward Ringwood Hewitt, father of the Bivisible. (March 1956)

FIVE YEARS ago, a vigorous and active man named Edward Ringwood Hewitt went from New York to Spain as the guest of General Franco to fish some of the northern rivers for salmon. *El Caudillo* had invited him because, next to running Spain with an iron hand, the chief likes best to hunt and fish, and he wanted Hewitt to test the salmon fishing potentialities of the Spanish streams. Hewitt fished 16 of the rivers which come pounding out of the mountains in the north, a most rugged job, and rated them among the best he had ever encountered. Four, he found, were especially good. "A five-year-old fish in these streams runs about 18 pounds to Canada's and Scotland's 15 pounds average, and there are practically no predators except human poachers," he said in his precise report. He pleased the general no end.

Hewitt returned to the United States with Franco's thanks, and devoted his time to fishing and improving the Neversink, his favorite New York state stream famous among fly fishermen. Although impeded by a leg broken while angling last summer, this spring he bought and imported 10,000 eyed salmon eggs from Scotland for experimental planting in the Neversink, and hopes to have results in a few years. When winter comes, he works wood as a hobby in his New York City home, runs soil analyses in his own chemical laboratory and keeps a sharp eye on trout and salmon fishing developments all over the world.

None of this would be especially remarkable, except for one thing. Seventy-two years ago this same Edward Ringwood Hewitt—then a youth of 17—caught fish in Germany for the breakfasts of Emperor Wilhelm I, and both the emperor and the great Bismarck used to watch the young American at his fishing. That was worlds ago and far away, but even then Hewitt was embarked upon a fishing career that has made him a legendary figure within his own lifetime, a distinction that comes to few men.

Hewitt, now 89, was born June 20, 1866, one year after Abraham Lincoln died, and has spent most of the years in that long span fishing for trout and salmon on both sides of the Atlantic. Most literate fly fishermen know of him as the author of several authoritative books on fishing. Many know that he invented the bivisible dry fly ("bivisible because both the fish and the fisherman can see it, even in fast water"), and sired dry-fly and nymph angling for salmon. Still others have been influenced without realizing it by his carefully tested theories on flies, colors, leaders and methods.

Nearly all, though, are a bit startled when they learn he belongs very much to the present as well as the past, because they feel he must have joined long ago such vanished giants of the fishing world as F. M. Halford, of England, Theodore Gordon and George M. L. LaBranche, men who were his contemporaries in an age when fly fishing came into its maturity. A personal preference for a serene life, alternating between seasonal living along the Neversink and his New York City house on genteel old Gramercy Park, and a disinclination to write further about fishing—"This must be my final writing on fishing," he said of his book *A Trout and Salmon Fisherman for Seventy-Five Years* in 1948—have kept him from the public eye. And surprisingly little has been written about this man who, I believe, had a greater influence on fly fishing than any other American.

He is a small man, courteous in manner but brusque of speech, inclined to be testy about some current trout stream management methods, keen and alert in mind, and energetic in body, showing no ill effects from his leg injury. "I stepped in a confounded ground-hog hole along the Neversink last summer," he told me recently, "and laid on a cot all fishing season without realizing I had broken a bone until I got back to the city for an X-ray." He obviously regretted the wasted fishing time. We were talking over tea—a daily ritual with him—in the second-floor sitting room of his Manhattan home. It was one of those late winter days when foggy daylight turns suddenly to evening's dusk, but the air "feels" like fishing weather, making a man impatient to get outdoors.

A huge and ornate, but blazeless, fireplace dominated the room, the walls of which were crowded with pictures and photographs. The room exuded old New York, as well it might because its owner belongs to a vanishing period in every way except for his vigorous throwing off of the years. I asked the first and most natural questions that could be put to a man who had caught his first fish more than 80 years ago on the family's 20,000-acre estate along the Ringwood River in northern New Jersey: What fish did he find most interesting to take with a fly, and what kind of fishing was most interesting among the many kinds he had time to sample in four score years?

Confirmed salmon anglers seldom admit that any other worthwhile fish exists, so his answer to the first part of the question came as a surprise. Without hesitation, he replied: "The Norwegian sea trout is the best, and strongest, fish I've ever taken in fresh water. It is a sort of silvery brown trout which runs up the rivers of Norway from the sea for spawning, and it is much better than the salmon. They run to 20 pounds, but most are 12 to 15, and even the natives over there prefer them to salmon. They put up a tremendous battle."

He chewed reflectively on a biscuit: "Do you know, there are two places where they occur in America, and if I wanted to have some real fun on a fishing trip, I'd go there to get them. They come up a couple of streams below Bangor, Maine, south of the Penobscot, and they enter a few rivers in Newfoundland. Those in Maine only grow to two or three pounds, and, unfortunately, they arrive only during the last few days of trout season, so few fishermen know about them. They get bigger in Newfoundland."

The second part of the question caused more mental debate. "The most interesting fishing I've ever found?" he repeated thoughtfully. "Well, I like all kinds of fishing, and find it all interesting, but casting in the chalk streams of England is probably the most interesting because it offers the greatest test of skill. It is difficult. However, I like our Eastern mountain streams, and the greatest trout fishing I've ever had was on the Nipigon in

Canada." He told of one day on the Nipigon—which he spells "Nepigon" in all his writings after an older version of the name—when he had "the greatest trout fishing in my life." He took 13 brook trout, six of them over six pounds each, and one which went an estimated 13 pounds in weight. His scales were lost, but the fish measured 26 inches in length and 20 inches in girth.

That occurred in 1891, but Hewitt first fished the Nipigon in 1887 —68 years ago!—at a time when it was a wilderness river in the wildest part of "settled" Ontario, instead of the much-harnessed stream it is today. Before he lost his scales, he weighed some brook trout that had been netted and kept on ice at a post of the Hudson Bay Company. They were cleaned with the heads on, and all ran between 10 and 12 pounds, after 11 months on ice.

Hewitt has fished the Test, Itchen, Kennet, the Gade and the Narr, among other streams, in England; the Beauly and others for salmon in Scotland, the Black-water and similar Irish salmon rivers, the famed salmon rivers of Norway and Spain, the salmon rivers of Newfoundland and New Brunswick in Canada's Maritime Provinces, and most of the great streams in the United States. "The Test and Itchen fish are the most difficult I have seen anywhere in the world, and for that reason the most interesting," he wrote in one of his outstanding books, *Telling on the Trout* (Charles Scribner's Sons, 1926).

It is hard for a person today to fix some of his exploits in time and space because they seem to belong to another world. Possessing money and social position, Hewitt was at home anywhere, and welcomed. While a student in Germany, he encountered—by a backdoor sort of introduction —Emperor Wilhelm I and Bismarck. He was fishing the River Lahn when he caught a large barbel. Immediately it was confiscated by a German officer, much to Hewitt's surprise. He thought he must have broken some law, but next morning he found himself escorted into the presence of the emperor who thanked him for a fine breakfast fish, and, after that, the two men who formed the old German Empire, Wilhelm and Bismarck, often accompanied him on his daily fishing.

Such a man, who has frankly made a lifetime career of fishing because he had the means, might be envied by less fortunate anglers except that few men, as free to do as they please as he has been, would devote as much time as Hewitt did to studying fish, as well as catching them, and thus helping all fishermen. Some other persons undoubtedly would have eventually discovered the bivisible fly, dry fly and nymph in fishing for salmon, and evolved the theories and techniques that Hewitt did, but the fact remains that he was the discoverer, and thus has added immeasurably to the pleasures of angling for all men.

Hewitt has never received full public credit for all he has done for fishing. I believe his little-known book, *Hewitt's Handbook of Fly Fishing*, is just about the best and most compact course on the subject ever published, but you have to hunt around in secondhand bookstores to find a copy. Another of his books, *Secrets of the Salmon*, gave the fishing world dry-fly and nymph fishing for salmon for the first time, and created an entirely new trend. About the only recognition Hewitt received was among his readers and through having a series of salmon flies named in his honor by the famed English firm of Hardy Brothers. On the other hand, LaBranche, a fishing companion of Hewitt's, will go down in angling history as the originator of LaBranche's Pink Lady, a noted salmon dry fly which is little more than a gaudy type of Hewitt's original bivisible fly.

"I tied the first bivisibles because I wanted a dry fly that I could see in fast water, and that also would be visible to the fish," Hewitt told me. "I never tied it any other way than brown hackle for the body, tied palmer, with a front hackle of white." Although tyers have deviated from this original with black-and-white, red-and-white, and various bivisibles, many a myopic angler has had reason to bless Hewitt's name—even if he never heard it—when able to follow a dancing bivisible in rapid water.

"I first met Halford (F. M. Halford, of England, who started the world dry-fly fishing), and saw my first dry flies used then on the Itchen around 1885, I think." He frowned over the effort to recall something that happened 70 years ago. "I also met Gordon (Theodore Gordon, who introduced the dry fly to America in the 90's, and who is remembered by the popular Quill Gordon pattern), but he was a very sick man then, and dying. He fished the Neversink, you know, and I've had a camp there since 1917, a few years after Gordon died. However, I first used dry flies on the Paradise at Henryville in Pennsylvania somewhere around the turn of this century. I had been fishing wet flies upstream, but they weren't quite satisfactory at the time, and I tried dries."

No dry-fly purist, Hewitt believes that wet flies will take more trout than dries through an entire season, and that a good nymph fisherman can clean out a trout brook if he wishes—"But he must be good with nymphs," he added firmly. Nevertheless, he knows dry flies as few persons do, even to taking photographs of what dry flies look like to a trout when viewed through the trout's-eye. He has given himself the dubious compliment of "being able to think like a trout."

I asked the usual questions that might be tossed at a man who has fished dry flies longer, perhaps, than any other angler in the country. His answers contain a wealth of information:

"With dry flies, a fine leader is much more important than the fly, especially if the water is low.

"Next most important is the size of the fly with regards to the kind of food trout are taking at the time.

"Next comes good stiff hackle, so the fly sets upright on the water.

"Color—*except for light or dark*—doesn't mean anything in dry flies. I have tied flies with yellow wings and red bodies, and various other unnatural combinations. The trout didn't care. But it is important to approximate light or dark flies on which the fish are feeding. It's a good idea sometimes to use a dark-winged fly in a light-colored hatch, because it will stand out, and occasionally trout will take a very large fly if it is put down on the water during a hatch of small flies, but these are exceptions."

Then we turned to wet flies for trout. "The best fly over the entire season is the Stone Fly tied with turned-down wings. Early in spring, the Blue Quill is best." He was talking about fishing Eastern streams. "The size is very important. Usually I use a No. 11 model perfect hook." He believes color is of considerable importance in wet flies, which are seen by the trout under water. He fits his casting and fishing method to the conditions at hand, but usually casts a wet fly across the current and lets it swing down-stream, straightening out and coming to the surface as it nears the end of the arc thus described.

His experiments with what dry flies—and trout fisherman—look like to trout led Hewitt to interesting conclusions. A dry fly should be smaller than the natural insect it imitates, he believes, because the way the hackles disturb the surface tension makes the artificial look larger than it really is. Anglers should wear light clothing against a light background, dark clothing against a dark whenever possible to be less visible to the trout. Some of the weirdest photos ever taken of Edward Hewitt show him as he looks to the trout.

For salmon fishing, the wet fly is best for the early-season runs when the rivers are swollen with rains. In fact, Hewitt considers such fishing too easy, and won't have much to do with it. Actually, Hewitt is in what he calls the Third Age of the Fisherman. The three ages he defines thus:

1. When he wants to catch all the fish he can.
2. When he strives to catch the largest fish.
3. When he studies to catch the most difficult fish he can find, requiring the greatest skill and most refined tackle, caring more for the sport than the fish.

"Easy" salmon angling naturally wouldn't appeal to him in his Third Age. He prefers a 14-foot leader for most salmon fishing, tapered from .020 to .012, likes brightness in wet flies, and considers size quite important, with the pattern of little moment. Casting and handling the fly properly are of prime importance. When fishing is good, he uses sizes No. 8 and 6, but carries a much wider range of flies.

He prefers the bushy, good-floating, all-hackle flies tied palmer as dries for salmon, sizes 10 to 6. It has been his experience that salmon won't take dry flies well when the water temperature is below 58 degrees F., and they strike best between 60 and 66 degrees. He caught his first salmon on a dry fly on the Indian River in Newfoundland, and developed the method on the Restigouche and Upsalquitch in New Brunswick, putting the knowledge he gained into his book *Secrets of the Salmon* which was published in 1922. Sometimes he uses dry flies as small as No. 16.

The development of theories and techniques was not Hewitt's only contribution to angling. As a youth on the family's New Jersey estate, he operated a hatchery and later set up one on the Neversink near Liberty, New York, where his camp is located. He does not have much respect for hatchery-reared trout that do not get natural food. "They never seem to learn how to feed properly in the stream," he told me, "and they never develop much, even in the second year if they hold over. In fact, they lose ground. The best trout I get for stocking come from a hatchery where the holding ponds are almost as natural as a trout lake, with trees and vegetation, and bottoms that provide natural food. They are equipped for growth and survival when put in streams."

He feels that it is better to stock fry than mature trout, although stocking fry was abandoned generally long ago. He believes fry learn from infancy to fend for themselves and forage for their food. Of course, he has in mind the permanent improvement of a trout stream, and not simply dumping in a load of fish for the put-and-take anglers. Neither does he believe planted fish must be doled out carefully along the entire length to be stocked. "I found one time that I could plant a whole stock of small fry at one place, and in a little while they would be scattered up and down the stream."

*

There is little guesswork about his theories. The third floor of his old home on Gramercy Park is given over to a chemical laboratory—and wood-working shop—which probably makes it the strangest house in that backwater of respectability in Manhattan. Here he analyzes soils and waters with regard to their effect on fish. The Neversink is a natural laboratory where he tests his ideas, and fishes occasionally in the morning and evening hours. His theories—some of which clash sharply with the practices of fish commissions, leading to a sharp exchange of letters with Hewitt in the only writing he does these days—are put into concrete form in his books, *Telling on the Trout* and *Better Trout Streams*. In more condensed writing, the theories appear in his more recent *A Trout and Salmon Fisherman for Seventy-Five Years* (Charles Scribner's Sons, New York) which could be read with considerable profit by anyone who fishes flies.

His last trip abroad was on the errand for General Franco. "The Spanish salmon rivers are the finest in the world," he said to me, "but they have been poached to death since the Romans. The natives are allowed to fish them, and have sort of ruined it for the rods because they scare the fish. However, my 1950 trip proved to me that they are capable of producing around 100,000 salmon a year for sportsmen. The rivers come down out of high mountain gorges where the salmon can spawn in peace, and there are no crawfish, kingfishers, cranes, seals or other vermin to destroy the fish or their eggs—and it is warm enough so the young salmon can feed all winter."

One of the many pictures on the walls of the room where Hewitt drank tea and talked shows him with General Franco. The Hewitt in the picture might be any age above 50. The Hewitt in the easy chair, beside the table he made himself, might be any age above 50. Some few persons achieve timelessness, and Hewitt is one of them. Perhaps it is due to his lifetime of fishing. Whatever the reason, he has not reached old age yet because he looks to the future more than he lives in his interesting past.

He even looks to the final future, and hopes that, when he dies and Charon rows him across the River Styx, "I may have one last chance to see if I can raise one there also." If he does, he will make a chemical analysis of the water, study its insect life, the soil it drains, and get into an argument with the Stygian Fish Commissioners over exactly how the Styx should be stocked.

THE OL' MAN TAKES UP
THE FLY ROD

Harry J. Entrican and
Farrell E. Lehigh

This duo was responsible for the hilarious "Ol'
Zip" series, about a hillbilly hound dog that liked
his moonshine. Surprisingly, one of their tall tales
has to do with flyfishing. (July 1957)

WILL SLID the package across the counter with an important air. Bein'
as it was from the mail-order house, you couldn't blame him. About a dozen
other fellers crowded around and Will grabbed his bung-starter. His Adam's
apple bobbed up 'n' down his turkey-red neck.

"This yere's th' Yewnited States Mail!" he bellowed, which was a little
unusual, for Will is noted as bein' a soft-spoken feller. "Don't any o' yuh
lay a liddle finger on hit, 'til hit passes into the Ol' Man's hands! Hit's
his'n!" He rapped the maul down hard and we all jumped back. We'd all
had enough trouble with the dang revenooers without gettin' the U.S. Mail
onto us.

Everyone bein' at a respectful distance, Will smiled and hitched up his apron. "Thet's better, boys. 'Tain't thet Ah don't trust yuh, hit's jes' thet yore so dang nosey. Then, again, one o' them dang Burrocrats from Washington might be apeekin' round the corner tryin' to git mah job; seein' as how Ah'm a Demmycrat." He jabbed his yellow pencil stub at me.

"You, Bud! Ah'm delegatin' you to tote the Mail. Seein' as how you, me and the Ol' Man is all related, Ah figger hit's all right." Shovin' the box into my arms, he pointed at the door. I trooped out with head high and jaw set. The package was about a yard long, a foot square and had enough stamps to take it clean to hell 'n' gone. I figgered it must be really somethin' to spend all that money. Since wondering wasn't goin' to tell me, I leant forward an' burnt the breeze.

I was puffin' a little when I cleared the fence and zoomed into the yard. The Ol' Man was sittin' there on the porch, rockin' and brushin' skeeters. His .30-30 was leaning against the porch and the ol' stone jug sat beside his chair. Ol' Zip, his hound dawg, peeked around the corner as I put on the brakes. Jammin' the box into the Ol' Man's lap, I wheezed:

"Clean from Chicago, Gran'pa! From the mail-order house! Open 'er up!"

"Whoa, thar, boy!" The Ol' Man pushed back his slouch hat and squinched his gray eyes at me. "Let's not be jumpin' over the wagon tongue. Simmer down an' quit yer jabberin'. Ah'll open 'er up in mah own good time."

Settin' down with my back against the post that held up the porch, I wondered if the Ol' Man was gettin' soft in the haid bone. I fairly itched to see the insides of that box.

I held myself in as he fished in his pocket for his hawk's-bill knife. He cut the string, wound it up in a ball, stuck it into his shirt pocket and then stroked his red beard and stared at me.

"Gittin' kinda curious?"

"Well, not too much," I lied. "'Cause, it bein' from Chicago, I reckon it's purty important."

"Ah reckon so, mahself." Tearin' off the wrapping paper, he tossed it aside and lifted the lid.

As he pushed away the tissue paper, Ol' Zip climbed onto the porch and shoved me to one side. Rarin' up, he hooked his front laigs onto the back of the rocker and peered over the Ol' Man's shoulder. Betwixt the two of us, we sorta got in his way.

"Zip!" he stormed. "Ah'm 'shamed o' yuh! Yer gittin' as bad as Bud yere!"

Reachin' down beside the rocker, the Ol' Man hefted the jug to his knee. He took a couple long snorts, and hauled out of the box a fishin' rod so small it looked like a toy in its glass case. For a long minute the Ol' Man just stared at it, then glanced at me.

"Purty fish pole, young'un. Orta run 'bout 3½ ounces or so. Leastways, thet's whut Ah ordered. Look her over." He passed it to me.

When I got my eyeballs back behind my lids again I looked up. The Ol' Man was tinkerin' with a little reel. Passin' it over, he lifted out a green tackle box and snapped open the lid. I never saw so dang many artificial flies in all my born days. They fairly bulged outa the box.

Diggin' into the box again, the Ol' Man came out with a leather-bound book. In gold letters it said *THE ART OF FLY FISHING.* I set the tackle box down and Ol' Zip stretched out his bony snout and gave it a sniff.

The Ol' Man tossed the empty package aside and looked at me. "Boy, whut yuh see yere is a sample o' whut Ah call takin' yore time. Since 1898 Ah've been readin' them sportin' magazines and Ah been meanin' to try this yere fly fishin' all thet time." He pursed his lips, looked around for a target and sprayed a fly 20 feet out in the yard. Stickin' his nose into the book, he began frownin'.

Finally, stabbin' at a page, he drawled. "This yere book relates all 'bout handlin' thet liddle fish pole, Bud. Hit sounds real easy, too." He looked away out across the valley and up to the hazy hills. "Ah'm thinkin' o' Ol' Oscar layin' up in Clear Crick. Ah've fed thet trout worms and crawdad tails nigh onto ten y'ars now and only hooked him three times. Ah'll jes' wager thet fish has been awantin' one o' these artyfishul flies."

That afternoon when the Ol' Man came out of the house he was totin' his jug and carryin' a pair of waders. The cane lunch basket he always carried when he was goin' fishin' was under his arm.

"Gimme thet thar pole, Bud," he said. "Soon as Ah git the hang o' the dang thing we'uns 'll go."

I remembered, as a little boy, thinkin' how the Ol' Man looked like the picture of Moses in the family Bible—with his red beard flowin' and his gray eyes aglintin'. 'Course Moses didn't have a red beard, but when the Ol' Man stepped into the yard, swingin' the tiny rod around, I knowed Moses must have looked the same way when he come stompin' down offa that mountain to whip his folks into line.

I watched from the porch for a minute and saw the Ol' Man wasn't havin' any luck. First he got the reel on the wrong way. Then the fly dribbled out a couple feet and wouldn't come any farther, though he whipped the rod back and forth somethin' fierce.

"Bud!" the Ol' Man yelled, "bring thet instruction book out yere and read hit to me. Ah'm all fouled up." He was snortin' like a grain-fed mule. "Find whar hit sez how to throw the dang line out, and Ah'll be all right."

Finally by feeding out line little by little, he got the fly sailin' around right purty. A smile seemed to grow through his beard, and he looked at me with his eyes twinklin'. "Thar yuh air, Bud. Ah got 'er now." He seemed real proud of hisself.

Ol' Zip had been watchin' from the porch. His bony snout was between his paws, and his mournful eyes were puzzled as they followed the Ol' Man's actions. Gettin' to his feet, he fell off the porch and staggered out into the yard. He stood by me for a minute and stared amazed.

Just then the Ol' Man picked up about 80 feet of line and sent it in behind him in a graceful backcast. Ol' Zip was comin' up from behind and, as those things go, he'd had to have his hind end at the right spot at the wrong time. As the Ol' Man lay into his cast, the fly sank into Zip's hide.

The ol' dawg just stood there a second, stock still. He hadn't seen the

fly nor the line. But somehow he just *knew* the Ol' Man had attacked him. Zip was born with about four times the Original Sin in him as other dawgs had, but he knew he hadn't done anythin' to deserve this. He let out a howl and went into a tight circle to see if there wasn't someone behind him. Findin' out there wasn't, really hurt him. A look of pained betrayal shot across his face, and he lit out for the back of the house.

The Ol' Man stood flabbergasted as the rod bowed in his hand and the reel started to sing. "Goldangit!" he bellowed. "Bud! Ketch thet fool dawg afore he busts muh fish pole!" He began runnin' after Zip, who thought the Ol' Man had a switch in his hand. Ol' Zip really outdid himself, for he was goin' in high gear—about five miles per.

Tearin' around the other side of the house, I met the dawg. He was leadin' the Ol' Man by about a length and a half. Zip bowled me over, but I hung on. Betwixt us we got the hook outa him, but it took some fussin' from the Ol' Man before he was able to talk Ol' Zip outa leavin' home. The ol' bony cuss looked up outa his mournful eyes, all bloodshot and sad, and after inspectin' his wound, he slurped at the Ol' Man's hand and forgave him.

We all trooped to the porch, where the Ol' Man took apart the rod and stored it away. He squinted at the sun that was about halfway up the sky. "Let's see now," he drawled, "go out back and git yore cane pole, Bud, and we'uns 'll go. Thar's a poke sack back thar too. Git hit, fur Ol' Oscar is a mitey big fish. We'll hev to use hit fur a net. On yer way back, holler in the back door and tell yer Gran'ma t' grease up the skillet!"

The Ol' Man was all set when I got back. He was carryin' his .30-30, and the jug was slung on a rope over his shoulder. I picked up the rest of the gear and the lunch basket. Ol' Zip sniffed to make sure we hadn't forgot the grub. Startin' off across the yard and into the brush, we headed down the valley.

It was a fine day for fishin'. A slow wind made its way through the notch at the head of the valley, bringin' the smell of pines way up on the ridge. We made good time in spite of the fact that the Ol' Man's waders were chokin' me, hangin' around my neck like they were. Besides, Ol' Zip was doggin' my heels, mumblin' and talkin' to hisself as he staggered along. He sounded like he wanted to gum somethin' to death. As I was closest, I kinda kept steppin' out.

Clear Crick was about two miles from home, and was clear and fast as we come out onto the bank. The wind rustled the leaves and a beech tree creaked. A partridge clucked back in the bushes. I could see Ol' Oscar sizzlin' in the pan.

Downstream we went, 'til the Ol'Man laid his .30-30 against a tree and unslung the jug.

"Wal," he smiled, as he uncorked it, "we're yere and Ah kinda figger hit's time fur a liddle o' muh relaxin' tonic." He took a snort and passed it to me. I shucked off my gear, and Ol' Zip flopped down on the grass with a sigh. Unlacin' his shoes and drawin' on his waders, the Ol' Man begun puttin' his rod together.

"Yuh know, Bud," he said, sightin' down the rod, "we ain't been fishin' together for quite a spell. Been meanin' to tell yuh 'bout the 'art' o' fishin'."

I nodded my head and started stringin' my pole. Out of the corner of my eye I saw Ol' Zip inchin' his way toward the jug. He yawned and got to his feet and, casual-like, strolled over and lay down beside it. Then he sighed and curled one paw around the neck.

"Now, you prob'bly figger in fishing the onliest idea is to ketch fish. Wal, hit's important all right, but thar's more'n thet." Diggin' out his Brown's Mule eatin' tobacco, the Ol' Man bit off a chaw. "Fishin' leads a man to peace and patience. 'Member thet, Bud, and be like me—peaceful and patient."

"Now, take Ol' Oscar down at the foot o' thet riffle. For years Ah been after him and nothin' but mah patience has kept me from usin' Giant Powder. Patience, boy, is a good thing to know." The Ol' Man finished threadin' his line and stood at the edge of the bank. Ol' Zip peeked over the jug and seein' the Ol' Man lookin' the other way, gave the stopper a couple of good yanks with his toothless gums.

"Ah've fought thet fool fish three times now and lost him every time," the Ol' Man went on. "He's a tricky one and he's been gittin' fat and growin' smarter and bigger all these years. Ah'll wager he must weigh 20 pounds or more. Thar ain't no fish like Ol' Oscar anywhar's else in Virginny. Bet he's alayin' thar right now waitin' for dinner." He shot a stream of juice into the water. "Ah'm fixin' to fool him this time." He grinned and pushed back his ol' slouch hat.

Just then the surface of the water broke just below the riffle. So did the Ol' Man's nerves.

"Great sufferin' succotash! Did yuh see thet, Bud! Gimme one o' them flies!"

I grabbed the first fly outa the box and handed it over. The Ol' Man's hands shook as he tied it on the leader. He waded out about 15 feet and flipped the pole to let some line out. Then he shot the fly in the general direction of Oscar.

Ol' Zip decided right then that this was a good time to git hisself a snort. He rassled the jug down, pulled the corncob stopper and was alappin' up the Ol' Man's good squeezings when the Ol' Man glanced over and caught him.

"Zip!" he roared, wavin' his fist, "Dang yore potlickin' hide! Ain't Ah got enuff on muh mind 'thout yuh astealin' muh likker! Bud, stop thet fool hound afore he spills hit all!"

Ol' Zip fought me like the town drunk as I tore the jug outa his paws. Then he tried to gum my arm off. After quite a set-to I whipped him and set the jug up.

"Much gone?" called the Ol' Man anxiously.

I shook the jug and it sounded pretty hollow. "'Bout a snort left."

Ol' Zip curled his lip in a silly grin and flopped down under a tree. His tongue hung out a foot and his eyes was kinda glazin'. He opened his mouth and let out a long belch.

The Ol' Man snapped the brim of his hat down over his eyes, and his beard fairly bristled as he ground his teeth. He rubbed his hand across his face. I could see he was bein' awful patient. "Dang thet dawg, anyways," he growled. "Ah've half a mind to wring him out like a mop."

The Ol' Man stomped off up the crick, cussin' as he went. It looked like I maybe might catch my breath before sundown and I laid down to rest a bit. I don't rightly know how long I'd laid there when all of a sudden the Ol' Man let out a squawk that would have done honor to a banshee.

"Gawdamity, Bud! Ah got him! Ah got him!" he shouted. "Whoa, thar, whoa! Yuh lowbred son-O-Satan! Ye ain't goin' no place but in the skillet!" He floundered around in a circle.

I jumped up and hied myself down the crick to where the Ol' Man had waded just below the riffle. He was standin' in nigh hip-deep water, an' Ol' Oscar was givin' him the fight of his life. I wasn't sure who had who. The rod was bowin' nearly double, and the Ol' Man, knowin' his dinkey gear wouldn't hold if he forced it, begun playin' that trout like he knew what he was doin'. I stood there on the bank with my eyeballs popped out when I realized that the Ol' Man was ayellin' somethin' at me.

"Bud, ye dang walleyed idjit, bring me the poke, cain't ye see Ah got him ketched! Hurry, boy! Hurry!"

I ran up the crick and got the gunny sack that we had brung along to put the fish in and tore back as fast as I could. The Ol' Man was still waltzin' around with Oscar. It looked like Oscar was tryin' to lead him into deeper water.

"Hold him, Gran'pa!" I yelled, splashin' into the crick, startin' to wade out to where the battle raged. The Ol' Man's beard was flappin' and his jaws were workin' up and down. The rod shivered and shook, and the Ol' Man's eyeballs run halfway down his line tryin' to find out where it might break.

Ol' Oscar was sure holdin' his own. He knew all the standard tricks of shakin' loose from a hook, and a lot more of his own. He was usin' them all. The Ol' Man climbed up on a big rock, tryin' to keep a tight line, and Oscar headed upstream. That throwed a lot of slack in the line and the Ol' Man stripped it in madly to keep pace with him. In his excitement he slipped off the rock and went *kurr-splash* into the crick. Ol' Oscar broke the surface just then to get a looksee, but the Ol' Man was just goin' down at that time so they didn't meet. I swear there was a grin on Ol' Oscar's face as he walked on top of the water with his tail. He was all brown, gold and orange in the sun, and his belly was as big as a nail keg. When he dove under again he whapped his tail, and water splashed ten feet high. The Ol' Man come rarin' up on his hind laigs, soakin' wet and mad as a hornet. He still clutched that little rod, but he'd got his long laigs tangled up in all that slack line.

Ol' Oscar had shore caught hisself a man, and I think the Ol' Man thought so, too, for he just stood there like a man what's bit off more'n he could chew. I thought maybe he'd hit his head on a rock or somethin', and I hurried out to him. When I saw that he wasn't bleedin' anywhere, I knew he wasn't hurt, just plum' flabbergasted and mad.

"Help me git ontangled, young'un," stormed the Ol' Man, "and Ah'll ketch thet ornery bowlaiged bait-stealer bar-handed, so help me Hannah!"

I started to help him, but Ol' Oscar took off downstream again and the line jerked so tight the Ol' Man lost his balance and set right down in the crick again. Utterin' an unprintable word he flung that purty little rod as far as he could fling it and grabbed the line in his bare hands. He was mad enough to pull it in hand-over-hand, but he knew that would snap his leader. Instead he started awadin' toward where Ol' Oscar was boilin' up the deep water. It looked to me like Oscar had him for sure. The Ol' Man was so riled he couldn't see straight.

I still don't see how that tiny leader stood all the pullin', haulin' and jerkin', but it did. The Ol' Man finally dragged Ol' Oscar into shallow water, with the fish afightin' every step of the way. I grabbed the sack from under my belt, dived on top of Oscar and tried to pull it over his haid. But he just wouldn't stand still long enough.

"Hold him, Bud," yelled the Ol' Man. "Put him in the poke!" I was tryin' but I was gittin' scared. I had the feelin' Ol' Oscar was tryin' to put me in the sack and if'n I didn't git help pretty soon he'd do it. I reckon the Ol' Man saw I was fightin' a losin' battle, for he jumped in, and for a few minutes there the water got real riley.

First me, then the Ol' Man, then Ol' Oscar was underwater. Most of the time it was me. Of the three I think I weighed the least. The Ol' Man finally got a bear hug on the fish, and I jumped forward with the open sack. Then real trouble started.

Ol' Zip, who had been staggerin' up and down the bank barking his fool haid off, decided the Ol' Man was being attacked and leaped in to help. Just as the Ol' Man had Oscar in the poke, Zip landed on top of the pile and the Ol' Man lost his footing and fell smack-dab into the open sack with Oscar. I fell, too, not being able to hold them all up—but I held onto the sack, determined not to let Ol' Oscar escape. Only now I had the Ol' Man's head in the sack, too, and Oscar was sure smackin' the tar outa him with his tail.

The Ol' Man's voice was muffled, but I could hear him ayellin' and asputterin' for me to come help him git out o' there. Ol' Zip must have thought that I was the cause of all the ruckus, for he jumped me and tried to gum my neck off. For a minute there I thought it was Ol' Oscar achewing on me.

After what seemed to me an awful long time the Ol' Man pulled his haid outa the sack, spit out a mouthful of fishtail and hauled Ol' Zip off'n me so I could git to my feet. There was a wild kinda look in the Ol' Man's eyes and he looked about as happy as a rooster that'd got caught in a cloudburst. He helped me tie the sack shut and we all staggered up on dry land like shipwrecked sailors. We shore was a mess to behold. The Ol' Man flopped under a tree, while I tied the sack to a root and let it dangle in the water.

I cut the fish line at the mouth of the sack, recovered the Ol' Man's pretty little rod and after carefully crankin' in all the loose line, I laid it up by him. He cut hisself a big soggy chaw of Brown's Mule and just sat there watchin' me, without a word, for a long time. Then he got up.

"Young'un, we got to git thet dang hook out o' Ol' Oscar's mouth."

I untied the poke and held Ol' Oscar just behind his haid while the Ol' Man carefully worked the hook out.

"Gosh! ain't he a whopper, Gran'pa," I said. Ol' Oscar was just as quiet and meek as a lamb all the while. He lay there in the water, gazing at the Ol' Man with eyes as big as nickels. The Ol' Man tossed the fly up on the bank and, just as I was closin' the sack again, danged if'n he didn't reach under the water and pat that fool fish on his silly head. I thought about it as I lay down in a sunny spot to dry out a little. I figgered mebbe the Ol' Man had hit his haid on a rock after all. Ol' Zip got hisself 'twixt the Ol' Man and me and just lay there, aglarin' at anything that dared to move.

In about ten minutes the Ol' Man had puffed hisself out. He got up slowly, walked over and stood lookin' down at Ol' Oscar. I got up and started gatherin' our gear, figurin' we was aheadin' home. "Gee, Gran'pa," I said, "Ol' Oscar sure will make a lot of good eatin', won't he?"

The Ol' Man didn't even answer. He stood there combin' his beard with his fingers, with a faraway look in his eyes. I came over, lifted the sack out of the water and held it up to drain. When the water had just about all gone, the Ol' Man suddenly reached out, snatched the sack and held it well out over the water. Before I knew what he was up to he spilled Ol' Oscar into the crick. With a flip of his tail Ol' Oscar scooted for deep water.

The Ol' Man stared at me for a minute, slowly chewin' on his cud of tobacco. "Ah don't 'llow yu'll onderstan', boy, but Ol' Oscar waren't ketched fa'r and squar'."

"Fair and square!" I yammered. "If it'd been any fairer he'd a drownded us all!"

The Ol' Man kinda smiled. "Hit took three o' us tuh ketch him, son," he said quietly. He picked up the fly pole and stared at it, then shoved it at me. "Hyar yuh air boy, and the flies too. Ah don't want hit. To my way o' thinkin' hit was a sneaky trick, usin' an artyfishul fly. Thet pore ol' trout has got plum' used to worms and crawdad tails in the ten y'ars Ah've knowed him. Ah jest cain't cheat him with a mouthful o' feathers."

EVERYMAN'S SALMON

Charley Dickey

*A native South Carolinian takes a look at Down
East Atlantic salmon fishing when "the
Narraguagus was having its best run in three
years." (April 1960)*

I HAD always heard that New Englanders were taciturn. When I hit
Maine last summer I managed to get "yep" and "nope" out of one down
Easterner and felt I had won a moral victory. Being from South Carolina,
it took me a little while to learn how to get these people to talk.

When I first entered the state I mentioned pickerel at a service station.
I got a grunt from the attendant. A little farther down the road, in a café,
I mentioned trout fishing and actually had two people smile at me. At the
next stop I asked how was the Atlantic salmon fishing, and people descended
on me from all sides! For the ten days I was in Maine I got a solid stream
of solid salmon chatter that about pulverized my eardrums.

"Salmon" is a magic word in Maine. Mention salmon and you'll see a
tight-mouthed old-timer take a tug at his britches, clear his throat and rear
back. You'd better hang on. Whether he has ever caught a salmon or not,

everyone in Maine is an expert. He'll tell you not only how to tie your flies but also how to cook the salmon.

Cherryfield, in eastern Maine, is a pleasant little town along the banks of the Narraguagus River. As I ambled along in the pleasant June sun, I stopped by a grocery store not far from the river. A bell rang as I pushed open the ancient door. The storekeeper didn't say a word as I began to prowl the shelves. I had noticed that the streets were empty and there was no one in the store.

I asked the grocery man if he had any soda pop. He didn't say a word, just pointed to the icebox. When I asked for bread, he again pointed. Although my brogue is not exactly Ogeechee, it definitely isn't Yankee. I could see that he knew I was a stranger. He didn't volunteer a word.

"Where's everyone today?" I asked.

"Fishin'," he replied.

"For salmon?" I asked.

"Yep," he said.

"Well, I was hoping to do some salmon fishing. Wonder if you could tell me someone I might go with."

He brightened all over. I was a salmon fisherman. I didn't bother to tell him I was a complete beginner and had never hooked one in my life.

"Just a minute, young feller," he said in his salty twang. He grabbed a nine-foot rod out of the corner, picked up a box of flies and started for the door.

We walked out into the 2 o'clock sunshine toward the river a hundred yards away. I was meeting Bud Leavitt of Bangor the next day but there was no point in wasting an afternoon. Bud is Rod and Gun Editor for the Bangor *Daily News* and a television sportscaster over the Hildreth network.

As we walked along the river, my new friend began a lecture on salmon fishing that was to continue for several hours. We stopped at the Academy Pool, famous for the number of fishermen who have killed their first salmon there. I was surprised to find a fishing hole practically in the middle of town. There were even wooden benches for the spectators. Wives, children and dogs lounged around the green banks watching the fishermen below casting their flies into the deep pool. I had the feeling that I was at a social rather than a fishing party. Up the river I could see more fishermen and more spectators. The whole town was out. It was just as if the Cherryfield baseball team was playing in the little world series.

I soon found out why. June is often a hot Atlantic salmon month and the Narraguagus was having its best run in three years. Ten salmon already had been killed that day in a two-mile stretch, and the whole town was having a ball.

My new-found friend didn't bother to introduce me. He didn't have to. The others knew I was a stranger and they were flattered that I shared their love and respect for salmon. I sat on the bank and watched the grocery man flip a tiny fly 100 feet as easily as I would spin a heavy plug.

In half an hour I knew a dozen fishermen and was talking with them as if I were an old veteran. Or rather, I was listening to them and nodding my head wisely at their sage advice. Once in a while a car would come by, stop, and the driver would ask how we were doing. Then someone from up the river would come by and give us the latest dope on what the salmon were hitting. There was a continuous parade of information marching from pool to pool.

I didn't even break out my rod that first afternoon. As the natives regaled me with salmon stories, I watched the constant flow of fishermen at the Academy Pool. When a new one came up, someone would leave his spot and the newcomer would move in. It was a leisurely type of fishing and no crowding. Everything was done politely.

From the bleachers there came a steady current of advice, funny stories and salmon lore. When one of the fishermen tied into a huge salmon, all the others quickly brought their lines in. They whooped it up and cheered the fisherman. It was like Casey at the bat. More people appeared from the town as word mysteriously spread that a salmon was hooked. For ten minutes the fisherman played the angry salmon, and then the line went slack. A great cry of sympathy went up from the crowd. The fisherman silently walked up the bank, smiled, and said, "Someone else give them a try."

I thought: "This whole town is ganging up on the salmon." And they were. But the salmon have every chance; the salmon also have the undying respect and admiration of the Maine fishermen.

In fact, I learned the next day from Bud Leavitt that the salmon cult is so fanatical that they call trout "rough fish." We were fishing farther upstream and I was constantly amazed by the interest people showed when they saw my South Carolina license tags or heard my brogue. They gave me their best information on flies, places to fish and tips on flycasting. They weren't know-it-alls; they were simply trying to be helpful. And I needed it all, including Bud's steady tips.

At one pool about two miles above Cherryfield, we met Norman Hathaway, a regular Horatio Alger of the Maine salmon world. Six years ago he had never fished for Atlantic salmon, but today he is the acknowledged champion salmon fisherman of the state.

Norman, a garage mechanic from South Brewer, Maine, visited a salmon river for the first time out of curiosity. After seeing one salmon caught, he got hit hard by the bug. He went to libraries all over the state and got books on salmon fishing. He even sent to England for literature.

After the 29-year-old caught his first salmon, he was hooked for life. He experiments constantly with line modifications and flies he ties himself. His favorite invention is the Orange Crate. It was named by his friend, Harry Smith, a salmon guide of more than 50 years and creator of the bear-hair Atlantic salmon fly.

The Orange Crate is a great blob of brilliant orange hackle that floats so high on the water it looks as if it is flying. When a salmon jumps, or Norman finds a likely spot, he dances the Orange Crate across the water to irritate the fish. He'll cast it three or four times into the same place, and if he sees a movement, he'll quickly switch to a more conventional fly and cast to the same spot. He has only killed one salmon with the Orange Crate but he has made dozens angry enough to hit the next fly.

When I first talked with Norman he was trying a ten-foot leader of ten-pound-test monofilament. Behind that he had 28 feet of B-level line. This led into 100 yards of 25-pound-test monofilament. That was backed with 100 yards of black silk line, 20-pound test. He had an eight-foot glass rod. Norman was casting the Orange Crate 120 feet as easily as I might cast a dry fly 40 feet.

Norman holds the Maine salmon record for modern times. In 1958 he killed 33 salmon in three of Maine's eight salmon rivers. Like most true champions, Norman is modest and completely unassuming. Although I was a stranger to him, he eagerly quit his own fishing to give me tips on tackle and casting. And during my stay in Cherryfield I noticed that Norman spent more time on helping others than he did on fishing.

Salmon fishing in Maine is only token fishing as compared with the bonanza that usually hits Gaspé or New Brunswick. But it's the last stand of the Atlantic salmon in the United States. The Narraguagus River is one of the best in Maine; other rivers which still get salmon runs are the Sheepscot, Pleasant, Dennys, East Machias, Machias, Little Tunk and a small run in the Penobscot.

The salmon fishing in Maine has one big advantage. It's poor man's fishing. While most people cannot afford the fishing in the spectacular streams north of Maine, anyone can afford the Maine fishing. The best waters of New Brunswick are tied up by wealthy clubs and private leases. There is open water in certain areas but by the time a visitor pays license fees, guide fees, board and lodging, he soon finds he is paying $50 a day or more to fish.

In Maine you do not need a special license for salmon. You can get a three-day nonresident license for $3.75 or a 15-day license for $5.75, certainly a reasonable fee. Great stretches of the rivers are open and there is no trouble in finding a place to fish. At Cherryfield the banks are cleared at many pools for easy casting. The town even has a free camping spot for visitors. If you want to cook your own grub, there's a place to do it. In fact, you can live as cheaply on the Maine streams as if you were at home. If you want an inexpensive boarding house, there are many scattered in towns near the rivers.

The salmon season in Maine is open from April 1 through September in one stream or another. Nearly every river has different regulations. If you plan a trip to Maine, you may get a free copy of the regulations by writing to the Department of Inland Fisheries and Game, Augusta, Maine. The daily limit is two salmon.

Working the banks of the Narraguagus with Bud, we saw Brud Davis, Cherryfield fireman, hook his first salmon. The magic word went out and soon there were spectators along the bank and on the bluff overlooking the pool. The salmon headed downstream for swift water and Norman came up to help. Harry Smith also came with his wading staff to offer counsel to Brud.

They told Brud to follow his fish downstream but the bushes stopped him and the huge fish became tangled in the rocks of the rapids. Norman hollered across the river to three fishermen to bring their canoe. They didn't ask why or balk. They put down their rods and started upstream where the canoe was tied. A fisherman was in trouble and needed help.

Harry, who has a face like a mischievous Santa Claus, gave the salmon a few seconds to work loose and then said, "Hold on, Brud, I'm going in after him."

The 74-year-old Harry hit the cold water and began wading through the slippery rocks. With his wading staff he eased along through the current. Halfway to where the line disappeared around a rock, Harry stepped in a hole but he kept going. Suddenly, the line slackened and the fish was gone.

Brud couldn't say a word. He had been calm through it all but then he began to tremble as the excitement caught up with him. Everyone had a kind word to say. There was no making up for the disappointment Brud suffered but everyone did his best to console him.

Jack Randolph, Outdoor Editor of *The New York Times*, who was in the group, came up to Brud and said, "Let's go over to my car. You need a bracer."

Everyone on the bank felt as if he himself had lost the fish.

I leaned against a big rock and Harry Smith told me of his lifetime of fishing for the Atlantic salmon. His experience has been that at least nine salmon are hooked for every one that is landed.

When Harry gets going on salmon, you can listen for hours. He not only goes into the merits of bear hair for salmon flies but tells you the best methods of getting the bear. As I relaxed there in the early summer sunshine, I marveled at this friendly cult of salmon fanatics along the Narraguagus. And suddenly I realized that it was hitting me too. I felt as if I had lived in Cherryfield for years, rather than a few days. I also realized that it was the most leisurely fishing I had ever done. Strangely enough I was spending more time talking with the natives than in actual fishing.

I yelled over at Norman and asked if he would catch me a salmon, for the sun was just right for color pictures. He had been loafing on the bank, but came down quickly and put on his Orange Crate made of hair from the tail of a deer. He had seen a salmon roll far out in the river just above the rapids.

For five minutes he whipped the Orange Crate near a big rock and then switched to a bear-hair salmon fly. The angry salmon took it on the first cast. The crowd let out a yell and the race was on.

Norman wanted the fish and he didn't fool with it long. As it swung downstream, Norman followed, leaping from rock to rock like a mountain goat. When the salmon would slow, Norman would pop the rod to him. The pressure he put on the line and rod was unbelievably strong.

The crowd was more excited than Norman. He settled down to the business of beaching the fish as calmly as if he were changing sparks back at the garage. Harry Smith came alongside and waited patiently with the gaff. He waded out into the water as Norman quickly worked the surfacing salmon nearer.

But it was too early. The salmon leaped out of the water and started back upstream. He leaped again, and then sounded. Norman pumped the rod hard and in a few seconds Harry made a quick lunge with the gaff and caught the salmon in the middle. He waded out of the river holding the fish high and proud. Although he had gaffed hundreds of salmon, Harry was having the time of his life.

Everyone crowded around, guessing what the fish would weigh. Norman smoked a cigarette and sagged a little from the fight. We all went up to the spectator shelter on the bluff to see the fish weighed. It went 11 pounds.

Norman scraped off a few scales to save for the Maine Department of Inland Fisheries and Game and put them in an envelope.

There were six salmon caught from that one pool that afternoon and the crowd was delighted. As it grew late, more fishermen came out. Silently one or two would leave the water's edge, and the newcomers would take over for awhile.

Bud and I had to go. We told everyone good-by and it was like leaving the old home place. As I sat there silently thinking about Cherryfield, Bud went into a monologue on why the salmon is the finest fish in the world. It lasted all the way to Bangor.

I don't know where people get that stuff about down Easterners being quiet.

WHITE BASS ON A FLY ROD

Byron W. Dalrymple

*One of this country's best-known outdoor writers
recommends a quarry seldom considered by most
flyfishing enthusiasts. (May 1961)*

FROM THE highway that crosses 265-foot Norris Dam in Tennessee you look downstream on a ribbon of icy blue water that makes you itch to put a fly into it. This is the Clinch River escaping from huge Norris impoundment, and in truth it is worthwhile to place a fly there. Rainbow trout swim in this exotic habitat made possible by the low temperature of water flowing from beneath this huge dam.

On this day some few years ago while camping near the dam I stood gazing at the river, wondering how far downstream the water was chill enough to support rainbows. Unwittingly, I was on the verge of a delightful discovery that had nothing to do with trout.

I thrust my strung fly rod into my car, drove along the highway with the river on my right. Presently it angled away. A side road turned here, as if as loath as I to leave the stream. I took it.

Down here a little way I could see from the high bank natural rock formations which thrust out into the stream from either side, almost like rough, nonsymmetrical wing dams. At the center of one such place water poured through a swift, narrow slide, and below roiled and brawled momentarily before flattening into a slick, clear pool. No angler has ever gazed at such a spot without a rise of temperature.

Ten cast lengths below that pool, a high, rickety old one-way bridge tottered across the stream. I drove onto the bridge and looked back upstream. The water was clear as sauterne. What I suddenly saw swarming in it gave me the heady feeling that I had just tipped a bottle of it over my nose. There were literally scores of fish fanning all over the river.

Not trout, surely! No, I was sure they weren't. Nor were they rough fish. I was too far above and downstream to make out for certain their species. But I was not long in getting closer. Presently I was back on that high bank, scrambling down it with my rod, walking out onto the rocks above the pool. I had a small white streamer tied to the leader and I whipped out line and dropped the fly on an angle across the pool into which the rolling water poured.

I jerked it under and managed to move it a few inches. Then something jerked back and a rollicking good fight was on. When I finally brought the fish into the slack water by my feet, there was the silvery side, the meticulously drawn dark longitudinal stripes, the wearily fanning pale powder blue fins of a white bass. What a surprise!

It would weigh about a pound, I estimated. When at long last I left those rocks, I had a Tennessee limit of 30. It was one of the fastest, most interesting fly-fishing sessions I had ever had.

Those were my first white bass on flies. But they were far from the last. Oddly, though much has been made of the white bass over the past few years, and much written about it, seldom are white bass and fly-fishing equipment mentioned together. There may be scattered anglers who have bent a fly rod over these fish, but certainly the practice is not common. Yet here is a species perfectly adapted to such light tackle, and exceedingly willing to prove it.

As most fishermen know, until a couple of decades ago the white bass was a rather inconsequential fish that was native to large clear lakes and rivers over much of the fairly temperate portion of the United States, mainly east of the Mississippi. But it began to come into its own with the building of the TVA lakes, and later more so than ever as impoundments began holding back rivers all over the country. The white bass, a most prolific, sweet-fleshed fish that runs in large schools, was tailor-made for the huge new impoundments. In most of these small gizzard shad soon became tremendously abundant, and the white bass, a predaceous species, established itself by gobbling the ever-plentiful shad.

Today white bass are extremely abundant in most of the large impoundments and their tributary streams. In some they were native, in some stocked. They reach from the Great Lakes clear to the Rio Grande, which gets a fabulous spring run nowadays from rather new Falcon Lake, in which the whites have built a vast population.

Thus they are available to fishermen over a great portion of the nation, and easily accessible as well. Limits are high or nonexistent, seasons long or open all year. Although white bass do not leap when hooked, as do trout and black bass, but fight a dogged underwater battle, they compensate by offering wondrously fast action because of their large-school habits. With black bass pressure at peak these days, and trout fishing unfortunately in difficulties over much of its range, the white bass is a species to which devotees of the long rod, the light leader and the fly may and should turn. The reward is plenty of fly-fishing fun.

Because white bass are almost wholly minnow feeders, sunken flies of one kind or another that mimic minnows do best on them. I use small bucktails, polar bear, standard feathered streamers or marabou. All do the job. There is not much argument as to what colors are best. White or yellow. A dash of red or other color is favored by some fishermen I know. But I stick to all white or all yellow. I don't believe a dash of this or that makes any difference. There are times, however, possibly because of water color and visibility, when white does better than yellow, or vice versa.

These flies should be tied to sink quickly, and to run from a few inches to a couple of feet below surface. Sometimes it is necessary to weight them slightly. I dislike casting them this way, however, and prefer to wait out the fish for near-surface feeding. A sinking line is a must for best results. Nowadays, as most fly-fishermen know, these can be purchased. Flies should not be excessively large. Of course, when you hit a school of big ones that go two or three pounds each, larger flies with larger hooks are advantageous. The mouths of white bass are ample. But I find that fish of average size— a pound and less—seem to whack a fly of modest size, let's say a streamer not over 1½ to 2 inches, best of all.

During that first experience on the Clinch I happened to have only that one fly with me (without climbing the high bank after more). The fish chewed it up until there were only enough feathers barely to cover the hook. It was worn down to three quarters of an inch. But they hit it just as well, possibly because there was such a concentration, thus competition for food.

This is something that always happens with these large-school fish. Competition within the school, remember, is bound to be severe. They may enjoy each other's company, but they all want to get to the grub first. That's what makes action so fast.

Paul Young, a Texas fisherman who uses nothing but fly-fishing tackle, taught me to use a "pork rind fly" for white bass. It's a good one. Tie a light wire hook to your leader, and if you cannot get pork rind small enough, trim one to about ¼-inch wide by 1½ inches long. Cut a forked tail in it and slip it on the hook. The white can't chew this up. It is practically indestructible, stays on the hook indefinitely, sinks well, has beautiful action and simply murders the fish.

Although the small shad on which whites habitually feed are fast travelers, as are these predators, you do not need to fish a fly swiftly. Just make sure they get a look at it, and then swim it along gently and they'll grab it. By varying the action you can soon catch on to how they like it best on any given day. Some days they will like it deep, on others they may take it right near the surface. Sometimes they will take it barely moving, drifted or all but inert. At other times they want it retrieved in "scared" fashion. White bass, you will find, are erratic in their behavior, feeding wildly one day, sulking the next. But they make up for it in flurries of furious action during their intermittent slashing sprees.

A curious habit they have, which fly-fishermen can use to advantage, is that of following a hooked fish. One time I stood in a stream in Kentucky where white bass were moving abundantly, and cast downstream and across for them, the standard practice with streamers. Ordinarily whites do not like to fight the fastest water, or lie in it beside a rock as trout often will. But they do fancy the slack edges of the very swiftest runs. Here they lie in wait, fanning without effort, until they see some hapless prey fighting up through the current. Then they make a dash and smash it.

This was the situation where I was fishing. And, the light was exactly proper so that I could see the fish while they were not aware of me. When I hooked my first one, I saw seven or eight others dart out and begin flurrying around it in a minor blizzard of fins as I worked it in. Whether this is curiosity, or whether they hope the hooked one will drop the hunk of food he is battling, I do not know. Many salt-water school fish react in this same fashion. Every dolphin in a school can be caught by leaving one hooked up near the boat and casting to those that swarm around it.

In this case, I work the fish up close by my feet, lift it suddenly, unhook it and pitch it quickly up onto the bank. I drop the fly again as quickly as possible.

Most of the fish by this time have turned away. But, instantly, when they sight the fly, they rush for it. They are already worked up to fever pitch and ready to compete. I have taken a dozen-odd by fast work, in this fashion, on several occasions.

Several standard habits of the white bass make it virtually a perfect fly angler's target, and it is puzzling to me that more fly whippers have not previously noted them. The first is that the white bass is a spring spawner that swarms into streams large and small to make its annual "run." This packs a tremendous concentration of fish into a modest area of water. Many of the spring-run streams are wadable. Stretches of the famed Dix River near Danville, Kentucky, are a good example.

In addition to the larger spring-run rivers, practically every small feeder creek emptying into an impoundment where white bass dwell gets its share. And, if streams are too large to wade, they can be floated and fly-fished, or one can anchor and do likewise. There are also spots like the one I fished in the Clinch where the wader or bank fly-fisherman can easily operate. Another I think of that is a real whizzer is located at Marble Falls, Texas, on the Texas Colorado River. It is below the Marble Falls Dam. You push up the river in a boat against swift run-off below the dam, and get out onto rocks beside which white water tumbles. Thousands of whites are taken here during their run, and it is made to order for fly-fishing.

But one does not have to fish *only* the spring runs on the streams. Wherever you find one of the big dams today, usually there are white bass in the stream waters below it. Whenever the turbines are running at the power plant—whenever they're "generating"—white water pours out from below and runs swiftly over the rocks. This well-aerated water draws shad by the millions. And on their trail come the predator whites. These will concentrate and gorge on shad for hours on end, thousands of them. A fly put down among them, regardless of the time of year, is eagerly snapped up. They seem to take a fly more readily than hard lures cast by the spinners and pluggers. Perhaps it is less phony in appearance, its intent so much better camouflaged.

The most delightful habit of white bass, as far as fly-men are concerned, is the way they feed in schools all summer in the big lakes. In many a quiet cove and bay, at dawn and again at dusk—and on overcast days sometimes all day long—schools of white bass will prowl. They jump schools of small shad, swarm around them, drive them against a shoal or bank or bar, or just simply engulf them from below, and proceed to cut them to pieces. Evidence of what is occurring shows in the wild splashing and swirling on the surface. I've seen schools that were making probably several thousand circles on the surface at any one instant. The average school, however, is smaller than that.

Last summer in August my boy Mike and I got out on a big southern impoundment just as dawn was breaking. There was no ripple on the water. We could hear the whites butchering shad all around us while we were putting the boat in. I eased out near where a school was working and laid a streamer down among them. It was instantly seized. By the time I had that fish in, Mike had caught two on his heavier gear. Then the bass went down.

This is routine. Either the anglers are spied and the fish take fright and sound, or else the surrounded forage fish break away and dive. But always, when this surface feeding is in progress, the school will suddenly show again, off some little distance. You can see the noses of fish as they thrust out of water in their wild feeding. Often a dozen small schools will be up and down within sighting distance of the boat. Sometimes we chase after them, but usually these will sound before we get there and we'll see another school on top where we just left. It's as good a plan as any to stay put and quiet and let 'em come to you.

This type of fishing is what all mid-South white bass enthusiasts call "jump fishing"—going from one school to another to fish "the jumps." Oddly, though I have fished white bass all the way from Wisconsin to Alabama and from Tennessee to the Mexican border, I have yet to see a fly-fisherman fishing the jumps. Yet this feeding habit of white bass is tailored perfectly all summer long for flies.

There is no specialized how-to in this case. Get the fly out among 'em and retrieve it with steady and fairly rapid pulls, and one will have it before it has gone far. The main thing is to be sure they see it. Many anglers, seeing a school at surface, actually cast behind. The feeding fish quite commonly move fast. You have to establish their direction correctly and cast ahead when this is happening, making sure the fly is well out in front, so it crosses their path. It need not be deep. Six inches under is usually enough.

One July morning I watched from a big rock beside a small cove as a school of white bass fed round and round out toward the middle of the area. Presently they worked in, driving the hapless forage before them. After a bit they had their prey penned against the shore. They were chopping them to bits, moving back and forth only a few yards away.

I began casting, placing a small white bucktail among them. There was no chance to sink it. The moment it touched water one had it. I hauled in without ceremony, for a few moments prior to this a nonfishing couple had come up behind me and I heard the lady remark:

"Oh, I wish he'd catch us some!"

"How many do you want?" I asked, kidding her.

She was embarrassed that I'd heard. She laughed and her husband said, "Enough for lunch would do."

I flipped the first one to them and shot the fly out again. Another struck instantly. Within minutes I had horsed in ten, pitching them to the people behind me as quickly as I could unhook. They were laughing now and protesting that they had enough. But I was curious to see how long the fish would stay and how many I could take.

It should be noted that a large "take" does not harm the white bass population. Quite the contrary. They need more catching in most areas than they get. They are awesomely reproductive. So, I did not feel badly when I heaved the 27th fish over my shoulder to be gathered by my fish-hungry audience.

"Will that do?" I asked.

Then as they laughed and said absolutely no more and headed for their camp to clean the windfall, I shot out one more cast. But the forage fish had broken out of the trap and the cove was again as calm as if it were fishless. I stood there, resting my tired casting arm, looking to see if they'd surface again, and reflecting that white bass plus streamer fly equals a veritable fusillade of fun.

FLYFISHING TIPS

Joe Brooks

*One of the most highly-regarded writers on
flyfishing of all time here offers a number of
beneficial tricks and gimmicks. (Sports Afield
1962 Fishing Annual)*

ON THE FAR side of Beaver Creek in Maryland, a four-pound brown
trout was taking naturals a foot out from the bank. Above him the boughs
hung down within two feet of the water and stretched out from the bank
with an 18-inch overhang. To reach him it would take a low shot into that
hole, with plenty of accuracy and a lot of luck.

I didn't have either. My too strong cast landed the No. 16 Red Variant
in the boughs.

I pulled back with the rod tip, very gently, and the nicely hackled fly
jumped from branch to branch, from leaf to leaf, then dropped to the
surface. That trout fell on it like a ton of bricks.

"If that had been me," said Paul Levering, who was standing beside
me, "I'd have hung up and probably lost my fly. You have all the luck. The
fly miraculously comes out of there and that trout is waiting with his mouth
wide open."

"Not all luck," I said, with a laugh.

"Why didn't you hang up, then?" asked Paul.

"I probably would have if I had jerked back hard on the rod when the fly lit in the trees," I answered. "The hook would have sunk into a branch for sure, then. But instead I gave a slow, even pull, which allowed the full hackles on the fly to push the hook away from the limbs."

Ten minutes later I threw one into another difficult spot. This time the hook went around a small but tough twig on the same side of the stream I was fishing.

I pointed the rod tip at the fly, grasped the butt in both hands and gave a hard up-and-down motion to the rod. The line began to undulate up and down, and its force moved the hook back and forth, back and forth, until finally it shook itself off the twig and shot back my way.

"One minute you say, 'Take it easy and you won't get hooked up,' " Paul snorted, "the next you act like you're trying to pull the tree down and it still comes off."

"It was a different problem," I explained. "This time the hook was around a small twig and just wouldn't have come off with a straight pull. The only thing to do was make it move back and forth on that twig until it loosened up so it would come off. Of course, sometimes it doesn't work, but more often it does."

The whole profit in such a maneuver is not just the return of the fly and the pleasure of avoiding a broken tippet. Many a time that kind of treatment of a fly that has hung up on a branch has saved me from wading across the river to get the fly and thereby downing all trout within 75 feet. Such vigorous manipulation of rod and line may scare trout within close range but not to the same extent as if you waded right into their lair.

If you watch your fellow fishermen on the stream, you'll soon find that there are dozens of such little tricks you can pick up to add to the success and comfort of your fishing.

Once on the Letort at Carlisle, Pennsylvania, I saw my friend Ross Trimmer land a 15-inch brown trout, then stick his finger down its throat.

"The hook is away back in its mouth," Ross explained. "I want to get it out without hurting the fish because I want to put it back in the water. So I'm using my finger as a hook disgorger. I run my first finger down the leader tippet until it hits the bend of the hook, then push. Nine times out of ten the fly comes out and rests on my finger tip. I withdraw my hand and there's the fly."

You can do this successfully with hooks in sizes from 20 all the way up to 3/0 and it saves digging into your pockets for a knife to cut the fly out, or for a regular disgorger, if you have one. And if you do it gently the fish will not be harmed at all.

In much the same way you can use your rod tip to free a fly which has caught on underwater bric-a-brac or on a log just beyond arm's reach. Reel the line and leader all the way in until the fly is against the tip of the rod, then give a gentle push forward. Often that little pressure will dislodge the hook. However, you must be careful not to push too hard, or you may break the rod tip. If the fly doesn't come free with a slight push, then pull straight back with the rod and break the tippet. Better a lost fly than a broken rod tip.

One of the fly caster's most trying moments comes when he finds himself in midstream with his leader tippet wrapped around the rod tip so thoroughly that he can't shake it loose. There's nothing close enough to rest the rod butt on so he can move up its length and release the tippet, and the shore is far away. This is the time, literally, to shoulder your rod. Put the rod over your shoulder, with the reel back of you, then gently slide the rod back till you can reach out and free the fly and leader. Even with a long rod and fairly heavy reel, your shoulder will absorb enough of the strain so that the rod will be in no danger of breaking.

Such a small item as the way you reel in your line can add to or subtract a great deal from your fishing pleasure and efficiency. For instance, not long ago I was watching a movie about trout fishing when the action of the angler began to bother me. His arm was pumping back and forth as he turned the reel handle, like the piston of a locomotive. He was working much too hard for the size of the fish. Mentally I began to go through the business of reeling and then I realized what was wrong. He was reeling with his entire arm. This was doing it the hard way, all right. Yet, since then, I have noticed a great many anglers doing that, when all they need is wrist and hand action, keeping the forearm still. That way you can reel faster and with far less effort.

You can also prevent line from piling up on one side or the other of the reel by the simple expedient of using the little finger of the left hand as a level wind, moving it back and forth across the spool as the line is wound in. It will save you an occasional lost fish, too, because a pile-up of line will often crowd against the reel braces and add just enough resistance when it hits to cause a broken leader tippet.

Years ago dry-fly anglers used a punky fungus called amadou to dry their flies. They pressed the amadou on either side of the fly and it absorbed the excess water. Then they could apply the dry-fly buoy (dressing), blow on the fly and have an offering that would sit up high on its hackles. Nowadays amadou is seldom seen but there are quite satisfactory substitutes. For instance, it doesn't hurt a fly if you squeeze it gently between thumb and forefinger and press the water out. Or place the fly in a tissue and, again gently, squeeze. This latter is my own favorite substitute for amadou. After you've removed this excess water, the fly is ready for dry-fly buoy.

If you should happen to be caught astream without any dry-fly buoy and your fly has become saturated with fish slime, try casting the fly in and out of the water, time and again—nine or ten times. Then blow on it hard. You'll find that after this treatment it will usually float very well.

Many a fly fisherman takes all kinds of care to be sure his fly is right, then ruins it all with a heavy, sinking line. One of the toughest situations a dry-fly man can run into is to find himself casting to a rising fish in slick water with a wet, sinking line. He can't cast lightly, the line pulls the fly off center and underwater so the float is poor, and he can't strike fast enough because the length of heavy, wet line slows up the strike impulse enough so that the fish has time to find out that the fly is a phony and eject it.

When you are fishing upstream, as you usually do with a dry fly, a sinking line is again a hazard, making it all but impossible to keep in contact with the fly. When the time comes for the pickup for the next cast or for a strike, the line is so deep in the water that you can't get it to the surface for a neat pickup. It falls in against you, hitting the rod or your forearm and making it impossible to achieve a decent back cast.

But with a dry, high-floating line you can strike quickly and effectively and can pick the fly off the surface with a minimum of effort and disturbance. For these reasons, it is essential always to have a well-greased, high-floating fly line. Even with wet flies, nymphs, streamers and bucktails, a well-greased line makes a great difference in line work, such as mending, and in the retrieve and quickness of the strike. In most fly fishing you seldom want the fly to float more than a foot below the surface. So even when the manufacturer says his line does not need greasing, I grease it anyway.

And to assure a full day of fishing with a nice, high-floating line, I usually carry a second reel spool, already loaded with line—this one greased, too, of course—so that halfway through the day I can change spools and start afresh. This extra spool I keep in a plastic bag so that it will not pick up dirt from the inside of my pocket.

If you do not have a second spool, it will pay you well to take half an hour out when your line becomes wet. String the line between trees, high enough so it is free of the ground where it might pick up dirt, and preferably in the sun. Or spread it out in big loops on a bit of dry, clean grass where the sun and wind can get at it. Or it can be coiled on a coat or anything else that will keep it clear of grit of any kind. To speed the process of drying, you can run your handkerchief along the line first, to remove the excess water. Do it twice more and your line will dry that much faster.

After the line has dried thoroughly, grease it again, still being careful that it does not come in contact with any dirt. If you have stretched the line between trees, you can easily walk beside it, greasing as you go, using a small amount of grease on the thumb and first finger. After going over the 60 or 70 feet you may expect to have in the water, rub the line with a cloth to remove the excess grease which, if left on, will get back on the rod guides, then onto the line and soon become dirty, causing the line to sink.

If in spite of all this, you find that you have still been too generous with the grease, you will notice that it begins to build up in the rod guides and gathers dirt. To get rid of this grease, twist one corner of your handkerchief into a point, stick it through the guide and pull the kerchief right on through. If you are caught along the stream without a handkerchief, a small twig or even a long blade of grass will do the trick.

When the day's fishing is over, the line should always be dried. It can be stripped off the reel and dropped in big coils, as for greasing, on clean papers, sofa or coat, or wound on a line dryer, and allowed to dry overnight. Just as much care should be taken then, as when fishing, that it is not stepped on. To do so will break the finish, as will dropping it in grease, gasoline or sand. Once a break has come in a line the entire length will soon deteriorate.

Flies are expensive, yet I have seen many a thoughtless fisherman throw away a fly because the hook had straightened out or become opened a bit on a strike. Yet it's an easy matter to bend the hook back into shape. Simply put the nail of your right thumb against the outside curve of the opened hook and press in. Keep pushing gently till it's back in shape. Despite the bending it will hold trout as well as ever.

Just as important as a properly shaped hook is a sharp point, especially if you are using a fine tippet. A hard strike on a dull hook may leave the fly in the fish's mouth, or you may not be able to sink the point. But with a sharp point, even if you are using a 6X tippet, all that is required is a slight lift of the rod to set the hook. Since a point often becomes dulled after several fish have been caught, I check often. If it is the slightest bit off, I pick up a thin rock from the streamside, grasp the fly by the shank of the hook and use that rock as a hone, running the point of the hook across and back, across and back. In no time at all it will have a point like a needle.

The joining between line backing and fly line is another possible weak spot that may cost you a fish, whether you use a knot there or a splice. Not long ago, while fishing the Gloppen River in Norway, I was going over my tackle preparatory to the next day's fishing. A couple of other anglers got out their equipment, too, because they wanted me to show them the nail knot, which is the one I use to put line and backing together. The first man stripped line off his reel, and when he reached the spot where line and backing were spliced he took one in each hand and pulled. They came apart. He took two more lines out and the same thing happened. The other man did the same thing with like result.

Here were two good salmon fishermen, ready to start the season on a wonderful river, with poor ties. The first fish that hit would have pulled line from backing and their whole day would have been ruined simply because they had not checked.

Rod guides can also be a trouble point and should be checked frequently. A line that has a hard finish will sometimes cut into the soft metal of the guides, and this roughness will then destroy the fly line. Rust on the guides will have the same effect. While most rods built especially for salt water now have rustproof guides, fresh-water rods do not.

In salt water, fly fishermen often cast from a skiff and look for fish which are moving toward the boat. This calls for a fast throw in order to reach the fish before he is upon you. For this reason it is essential to have the decks cleared so that there are no obstacles for the line to whip around as you cast, to stop the line short of your mark, or worse yet, to catch on something when you have hooked a fish and he's running—phut! he breaks your leader against the purchase of that snag. When you are standing in a skiff and have cleared the decks, the shooting line can be stripped off the reel and dropped into the bottom of the boat so you are ready for a couple of quick false casts and then can shoot the line out at once. A large landing net placed flat on the floor boards where your stripped line will lie will help keep the line from being flipped around; and if you push a couple of feet of the line where it comes off the reel into your right-hand trousers pocket, that will keep this part of the line from twisting together in the wind.

be amazed at just how thrilling and productive this cold-weather sport can be—provided, of course, that he equips himself properly and employs effective winter angling techniques! Let's examine in some detail these important requirements for fishing the winter trout stream successfully.

Winter Fishing in the Lower Trout Stream

The lower stretches of typical trout streams—those below the high mountains and flowing across sun-warmed flats—usually provide excellent trout fishing throughout the cold months. Winter angling in these lower, warmer waters has many advantages. Because the water is warmer, winter trout are more active in the lower streams; therefore, the trout feed more heavily and strike better here than in the higher and colder waters. And most trout taken from lower waters in the winter months are far heavier than trout taken from the high streams.

Lower streams that are very marginal trout producers during the hot months and that are difficult to fish in the summer because of heavy populations of hungry rough fish are often the best of winter trout waters. The big "carry-overs," especially rainbows, tend to migrate down to these warmer waters in the cold months. And here the same winter water temperatures that keep the trout active keep the rough fish inactive.

Best of all most lower trout streams are surprisingly accessible as well as comfortable and easy to fish. During most of the winter there is little or no snow in the vicinity of typical lower streams, and most of them can be reached easily in the family automobile. It's just as easy to get up and down the banks of many lower trout streams in the winter as it is in the summer. Even ice on the water is rarely a major problem on the lower winter stream, especially in sunny late afternoons.

Selecting and Rigging Tackle for Lower-Stream Fishing

Most trout taken from lower trout streams in the winter months are belly-full of small rough fish, usually suckers or chubs. This is a clear clue as to the best baits and lures to use. Live minnows are always deadly for all species of trout, especially lunkers, in the lower winter waters. In streams where the use of live minnows is not permitted, dead minnows that have been salted down and frozen are often nearly as good. Worms and night crawlers rank third as winter brown and brook trout baits in most lower streams—and salmon eggs rank third as winter rainbow and cutthroat baits in these same waters. Wet flies, nymphs and streamers will take winter trout from the lower streams; but spinners, spoons and minnow-imitation plugs, are superior.

Spinning and bait-casting outfits are the most effective weapons for presenting natural baits to winter trout in most lower streams. The typical lower stream is of considerable size, and these long-range casting outfits enable the angler to fish far more water than he could with a fly rod—an important advantage in fishing for widely scattered trout in the winter stream. Of course, the heavier artificial lures that pay off best on the lower winter stream must be fished with the spinning or bait-casting outfit.

The new, highly pliable and small-diameter monofilament lines add new ease in winter to both spinning and bait casting. Such lines cast easily even when temperatures are frigid and when rod tips and guides are clogging with ice. These lines, in eight- or ten-pound test, are strong enough to land lunkers and to pull most snagged lures loose, yet they cast light lures as easily as most conventional lines of lighter test.

For fishing the lower winter stream with live minnows, a No. 5 split shot clamped on the line about 18 inches above a No. 4 hook is an effective rig. For stream fishing, live minnows should be hooked through the lips so that they stay alive and float naturally with the current. With this single-hook rig, it is necessary, of course, to delay setting the hook until a striking trout has time to get the whole minnow into its mouth. With salted minnows, a deadly tactic is to tie a No. 8 treble hook to the line just above the No. 4 single hook with a simple overhand knot. The treble hook, with slight pressure, can then be moved up and down the monofilament. The salted minnow should be hooked through the lower back with the large single hook. The minnow's head should be pointed up the line, and the treble hook should then be moved along the line to a position opposite the minnow's head and hooked through the minnow's lips. The line pull will then be on the treble hook, maintaining the minnow in a natural position. With this salted-minnow rig, the hooks may be set immediately when a trout strikes, and either the treble or the single hook will usually drive home. It is very important to use this rig when fishing dead minnows, for trout will usually reject a dead minnow shortly after the strike—and applying line pressure immediately when the fish strikes will seldom hook a trout when a conventional single-hook rig is used.

A No. 5 or No. 6 hook about 18 inches behind a No. 5 split shot is a good rig for fishing night crawlers and large earthworms in the lower winter stream. A No. 10 or No. 12 hook is usually best for fishing salmon eggs.

Quarter-ounce spinners, spoons and balsa-wood plugs in silver or gold are top artificial-lure choices for cold-weather angling on the lower stream. All these lures should be tied *directly* to the line. *No* snaps or swivels should be used. The buoyant balsa-wood plugs are usually most effective when *two* No. 5 split shot are clamped to the line about 18 inches above the plug.

Tactics for the Lower Trout Stream

The new angler cannot expect any trout stream to be as thickly populated with trout in winter as in summer. This is true whether the stream is inhabited by wild trout, stocked trout or a combination thereof. And this is especially true of the lower stretches of streams, for most pan-size trout will hold throughout the winter in the higher waters. The angler headed for the lower winter stream must realize that the delightful problem he faces is one of locating and outwitting a few scattered, large and lure-wise fish.

A big key to successful angling on the lower stream is concentrating casts in *water likely to contain trout*. Only the deep pools, and shallows immediately adjacent to them, are likely to contain lower-stream trout in the winter months. Fishing any other kind of water is apt to be a complete waste of time. During most of the typical winter day, trout in the lower stream will hold at the bottom of the deep pools. On warm, sunshiny days, however, they will often take up feeding stations in the late afternoon in nearby shallows—usually the tail of the pool or riffle just above the pool's headwaters. Therefore, when fishing the lower winter stream, the wise angler will work the deep pools thoroughly throughout the day. During late afternoon, he will also comb the nearby shallows.

Since trout tend to be widely scattered in the lower stream during the winter months, it is usually necessary to work several pools for each trout taken. Therefore, the most action will go to the angler who moves rapidly from pool to pool. Whether he's fishing bait or hardware, it is also important for the angler to work upstream. Casts should be within 45 degrees of straight upstream. The weighted lures should be allowed to bounce downstream along the bottom. Spinners should be retrieved downstream slowly, evenly and just faster than the current. Spoons and weighted plugs should be *jigged* downstream, slowly and along the bottom.

There is a decided advantage to concentrating winter fishing efforts on one or two good lower streams. In any such stream, the angler will find that the same pools will often hold big trout year after year. He will also become intimately familiar with the best approaches to those pools, where the trout in them prefer to lie and even where each underwater snag is located. A large percentage of winter lunkers will not be landed the first time hooked, or will be returned to the water—and the angler may return to the same pools, knowing with certainty that respected opponents lurk there, and enjoy the challenge of trying for them again and again.

Winter Fishing in the High Trout Stream

The higher stretches of typical trout streams usually flow through lofty mountains where winter temperatures are severest. Here stream banks are fringed with deep snow during much of the winter, making fishing difficult and access a major problem. Because of these obstacles, most higher trout streams are rarely fished during the cold months. But these same conditions make the high trout stream an exciting place to visit. No winter wonderland is more breathtaking than that in which the typical high stream nestles. In winter, there is rarely *any* competition on the high trout stream. And winter fishing in these icy, snowbound streams can be productive.

Winter trout in the high stream are not so active as trout in the lower and warmer waters, and the high stream is not populated by so many lunkers. However, it usually contains *more* winter trout—and these trout can be taken by the resourceful angler.

In order to fish most high trout streams, the angler must first beat the problem of access. A set of chains on the family auto will get anglers into most high eastern streams even during severe weather. However, to fish most high western streams in winter, at least the last several miles of each journey must be conducted by four-wheel-drive vehicle, snowmobile or a combination of the two. This transportation requirement, however, need not be a major obstacle to the determined angler, for today these snow-defeating vehicles can be rented for very reasonable fees in almost every mountain town in the West.

Deep snow along the stream bank probably deters most anglers from fishing high streams in winter. In most cases, they can very easily solve this problem by donning a pair of waders and wading the stream, rather than walking along its banks. Of course, there will be times when large and deep high-country streams cannot be fished because of heavy ice— ice that is too thick to break through while wading, yet too thin to walk upon safely. *Most small high-country streams, however, will have little ice or ice only on the still pools during most of the winter and can be safely and easily waded and effectively fished.*

Selecting and Rigging Tackle for High-Stream Fishing

High-stream trout feed sparsely in the cold months, rarely on minnows and on no single predominant group of aquatic insects. Therefore, although a wide variety of baits and flies will take high-stream trout in the cold months, the angler using *any* fly or bait will have to work for his trout. Soft, oily salmon eggs are the top winter bait for high-stream rainbows and cutthroats. And these same eggs are sometimes fair winter baits for high-stream brooks and browns. Small native earthworms, however, are the unbeatable brook and brown trout producers on the high winter stream. As a rule, the best fly choices for this specialized brand of fishing are tiny nymphs and wet flies tied on No. 16 to No. 20 hooks.

The fly rod, of course, is the best weapon for fishing the small, high stream using any of the baits or flies described above. The use of small-diameter leaders, tapered down to not more than one-pound test at the tippet, is almost essential for fooling finicky frigid-stream trout with either bait or flies. On the small stream, however, leaders need not be long. Three- or four-foot leaders are ample for taking trout in most small high streams—and short leaders, of course, make casting along the brushy banks of the typical high stream much easier.

Those best icy-stream baits—soft salmon eggs and small native worms—should be fished on No. 12 hooks tied directly to the light leader. Snelled hooks in this size are usually tied on excessively large leader material and should *not* be used. For fishing nymphs, flies or bait in the high winter stream, as unpleasant as it may be, the use of a small split shot positioned about six inches above the hook is usually required to slow down the drift of the fly or bait and to keep it on the bottom—requirements that must be met to take many sluggish high-stream trout in the cold months.

Tactics for the High-Stream Trout

When the high stream is not frozen over or only fringed with a little rim ice, the angler should work upstream slowly making fairly long casts. This tactic will keep him concealed from most sharp-eyed stream trout he's casting to. Casts should be concentrated in the deeper pools, for winter trout in the high, cold streams inhabit such pools almost exclusively.

The weighted bait or fly should be allowed to drift back downstream slowly and along the bottom of the deep pools. At least a dozen casts should be made into each good pool, for often finically feeding winter trout must be teased into striking by this tactic. When a strike occurs, the hook should be set immediately, for winter trout in the high stream are quick to feel the hook and to reject a fly or bait.

When a high stream is iced up, the ice will usually cover the still water surface above each of the deep pools harboring fish, but the fast water entering and leaving the pool will usually be ice-free. In this situation, the angler's basic problem is getting his bait or fly under the ice and to the bottom of each pool where the fish are. To accomplish this, the fly or bait must be dropped into the fast water at the head of the pool, then allowed to drift under the ice. There are two methods for executing this neat trick. One is to cast from a downstream position over the ice and into the fast water entering the pool, then strip out enough slack line to allow the bait to drift under the ice and into the pool. The other is to climb into the deep snow on the stream bank and to waddle up the bank to a position where the bait or fly can be let straight down into the headwaters at the edge of each frozen pool. Either of these methods will work, and there is no *effective* option to them. Wading downstream sends a wall of broken ice ahead of the angler, which alarms trout and further complicates fishing. And working downstream along the bank for even an hour is far too exhausting in those waist-deep snowdrifts.

Yes, the skillful and hard-working angler should take trout from any trout-populated stream, high or low, during any month of the winter and during any hour of the day. There are predictable periods in the winter, however, when stream trout usually strike best. Any winter day following a week or so of unseasonably warm weather will sharply increase the appetite of stream trout. And as previously indicated, late afternoons are usually the best fishing hours for stream trout during any sunshiny winter day.

Finally, a shortage of adequate clothing can make winter trout fishing a miserable experience—and so can clothing that is excessively warm.

When heading for the winter trout stream, the wise angler will have adequate clothing along for both warm and extremely cold weather—because either condition, or any in between, may prevail. Of course, extreme cold is the most critical condition to prepare for when heading for any winter stream. Two sets of thermal underwear, wool shirt and trousers, a heavy wind-and-waterproof coat with warm hood, light leather gloves, insulated waders and wool socks are minimum cold-weather clothing requirements on most winter streams. A knowledge of angling tactics can make fishing the winter trout stream productive, but only adequate clothes make it pleasant.

THOSE VERSATILE BLOSSOM FLIES

Mark Sosin

Orange, lemon, apple, cherry—there's a flavor to match almost any situation, freshwater or salt, according to this gifted angler. (March 1967)

GEORGE CORNISH huddled over a small plastic box, concealing its contents in cloak-and-dagger fashion as he carefully lifted the lid. I leaned forward, struggling for a peek; but Dick Wood stepped between us, blocking my view. To the uninitiated, it might appear that we were foreign agents bartering over a closely guarded secret. Actually, this gathering was nothing more than three fly fishermen inspecting a fly box that contained a very effective pattern.

"What did you say this fly was called?" I asked.

"We call 'em the Blossom series," Dick answered, "because of their pronounced opening and closing action in the water."

"You've used them in both fresh and salt water with equally good results?" I persisted.

They knew I was hooked by their clandestine presentation, but that was only the beginning. George smiled and bellowed in his own inimitable way, "Why do you think we're showing 'em to you?"

Fly fishermen are generally a peaceful lot, exhibiting patience and poise in the most trying situations. But a point can be reached that will tax even the most dedicated of the light-wand set. This seemed to be my breaking point, and I gently wrested the fly box from George's grasp so I could see what this mystery was all about.

"That pattern is similar to Lefty Kreh's Chesapeake Eel," I said as I finally got a glimpse of the flies. "Only there are more sizes and more colors.'

From the grins that drifted across their faces, I felt as though I were dealing with two Cheshire cats.

George Cornish and Dick Wood live in Cape May County, New Jersey—a mecca for the light-tackle salt-water angler as well as one of the finest black bass and pickerel areas on the entire East Coast. It was here that the Blossom series received its baptism of fire. You would think that Dick and George would first try it along the sedge banks and tidal flats that are constantly patrolled by stripers and blues, but this was not the case.

Instead, they took their discovery to the shallow ponds that dot South Jersey to try it out on large-mouth bass. A five-pounder is not uncommon in these still, dark waters, and some bruisers can pull a scale to seven pounds or better. To hear these anglers relate how bass after bass charged an Orange Blossom or Lemon Blossom would make any devotee of the sport forsake wife, family, friends and business for a day on the water.

Add to this the torpedolike pickerel, sometimes almost as long as your arm, inhaling a bundle of marabou and you have the makings of an extremely productive artificial.

I had first seen a fly resembling the Blossoms when Lefty Kreh fished Jersey waters for stripers with a black-marabou fly designed to represent a small eel. George, Dick and I had tied up several of these and used them for a couple of years with tremendous success on striped bass and bluefish. George had then decided that the same fly could be tied in a multitude of colors and sizes for different species—and with Dick's help, the Blossom series began.

Currently, the flies are tied in six colors, with each bearing the name of a different blossom. The all-white fly is known as an Apple Blossom; pink is a Cherry Blossom; yellow, Lemon Blossom; orange, Orange Blossom; blue, Plum Blossom and black, Blackberry Blossom. Other variations are already being created, and there is no reason why you can't come up with your own combinations of colors.

The secret of the Blossom is the life-like, "breathing" action of the marabou, probably the deadliest of fly-tying materials. Trout fishermen have favored marabou for generations, and the Blossom series has taken its toll of brooks, browns and rainbows. Nothing exceptionally big, mind you, but only because large trout are scarce in the heavily fished eastern streams where these patterns have been used.

The East Coast has become a hotbed of salt-water fly-rodding activity, with stripers, blues, bonitos and albacores the mainstays of the double-haul enthusiasts. Just last summer, three of us nosed our boat up to a school of rampaging blues and tied on Apple Blossoms. The six- to eight-pound choppers were tearing into herds of terrified baitfish as I roll-cast 25 feet to the edge of the carnage. I watched the fly hit the water and seven blues instantly peel off for the attack. The sight was so awesome that in the excitement I almost forgot to move the fly. Abruptly remembering the task at hand, I pulled the fly away rapidly, and a cloud of spray and arched rod left six fish looking for other food and a seven-pounder trying to rid himself of a mouthful of marabou.

That was an afternoon such as you dream about, with bluefish after bluefish slugging it out against the light tip of the fly rod. Their dentures made confetti of the feathers, and we changed flies often. Almost any pattern would bring a strike, yet the Blossoms seemed to elicit the greatest response. Throw a Blossom into the water and five to ten fish would gallop after it.

Take the case of New York City sportsman Bob O'Byrne. Bob and I met at Stuart, Florida, when someone told him I had a supply of salt-water flies with me. Bob hadn't expected to fish and had left his tackle home. Then he had received an invitation for an offshore trip. He quickly borrowed a fly rod and reel and asked if I could lend him some flies. "Just in case," he said, "we run into something good out there."

I never did get the full story of that trip, but Bob returned my flies gingerly holding a chewed-up Lemon Blossom with enthusiastic comments about having run into a school of dolphins.

There are other gamesters in Florida waters that will all but stand on their heads to grab a fly, and this became our next test. Tarpon seemed to favor the Orange or Lemon Blossom, although the Apple and Cherry models worked well on the smaller fish. White or pink became the nemesis of bonefish, while snook preferred the white. Redfish and jack crevalles didn't indicate favorites, being content to engulf any of the feather dusters placed in front of them. Of course, there were ladyfish, weakfish and an occasional barracuda, with the Apple Blossom holding a slight edge on these species.

The key to success with the Blossom series lies in the retrieve. There is certainly enough natural action built in to catch fish, but skillful manipulation on the retrieve can enhance your chances and add to the appeal. When marabou is pulled through the water, it has a tendency to flatten against the hook, presenting the appearance of a darting baitfish. Once you stop pulling, the feathers will blossom out and undulate, imitating a small fish finning in the current.

The idea is to swim the fly by retrieving in slow, foot-long pulls, with momentary pauses between them. This allows the Blossom to close and then open again, creating a wiggling motion. At times a faster retrieve is necessary, and this you can achieve by pulling for several feet before pausing. You can also impart life to the fly by continually lifting the rod tip and dropping it.

If there is a salt-water current flowing or if you're fishing a river or stream, the technique differs. Remember that fish almost always face into a current, looking for food to be swept by them. Cast across the current and slightly upstream. The thought here is to work the fly broadside to the current. The fly should give the impression of a struggling fry being swept along, yet trying to reach the safety of the shallows or to buck its way upstream.

Work the fly in short jerks toward you as the line arcs downstream. It might even be necessary to mend the line on occasion to eliminate drag. If this doesn't work, let the fly sweep along with the water and then work it toward you slowly. You can even let it hang in the current, moving it only slightly—the marabou will breathe beautifully and appear to be struggling against superior forces.

The important consideration is to keep the feathers opening and closing. If you're blind casting from a boat or wading the shallows, develop the habit of fishing the fly right up to you. Very often a gamester will follow the Blossom for a long distance and strike just as you're lifting it for another cast.

Speaking of casts, wet marabou is not the easiest material to cast, since it offers resistance to the wind. Nevertheless, it is often worth the extra effort; and with a bit of planning, casting will not present too much of a problem. Position yourself so that you don't have to cast directly into the wind; instead, try to use it to your advantage. Your best situation if you're a right-handed caster is with the wind coming across your left shoulder. This will keep the fly away from you.

If you can cast 50 feet, you can use a Blossom for most situations in fresh water or salt. Of course, longer casts are sometimes required, but in 95 percent of the situations, a comfortable cast of 50 feet will let you work an area thoroughly.

Perhaps the greatest feature of the Blossom series is the ease and speed with which they may be tied. Even someone who has never tied flies before can cut his teeth on this pattern and be assured that his efforts will catch fish. You might want to use small hooks for trout or panfish; but for largemouths, pike and the salt-water species, a 1/0 to 4/0 hook works well. Anything over 4/0 is extremely difficult to set with a fly rod and is heavy for casting.

Starting on the shank opposite the point of the hook, tie in your thread. Select two marabou feathers and place them face to face. Blood feathers work best, because they don't have a quill running to the end that prevents a free-flowing action. If you can't find blood feathers, look for those with the smallest and limpest quill.

Lay the feathers evenly on top of the shank, adjusting them for length, and tie them in with the thread. At the same place where you just fastened the marabou, tie in a piece of chenille. Now wrap the chenille toward the eye of the hook, secure it to the shank with thread and finish off the fly. There is no need to produce a fancy head or paint eyes unless this pleases you. The whole fly can be tied in less than five minutes.

One evening, George Cornish located a school of stripers up to 25 pounds under his pier. Every time he threw an Orange Blossom, a bruiser walloped it, promptly ran around the nearest piling and broke off. It wasn't long before George had lost every fish that hit—and every Blossom he had in his box. He then resorted to running to his office, tying a Blossom and running back to the dock only to lose it. George claims he spent most of that evening running, because it took him less than a minute to tie the fly and about the same time to lose it. He's now looking for a way to secure his pier without pilings.

There is no fly pattern that will invariably work in every situation. Nevertheless, the Blossom series has proved to be more versatile than most and will often produce results when other patterns fail. Remember to carry an assortment in different sizes and colors with you at all times. There might be an occasion when the Blossom series can save the day—and you'll be the first to bless those Blossoms.

12 LESSONS FOR A TROUT-FISHING FRIEND

Ernest Schwiebert

A writer, whose name is synonymous with trout,
offers advice designed to fine tune your skills.
(March 1971)

THE LAST time I fished with you, Don, it was a bright spring morning in the Appalachians. The bitter weather had finally passed, and the dark branches were turning olive with their first budding leaves. The first *Epeorus* hatches were coming. Swallows and fly-catching phoebes were waiting anxiously for afternoon, when the slate-colored mayflies would come off the riffles.

It's hard to believe, Don, that ten years have passed since we first started fly-fishing together. Although you could be classed as an expert, you say you're not satisfied with your progress.

Perhaps, like many another angler, you have become set in your ways and have lost the adaptability needed to meet the various conditions that occur at streamside. Therefore, I would like to take this opportunity to list a few of the things that sometimes make the difference between an exciting fishing day and an empty creel.

Since my father and his trout-fishing friends introduced me to their sport on a marl-bog creek in Michigan, where the fish darted nervously under the quaking banks, learning about the intelligence and spookiness of trout came naturally under these angling experts' patient instruction. But trout-fishing beginners are often less lucky, and usually try trout after learning basic techniques on easier species. Novices are seldom taught to stalk meadow trout infantry-style, crawling and hiding behind bushes and trees. My father taught me those lessons almost 35 years ago, and sometimes we forget that most beginners approach a trout stream without knowing its most basic lesson: Trout are perhaps the craftiest species of all, unless they are fresh from a hatchery, and stalking them successfully means using all the guile of a cat-burglar.

Our fishing experience is filled with hard-earned lessons. Much of our stream-wise knowledge is accumulated after years of trial-and-error, and it took me years to learn many such lessons.

It's surprising how many trout fishermen fail to understand that the nymphs and larvae of aquatic insects are in the water all year.

Several seasons ago, I sometimes fished Prospect Lake in Colorado Springs all winter. It was the only water open twelve months a year. The earthwork dam along the south shoreline of the lake was a favorite place for bait-fishermen when the weather was good, and I fished my flies there too.

We waded the icy water in the weak sunlight, casting our flies in a clockwise pattern, and allowed them to sink until our slow hand-twist retrieves ticked them back along the bottom.

"What're you using?" The fishermen on the rip-rap dam yelled.

"Wet flies!" I yelled.

The bait-fishing regulars never believed me. "There ain't no flies around this time of year," they grumbled among themselves. "Can't catch no trout on flies in February."

Those fish in Prospect Lake were usually full of caddis worms, back-swimmers, nymphs of damselflies and dragonflies, beetle and larvae and snails, but the old-timers who fished the dam never checked the stomachs of the fish they caught. They never knew about the insect nymphs and larvae that thrive in trout water all year, and that flies work anytime the water is clear and the fish are feeding.

The old-timers believe in another myth that is often heard when the fish are really rising. Such feeding usually frustrates the average fisherman, because the trout are boiling and nothing can touch them. Fishermen respond like the chorus girl who stopped reading altogether because she tried one book and found it boring.

"Tried flies and them fish just kept boiling away!" they sigh. "They probably ain't taking flies."

"They're just *playing*," somebody usually adds.

The life of a trout in the river is a precarious balance between calories ingested, rising to hatching insects or rooting for larvae among the stones, and calories expended in the current. It is an existence filled with fear, searching for food and avoiding danger, and the fish are never playing. When the water boils with rising trout, you have a unique opportunity to catch them, if you know what food they are taking and can imitate it successfully.

That cause-and-effect pattern between aquatic insects and the feeding response of the trout is the key to success, but there are other important variations on this theme. Most fishermen believe that rising trout always mean surface feeding and dry-fly fishing.

"Tried every dry in the box!" I explained to an old-timer on the Pere Marquette in Michigan. "They were rising everywhere."

"They weren't rising," he smiled.

"But they *were* rising everywhere," I said.

"Rising but not feeding on top," he explained. "They were taking something just under the surface."

Few fishermen know that trout often take hatching nymphs and pupae just under the surface, and make rise forms every bit as showy as fish taking adult flies riding the current. Such fish are taking aquatic insects as they migrate up toward the surface, and their porpoise rolls and swirls cause most fishermen to waste their time with dry flies when a wet fly or nymph is needed.

Another common error that took me many seasons to correct was observing the hatches in the air, and making judgments about their color without actually catching them. More than 20 years have passed since the summer on the Frying Pan in Colorado when I finally learned my lesson.

Early each summer that little river has a fine hatch of small *Cheumatopsyche* caddis flies. These insects move upstream in clouds each evening and the trout bring the current to a boil. The caddis flies look like a straw-colored blizzard in the sun, and we tied pale little imitations for days, hoping to find a fly pattern they would take consistently.

"Can't understand it," said Frank Klune, "they should take these pale little flies we're using!"

"Seems like it," I said, as I stayed at the fly vise.

We took a few fish each evening, but our results were meager compared to the number of trout busily rising. Finally I found two caddis flies crawling on my fishing vest.

"These flies are dark!" I yelled. "Dark mottled brown!"

Caddis flies usually have darkly mottled fore wings and paler wings at the rear, and like most flies in flight, they look pale against the light. We quickly dressed darker imitations and took trout as quickly as we could land them and cast again. The good fishing lasted until the hatch ebbed and stopped at the end of the week. It taught me an important lesson— never match the hatch watching the naturals in the air.

Terrestrial insects are another riddle to many anglers. Most fishermen have seen trout busily taking flying ants in their mating swarms when it is impossible to miss the patterns of cause-and-effect. But few trout fishermen are aware that the constant, unobtrusive rises to ants, leafhoppers and tiny beetles are a staple of hot-weather activity for the fish.

Such feeding is subtle and puzzling. Terrestrial insects drift flush in the surface film, and although a trout taking them is clearly engaged in surface rises, the fisherman can see nothing on the water. There are two principle clues. Drifting terrestrial insects are trapped in the surface and cannot escape, and the fish inhale them quietly. Such insects are seldom extremely active except on warm days, and they get into the water most often in windy weather. Quiet rises and hot gusty days are the most reliable clues to terrestrials on the water.

Trout feeding on terrestrials are never easy. Such insects are usually small, and imitations must be fished on relatively delicate leaders. The silhouettes of ants, leafhoppers and beetles are all radically different, and make different patterns of light in the surface film. Therefore, color and silhouette and size are equally important.

There are many examples in my experience. Perhaps the most striking occurred years ago on the famous Big Hole in Montana. Gene Anderegg was fishing with me above Twin Bridges, and we were waist deep in a huge, smooth-flowing flat. Trout were sipping and swirling quietly in the current, but they consistently refused our flies.

"What're they doing?" yelled Anderegg.

"Strange!" I answered. "They're usually not this picky!"

It was hot for October, and the wind eddied and gusted in the cottonwoods and willows along the water. The rises picked up intensity every time the wind riffled across the pool.

"Terrestrials!" I finally guessed.

Anderegg waded upstream to join me. "Ants?" he asked.

"Maybe," I said, as I tied a delicate No. 20 ant on my tippet and placed it softly above several rising fish.

They refused it. "It's not ants," Anderegg laughed.

Leafhoppers were another possibility. We clipped the ant from my leader and I knotted a No. 18 black Jassid on the fragile nylon. The trout inspected it and refused it too. "It's not jassids either!" said Anderegg. "What do we do now, Professor?"

"Might be bark beetles," I guessed.

There was a small No. 18 beetle in my box, and I trimmed it smaller with the scissors of my English knife. It settled gently in front of the closest fish and disappeared in a lazy swirl.

"That's it!" I shouted happily.

Another baffling rise of trout often comes when a flight of mating mayflies fills the air. These spinners rise and fall in the rhythm of their mating swarm, dropping their egg-sacs or dipping them off in the current. The fish slash and roll at these egg-laying drakes, frustrated with so many flies in the air.

"That's the trouble with spinner flights," Art Flick said as he smiled across the bar in his Westkill Tavern, "the flies are in the air and not on the water!"

Some mating mayflies get into the water, but until the egg-laying is finished and they begin to fall spent on the current, spinner flights fill the air with insects—but seldom put weight in the creel until their mating is over and there are more flies on the water.

Another common enigma is a session of midge-pupa feeding on a lake or slow-moving stream. There are times when these tiny insects change from their delicate threadworm stage to millions of tiny pupae breathing under the surface film. The trout range widely in lakes and ponds, sipping them softly by the thousands, or hang lazily in the smooth current and sample them like a coffee taster with caffeine fever.

Successful imitations are usually tiny flies dubbed with olive, black, brown or lead-gray fur ribbed with dark quills and a collar of a few soft hen fibers. Such flies can be deadly. The best example that comes to mind occurred in late October above Deckers on the South Platte in Colorado.

Beno Walker and Jim Wallace of Colorado Springs were fishing with me, and the trout were preoccupied with midge pupae. Their rises covered the smooth current. Heavy autumn rises of trout are often caused by these tiny *Chironomidae* on western rivers, and millions were apparently coming through the penstocks of the Cheeseman Dam. It was easy fishing once I selected a tiny pupa dressed with black seal fur, and I took trout after trout all afternoon.

There are a lot of dogmatic rules in trout fishing, and there are times each season when they should be ignored. Some of those standards include always fishing streamers downstream; the idea that wet flies should sink; and that dry flies should always be fished upstream without drag.

Most fishermen fish their streamers conventionally, casting down and across stream, and letting the current give them life against a rhythmic pumping of the rod. It works well most of the time. But since trout lie facing the current and a streamer is fished downstream, in some pools it is possible that the fish see you before you can cast to them. Such pools call for a radical change in tactics.

There is a pool on my favorite reach of the Brodheads, where the current turns sharply under a dense thicket of rhododendron. The hillside rises steeply behind the pool, and it drops off into six feet of slow eddying currents. It always holds big browns. But most of the day a fisherman working his streamers there is spotlighted in the bright sun, walking down an open gravel bar in plain view of the fish. It is rare that the pool surrenders a big fish before evening, when the shadow of the mountain falls across the current.

One season the pool seemed empty. "There's a buster in there!" said Henryville Charlie Ross as he rifled a stream of chewing tobacco into the nettles. "He's chasing all them smaller fish out!"

The problem of removing the cannibal fell to me. Finally I decided to tie a huge Supervisor, with four-inch wings of polar bear and olive grizzly hackles mixed with blue saddles. Its slender silver body glittered in the sunlight as I clinched it to the leader. Henryville Charlie led the assault, swinging wide around the pool through the trees.

"Fish it like a crippled minnow!" he grinned conspiratorially. "Big browns can't resist a cripple!"

I crawled slowly into position in the tail shallows, careful not to disturb the current or displace the stones. The big rod worked out eighty feet of line and dropped the huge streamer into the fast water above the pool. I let it sink in the current, and then I stripped it back wildly with my left hand, fishing it with an irregular retrieve—darting and fluttering and sinking along the bottom. Then the pool exploded.

It was a sailfish-size strike. The heavy leader sheared like a cobweb, and a pot-bellied brown tailwalked angrily up the pool with my gargantuan streamer dangling in its jaws. "My God!" Henryville Charlie croaked. "You hooked a killer whale!"

We never saw the big brown again. Smaller fish, however, began showing in the pool. It seems likely that the fish migrated, or was killed by an otter or raccoon, but I have never forgotten our experiment with the upstream streamer and I've used the trick on other occasions.

Most fishermen believe wet flies should sink, and spend a lot of time soaking leaders and flies in soap, special solutions and silt to take them under. But there are times when that rule should be ignored too, when a wet fly drifting awash in the surface film is very effective.

Old-time wet-fly fishermen knew about fishing in the film. Long ago Stewart used the method on the rivers of southern Scotland, and Thaddeus Norris mentioned it also when writing about the Brodheads and the Willowemoc in America a century ago.

The secret is simple. Many kinds of aquatic insects drift several feet in the surface film while their nymphs and pupae escape from their nymphal skins. Their life is brief, a matter of seconds in transition to the adult stage, and they drift helplessly in the current, where they are easy prey for the fish.

Typical examples are the *Stenonema* mayflies and most *Trichoptera*, which struggle half-pinioned in the surface film while they escape from their nymphal skins. Bedraggled and floating awash, they are neither immature insects nor adults—a stage of the hatch when a wet fly should be fished almost dry, but sodden and shapeless to suggest an emerging hatch.

Old patterns often work best at such times. Flies such as the English March Brown, which can trace its lineage back six centuries to the *Treatyse of Fysshynge Wyth an Angle*, and the slightly younger Hare's Ear are excellent hatching mayflies. Caddis flies are perhaps best imitated by flies such as the Woodcock-and-Green, Partridge-and-Olive, Woodcock-and-Brown, Woodcock-and-Orange, and Grouse-and-Gray.

Another truism of modern trout fishing is the dry-fly practice of achieving a dragless float. Most times a floating fly should be fished dead-drift, because many aquatic insects ride the current like drifting sailboats, and a dragging fly will frighten a sophisticated fish. But there are other times when the naturals flutter across the water before they can fly, skittering and skipping and laying their eggs, or actually dragging in the current.

Fishing a fluttering fly is a technique as ancient as the three-snell leader, when old-timers skittered the droppers in the surface, using the tail-fly as a sea-anchor. Although a crude three-fly leader is quickly detected by trout these days, it is still possible to fish a dry fly this way with fine modern monofilament, holding the rod-tip high. Mayflies such as the March Brown and Green Drake often ride the current some distance, and should be given an occasional twitch like a grasshopper. Some caddis flies actually run on the surface when they lay their eggs, and everyone has watched the green inchworms trail in the current at the end of their silken webs. Those are times when the twin dry-fly commandments of the upstream cast and the dragless float should be broken—and a floating fly can be fished downstream.

The final lesson is so basic it must be ranked with respect for the spookiness of trout as a species. It is as little understood by many experienced fishermen as it is by beginners. I'm referring to selective feeding behavior.

Selectivity is a simple reflex pattern. The cycle of the season is an annual recurrent emergence of insect species, one after another from the river. When each appears it takes a little while before the trout get accustomed to seeing it. Finally they sample the new insect, find it is safe and palatable, and begin to take it regularly. Each hatch can last from a few days to a few weeks. Before a hatch is finished, the reflex patterns of the trout are so focused on a particular species, in terms of its size, configuration and coloring, that they sometimes ignore other types of insects completely.

Six years ago on the Collon-Cura in Argentina, the wilderness rainbows were so preoccupied with olive caddis pupae that they ignored all other patterns. The river is legendary for two-pound fish that rise freely to almost anything, and this was on a pool accessible only after a two-day float. Such things have occurred from Labrador to Lapland, and catching selective fish consistently is a matter of matching the hatch—fishing flies that imitate the insects they are taking.

Believe me, Don, these 12 lessons can make considerable improvement in your fishing. Study them and apply them. I hope you have phenomenal angling success in the season ahead.

TACTICS FOR TAIL-WATER TROUT

Dave Whitlock

High water, low water, fast water, slow water—
trout and other aquatic life must adapt and so
must the serious angler. (April 1971)

THE BOAT landing outline was softly backlighted by the orange glow of the setting sun, otherwise it was almost invisible to sight in the purple shadows and veil-like fog that hung in a thin layer just above the moving river. We were reluctantly guiding our canoe toward the finish of another mild January day of trout fishing on a fine stretch of the White River some 25 miles below Bull Shoals Dam. I had taken fine fish almost all day on tiny midge flies while my companion had worked a degree of magic with ultralight spinning lures on other plump rainbows that bounced in and out of the cold, pure river.

We were beginning another year of trouting on a most unique and productive fishery. For the last 15 years I have been experimenting with tail-water trout. I have made the costly mistake of relating these waters to the fine northern and northwestern trout waters I had been privileged to sample. It is the purpose of this article to help others to avoid making the same mistakes that I have. Tail-water trout fishing is unique, requiring revised thinking and tactics.

American fishermen have been pursuing trout across our continent's northern streams and lakes. Now there exists a third dramatic cold-water fishery that has expanded the trout's ranges deep into the South. Just as tackle and techniques differ with lake and stream fishing, so does this new fishery call for specific methods if you wish to meet with reasonable success.

One of the first significant steps in developing this new trout fishing occurred in the early 1940s as the TVA lakes were built to control the Tennessee River's floods and to harness the hydroelectric potential of these waters for public and industrial uses. Perhaps a few farsighted biologists foresaw the advent of ideal environmental conditions for stocking trout, but this was certainly not the motive that inspired the projects in Tennessee as well as in other surrounding states. Later, it was noticed that these tail waters soon became almost void of native warm-water species as cold water was released from the hydroelectric facilities. This situation encouraged experiments and eventually rainbow and brown trout were introduced. But it has taken years to fully understand the new problems, to adopt practical stocking programs, to adjust laws and seasons and to use the fantastic potential of this infant fishery.

During the 40s, 50s and 60s practically every state south and west of the Mason-Dixon line has experienced dam building across many of its free-flowing streams and rivers. Many of these created suitable conditions for tail-water fisheries. The prime requisites briefly are these. The resultant reservoir of water trapped by the dam should contain sufficient depth to create a substantial volume of stratified water in the 50-to-60-degree range. This cold layer of water must be free of organic nutrients and micro-organisms to the degree that it is relatively rich in oxygen and free of other dissolved gases such as CO_2 and SO_2.

Water releases at the base of these dams must contain enough of this cold water to ensure a day-to-day, year-round environment in the temperature ranges which trout must have to survive and thrive. The latter requisite is particularly important in the southern states which commonly have summer-month temperatures of 90° to 100° and normal water temperatures that would boil a trout.

When suitable conditions exist, there are several other bonus conditions which are not usually experienced in a natural trout fishery, with the exception of certain large spring creeks. These are: Water temperatures are in the most ideal ranges (50° to 60°) throughout the year. Dissolved minerals such as carbonates run very high due to runoff-water leaching and the distilling action of warm climates on the surfaces of these lakes. Water clarity at the dam is usually excellent due to the lake's setting action on inflows. Water releases usually are gradual and the stream beds of the tail waters remain quite stable. It doesn't take further explanation to show that these bonus advantages set the stage for ideal survival and growth rates. Certain tail waters yield phenomenal production due to these advantages.

However, a specific problem exists that must be carefully dealt with in order to maintain a successful fishery. First, due to the nature of daily elevator-like water fluctuations and the absence usual of cold feeder streams, little or no natural reproduction occurs. Maximum and mimimum flow levels threaten stocking success if not carefully controlled. Thus month-to-month survival is almost entirely in the hands of the state and federal authorities responsible for the operation of these projects.

Frequently hatcheries are constructed directly below the dams to provide a constant source of stock for the fishery. This solves many problems and results in two major types of fishery aptly described as "put and take" and "put, grow and take." When ideal conditions occur the latter exists, which is a far less costly condition. The 8- to 4-inch hatchery-raised stockers remain in the stream over periods of several months to several years and grow into beautiful heavyweights worthy of any angler. One inch per month growth rates are not unusual and rival the best hatchery feeding programs.

Most tail waters are stocked with rainbow trout because they have proved to be a good fish to raise in hatcheries and they assure a high return rate when stocked. However, where brown trout are also stocked, they have shown a marked ability to avoid being taken quickly and usually reach considerable size before they are lured to the hook. Unfortunately browns do not enjoy much favor with most hatchery stocking programs since they are more difficult to raise, and after they reach the stream are usually branded as cannibals, a reputation which I feel is not entirely justified. Hard-pressured tail waters usually produce rainbows to not much over 10 pounds; browns often manage to double that growth in the same water.

Fishing tail waters the first four or five years, my catches were extremely unpredictable, ranging from feast to famine on waters loaded with fish. The primary mistake I made was failure to understand and cope with the constant changes in water levels. Over a 24-hour period levels often varied as much as 6 to 12 feet as need for power generation or lake-level control was met by releasing dammed water.

Since those early frustrations I have discovered how to use these changes to my advantage, just as those trout living there have learned to do. Basically, the release schedule begins at 8 a.m., and water quickly rises from minimum flow to levels determined by the number of turbines or gates opened. Generally these releases continue until 5 p.m. when they are reduced or turned off completely. From that point until the following 8 a.m. you have minimum flow or "low water."

I realize by analyzing the changing levels that a tide effect is experienced during each day of normal operation at the dam site. Each section of the river experiences a rather rapid water rise, a period of high tide, then a falling water level and finally a period of low tide. This tide effect progresses down the river at rates proportionate to the amount of water released. So with a little experience you can fish low, rising, high, or falling water almost anytime of the day. Each of these conditions offers a special type of opportunity to take good fish.

Over the yearly seasons these flows will vary naturally due to the amounts of rainfall and needs for hydroelectric power. Across the country there will be a natural variation due to geographical and climatic differences. Generally the water-level fluctuations I've outlined hold true for all the tail waters I have fished.

There seems to be two basic classes of tail waters. Since both require certain different techniques, descriptions and comparisons of the two will be useful in further understanding about how to fish tail waters. I'll classify the first type as Class A: a large, clear, river system, creating a deep pure-water lake relatively free of turbidity caused by organic content. This type of tail water usually provides ideal conditions for trout support for 30 to 60 miles of river. Its average width will run 150 feet or more at normal flow levels. Generally four to eight turbines are installed at the dam, but operation is seldom more than 50 percent. Due to released water volumes and speeds, only a small amount of aquatic vegetation exists on a basically freestone bottom.

The second type—Class B—is a smaller river system creating a moderate-size lake with sufficient depth to provide the temperatures needed at the tail water's origin to support trout. Usually the water clarity is less than in the first type and provides a tail-water length for trout support for 5 to 20 miles below the dam. Average width at normal flow will be from 50 to

100 feet. Two to four generators will handle the lake's potential. The small number of generators and less volume force as well as higher organic content afford conditions for high aquatic plant growths on the stream bed.

Ideal examples of both A and B tail waters are found only minutes apart in northwestern Arkansas and have provided me with an excellent opportunity to study and fish both at the same time periods and seasons. The White River below Bull Shoals Dam would be classed as an A type, and the Norfolk River below Norfork Dam fits perfectly into the B classification.

Both examples are well established and maintained tail-water fisheries of the "put, grow and take" category offering a range of trout from eight-inch stockers to trophy fish that dreams are made of. Open season extends 12 months each year and no restrictions are put on normal sport angling methods. Bait, artificial lures and flies are all quite successful when fished properly. Weather extremes are within bounds to enable enjoyable angling almost every day. Thus a near ideal situation exists.

Trout are acutely aware of these fluctuations. Evidently they accept them as facts of life and soon learn to use each stage to their advantage. Such frequent changes might quickly cause a natural-stream-bred trout to become neurotic, but not our tail-water inhabitants.

During low water, which usually lasts about six to eight hours trout move into deep pockets, riffles and pools, especially favoring cover areas such as moss beds, boulders, logs, ledges and cutbanks. Feeding becomes selective and food forms are usually smaller than during any other period. Large fish usually are not as active now as at other periods.

During rising water—a period that usually exists 30 minutes to one hour each day on any one area of the stream—all fish, large and small, become extremely active, moving into unprotected areas and feeding quite enthusiastically on most food forms. Undoubtedly this period is the angler's best bet to hook large fish in a given area.

During high water, which extends from 6 to 12 hours, trout usually move to edges of the stream and hold in deep main channels. Feeding varies throughout this period; usually the first half is most productive since more food is available due to the fast level change and flushing action. Large food forms are most productive and fishing deep or on the bottom scores best.

Falling water, which extends from one to six hours, will find fish almost anywhere and moving, as water recedes and flow speed reduces. Feeding varies according to the location of the fish. Often big fish will hold in the open until water becomes too thin to provide decent cover. They will feed well during falling water until they are forced to move to low water stations.

On a Class A stream these periods vary greatly according to time of day and water level, since speed of water flow ranges from 2 mph up to as high as 12 mph. Therefore, at noon, with a four-mile current speed, which is about average on the White River, the water will still be at low tide 16 miles downstream if the water isn't released until 8 a.m. at the dam. So if you wished to take advantage of low-water-period fishing at daylight, then positioning yourself downstream from the dam at a proportionate distance will put you into the right levels over a maximum length of time. A second move downstream another 10 to 20 miles at noon and subsequent moves will provide additional afternoon low-water fishing.

However, this sort of tide-level choice is not as possible on our Class B stream since it is more limited in length which prevents any considerable time lapse between the outlet and its downstream tolerable reaches. Thus what daylight hours exist on this smaller water respond quickly to what is going on at the dam and for the most part we must fish the water as it exists, high or low.

The options described for fishing these tail waters are the same for any other water—that is, from the banks, wading, or by boat. For both tail-water classes the very best choice and the most versatile is to use a boat and to wade. Regardless of water levels, a john boat, powered by an outboard motor, will easily reach the best runs and carry all the equipment needed. If the water should start to rise while you are wading a particular stretch, it is a good safety convenience to have your boat near you in case you are on the wrong side of the stream or wish to fish the higher levels.

Bank fishing leaves you at the mercy of high water which more often than not creates deep unfishable torrents and dangerously slippery banks. If a good fish is hooked you are almost certain to lose it if you are bank-bound. Low-water periods, however, enable the bank angler to fish easier and to have a bit better success.

The choice of tackle to use, depends on water conditions. Generally, high water is best worked with a medium-weight spinning or bait-casting rig which will handle lines from 6- to 12-pound test and cast weights from ¼ to 1 ounce. Fly-fishing during this water level is a tough challenge even for the expert because the flows often equal the force and depth of large western steelhead rivers. Sinking lines and large wet flys and streamers will produce. Bait and hardware will get down to the fish and match the good forms that usually drift with the flood. The techniques are similar to those used on large natural rivers.

Low water is another story, however. Now tackle refinement is in order. Riffles and pools are more defined and resemble those found in natural trout streams. Fly and ultralight spinning outfits are the most effective tools because the trout are holding in shallow but protected areas concentrating on smaller food forms. Coarse tackle methods seldom take fish, unless bait is used if the fish have just been stocked. Most of the methods used for small stream fishing will work under these circumstances and conditions.

Changing water levels, either rising or falling, are difficult to characterize, since it seems to me that the fish are moving and in a varied mood, holding no special feeding stations. Riffles and pool tails are the most consistent action areas, depending on what baits or lures you are using and at what stage the changing levels are in. Rising water, especially during early stages, produces best for me if I'm looking for trophy fish on light tackle. The only drawback to this period is that it lasts for too short a time and wading becomes increasingly difficult as the water becomes higher and swifter.

A technique which I call "jump fishing", involving either a powerboat or a car and a good knowledge of the river's hot spots, is the answer for fishing the prime-rise period. I simply begin a short distance below the dam and fish a riffle until the water rise there eliminates wading, then a fast boat or car ride downstream a mile or so again puts me on or ahead of the rise for another prime period. This is repeated for several miles. Usually each stop allows 15 to 30 minutes of fishing before it is time to race on. This is an energetic and exciting way to fish and it really produces fine catches once you have the spots and the timing adjusted. Two or three anglers can work this tactic most efficiently since they can cover the best water more quickly and without passing up any hot spots. Flycasting is my favorite method while jump fishing.

Most tail waters, because of their frequent water fluctuations, limit natural foods to forms of life that can move freely and are strong swimmers. Chubs, shiners, shad and sculpins are almost always plentiful as they have no problems changing living quarters every few hours and thrive well in the rich water. The same is true with various crustaceans such as crayfish and fresh-water shrimp which also flourish well in most tail waters despite level changes. Aquatic insects and snails are another story however, since low water often exposes their prime living quarters (gravel and moss beds) to a high and dry situation. If however, minimum flow levels do not shrink the river's width and expose the gravel and moss, a good population of aquatic insects usually exists. The Norfork and Little Red in Arkansas are good examples of tail waters harboring a high aquatic insect population and the White River is an example of extreme bottom exposure and low numbers of snails and aquatic insects.

Midges and terrestrial insects are two additional food forms providing frequent meals for tail-water trout. Midges hatch almost the year round, but especially provide extremely fine low-water winter fly-fishing when other insects are scarce. The constant flushing of the bank areas washes hordes of ants, beetles, worms and grasshoppers into the stream daily during long warm-weather periods. Trout love this wonderful variety and it is easy to see why they aren't usually selective about various flies, lures or baits.

When fly-fishing I generally find wet flies to be most effective, especially the Woolly Worm, large nymphs and shrimp patterns. Dry flies and streamers are fine under the right circumstances. Colors that work best are olive, brown, black, grey and yellow. Two-fly casts are quite effective; I favor either a Woolly Worm and nymph combination, or a nymph and shrimp. Spinning lures are always productive, especially small gold or copper spoons; yellow, orange, or metallic banana-shaped plugs, and weighted spinners in gold or silver. Slow and deep-drifting retrieves are best.

Live baits are usually local choices. Most waters I fished produced well when I used angleworms, crayfish, crayfish tails, sucker meat, sculpins, small minnows and grasshoppers. Corn, cheese, marshmallows and salmon eggs produce well but somehow it seems almost a crime to kill such a fine gamefish as trout with these crude baits, especially when they will rise to a fly or tiny spinner on sensitive, light tackle.

Since trout stocking is an expensive method of maintaining tail-water or natural fisheries, it is a costly waste to kill all the trout we do by carelessness. Baited hooks and the treble-hook artificials harm smaller fish that might not be included in your limit. I would like to recommend several methods to eliminate undue hook damage. Always use a large bronze hook with bait. Small trout will be less apt to swallow a No. 2 hook than a No. 10. Replace trebles with a single hook on spoons or spinners, this will cut mouth, gill and eye damage at least 60 percent.

If the freshly stocked rainbows or browns survive the offerings of tail-water fishermen for a week or so they quickly begin to change their color inside and out. Initially there is a slight weight loss before these trout adjust to hustling their own food, then they begin to put on solid flesh and their coloration improves daily. After a few months they resemble lake fish more than stream fish in their shape: Their bodies become wide and thick with a tiny head and their fins grow long and transparent. This is a result of the high intake of protein and minerals provided by the rich native food sources and ideal water temperatures.

These fish soon learn to let the varying currents bring food to them and move only to adjust to water levels. Therefore, the best carryover fish are usually taken using a natural drift. I always cast up and across stream and allow little or no drag to develop as my fly or lure is carried downstream. Otherwise, a lure retrieved upstream will attract and tempt mostly the hungry, anxious, freshly stocked trout and your sport will be less exciting as a consequence.

Fishermen will find that all of the better tail-water fisheries offer excellent living accomodations in the area and boats, motors, guides and tackle are usually available. Most owners of the river docks can give you accurate information on water levels and access points. I'm convinced that the worst mistake made by inexperienced anglers is that they almost always fish directly below the dam on their tail-water trips. These places are hard fished and have less ideal holding water than can be found further downstream where riffles and pools provide a more natural environment for trout.

Float-fishing is an extremely popular way to see and fish the rivers. Floating provides a quick course in becoming familiar with a long stretch of the river. Usually float-fishing is less productive for the serious angler than concentrating on one or several choice runs. Most float guides encourage the use of live bait rather than artificials. If you can retain a guide who prefers artificial lures, chances are you will learn more about the tail water and have a more enjoyable and productive day on the river. Dragging a weighted, baited hook down the river is less fun in my opinion.

Tail-water fishing has introduced the trout to a lot of southerners in the last two decades and has encouraged many northern anglers to go south for action. The damming of free-flowing streams has long been a bitter pill for many of us but the creation of new, cold-water fisheries has certainly made the pill a bit easier to swallow.

If tail waters are recognized as a unique public cold-water fishery and proper methods are used to maintain them, surely they will be one of the few good results of civilization's progress. Perhaps the next hundred years of angling history might well record the names of famous rivers and pools in these tail waters when our present natural streams have been lost to pollution. I hope this will never come to pass, but at least we are holding an ace in our hand.

LONG LIVE THE LONG ROD

Leonard M. Wright, Jr.

One of America's most respected writers on trout fishing has some very definite views on fly-rod length. (February 1974)

THE MOST overrated piece of fishing equipment in America today is the short fly rod. It is the least effective, least comfortable and least sporting angling tool ever invented. I know it's risky to knock another man's woman, dog or favorite rod, but a close look at the evidence will only confirm my position.

At first glance it may seem that the choice between a short or a long rod for stream fishing is simply a matter of whim. After all, it is less visible, and a fairly skilled caster can lay out 60 or 70 feet of line with a tiny rod—more than enough distance for most trout stream situations. But, keeping out of sight of the fish is only a small part of the game. What is important is the ability to present the right fly in a way that deceives the trout, and then to hook those you've fooled. This is what separates the anglers from the casters. And it is exactly here that the stubby rod short-changes you.

A short rod leaves far too much line on the water while you're fishing out the average cast. Every extra foot of this is a crippling disadvantage, whether you're presenting a dry fly, wet fly, nymph, streamer or (forgive me, Federation of Fly-Fishers) live bait.

Suppose, for example, you're casting to a fish 30 feet away. With a six-foot rod, tip held high, you'll probably still leave 18 feet of line and leader on the water when you make your presentation. (A bit more when fishing upstream, a bit less when working downstream.) On the other hand, with a ten-foot rod, casting under the same conditions, only about ten feet of terminal tackle—perhaps just your leader—would be lying on the surface. Judge for yourself which presentation is most likely to give you a badly dragging dry fly or an underwater fly that's moving unnaturally and out of control.

Admittedly, the amount of line on the water isn't a critical factor when you're fishing a still-water pond or lake. But on streams with braiding currents, tongues of fast water and unpredictable eddies, the more line you have on the water the more likelihood of an unappetizing presentation of your fly.

It is also much easier to hook a fish when most of your line is off the water. You're in more intimate touch with your fly and you don't have to guess at how hard to tug to straighten out the esses in your line, overcome the friction of water and finally set the hook. Over 90 percent of the trout broken off are lost at the strike. Examine the circumstances the next time you leave your fly in a fish; the problem usually is too much line on the water when the take occurs.

It took me years to learn these simple fly-fishing facts of life. The truth started to sink in only about a dozen years ago when I was fishing in the mountains of Southern France. I was using a snappy, eight-foot rod (certainly a sensible length by Eastern U.S. standards), but I wasn't catching many fish and almost no really good ones. This was slow, clear, limestone water, heavily fished by vacationers and constantly harvested by a troup of professional fishermen who supplied the local hotels. Any fish that had run this gauntlet and grown to decent size was as thoroughly trained as an astronaut.

The professionals finally showed me their secret—which they regarded more as common sense than as an ingenious technique. They'd learned that, in this clear, slick water, they couldn't approach these fish from upstream. Neither could they give the trout a look at their leader. So they cast upstream to a rising or observed fish, but with a variation of the conventional method. They'd drop their fly—usually a sparsely dressed wet pattern on a light hook—just downstream of the trout's tail so the leader wouldn't pass over his head. When the tiny ripples from the fly's entry passed over the trout's nose, he would usually turn around to see what sort of insect had fallen into the water behind him. If the stunt was pulled off perfectly, all the trout could see now was the artificial sinking slowly down-current.

Any line splash or drag meant instant failure, and I began to see why these experts used long rods—10 to 10½ feet long, in fact. "With a rod of three meters (nine feet, ten inches) you are just beginning to fish," they told me.

I finally learned how to execute this presentation with occasional success after days of practice. But my eight-foot rod, even though it could throw 70 to 80 feet of line with ease, was a big handicap.

Fishermen I saw in the Pyrenees on the Spanish border had taken this theory one step further. They used rods 12 to 14 feet long on those tumbling mountain streams and these kept so much line off the water there wasn't even a word for "drag" in their local *patois*. They would simply swing their fly (or more often maggot) directly up-current and let it drift back naturally, keeping in touch by raising the rod tip. They neither added nor took in line. And they took in trout with unbelievable regularity.

The implications of all this to the dry-fly man, with his almost paranoid fear of drag, are enormous. The perfect presentation of his fly has to be one dapped on the surface with no leader at all touching the water. This is true whether the offering is to be made dead-drift with the natural flow of the current or simply bounced on the surface like an egg-laying insect.

I proved this to my satisfaction several years ago after a neighbor had been given an ancient and enormous English fly rod. This awesome wand was a full 20 feet long, made of a solid wood called greenheart, and must have weighed over three pounds. However, it had a light, flexible tip, having been built when single strands of horsehair were used as leader tippets.

I found some pretext to borrow this rod for a couple of hours and, after I'd rigged it with a light line and fine leader, I headed for a nearby river. Once I got the hang of it, I could dap a fly on the surface 30 to 35 feet away and make it dance and hop there with no leader at all touching the water. Smart, overfished trout nearly herniated themselves to grab my fly. If I'd continued to use that rod the State Conservation Department would have named me Public Enemy No. 1. However, my friend soon retired that rod to his collector's case and perhaps that was just as well. After two hours with that wagon tongue, I felt as if I'd slipped every disk in my back.

Going to the opposite extreme, you can cast and catch fish with no rod at all. This would give you a rod some 20 feet shorter than the old English muscle-builder I just described. Of course this would have to be the worst possible tackle for trouting, but not because you couldn't cover the water or land the fish.

The late Ellis Newman could take the reel off the rod and with his bare hand work out all 90 feet of a double-taper and keep it in the air, false casting.

Similarly, Lee Wulff once hand cast to a nearby salmon and played that full-grown fish to the beach with just the reel in his hand. No rod at all. Again, you might do that, too, with practice. You might even be able to dine out on this feat for weeks if you could tell the epic story with enough suspense and gusto. But I don't think you'd want to make a habit of fishing like that.

So you see, a fly rod isn't a necessity. It's merely a convenience and a comfort.

How can I say "comfort" after that 20-footer nearly put me in bed under traction? And doesn't a long rod have to punish the angler more than a short one? Well, yes and no.

In the first place, sheer lightness in a rod doesn't necessarily mean less effort. The difference between a two-ounce rod and a longer five-ounce model, compared to the angler's total weight on the scales, is negligible. So rest assured that the longer, slightly heavier rod won't weigh you down.

I have fished with many superb casters who said they reveled in the lightness of their short rods. But how they huffed and puffed and sweated. They were using both arms, both shoulders and their back to make those long casts with toy tackle. Double-hauling may be the ultimate technique for tournament casting, but it's about as placid a way to enjoy a summer evening as alligator wrestling.

The point is, ask not what you can do for the rod, but rather what the rod can do for you. With a long rod, a small movement of the arm or wrist will take any reasonable length of line off the water for the backcast because there really isn't that much line clutched by surface tension. The line then goes back over your head, straightens out and bends the rod backwards. Now a minimal effort forward with forearm, wrist or both and the rod snaps back, propelling the line forward again. What could be easier than that? The rod has done most of the work for you. Your hand has moved a foot or so with very little exertion instead of moving three feet or so and bringing shoulder and back muscles into play, as well.

My experiences in France were not the only reason why my rods became longer about a dozen years ago. At approximately that time, I read an article in an outdoor magazine extolling the joys of mini-rod fishing. The author honestly admitted that he did, at first, have trouble avoiding drag with his shorter rod, but that he had solved this problem by holding the rod high above his head as he fished out every cast. Thus this six-footer, he claimed, was every bit as effective as an 8 or 8½-footer and (get this), because his rod weighed only 1¾ ounces, it was far less fatiguing to fish with. Anyone who subscribes to that theory should now hold his right arm fully extended over his head for two or three minutes and tell me how it feels. I can't recall seeing any more articles from this man and I can only assume that acute bursitis has prevented him from taking even a pencil in hand.

If a 20-footer can break your back and a six-footer gives you too much drag and too much work, what should be the length of an efficient and comfortable fly rod? A lot depends on your physical makeup and your style of fishing. If you're a continuous and compulsive false caster who likes to fish pocket water upstream, where the effective float is a foot or less, any rod over eight feet might put your arm in a sling. If, on the other hand, your style is more deliberate and you spend most of your time on slower water where you may make less than ten casts per minute instead of nearly 100, you could probably handle a ten-footer with ease for a whole day's fishing.

And don't be misled by the "bush-rod" addicts. They argue that you get hung up too often fishing small, overgrown streams if you use anything longer than a five-footer. But the fact is, you'll get hung up a lot with a very short rod, too, because any form of true casting here will put your fly and leader in the branches. A long-line presentation is seldom an effective way to fish a string of small potholes, anyway. Drag is instantaneous and disastrous with a lot of line out on this type of water. Here, you're far better off with the long rod, flipping or swinging your fly to the chosen spot while you make the extra effort to conceal yourself.

Use as long a rod as you comfortably can. I have been fishing for the past several years with an 8½-foot bamboo that weighs 4½ ounces. I am now going through a trial-marriage with a 9½-foot glass rod that weighs about the same. This liaison has been so enjoyable that I'm now searching for a ten-footer with the same qualities.

On salmon rivers where I make only four or five casts per minute, my favorite wet-fly rod is a 10½-footer that works beautifully with a medium weight No. 6 line. But I'll admit that I have to drop back to an 8½-foot stick for dry-fly fishing. I just can't false cast that often with the long rod —although that 10½-footer is the most effortless wet-fly rod I've ever hefted. And let me repeat: I find all these rods, both trout and salmon models, comfortable for a full-day's fishing.

In case you're interested, the man who wields these monster rods bears no resemblance to King Kong. I don't tip the scales at 140 pounds with chest waders, spare reels and enough assorted fly boxes to drown me if I fell into deep water.

I'll have to admit, though, there's one disadvantage to long fly rods— and it's a beauty. When you've finally hooked a fish, the long rod makes the fish grow stronger. That extra length gives the fish greater leverage against your hand.

Isn't this precisely what the short-rod people are espousing? That fish are now smaller and tamer so we must use tackle that magnifies the quarry? But aren't they actually doing just the opposite?

There are only two basic ways to measure a rod's ability to glorify the struggles of a fish. One is the weight or force it takes to bend the rod properly. This factor is usually printed on the rod, just in front of the cork grip, in terms of the weight of line it takes to bring out its action. I've seen a lot of six-foot rods that call for a No. 6 or No. 7 line to make them work properly. This means that it takes between 160 and 185 grains (437½ grains equal one ounce) of moving line to flex the rod adequately. My 9½-footer, on the other hand, needs only a No. 4, or 120 grains to flex it to its optimum.

But there's still another factor that makes one rod more sporting than another for playing a fish. That's the leverage against your hand. With a fly rod—which must be considered a simple lever once a fish is hooked— the fulcrum is where the hand holds the rod. You don't need an M.I.T. degree to see that the mechanical advantage is approximately 66.66+ percent greater in favor of the fish and against the sportsman with a ten-foot rod than it is with a six-footer.

Despite this elementary fact, I am often accused of derricking small fish out of the water with a whacking great salmon rod. Fault my reasoning if you can: I'm convinced the shoe is on the other foot. I maintain that short-rodders are not only selling themselves short on presentation and overexercising themselves needlessly, but grinding down small fish with mechanically superior weapons, as well.

If you have followed my argument carefully so far and, hopefully, found it airtight, you're probably asking, "How can so many of nature's noblemen have been taken in by this cruel hoax?"

In the beginning, all rods were long. They were used to swing some lure out to the unsuspecting fish and to haul the catch back to shore again. They were very much like our present-day cane poles and probably just about as long.

Rods were still very long in the 17th Century. Izaac Walton recommended a snappy, 18-foot, two-handed model as the best choice in his day. He and Charles Cotton dapped, dibbled and dangled their flies (and worms and maggots) on the water with these mighty poles with killing effect on the trout.

In the following century the scientific progress of the industrial revolution reached the angling world. Fishing reels appeared on the market and soon became popular because they allowed fishermen to lengthen or shorten line easily and to play larger fish more effectively. But the rods themselves remained long.

One hundred years after that, in the not-too-distant 1800s, rods still averaged a sensible 12 feet. When dressed-silk fly lines and split bamboo were introduced, just after the midpoint of the century, rods grew shorter and lighter. After all, why should the angler stand there waving half a tree over the water when he could cast to the far bank and beyond with a zippy little ten-footer?

But along with these advances came another type of progress: overpopulation, overfishing and pollution. Trout became fewer. Fishing no longer was the simple culling of nature's bounty as it had been in Walton's day. It needed a mystique, a philosophy, a reason-for-being. This Frederick M. Halford and other British Victorians readily provided, and their code soon spread across the Atlantic in a slightly modified form. If the sheer joy of catching fish was not a sure thing, at least there was the joy of casting. A day astream . . . the play of the sweet bamboo . . . the lovely hiss of the line . . . the fly cocked perkily on the sparkling riffle . . . who cares for a full creel with all this?

All the while, of course, anglers still secretly wanted to catch fish— and I suppose you do, too. But our artificial Victorian code insists that this be done only by improving our casting or presentation, or by tinkering up a bit better imitation of, say, the female Iron Blue Dun. Reverting to aboriginal tackle and the more varied presentations it puts at your fingertips has been unthinkable.

Well, I think it *is* thinkable. And, if you really want to catch more trout and enjoy more sport doing it, perhaps you should think about it, too. Going back to 18-foot poles might be a bit too much. But do try a new nine- or ten-footer. If a ribbon-clerk like me can swing one all day long, you may be able to handle one like a conductor's baton.

Can't I, after all this, find at least one kind thing to say about our new short fly rods? Well, yes. Perhaps this.

I am reminded of the country sage's defense of bad breath. "It's mighty unpleasant, but it sure beats no breath at all." Same goes for short fly rods. They beat handlines, or no rods at all.

FLY ROD BASS

Homer Circle

Bugs, poppers, spinners, even plastic worms can transform a fly rod into a powerful piece of bass-catching equipment, says SPORTS AFIELD's current angling editor. (February 1975)

FLY-RODDING quite possibly is the best all-around method for catching bass. This conviction grows on me with each passing season. And yet it is rare to see one good fly-rodder among thousands of bass fishermen. Why?

Well, one can only conjecture that (a) most tackle salesmen know little about it and therefore avoid talking about it; and (b) most fishermen believe a fly rod is a tool for casting flies and not many bass are caught on flies. Trout yes, bass no.

Let's examine (a) first. As one who spent, nay invested, eight years as a fishing-tackle salesman I remember the difficulty I encountered trying to sell fly rods, reels, lines and lures.

So, we held fly-fishing schools at the Y.M.C.A. and exposed the technique's values to large groups of interested anglers rather than talking to one customer at a time.

Various companies sent in their fly-fishing experts to do guest shots at our clinics. But, although we had one river in our area that once produced fine trout fishing, it was ruined by effluents from a strawboard company.

Therefore we switched our teaching emphasis from trout to panfish and bass. With the emergence of weight forward lines there came a wide range of bass bugs and poppers. The fly rod grew in stature and usage as a productive fishing method, and I pursued uses of the fly rod beyond the usual concepts.

This leads us to (b). If the fly rod were a tool for casting flies only, I could understand its narrow profile. But today, when fly rods are used for all species of fish from sailfish to panfish, it follows that the long rod must lend itself to a lot of ways for taking bass. And it does!

First and foremost is bass bugging. As I have stated with sincerity, in a contest to see who could catch the most bass I never would bet against the fly-rod man who knows the art of bass bugging.

The method is so deadly and efficient that it tops anything I'm familiar with. Let me give you a rundown on the basic approach to see if it draws on you. If it does, I recommend you give it a go and watch your take of bass double, even triple, over whatever other method you might be pursuing.

Bass Bugging

The Tackle: Make the fly rod an eight or nine-footer with muscle, maybe even a slightly clubby feel so long as it has an even overall bend. An L10 line will bring out the action when you get at least 30 feet of line into the air.

Acquire a moderately priced single action reel, and a ten-yard coil of 20-pound monofilament line to use for leaders. Tie six feet of leader to the end of your line and practice fly casting in your yard until you can lay a flat line 30 to 40 feet long.

That basic outfit needn't cost you more than $20 to $25. Bass bugs will run the tab upwards in a hurry but don't go hog wild, just start with a few proved patterns.

Bass bugs are large, floating imitations of insects, mice and other critters bass go for. My best all-time producers are: a gray deer-hair mouse, black and white spent-wing moth and an assortment of wild-looking poppers. I recommend you begin with no more than two each of these.

During your first half hour of fishing, forget about catching bass and concentrate on working those bugs. Tie a short leader to your fly-rod tip and secure the bug to the end of it. Splat it down close to you so you can hear and observe its fall on the water.

Notice how little movement it takes to cause the bug to make a commotion. Remember that a bass has sensors which enable it to detect the most minute motion of any creature that drops into its domain. Become thoroughly familiar with what it takes to make the mouse swim, the moth flutter and the poppers pop.

Now assemble your fly rod, still staying with a six-foot leader, which is long enough for a beginner. And remember, bass are cover creatures. They conceal themselves in, around, under, beside and behind such features as lily pads, weeds, rocks, trees, logs, stumps, pilings, etc.

Approach quietly and select one of your bugs. Be certain that the knot you use is a strong one. If in doubt, use a keeper knot in the end of your leader to prevent slippage. Here are proved ways to work each bug.

The Mouse: Learn how to make it do everything but squeak. When a mouse falls into the water its only thought is to get the heck out of there before it gets gobbled down.

So, motivate it with this intent. Swim it with mini-twitches on your line, either impulsed by your free hand or the rod tip. Stop it occasionally for a rest, then move it along. A strike can come anywhere from the second it lands until you have it only a rod's length away from you. Stay alert!

When a bass strikes the lure, you must have a fairly tight line in order for you to strike the bass. To do this, keep your rod tip low and the line fairly taut as you work the mouse.

The Moth: Deer hair floats because it is hollow. But it doesn't float high like a cork-body popper. And therein lies its seductiveness. Many times I don't begin catching bass until the moth gets a bit waterlogged and barely floats.

Also, in this state the moth alights on the water softly and quietly, just as a live moth would do. You must remember how a moth usually acts when it falls onto the water. Its instincts tell it to remain quiet or be eaten. Sometimes it is too stunned by the fall to move.

Let your imitation lie quietly for ten to 15 seconds. Then, when you move it, see how little you can get by with. When the water is dead calm, here is a little technique that works regularly. Tap on your rod butt with anything metallic, like a clipper, knife, fly box, etc. Even your thumbnail snapped against the butt works effectively.

This transmits a perceptible vibration to the moth and will trigger even a man-wary bass into busting it. Normally, just an occasional nudge to make the moth push up a ripple will impulse a strike.

The Popper: This type of lure works on the noise principle. No creature I'm familiar with makes a loud "pop!" on the surface. Yet, bass go for it repeatedly. Here's how to take a whopper on a popper.

With all the slack out of your line and your rod tip low, a terse, short snap of the rod tip will cause the popper to pop. Also, you can do it with sharp jerks on the line.

Pop the lure, then let it lie motionless. Follow with barely perceptible nudgings. Swim it a few feet by drawing it toward you with your line hand. Then pop it again. You'll soon learn many ways to work a popper and that some head designs work better for you than others.

To hook a bass on a popper, keep your rod tip low and line fairly taut as you work the lure. The instant you see a swirl at your lure, or hear a bass bust it, tightly grip the line in your free hand and sweep the fly rod backwards with all the muscle you can muster. You'll know if you hooked the bass, quick like.

You now have a choice of two ways to land that bass. One is to simply reel it in, letting the rod tip play it all the while. If the fish surges and demands line, the drag on your reel should keep the line from fouling as the bass takes line.

Some reels are so designed that you can gently brake the revolving spool with your free hand. I prefer this type, although they cost more, because I can sense just how much pressure to apply.

The other way to bring in a bass is to strip the line in. To do this reach up to the first guide, grasp the line and draw it downward toward your rod hand. Grip the drawn line between the thumb and forefinger of your rod hand. Repeat until the bass is landed.

The advantage of stripping in line is that after you've subdued the bass, you know how far away you caught it because that precise amount of line is on the water around you, or in the boat. If you are fishing in weedy cover, it can become entangled, so be cautious.

About Good and Bad Bugs: Shop around when buying deer-hair mice and moths, as well as poppers. You can spot a shoddy tying job on the first two simply by grasping the head of the lure in one hand and the rear end in the other. Gently twist in opposite directions and if the bug body turns on the hook, look for one that won't.

Poppers should pop, even at the most delicate jerk. If they are im-

properly balanced, float too high, or have the hook eye in the wrong place, they will not yield that sharp bloop you want. Return them until you find some that do. Then stay with them.

So much for bugs. Now let's talk about other ways to catch bass on the versatile fly rod.

Spinner Fishing: There is an art to spinner fishing with a fly rod. If you don't learn it you are a good candidate to wind up with a spinner and hook stuck in your ear, back or fanny.

Where you can keep a fly moving overhead because of its lightness, you must lob a spinner because of its weight. By lobbing I mean keep your cast low, flat and away from you, like a side cast.

Watch the spinner, and when it reaches the end of the line on your back cast, just lob it forward and onto target. A little practice will find you doing a passable job your first trip afield.

This technique demands a little more work than bugging because you've got to keep the lure moving through the water in order to keep the spinner spinning. Most fly-rod spinners weigh from 1/20th to 1/30th of an ounce, have a minnow shape or hackle body ahead of which is a spinner blade. The spinner is the attracter and the body the target for the strike.

Why spinners take bass is a mystery. Nothing the bass eats looks or swims like a spinner, but they surely take fish when nothing else tempts ol' lanternjaw.

The technique is simple. Cast the spinner near bass cover, allow it to sink a few feet, then start a steady retrieve. If no strike results in the first six or eight feet, pick up the spinner with a lateral sweep of your rod tip and splat it onto the next target.

Because of the efficiency of this method a lot of water can be thoroughly covered with minimal time and effort. I especially enjoy fly-rodding a spinner while wading a stream. You can work a rifle or undercut bank and take bass that won't respond to plugs or live bait.

Plastic Worming: If you've never tried this tactic you've missed a lot of big bass on a fly rod. Use a sinking-tip fly line and a ten-pound leader the same length as your rod. I prefer a weight forward line, although a level or double taper will do.

Rig a floating, six-inch worm on a single hook and bury the hook in the body so it will be weedless. Add a split-shot just heavy enough to sink the worm, about six inches ahead of the hook.

Using the lateral cast, splat the worm close to cover where the water deepens enough to be dark. Let the worm sink to the bottom, then retrieve it with sharp upward sweeps of the fly rod. Now pause right here and pay attention.

The trick is to feed the worm back to the bottom with your rod tip, keeping the line always under tension so you can feel the bass inhale that worm. This is necessary because the split-shot tends to dampen the feel of the pickup.

The instant your line does anything different, like hesitate, move sideways or backwards, or go slack, set the hook with a backward sweep of the rod, then do it again for good measure in case the bass was moving toward you as you set the hook.

This is an excellent way to fish live night crawlers, too, if you have no aversion to feeding bass live meat. In fact, during dog days when bass aren't eating much of anything you'll find that fly-rodding night crawlers can be the *only* way to outfox them.

When It's Too Windy: You'll hear it said that fly-fishing is not worth a hoot when a breeze rises. Admittedly, it makes more work out of it, but you still can find sheltered covers to fish.

When the wind gets its back up to where the water is just below white-capping, it's no fun to fight it. Then don't. Let the wind help you catch fish.

Use a motor to run upwind and make a drift across the lake as the wind propels your boat. Use the fly rod for trolling. You can use a plastic or live worm, a minnow, a spinner, a jig or a weighted streamer fly.

Double-Barrel Fishing: While I wouldn't recommend this for all fishermen, if you're the innovative and versatile type, you might try what I call "double-barrel" fly-rodding.

I didn't originate it, but a friend of mine who catches a lot of fish came up with it. First, he replaces the first guide on his fly rod with a larger spinning-type guide.

When it's too windy to bug-fish, he takes off the fly reel and puts on a hangdown type spincasting reel, one with an enclosed face. He does a surprisingly proficient job of spinning. The larger first guide throttles down the line so that the fly-rod guides let it flow to give long, smooth casts.

Habitually, he bug-fishes early and late in the day, when the water is usually calm, and converts to spinning during the windier parts of the day. He does most of his fishing afoot and carries his total assortment of lures in two small plastic boxes. And, man, is he tough to top!

By now I imagine you have deduced that I think a fly rod is for more than flicking flies around. Once you acquire an outfit and become skilled in using it, you'll find it has endless applications.

THE DANCING FLY

Robert Traver

*Never make a wager with an angler who has a
secret—as in this tale by the famous author of
ANATOMY OF A MURDER and TROUT
MADNESS. (February 1975)*

MY NAME is Al and I'm here to tell my fellow anglers—wups!—and
all those dear lady anglers, too (if the former will please kindly forgive this
old bourbon bibber his sly Women's Libber bow to the latter)—that
Frenchman's Pond is by all odds the most fascinating and frustrating trout
water I have ever fished—and I've been angling like crazy since before I
could spell it.

Fascinating I find Frenchman's because I am one of the few fishermen
in these parts who happens to know the place is simply crawling with
lovely wild trout (most fishermen not even knowing of the pond's existence);
frustrating because my pals and I can't catch them—with sufficient regularity, that is—to avoid the sneaking suspicion that on those rare occasions
when we do catch a few it isn't all blind luck. Frenchman's Pond, in other
words, gives graduate courses in fisherman's humility on almost any old
day a guy dares visit it. Tuition-free courses.

My old fishing buddies Timmy and Pinky share my views about the pixilated place and in fact we three were together the first time we ever laid eyes on it. This memorable visit occurred last summer on a warm evening in mid-June when we slugged our way in there on foot, all on a hunch of little Timmy's, who is forever collecting and poring over tattered old maps in the hope of discovering some remote and overlooked trout Shangri-La.

Our first trip in was one prolonged fight—fighting brush, fighting clouds of fisherman-starved insects, fighting hidden sump holes in the swampy stretches we had to hack our way through. Our leader, little Timmy, disdained using a compass and instead led us over a tortuous and indistinct old tote road which he was positive would lead us straight to our latest trout paradise only because his latest antique map said it would.

About the time a puffing Pinky and I were almost ready to conclude that Timmy's ancient cartographer was taken drunk the day he drew his map, Timmy stopped and held his finger to his lips and whispered "Listen!" We gratefully stopped and listened and, sure enough, heard the shrill insistent cries of what must have been a million frogs, sounding at first for all the world like an army of vying youngsters blowing toy whistles at the top of their lungs.

"Can't be far," Timmy whispered, pushing on and, again sure enough, we hadn't gone 50 paces when our road ended abruptly on a granite bluff overlooking a lonely and desolate expanse of water. Our presence disturbed a pair of blue herons below and they arose with great comic commotion, threshing extravagantly for altitude, and then, with all the languor of a slow-motion movie, flapping silently away on oiled wings.

"See!" Timmy announced triumphantly, complacently folding his map and patting it. "Old tote road ends exactly where old map says it should. How about that?"

"First there was Magellan the Magnificent," I intoned, "followed by Timmy the Intrepid."

"Look, fellas!" Pinky suddenly croaked, pointing bug-eyed at the pond below. *Look what I see!*

Timmy and I looked—and saw unfolding on the water below us the wildest rise of trout any of us had ever beheld. As far as the eye could see scores of trout were dimpling and sending out widening magic rings, and for a moment I had the illusion we'd been caught in a freak hailstorm. But no, for in their eagerness some of these trout were leaping clear out of water—just like on the outdoor magazine covers—and landing with a smack we could hear on our bluff.

For a long time we stood there, still panting and perspiring from our trek, watching the crazy piscatorial fireworks. Yet even as we gaped I felt the first small premonition that this place just might not yield its trout gladly—an intuition we had ever so richly confirmed.

First of all I could see at a glance that Frenchman's Pond wasn't truly a pond at all—Timmy's treasured old map to the contrary—but rather the long, narrow meandering backwater of an old inactive beaver dam originally built on a flowing stream. Down on our left we could see the faint brush-covered outline of the old dam itself while the serpentine backwater seemed roughly to follow the wavering contour of the granite range on which we stood. Another clue that the fishing mightn't be easy—at least from shore—was that the pond was heavily forested mostly by tall spruces to the very waterline on the far side while on our side, though fairly open, it was boggy-margined clear back to our granite range, with ominous patches of open water showing through—sometimes a real quick way, I ruefully knew, for a careless fisherman to disappear abruptly and maybe not emerge until weeks later in droll places like Singapore.

"Looks sorta kinda like tough fishing," Timmy said, reading my thoughts.

"We might try dapping flies from a balloon," Pinky suggested helpfully. "If only we'd brought a balloon."

All of us were sufficiently battle-scarred veterans of past collisions with old beaver dams to suspect that the water would also probably be shallow (thus making these spooky wild trout all the more scary) as well as unwadable from the long accumulation of silt. Meanwhile the frogs kept up their shrill clamor and the trout their steady feeding so we banished our suspicions and rigged up with trembling hands.

"Looks like Frenchman's got us hooked," Timmy murmured prophetically as, our bamboo wands assembled, we slid our way down the steep hill on an old deer trail to join the fray.

Once out on the wobbly bog we quickly separated, as fishermen do, Pinky taking up his stand on the wide watery margin and immediately uncorking and starting to flail away. Timmy shrugged and headed upstream and I nodded and hooked my thumb and headed for the old beaver dam below, fishing as I went.

Soon we lost sight of each other, and as I staggered and reeled my way along, occasionally pausing and balancing myself enough to paste out a fly, I felt less like a fisherman than a gesticulating drunk on a trampoline.

Keeping in character I presently contrived to step in a hidden bog hole, sinking well over one hip boot. After I'd wallowed my way out, holding my rod high like an Olympic torch and still gasping from the shock, it quickly swept over me that among its other allurements the waters of Frenchman's were colder than the deep-freezes of hell. . . .

Hours later we met back up on the bluff, chilled to the bone, our hands shaking so much that our wavering flashlights looked more like blinking fireflies.

"Confess!" Timmy said, his breath emerging in thin vaporous jets. "I didn't catch a bloody fish or get a bloody pass."

"Me too," Pinky confessed.

"That makes us even," I said, cupping my ear. "And you can still hear 'em flopping down there." We listened, and sure enough, even above the din of the frogs mixed now with the shrill cries of nighthawks feeding overhead we could hear the steady *slurp-slurp* of the still-feeding trout.

"Frenchman's may have us hooked," Pinky remarked as we came to the first swamp, "but we sure in hell haven't its trout."

"There's gotta be a way," little Timmy murmured, plunging into the maze of tag alders.

The next evening we were back again at Frenchman's, of course, and the next evening after that. But the verdict remained the same: still no trout and no offers.

"At least we're hacking out a pretty fair hiking trail," Pinky said. "For water buffalo, that is."

So excited were we over the pristine fishing we'd found if not solved at Frenchman's that we decided not to risk reopening the old tote road so that we might drive our bush car in. For if we could drive in so might curious rival fishermen, we figured, and if they did pretty soon our precious pond would inevitably land on the tourist beat, complete with ambulant septic toilets. This prospect so scared us we took to hiding our parked car, the better to cover our tracks, as well as leaving the first quarter mile or so of the old tote road in the tangled state we found it so that no prying hardier souls might be tempted to hike in and so spread the word.

Our strategy worked and no fishermen bothered us, but the hell of it still was, neither did the trout. This virtually fishless state of affairs ran on so long that first summer that finally we limited our visits strictly to weekends. This we did not simply to solace our tattered pride but to preserve also at least a smidgen of domestic tranquility. After all, if three braggy fishermen couldn't occasionally bring home at least one wizened trout mightn't the home front naturally begin wondering what other dark shenanigans we might be up to?

"Anyway we mustn't be too greedy," Pinky said. "Seven pratfalls a
week is too much for any gentleman angler."

Despite all our frustrations at Frenchman's we naturally learned more
about the place as the summer wore on, including gathering more clues to
help solve the baffling enigma of why its trout were so reluctant to commit
suicide with any degree of regularity. Two of our biggest finds came the
day we toted in our inflatable wading floats and swiftly confirmed our suspicions that the water was generally too shallow and the silt too thick to
use them for fishing.

But this day was devoted to exploring, we told ourselves, and so, eyes
glowing with scientific zeal, we had not even uncased our rods. Instead we
sweatily persisted, kicking and churning our way through spreading clouds
of silt like a marauding trio of ink-ejecting squid. From our exhausting
labors we learned two things we felt helped mightily to explain our astonishing run of fishing disasters.

First we found the place abounding with easily accessible natural food,
principally hordes of minnows and scads of tiny freshwater shrimp burrowed
in the silt. Our next benumbing eye-opener—in more ways than one—
was the further discovery that the water in Frenchman's was incredibly
cold—I'd had a taste of it on that first day—in turn doubtless accounted
for by the fact that for its entire winding length the place abounded with
scores of bubbling underwater springs, both large and small. Timmy, our
acknowledged intellectual, quickly enlightened us on the ominous consequences often attending such a combination.

"All this easy grub makes it all the more easy for the trout to ignore
our flies," he declaimed as we shivered and danced around an open fire on
our cliff top while thawing out. "At the same time this frigid water naturally
sharply lowers their metabolism—"

"I was a kindergarten dropout, p- p- pal," shivering Pinky broke in.
"What's this here now fancy m- m- metabolism?"

"Means the little bastards never get so hungry, stupid."

"Sorry, Herr Doktor. P-please proceed."

"Which in turn, means," Timmy concluded, "that naturally our poor
little fake flies don't even have the usual Chinaman's chance to attract them."
He widened his hands. "It's as simple as that."

"One thing puzzles me, Timmy," I said, putting in my oar. "Granting
all you say, why is it these presumably anemic and easily gorged trout at

Frenchman's continue to spurn our flies and yet hit the naturals here like crazy?"

"Beats me, too," Timmy admitted, wagging his head. "All of which puts a finger smack on the big problem we gotta solve." All of which in turn brings me smack down to the most baffling enigma of all at Frenchman's.

For good old Frenchman's—as if all its other afflictions weren't enough to drive us screaming from the place—had one final trick up its sleeve calculated to preserve its trout and sap our waning sanity: its fly hatches were like no other fly hatches any of us had ever seen. Instead of the widely varied and predictable succession of aquatic insects that occur annually on most trout waters all season long, year in and year out, only one species of fly kept hatching over and over on Frenchman's, or so it seemed. Not only that but this unique Frenchman's fly was almost too tiny to be seen by the naked eye and moreover it looked more like an animated ball of fur than a fly. Finally, to top things off, the damned thing danced—ah yes—forever it crazily danced and danced, up and down, up and down . . . In fact in a sunburst of creativity we immediately christened it the Dancing Fly.

While none of us was really up on our entomology or for that matter more than passably savvy amateur bug men, all of us had seen midge flies before, of course, and even carried a small emergency assortment of "boughten" imitations in our boxes—all of which the trout at Frenchman's disdainfully ignored.

So stubborn Timmy, by far the best tier among us, reassaulted the pond in a wading float (we now kept one cached there) and gathered up specimens of the Dancing Fly in a bottle and took them home to tie up some imitations. Two days later we tried them out but either Timmy's hooks were too big or Piscator had a bellyache that day or something went haywire—for they too were spurned like all our other offerings.

"I'll order some smaller hooks first thing tomorrow," Timmy promised.

"If they get much smaller I'll have to hire a small boy to tie them on for me," Pinky said, squinting wryly.

We wound up that first season at Frenchman's, of course, valiantly trying out Timmy's latest midges, this time tied on the smallest hooks he could find.

"The man wrote they don't make eyed hooks much smaller," Timmy explained as we rigged up for the final assault of the season. Box score: Timmy got cleaned out overstriking a dandy; Pinky got one feeble pass; while I, virtuously shunning the obvious rhyme, fell quietly on my can.

"Damned funny thing," I said as we dragged ourselves out to the car. "While I'm no Art Flick, I'd swear your flies were almost exact imitations of the Dancing Fly, Timmy."

"Scarcely, but thanks anyway for the compliment, pal." Timmy said, modestly fluttering his eyelashes. "But even supposing we *could* tie an exact imitation of the little devils, tell me, how the hell we ever gonna make 'em dance?"

"Look, fellas," I announced casually on the first day of fishing the following spring, when once again we stood on our new granite bluff looking down at our tantalizing pond, "last winter I gave a lot of thought to this baffling Frenchman's place, and while I don't claim to have all the answers I do have a little suggestion to make before we launch the new season that just might help ease our pain."

"Let's have it," Timmy said, lowering his packsack and listening politely.

"I've got it," Pinky said, slapping his thigh. "This season we're gonna start hitting the bottle *before* we start fishing."

"Let the man talk," Timmy said. "Do please reveal your little pain-killing plan, comrade."

"First I want to make it perfectly clear," I said, "that I don't aim to commercialize our fishing or turn the place into a gambling casino."

"Hear, hear," Pinky said. "Ol' fishing pal shuns gambling hell."

"But I do think my little suggestion might not only help us over some of the balder fishing spots but, who knows, even improve the results."

"Goody, we're gonna plant a troupe of topless mermaids in the place," Pinky broke in, clapping his hands.

"Will you *please* let the man say his piece," Timmy said, frowning at Pinky. "Though I got a faint inkling we're gonna hear a quaint tinkling involving a swap of the coin of the realm."

"That's *it*, Timmy!" I said, nodding brightly. "You just put your finger on it. My little suggestion is that it might be good fun and also stimulate our fishing if we put a friendly little daily bet on the results."

"Like how small?" Timmy said.

"Oh," I said, shrugging. Something say like five bucks a head to the guy who catches the biggest fish."

"My, my. You mean the winner'd dance outa here waving ten bucks —five each from his two pigeons?"

"The daily winner would get his ten bucks, all right," I agreed, "but it might be fairer and even more stimulating all around if we agreed that the guy with the second biggest fish would at least be rewarded by not losing anything, the last guy paying the full shot."

"I don't quite follow."

"Look, supposing here today Pinky up and caught a 12-incher—"

"First I'd frow up an' then fall down in a heap," Pinky said, pouching out his cheeks and staggering around drunkenly.

"And you, Timmy, an 11-incher," I ran on, "and me a ten."

"Go on, dreamer."

"Under my plan Pinky would cop the ten bucks, all right, you'd neither win nor lose a dime, while poor little me'd have to fork over the full ten."

"I get what you mean, all right, but supposin' Pinky caught a mere eight-incher, you a seven, an' me somewhere in between? Isn't ten bucks a pretty elegant reward for catching a trout of a size all of us usually returns?"

"I've thought of that, Timmy," I said. "We could solve that by setting a pond minimum of, say ten inches. No ten-inchers caught, all bets off."

"Fair enough, but supposin' only one guy catches a ten-incher or better? Do the other two each pay five though one catches an eight-incher and the other a seven?"

"It's all what we agree to, Timmy," I said loftily. "Personally I think it'd be fairer and even more fun to say that the only way a nonwinner can save himself five bucks is to at least catch a qualifying trout, even if it's finally nosed out."

"Well I'll be damned," Timmy said, wagging his head. "Did you dream all this up or run across it somewhere?"

"It's all my baby, Timmy," I said. "I thought a lot about Frenchman's last winter and in fact I often *did* dream about it."

"As who didn't?" Timmy murmured, rubbing his chin. "But under your bet wouldn't we still be killing fish we'd otherwise like to return?"

"How do you mean?"

"Like say I catch and creel a qualifying ten-incher on my first cast here today and then, just before quitting time, latch on to a 12."

"I've thought of that, too," I said. "We'd fix that by keeping our qualifiers in live traps. That way everybody could return all or any of his fish, the winner out of sheer euphoria, the losers in bleak despondency."

"I've got a drinkin' uncle down in Peoria," Pinky said, "but no kin I know of in this here Euphoria."

"You've also got a bug up your Emporia," Timmy said scathingly, turning and shooting me a shrewd glance. "Looks like you've thought of just about everything, eh, comrade? Beats me how you ever found time to work last winter."

"I've tried to cover every foreseeable contingency, Timmy," I said, laughing, at the same time feeling myself flushing guiltily over all of the things I *wasn't* revealing. "What do you say?"

"I'm on," Timmy said, shrugging and spreading his hands. "Can't think of a lovelier way to go broke or else make an easy buck. What hour is the bet off?"

"That would depend," I said, "on when we arrive, the state of the weather or our hangover, how long we want to fish—variable things like that to be determined each trip. Since today is warm and pleasant and it's still early, how about our closing the bets at five?" Timmy nodded. "After that a guy can suit himself, either keep on fishing a bit or hit the jug or maybe even take a nap." I turned to Pinky. "How about you, lucky?"

"Why not?" Pinky said, nodding. "It'd be worth five bucks just to see a decent trout caught outa this haunted place—though the Lord knows they're here. When do we start?"

"Minute we're rigged up," I said, unscrewing my rod case.

Shrewd little Timmy had been righter than he knew in guessing that I'd thought of just about everything, I mused to myself as I bounced my way along toward the dam. But the poor man really didn't know the half of it, I guiltily reflected, because in all truth I had devoted far more time and thought to solving the problem of the Dancing Fly before ever I dared think of broaching such a risky bet to the fast fishing company I kept.

As I inched my way along the trembling bog, avoiding water traps, I reviewed some of the high spots of my busy winter. The first important decision I had made, I recalled, was the uncharacteristically modest one that I was probably not good enough either as a fisherman or fly tier ever to solve the problem on my own—I'd simply have to seek help from someone. But who? I pondered—or maybe I should better have pondered whom! True, there were a number of first-rate fly tiers in my bailiwick, most of whom I knew, but I also knew that all of them were avid fishermen. And I felt in my bones that any local tier smart enough to solve the problem of the Dancing Fly would likely also be smart enough to track down where the little devils danced. No, it was plain I needed outside help.

It was then the inspiration hit me to avoid the obvious approach—such as combing the outdoor magazines and popular fishing books and the like—and instead visit the library of a nearby college. There I was shortly poring over a whole raft of technical articles and books devoted to the esoteric subject of freshwater aquatic entomology. This I did not to seek enlightenment by actually *reading* the baffling material I'd dug up, heaven knows, but only to find one solitary clue identifying one single author who also both fished and tied his own flies.

It was almost Valentine's Day before I'd tracked down such a gifted soul—a teacher in a happily remote northern New England college—following which I *did* read his article, some of which I even faintly grasped. Next I wrote him a glowing fan letter, naturally telling him all about Frenchman's Pond, of course, and especially about the riddle of the Dancing Fly. Finally I pensively wondered whether he might possibly be able to identify the fly from my crude description and, if so, wondered ever so wistfully whether he might not be prevailed upon to tie up some working imitations, cost of course being no consideration . . .

I so fancied the light air of fishing camaraderie in my closing paragraph I even learned it by heart. "The elusive trout at Frenchman's all seem to arrive in their watery world sporting framed master's degrees in evasion," I wrote, "so if you can possibly solve the mystery of the Dancing Fly you will not only make one distracted fisherman eternally grateful but also perform the humanitarian act of likely saving him and his two fishing buddies from the booby hatch."

It was only after I'd received the good professor's diabolically ingenious flies, along with his revealing letter, that Satan first reared his ugly head and sorely tempted me. Or was it cupidity? In either case I'd awakened one recent morning with my little betting scheme laid out cold.

By now I'd reached the old beaver dam, which had become my favorite fishing spot in the pond—just as Pinky's was the wide midpond area he had dubbed the "Big Spring" and Timmy's his coveted "Top Log." Moving carefully now lest a sudden jarring step alert the lunkers I knew dwelt there, I moved over to firmer ground, rested my rod, glanced around to make sure I was alone, and then produced my brand-new pruning shears and went to work.

In less than an hour I'd cut out a wide swath of casting lane in the maze of slender alders and willows behind me, during which I heard at least a half-dozen exciting splashes and had wheeled in time to see the out-rolling rings—all in the same magic spot. This spot I'd privately named the "Hot Spot" because, I'd learned the season before, it was not only one of the deepest pools in the pond but also harbored a hidden protective maze of ancient submerged logs under which lurked some of the loveliest wild brook trout I'd ever seen.

Scanning the dam closely I could see no sign of our Dancing Fly or indeed any insect life on or above the surface (not too surprising in view of the earliness of the season), and I speculated that the dramatic splashes I was hearing might be the occasional over-leaps of hungry trout charging after foolish minnows which had strayed too close to lurking danger.

My labors done I sat down and took a breather before tying a fresh tippet to my leader. Then I unzipped my vest and pulled out my newest fly box and, again glancing furtively, with a tweezers removed and held in my palm a single fly, rapturously admiring it. For this was my talented professor's exciting imitation of the Dancing Fly which, along with his letter, I'd received only the week before.

While he rarely attempted to identify any aquatic insect without first seeing an actual specimen—the good professor wrote—my Dancing Fly was at once so rare and so uniquely distinctive, and my letter to him so revealing (ahem!), that he did not hesitate to identify this one as a certain rare species of midget mayfly (giving me the impressive Latin name and stressing that it shouldn't be confused with common midges, which are *not* mayflies) noted chiefly for its affinity for extremely cold fresh water accompanied by loads of overripe silt—which twin distinctions Frenchman's, of course, possessed just oodles and oodles of.

Other distinctions, he explained, were the insect's unusually long hatching period, sometimes running for weeks; its further post-hatching lingering on the water; and, above all, its eccentric, skeetering, up-and-down movement upon the surface. Few "normal" insect species were ever found where my Dancing Fly dwelt, he further explained, because so few of the former could live in such an environment while the latter couldn't seem to anywhere else.

There was another big splash at the hot spot and so, with trembling hands, I tied on the professor's imitation for the first big test. As I did so I saw in the clear daylight that only superficially did it resemble the real Dancing Fly, having indeed at its center the same darkish furry balled look but lacking the tiny wings. Beyond this wingless center I saw protruding an almost invisible pattern of fine hairy tendrils of a neutral color. These, his letter explained, gave his imitation the buoyancy subtly calculated to make it dance—but only, mind, if I explicitly followed his accompanying directions.

Two fish rolled suddenly at the same hot spot and, my heart pounding, I jumped up and started feeding out line and, after a quick backward glance, prepared to launch the great experiment.

Out, out flew my line with the speed of a dart and then I saw my leader lazily folding forward and, last of all, the professor's Dancing Fly floating down and gently kissing the surface.

Nothing happened, as the professor had warned, so, still following directions, I waited a full minute before making any move, listening only to my thumping heart. Then, slowly raising my rod tip to about 9 o'clock (as old-time fly-casting directions so quaintly used to put it), I took up the slack between me and my fly. Then, still following directions, I brought my rod tip down sharply, almost slapping the surface, and my line rippled out like a fleeing serpent and, as the serpent gradually disappeared, lo, before my very eyes my fly began merrily to dance, up and down, up and down . . .

"One fly gone and 23 to go!" I yelped when, all in one blinding flash, a glorious trout rose and engulfed my fly and I reared back like a goosed shot-putter and—*ping!*—found myself gloriously cleaned out.

Shortly after five I found Timmy and Pinky waiting for me on the granite bluff, standing before a little fire, both of them unrigged and champing to leave.

"Hi," I greeted them cheerily. "How's the old luck?"

"Can't you tell by lookin'?" a dejected Timmy said.

"Same old nonsense," Pinky said, making a face. "Not really a big rise but slow and steady all day, some of 'em dandies." He widened his hands. "But good ol' Frenchman's, true to tradition, turned us down cold. How about you, smiley?"

"I'll show you," I said, my grin widening, and I found a mossy spot and undid my creel and poured out a small avalanche of glistening trout running from ten to 14 inches. "Thought I'd keep a few on account of it's the first day and all and further I had no live trap."

"Of course you hadda keep a few," Timmy murmured, still staring and then gesturing, "but tell me, did you do all *this* with that one little Adams you got on?"

"Mostly," I lied steadily. "But that next biggest one there came on one of your own small weighted Muddlers," I ran on, piling on the falsehoods, at the same time telling myself that after all I'd done nothing more than my pals could have done on their own with a little imagination. Moreover, I further moralized, since actual money now rode on the result, why should such a dedicated free-enterpriser as I be expected to share a secret that might cost him dough?

Pinky made the first move, fumbling in his jumper and handing over a crisp new bill. "Hope you got change for a ten," he said.

"Sure thing," I said, making change deftly as a carnival barker.

"So the little Adams turned the trick, eh?" Timmy said, thrusting a wad of wrinkled ones at me along with a piercing glance.

"Sure did," I said, stashing my winnings and gathering up my fish. "But, who knows, maybe tomorrow it'll be something else," I philosophized. "Part of the challenge of the place, don't you think?"

"Also its charm," Timmy said, rubbing the stubble on his chin. "Well, at least tomorrow is another challenging day, so let's get the hell outa here and get some sleep."

My luck held miraculously on succeeding days at Frenchman's. In fact I kept winning so monotonously that it got so at quitting time the only question became not whether I might win but whether one or both of my pigeons would have to pay. Meanwhile I wrote the good professor an ecstatic letter telling him all about my wild success with his fly. In it I also wondered if he might find time to tie up a few more. And since in his earlier letter he had said he never tied commercially, I cagily enclosed a rather handsome contribution (out of my winnings!) to his college library.

That summer, with the aid of my trusty live trap—which I now kept stashed at the dam—I caught far more lovely trout than ever I took home. This Spartan self-denial I exercised largely for sporting reasons, of course, but I must confess that one tiny factor might have been that to do otherwise was akin to robbing one's own piggy bank.

Of course occasionally there were those inevitable days when none of us qualified for the bet, when indeed one found oneself wondering by day's end if the temperamental place still harbored any trout. On such days I usually sorted out my fly boxes or rearranged the unused decoy flies on my drying pad (for the further confusion of Timmy and Pinky, of course) and sometimes even visited my pigeons at their favorite spots—always ostentatiously sporting almost any fly but my secret pet.

One day about mid-June my pals almost caught me flat-footed. I'd just cast out my secret weapon and was about to make it go into its dance when I heard a twig snap behind me, followed by a muffled curse. So quick, without turning, I whipped in my fly and snipped off and stashed my treasure and was absorbedly tying on a No. 18 Jassid when Timmy and Pinky popped up behind me.

"Oh, you guys sure startled me!" I squealed and giggled like a girl, elaborately surprised. "Out for a little stroll, boys, or just drop by to spy on the master angler?"

"Little of both," Timmy said, squinting. "What's that you got tied on?"

"Orange-bodied Jassid," I said, showing him.

"Thought I just saw you changing flies," Timmy persisted. "What'd you take off?"

"Same favorite li'l old Adams, but it seems to lack its magic touch today," I lied without blushing. "See," I ran on, displaying my sheepskin lapel pad like a convention badge, "It's still drying out. What's up? You boys ready to quit?"

"Still got about an hour to go," Pinky said after shooting his cuff and consulting his wrist. "Just checking to make sure you weren't being seduced by a nearsighted mermaid. Have any luck?"

"Pretty slow today," I said, shaking my head. "No seduction offers and caught only one barely 12-incher on the li'l ol' Adams."

"Still got us beat," Pinky said with a sigh. "Neither of us has caught even one regular keeper. We really came to take lessons from the master —that's if the tuition's right."

"Wanna try it here?" I said, knowing they wouldn't, making as though to reel in and generously move aside.

"Hell no, man," proud Timmy growled, moving on upstream. "Just checkin' to see if some lunker trout had mercifully pulled you in but no such luck."

It would be too cruel and too boring to recount all the trout I caught that summer and all the wagers I won. Up until August, in fact, neither Timmy nor Pinky had won a single bet, incredible as that may seem, against such crafty old fishing hands. Indeed on those few occasions when one did catch a qualifier it simply meant double trouble for the other since under our ground rules he then paid the full shot. Modesty compels me simply to say that by the time August rolled around I'd already won the price of a new fly rod and had my eyes covetously glued on some elegant felt soles. Then on the first day of August—"black August," I came to call it—like a bolt out of the blue, calamity struck—*bang, bang*—twice in quick succession.

First I lost *all* my precious Dancing Flies—a zipper had worked open and (while naturally nothing else did) out popped their special box. Second, this seemed to be the signal for twin disaster: overnight Timmy's and Pinky's own luck soared off into space. The details are too horrifying, so I'll spare them, but during the first days of my black August I lost half a dozen double bets in as many days. Three of these melancholy days I spent virtually on my benumbed hands and knees vainly scouring the chilly bog for my lost treasures—and the next three fighting the wretched summer cold I'd caught for my pains.

The following week I had a brief financial reprieve, spending most of it in bed recovering from my cold and cursing my stupidity in failing to cache at least one sample fly safely at home. My main exercise that week consisted in tottering to the phone trying to reach my professor and plead for replacements. "Sorry, but that line is temporarily disconnected," a taped voice of doom kept monotonously parroting. But still I kept trying until a cheery postcard from Canada broke the bad news: my errant professor was off on an extended field and fishing trip there and wished me good health, tight lines and aloha—whereupon I had a relapse.

It was nearly mid-August before I rejoined the boys at Frenchman's, considerably more wan if not wiser, and proudly spurned their offer to call all bets off until I felt less rocky.

"Thanks, chums," I said, "but my fragile health may be just the handicap you've needed."

"Your dough," Pinky said, shrugging. "Anyway we offered, and maybe your luck will turn."

"You haven't won yet," I said, heading downhill and shakily groping my way toward the dam—after checking all zippers. There I tried out some dainty new spiders I'd got hold of locally, and while they danced fairly well, they simply didn't *look* like the Dancing Fly—which of course the smart trout at Frenchman's divined before ever they landed.

Pinky was dead right in his intuition that my luck might turn. It did, all right—it steadily turned worse. For the next nine days running, although I fished as if my life depended on it, I lost nine straight bets—all of them double. Nothing seemed to work. Though twice I managed to catch decent qualifying trout, both times during the final calibration scene Timmy's and Pinky's challengers nosed mine out. In fact so monotonously did they split my boodle, along with little pieces of my heart—one day Timmy, the next day Pinky—that it looked almost as if they'd planned it that way.

On the tenth day a mounting curiousity, mingled with a dash of cupidity, overcame my pride, and along about mid-afternoon I deserted my favorite dam and sashayed upstream to take a look. While I won't quite say I meant to spy on my pals, I did move with extra care, avoiding the more open bog and taking the granite ridge instead, which just happened to have more cover.

My first inkling that something might be afoot was when I peered down looking for Pinky and discovered he was not at his favorite "Big Spring," where he usually remained glued. Shrugging, I pushed on up the ridge to go discreetly visit little Timmy at his favorite "Top Log." When I got there, peeking from behind a protective balsam, I saw little Timmy was there, all right, but, contrary to his usual practice, fishing from the heavily forested far side, our spare wading float parked on shore beside him.

"My, my," I murmured to myself, noting the tall wall of spruces virtually nudging his back. "How the hell does the man ever make a decent cast?"

Peering closer I next picked up the missing Pinky standing on the near, or bog, side, right down below me, also busily fishing Timmy's same coveted area from the opposite side. But ever fishing the same place at the same time whatever angle was such a startling procedure for any of us, all prickly loners, that on a hunch I refrained from hailing them, as I was momentarily tempted, and instead silently withdrew behind my balsam.

It was well I did because what I next witnessed was the strangest sight I've ever seen out fishing, and I've beheld some quaking dandies: two fishermen, their rods pointed straight out at each other across the intervening 70-odd feet of open water, like duelists with bamboo weapons, slowly raising and lowering their rods in rhythmic unison, up and down, faster, ever faster. As I gaped, for a resentful instant I thought they were stealing my rippling-line stuff. But no, for as I leaned farther out for a better look I saw that, whatever in hell else they were up to, their two lines seemed most definitely joined.

Just then a gorgeous trout rose and struck savagely at one or the other of their flies, which I could not tell, and I almost fell off the cliff when, amidst all the wild threshing, I saw *both* fly rods hooped and vibrating from the strain. Retreating quickly behind my tree I froze in my tracks when I heard the following strange dialogue:

"Whose turn to reel in?" Pinky called across to Timmy in a sort of cross between a hoarse whisper and a strangled shout.

"Yours," Timmy hollered back in the same muffled fashion. "I landed the last dandy, remember?"

Then before my incredulous gaze I beheld Pinky reeling in a superb trout while Timmy's reel fairly sang as he busily stripped off line down to the backing. "Good God," I murmured weakly as the truth suddenly dawned: *my pals' leaders were not only joined but they were fishing the very same fly!*

I heard myself sort of moaning when next I saw Pinky coolly land

and release at least a 12-inch dandy, just like that, at the same time hollering, "Whaddya know—another fightin' rascal just busted another hook."

Held now in a fiend's clutch, I watched, fascinated, as Pinky tied on a fresh fly, blew on it daintily and hollered "Ready?"

Timmy nodded and this time Pinky paid out line while Timmy busily reeled in until I saw both lines held taut and a solitary fly dangling from its dropper, poised directly over Timmy's hot spot.

"Say when," Pinky hollered.

"When," Timmy hollered back.

Then, while I watched with glazed eyes, my pals began raising and lowering their rod tips in stately unison, up and down, up and down, faster and faster, while their little fly dapped the surface, first lightly here, then over there, all the while ever so gaily prancing and dancing and soon outdoing even *the* Dancing Fly itself.

"A little to your right," Timmy called, and Pinky moved a little to his right. I was dazedly rubbing my eyes with the back of my hand when I heard a watery explosion and then Pinky laughing and hollering, "Cleaned out our last pattern, Timmy, so I guess you gotta tie some more."

"Near quittin' time anyway," Timmy called back. "Better we get movin' before our pigeon does."

"Pigeon has already moved!" I hollered, popping out from behind my balsam and standing with proudly folded arms. "And thanks awfully, fellas, for reminding me there's more than one way to skin a cat."

Pinky wheeled and waved at me and sedately tipped his hat. "Hi!" he hollered. "You been eavesdropping up there very long?"

"Frenchman's biggest pigeon has seen all and heard all!" I cupped my hands and bawled like a train announcer in an empty station, my words echoing and echoing . . .

When finally they joined me up on the ridge and I'd resignedly paid off Pinky his double bet—it being, as I'd guessed, *his* turn to win—I cleared my throat and managed to inquire without my voice cracking just what magic fly had turned the trick.

"Your little Adams, of course," Timmy said.

"*My* little Adams?" I repeated dully, momentarily forgetting.

"Sure, sure, the very same fly you so generously told us about weeks ago but we so foolishly wouldn't believe you until approaching insolvency and desperation drove us to it." He wagged his head. "Trout simply go nuts over it, especially when it goes into its polka."

"Tell me," I murmured when I was able to go on, "how in the world did you ever dream up your astonishing joined-leader dropper-fly ploy? Or did you run across it somewhere?"

"Hell no," Timmy said. "One day I simply remembered Pinky's joshing remark last year about dapping flies from a balloon."

"I don't see the connection."

"Well, I figured ballooning really *was* one way to suspend a fly and also make it dance, however awkward." Timmy spread his hands. "Then I got to thinkin' about other possible simpler ways to do the same thing—an' it took no great burst of Yankee ingenuity to come up with what you just seen."

"You're way too modest, Timmy," I said fervently. "I've been fishing ever since I shed diapers and never have I seen or read or so much as heard of such a fantastic thing in all the ancient lore of angling. Why, it could revolutionize fishing—either that or ruin it." I wagged my head. "You— you ought to be in Congress, man."

"Don't get nasty."

"One more thing," I persisted weakly. "How do you guys ever get the damn leaders joined in the first place, fishing from opposite sides? Sounds like a real big deal."

"Easy, man," Timmy said. "When we start fishing one of us casts a big bushy dry fly out maybe 30–40 feet, somewhat at an angle, then the opposite guy pastes out a weighted nymph *over* the first cast and then we both tighten and—bingo—the flies naturally hook and one of us simply reels in."

"But then you gotta tie on a dropper and all that," I persisted, morbidly determined to learn just how far I had been taken.

"No," Timmy said. "One of us keeps a permanent dropper on his leader, tied up about a foot or so. So all the reeler-in has to do is remove the old flies, join the two leaders, clap on a li'l ol' Adams—an' we're all set." He sighed. "Actually it's kinda like shootin' fish in a rain barrel an' Pinky an' I been talkin' lately about goin' it alone."

"I've not only been taken but took," I said as I stared at the little man and wagged my head. "Indeed there *is* more than one way to skin a cat," I dully repeated, screwing my rod case shut and hoisting my pack with a sigh.

"You're dead right there, pard," Timmy agreed, giving me a quirky smile and a wink, "just as maybe there's more'n one way to dance a fly."

"So I see," I said, for I saw.

FISHING WILD

Ted Williams

An outstanding outdoor writer tells what it was like
to fish secret backcountry ponds in Maine,
restricted to fly only. (May 1976)

DOWN IN Maine, when they say "fly-fishing only" they mean fishing only the way a gentleman would fish, for fish only a gentleman would fish for. In other words, casting dry flies to trout or salmon and—if one must —wets, too, though the latter act is regarded as questionable at best, somewhat akin to picking up chicken wings with one's fingers.

If you troll a fly on fly-fishing-only water or even drag a sloppy backcast with the wind, there is always the possibility that a Maine warden will pop out at you from the bank cover. Hidden, they will watch you for hours the way eagles watch dead deer. For them there is no such thing as a "secret" pond, and they think nothing of hoofing five miles through thick woods.

Most of the East's truly great brook trout water is in Maine, and most of that is restricted to fly-fishing. There are those who regard fly-fishing-only regulations as patently un-American. It is easy and, I confess, rather fun to infuriate them with a charade of country-club snobbery. They wax wild and irrational, spewing Jeffersonian democracy. Most of them are gentle, beautifully innocent souls, and I am burdened with the lasting shame of having baited them. Still, I can't help noticing them among the opening-day horde that waves stubby, stout-lined spinning rods and vies gull-like for domestic trout that the state doles out each spring like so many haddock heads. In no way do I mean to assert that such carnivalizing is wrong, but in no way should it be confused with trout fishing.

Ironically, few vociferous critics of fly-fishing-only have ever fly-fished themselves, or at least experienced fly-fishing as an art form. Few have ever navigated through the big woods to fish a real trout pond for real trout. And yet they rail against the state for pandering to "blue-blooded elitists," charging that the ponds are restricted because they are great, never considering the possibility, and indeed the fact, that they are great because they are restricted. They have difficulty in understanding, for instance, that flies simply do not kill trout and that it serves little purpose to release fish whose gullets or gills have recently been festooned with big, thick-wired hooks. Nor do they easily understand that ten fly-fishermen can work an evening rise together (if they have to) and that one spincaster can slosh along, launch a door hinge into the middle of things and send every trout in the pool screaming for cover. Too much of any good thing is bad. This is a fundamental law of the cosmos that may be applied to everything from waffles to personal liberty.

I began fly-fishing Maine trout as an errant freshman at Colby College in Waterville. When the willows began to yellow along Johnson Pond, we would shake the leaders from our dusty books and jeep northward to begin what I considered then and consider now to be the most valuable part of our education.

We had our favorite spots which we renamed as a precaution against careless barroom conversation. There was "Split-Mountain Sump," "Boty" and, most treasured of all, "Secret Pond" within a morning's walk of the fabled St. John River. The best was always "secret" something. The finest grouse covert we ever found, a popple-laced tote road teaming with "pat'ridges," was known around Waterville (after we'd graduated of course) as "Secret Road." The name stuck until 1973 when the pulpmen thoughtfully moonscaped it.

We discovered Secret Pond the same way we discovered all our ponds—scowling over a topo late into the night and checking ponds in steeply contoured, roadless watersheds against the list of fly-fishing-only ponds in the booklet that comes with your fishing license.

I cannot, of course, tell you the real names of any of the ponds we fished or fish. Not only would it be a nefarious offense against common angling decency, it would ruin your fun. Choosing a pond for yourself, finding your way into it and emerging full-creeled from the wilderness is all part of the magic that makes Downeast fly-fishing the poignant and intensely personal experience it is. Though my fishing accomplices will furiously deny it, the hard truth is that the trouting in our ponds was, and is, not a whit better than the trouting in most of Maine's 153 fly-fishing-only ponds. All have healthy populations of squaretails that, thanks to flies-only and remote settings, are not significantly affected by fishing pressure. On many, one can fish a whole season without seeing a dozen anglers.

Finding your own pond in Maine is like finding your own woman. Basically, they're all put together the same way, but you become attached to a particular one for her individual topography. After you have lived with a few (ponds that is) you will be able to identify subtle variations in the trout from each. Split-Mountain Sump's, as I recall, were plump and black, Boty's sleek and silvery, Secret Pond's very orange. Obviously, some differences reflect the physiological response of the individual to his environment, but others reflect the evolutionary response of a population. Wisely, Maine has never stocked any of her truly wilderness trout ponds. To do so could bring about the destruction of a pond's genetic identity established over millennia. The trout inhabiting such ponds are uniquely suited to their particular environments as are no other trout on earth.

I remember vividly the first day I fished Secret Pond. I was with my old roommate, Bob Daviau, a lifelong resident of Waterville who believes in his heart that Maine is supported by giant tortoises and that her borders fall away into primal chaos. Bob had pilfered the pond from his father, Jerome, one of Maine's renowned fly-fishermen, an attorney and author of *Maine's Lifeblood*—an exposé of the paper industry's hog-greedy assault on the state's rivers and watersheds and of the spineless politicians who have permitted it.

Bob and I packed our gear late into the crisp June night, then left without having slept. All the way up, he was swearing me to secrecy. Mostly, he was afraid of his father's finding out he had betrayed the pond to an out-of-stater. An in-stater would have been bad enough—grounds for disownment at the least—but an *out-of-stater*. It was unspeakably heinous. I was not to let on I had even fished with Bob. And *never*, under any circumstances, was I *ever* to tell *anyone*, even my wife, should I ever have one, the location of Secret Pond.

In the predawn, with northern lights still flickering ahead of us, we pulled onto a rough logging road and jounced 20 miles into black wilderness. A woodland jumping mouse bounced down the headlight beam like a miniature kangaroo. Wood thrushes fluttered up like moths. We saw the glowing eyes and frozen silhouettes of deer, and once a young moose crossed casually in front of us.

We hid the jeep behind dripping spruces, brilliant in the breaking dawn. For long seconds, we inhaled the heady fragrance of balsam and wet, fresh earth, then walked backward into the woods, sweeping away our spoor with spruce bows. After the first blowdown, we turned and settled down to a fast-clipped hike over two miles of ancient, ingrown tote road, up one mountain, down another and, finally, by compass through thick trailless puckerbrush.

We panted over a ridge, and there it was, rippling here and there in the morning wind, but mostly dark green and glassy in the shadow of protecting conifers.

I took a deep, steadying breath and started rigging my fly rod. Then we walked quickly to the rafts—two ponderous affairs with precarious birch-limb seats and long poles of black spruce.

Rafts are a tradition on Maine's fly-fishing-only ponds. They last about eight years, then someone makes another pair. Secret Pond has probably a dozen devotees who know each other only vaguely but who are strangely close in a common love for the pond and a knowledge that they are among the very, very few who have come to understand the meaning of the Maine woods. When someone builds a raft, it goes without saying that it belongs to everybody. Usually, there are two just in case there's someone in ahead of you, though it rarely happens.

Bob set me up near some dry-ki in the spring hole, and, with the kind of certainty that makes Downeasters impossible to argue with, announced that we'd really be wasting our time until 9 a.m. when "she turns on like an alarm clock." With that he poled for the big pond, back through the shallow thoroughfare whose mud bottom was a mass of moose prints, some still cloudy.

I started fishing grasshoppers on top. ("Anybody who don't go into them woods with a pocketful of grasshoppers ain't been fly-fishin' in Maine," I was once informed.) For half an hour, I bounced them off the dry-ki and skittered them around, so that they sent inviting little circles radiating out to blend into the moss-lined banks. Ravens croaked. After a long squint skyward I spotted them, two pencil dots on unbroken blue. Over on the big pond I could see a pair of loons and, in a cove near the beaver house, Daviau casting rhythmically. I had to admit that he handled a fly rod well. His backcasts were long and slow and powerful. They never even nicked the surface.

Without changing the 6X leader, I tied on a little Mickey Finn. On the third cast, a big squaretail floated up through ten feet of transparent spring water, sliced the surface like a shark and sucked in the fly a rod-length from the raft. I struck, and he bored deep.

The winter had been long, and I rejoiced in this strange rite of spring—the sight and the feel of an arching rod, the tip dancing to the surface and below, and the yellow line slipping irresistibly down until it faded into dark refractions. I could feel heat between my thumb and fore-finger, then the lump of the backing splice. I turned him with the splice halfway through the guides, marveling at his strength. At last I could see him spinning slow figure eights under the raft with two lesser trout attending on either flank like pilotfish. A minute later, I was gliding him into the wooden landing net. A gaudy cock fish, bass-fat and long as my forearm. I looked at my watch. It was 9 a.m.

The trout came fast for the rest of the morning, smaller than the first but all bright and in superb condition. Once, during that magic first day when I lay on the raft, viewing the bottom through cupped hands, feeling my belly tighten as the water between the logs soaked into my shirt, I saw something I have never seen before or since. A school of brook trout, perhaps 100, from a few ounces to several pounds, flowing along in close formation halfway between the surface and the bottom.

By noon, we had killed all the trout we could use and had released many more. There had even been a brief hatch of midges, and we had had a few minutes of fast action on top with No. 18 Black Gnats. For once we were sated.

We poled to shore and anchored the rafts by pushing the poles between the logs and into the mud bottom. We hung on them so that they sunk in another foot, then swung ourselves onto the bank.

In a spruce-needled clearing, we munched sandwiches and sucked water from an icy brooklet black with trout fry, just touching the surface with our lips so as not to disturb the bottom silt.

Northern Maine is among America's last big tracts of wild land. It exists in its present form not because its residents differ significantly from other Americans in their feelings toward the land, but simply because they are few in number. In Maine, as elsewhere in the U.S., rivers, lakes and forests are just commodities to be disposed of whenever the economic whims of special interests dictate.

If the Army Corps of Engineers gets its way, 90,000 acres of Maine wilderness, including the upper St. John River—one of the nation's last blue-ribbon brook trout streams—and its network of trout-filled tributaries will be drowned. Capitalizing on the hysteria brought on by the contrived gasoline shortage, the artful Engineers managed to wangle the support of many otherwise environmentally responsible legislators for this decade-old boondoggle, the annual scuttling of which had become a House tradition.

Actually, the two dams at Dickey and Lincoln, which would cost us working folk at least $1 billion, could not even provide a pathetic 1 percent of New England's energy needs.

Residents of the village of Fort Kent, which nestles deliquently into the St. John flood plain just north of Eagle Lake, are eager for their little share of the federal pork the project is supposed to pump into Maine. They maintain that the dams are necessary to protect them from spring floods, though the Corps used to say all they needed was a $500,000 dike. It would be far cheaper for us to allow the river to reclaim its ancient flood plain and buy each villager a San-Clemente-style mansion in the state of his choice.

Massachusetts Congressman Silvio C. Conte, who led two unsuccessful floor fights to kill appropriations for preconstruction planning, calls regionalism the biggest problem he has faced in educating the public to the real costs of the Dickey-Lincoln dams.

"Many residents of Maine think the dams are going to be a cure-all for their problems," he says. "'Who are you from Massachusetts coming up here to tell us what to do with our river?' they say. What these people don't realize is it's not just their river; it belongs to the whole country. It's yours and mine, and once it's gone, it's gone forever."

According to former Massachusetts Fish and Game Director James M. Shepard, this is what the Dickey-Lincoln dams will cost America: "90,000 acres of fabulously productive wildlife habitat supporting bald eagles, moose, an estimated 2200 deer (enough to provide 30,000 hunter days per season), black bear, ruffed grouse, woodcock, thousands upon thousands of woodland birds (especially warblers); 17,600 acres of top-quality deer yards vital to deer miles away from the project area, 2800 acres of prime waterfowl breeding ground which unleashes on the Atlantic Flyway a steady stream of blacks, woodies, blue-winged teal and ringnecks; about 50 miles of super brookie fishing on the Big and Little Black rivers and many miles of smaller but equally productive feeder streams; about 57 miles of upper St. John which now offers wild trouting and canoeing at its absolute best; the natural beauty and wilderness value shattered by 150 miles of new power lines; much of beautiful Deboulie Mountain with its 24 pristine trout ponds. (The mountain will be carved up for fill. To give you an idea of how much will be needed, the dam at Dickey will be 1¾ miles long, 300 feet high and substantially bigger than Egypt's infamous Aswan Dam.) Finally, a timber resource yielding $666,000 a year will be drowned, and 30,000 acres of ugly 'bathtub ring' intermittently exposed as the reservoir fluctuates."

Secret Pond and the vast wilderness that embraces it may die with the St. John. But one thing Congress and the Corps cannot take from me is the memory of that first day with Bob Daviau—how we caught orange, porcelain-finned brookies until our wrists ached. How we cleaned them by the beaver-blocked outlet and packed them away in corn snow and sphagnum moss. How we lay on our backs, catnapping and listening to the warblers rustling through the spruce trees. And how we trudged out in the late afternoon sun with our jackets tied around our waists, spitting blackflies and saying nothing because Secret Pond and the sacred Maine woods had said it all.

THE EMPEROR'S NEW FLY

Nick Lyons

*Not all fishing forays end in success. Even though
the conditions were perfect, this one concluded in
mysterious failure. (January 1977)*

MICHAEL was an hour late. It was all right because he's often late, and the fishing didn't start, he had said, until "very late in the day." Then he became two hours late and it was ten o'clock. By the time his dark-blue Pontiac rounded the corner of my city block, I would have given up the trip and gone back to bed had my expectations not been so high.

We were going to fish the big Delaware for rainbows with Ed Van Put, and I'd been looking forward to the trip for weeks.

As we headed out over the George Washington Bridge, up the Palisades Expressway, Michael told me he'd left the car in front of his apartment building for a few moments to go back for some forgotten equipment. When he returned, the car was being lifted behind a police tow truck. His protestations were futile. He had to follow the truck by cab to the city lot and pay a $75 fine to retrieve it. One never extricates oneself from the city easily. It must love us too well.

Well, there was still a long, rich day ahead of us and those muscular rainbows Michael had described danced in my imagination. I speculated, as we drove, that for the overworked inner-city angler fishing often depends less on what than who you know.

No more, for me, the long disastrous escapes from the city—driving hundreds of miles to barren water, meeting crowds or poor conditions, fishing an hour too late or leaving an hour too early, arriving a day after construction started upstream and the water was in cocoa-colored spate. No more the exhaustion and frustration and discovery, three hours from New York, that what I'd labored so hard to get was not really there.

What with the busyness of urban life and the complexity of arranging even the shortest break, I'd fished too little. And when I did, something always went wrong. No more of that.

As an editor of angling books I was corresponding with such resident experts as Art Flick in West Kill, New York; Frank Woolner in Massachusetts; and Charlie Brooks in West Yellowstone. Hearing and reading so much about their successes whetted my desire to be out more. When suddenly my angling success took a dramatic swing upward I thought some of their words had rubbed off on me. Later I had to admit the source of my triumphs lay elsewhere.

Instead of trips stolen randomly from the maelstrom of the city, I selectively made those long upcountry pilgrimages to Vermont or the Catskills only when induced by an authority.

"Hi, Nick, my boy," came Art Flick's hearty voice on the phone. "They started coming off today. You ought to get up within the next few days while they're still strong. The 'Kill eight miles below the bridge, above Old Oak Pool. I'll be there tomorrow at noon if you want to meet me."

"They" were the Hendricksons. It was early May and they came off about midday. Hadn't I reissued Art's little *Streamside Guide to Naturals and Their Imitations*? And the spot pinpointed? And the master near at hand? An offer too good to refuse.

So I made the emergency preparations, drove up the next day, and at 1:30, just like the book says, the Hendricksons began to hatch and the fish rise. I was actually there, at the right place and right time, with the guy who wrote the book and who had given me some of his Red Quills, which imitate the male of the species—as all of the initiate know. Who couldn't have caught fish? Even I caught a few.

With that kind of advice, one forgoes the sage adage that the best time to fish is when you can. The best time to fish is when Art Flick tells you to fish.

This remarkable principle worked when I managed a long-overdue trip out West and Charlie Brooks, whose book *The Trout and the Stream* I was preparing for publication, put me on the Yellowstone River during a tremendous caddis hatch which brought literally thousands of trout to the feast. They began to appear just as we arrived, as if his lifted rod indicated the music should commence. Up and down the river, as far as I could see, hefty cutthroats were rising freely in the clear, long glides. I had fished alone in that trout Mecca for three days without taking more than a few miserably small rainbows. This was awesome.

I was again there at the right time and place, with the right caddis imitation, and though the fish-expert's editor disgraced himself by first putting a fly in a big hemlock, then another in the hemlock, then one in his ear (which Charlie hauled out with a brisk straight tug of the pliers—"The way we do it out here!"), I caught more trout in two hours than I'd caught in the previous five years. These cutthroats were 14 to 17 inches.

Clearly I had the system beat, the inscrutable mysteries of trout fishing solved. Or thought I had.

When Frank Woolner, the swami of the surf, advised me that stripers and blues were heavy in the rip off Provincetown, and sent pictures to prove it, I literally threw all my manuscripts onto the shelves and my family into the car on a few hours notice. I told my wife and children only that they were getting an unexpected Cape Cod vacation. We were hit by the worst hurricane in years. I can't blame Frank. It was only those old Furies of Fate, pricking my cockiness.

For years I heard rumors about the increasingly good fishing for large rainbows in the Delaware, and the name Ed Van Put came up repeatedly. As a Catskill-region fish and wildlife technician, he was a knowledgeable biologist as well as an angler with regular access and knowledge of the river. Michael had met him, and that's why we were going: to be taken by Ed to one of the best pools on the Delaware.

There were a few chores first: to visit a house Michael might want to rent, then over to Len Wright's cabin on the Neversink, to pick him up. By the time we finally met Ed at four o'clock at the Roscoe Diner, I was exhausted; it had been eight hours since I'd officially started this fishing trip, and though the company was good, I was anxious to be on the water. I always am. If I fish a million times, it will never be to satiety; I will always shiver with expectation before I fish.

It had started to rain—first steadily, then fiercely, then not at all, then steadily again. We packed into two cars and Michael followed Ed along

Route 17 to the Delaware. An hour later, about five o'clock, we turned down a dead-end dirt road, stopped, stretched, suited up and headed for the river.

What a river! Its huge sweeping turns were more than a half-mile long; where we came out of the woods, there was nothing more human to be seen than an old railroad track. Aspen, willows, birch and alder graced the far side of the river. Some rhododendron was in bloom. This was a gloriously wild stretch, equal to anything I'd seen out West.

We marched slowly down the tracks, in the rain, watching the water constantly. This was as lovely a stretch of river as I could remember ever having seen. Ed said it would be lovelier if reservior people let out a steady flow of cold water from the bottom of Cannonsville and Pepacton. He said that in another week or so the water would become so warm that fishing would be impossible and fish might die. It sounded criminal.

"What's the drill?" Len asked when we got to the bend Ed wanted to fish.

An Adams or Grey Fox Variant, about size No. 16, would be best; we might pick up a fish or two during the next hour or so, but the real fishing would start at dusk. Ed did better than catch a fish or two. In ten minutes he was into a really large rainbow that took him into his backing. Then he had another on, then another. Earlier he told me he had caught more than 200 rainbows each of the past two years, most of them over 15 inches and at least 40 or 50 over 18. Today, no one else caught even a chub.

I fished from the tail of the sweeping pool up into the run where the current struggled to keep its definition, then into the fast, choppy water, then into the head of the riffle—thinking that the rainbows might go into the fastest water during the day.

The trouble was, besides not seeing a fish—except those on Ed's line—I couldn't keep a cigar lit. Either I would get one started and have the rain snuff it out a moment later, or I would spend ten minutes trying fruitlessly to light a soggy cigar with damp matches. I fish better with a lit cigar; some people fish better with talent.

I fished downstream diligently with a large Whitlock bronze nymph and watched Ed catch another muscular rainbow. He casts an immaculately slow and graceful line, and I had the distinct impression he was also doing something I didn't see—like humming or whistling to these old friends to perform for the crowd.

As for me, I sloshed about despondently, bone-tired now, slashing the water to a froth, getting wetter by the minute, wondering precisely why I wasn't home reading Jane Austen or Henry James instead of making such a fool of myself. This was strictly a regression.

But finally, at about 8:40, just after the light grew dim, two splendid events took place: the rain stopped and the fish began to rise steadily, dozens of them. I promptly lit a new cigar, clipped off my large nymph and rummaged in one of my fly boxes for a No. 16 Adams. Well, I was going to make a day of it at last—or at least 15 minutes of it. I could *taste* the rise and run of one of those sleek rainbows.

My hands began to tremble. All the fever and expectation returned; all fatigue vanished. I fumbled with the fly, couldn't get the leader point through the eye of the hook, raised the fly against the dun sky, manipulated the thin monofilament with the deftness of a surgeon and got the pesky thing done. It was 8:45. And nearly dark.

The circles—rhythmic and gentle—continued to spread in the flat water where the current widened. Ed was at my left shoulder now, willing to forgo these fine last moments of the day so he could advise me. A saint.

"Cast to specific rises, Nick—as delicately as possible. Some of these are really big fish. Strike them lightly."

With not a second to lose, I took my dry-fly spray from my vest, held the Adams up near my face, pressed the plunger, and went stingingly blind. The little hole had been pointed in the wrong direction: I'd given myself a triple shot of fly dope in the eyes and, even after I doused them with a bit of the Delaware, I could barely see.

But I squinted bravely, puffed with vigor on my cigar—whose tip now glowed like a hot little coal in the dark—and cast in the general direction Ed was pointing.

"That looked about right," he said as I laid out a surprisingly accurate cast to one of the inviting circles. "Can't imagine why he didn't take it."

When I miraculously repeated the feat, he said: "They're awfully picky sometimes. What have you got on?"

"A 16 Adams."

"That *ought* to do it."

Another cast—my third good one in a row, a new record. It was a magical, witching moment—the far bank receding in the swirling mists, the river sounds filling my ears, my squinting eyes seeing only that faint multitude of spreading circles. I could not see my fly but I knew where it was by estimating the distance from the end of my bright-yellow fly line.

Nothing.

"Strange," said Ed.

"Maybe this time."

Still nothing—and nothing for the next ten minutes, when a moonless sky finally rang down the curtain. We headed back up the railroad tracks to the cars.

In the headlights, I found a strange sight, which I took the liberty of not reporting to my fellow anglers. There was no fly on my leader. There was only a blackened, melted end—as if it might have been burned through by a cigar.

Michael and I made the long trip back in silence. Had I really fished through the entire rise, those 20 minutes I'd waited for all day, with no fly? No doubt.

My face still smarted in the dark car with embarrassment, my eyes still stung. I tried to keep my eyelids from drooping, and I tried to talk because good talk with a good friend after a long day on a river is one of the best parts of such trips. But I was bushed.

I closed my eyes and dreamed of muscular rainbows dimpling to the No. 16 Adams, then skyrocketing out and taking me into the backing. That huge bend in the river was alive with rising fish and each cast was true. I heard Ed say, "They're awfully picky sometimes. What have you got on?"

And I answered, moaning, knowing I had developed a pattern even the experts had never thought of, "The emperor's new fly." (*With apologies to Hans Christian Andersen.*)

BRIGHT FLIES FOR BRAWLING SHAD

Charles Waterman

This gifted outdoor writer uses flies for St. John's shad in spite of snide remarks from the spinners and trollers. (December 1978)

"THAT," SAID the fellow in the bow of the skiff, "is a typical Yankee fisherman. Rubber pants, funny hat, fancy vest and a fly rod."

He pulled expertly at the can of beer in one fist, waggled the spinning rod in his other hand and added, "Crazy as a bedbug!"

He was talking about me. Several generations of occasional fishermen have failed to learn that what they say loudly over the chuckle of a trolling outboard motor can be heard across a river. This guy and his partner were in a procession of boats trolling little spoons and darts for Florida's St. Johns River shad.

After that, all afternoon, I heard the same comment each time that particular boat passed. As the day and the beer wore on, the words became a little blurred but it was always the same: "Crazy as a bedbug!"

Florida isn't really much of a flyfishing state. They talk more about it than they practice it. I never invented flycasting for Florida shad but I'm one of a very few practitioners, and the fact that I'm doing something different doesn't boost my popularity. Since I'm using a different method I'm obviously a smart aleck of some kind.

"Lookit that guy way out there in the river!" yelled the jockey of one outboard cruiser that pulled a big swell. "Watch me fill his pants with water!"

And the repeated comment about what would happen if a *shad* grabbed that brim fisherman's fly was accompanied by loud laughter.

But don't let this scare you away from using flies for shad. The best flycasting for them is in places where there are no daisy chains of trollers.

Shad come up the river every winter, and the best fishing begins more than 100 miles from the river's mouth. Now and then a tourist black bass fisherman far downstream toward Jacksonville will hook a shad on a ⅝-ounce bass plug and wonder what it is, but if you want to do it right it takes little spoons, jigs and flies a little more than an inch long. Some jigs and spoons have No. 10 hooks; the flies we use are generally on No. 2s.

For some reason authors tend to associate the shad with angling poverty. I have read colorful prose calling them the "poor man's tarpon" and the "poor man's salmon." On the Pacific Coast, Russ Chatham (who loves to fish for them) calls them "stink salmon." Admittedly, a shad is no chrysanthemum but neither is a black bass or even a rainbow trout.

The first sportfishing for shad along the Atlantic seaboard was evidently with fly rods because there was no other way of throwing tiny lures. Boyd Pfeiffer, who recently wrote an informative book on the fish, says anglers were flycasting for shad in 1880 and using shallow-running flies. They probably did it long before that.

If you want to catch shad today you'll generally have to go deep for them. I don't say that the shad have changed their ways, and you can catch one occasionally near the surface. Probably there were just bigger runs in 1880. A lot of things have happened to rivers since then.

Where the water's slow and fairly shallow, a sinking-tip line will work on your fly rod but the most consistent winner is a fast sinker, either in a whole line or as a shooting head. A steelhead fisherman would feel right at home if the water were colder.

Seth Green, the genius of American fish management, introduced shad on the Pacific side in 1871 and there was commercial fishing there only eight years later. The Pacific Coasters have been strong on flyfishing for them right along. When spinning came in after World War II it crowded much of the flyfishing off the Atlantic rivers.

It was in the early 50s that I first saw Norton Webster catching shad on the St. Johns. He used a little wood and canvas boat and a light outboard, and he did his trolling with a fly rod and monofilament line. A master angler who fished over much of the United States, he is best remembered in Florida as the father of St. Johns shad fishing. The shad had been there all along but Webster really started the sport in the 40s.

He caught most of his shad trolling, I think, and he cheerfully shared all of his discoveries with any and all. That was before the fast-sinking fly line took hold and without it the flyfisherman was handicapped.

St. Johns shad history had another mover in the late Joe Cather, who originated the little Cather spoon that still takes its share. Cather, too, trolled with a fly rod and monofilament, but he would also cast the little spoons with his fly rod and a regular fly line.

When I went shad fishing with Cather he was businesslike and deft in his trolling until he had caught a fish or two—then he knew he had the right trolling speed and depth and the right spoon and jig combination, so he'd relax to watch the other boats.

The flyfishing technique that has worked best for us is borrowed from the steelheaders. In fact, the first flies that worked well were small steelhead patterns—mostly just a little bright yarn and some weight on a No. 4 hook. Orange and white proved good colors right off.

When I discovered flyfishing for Florida shad I first cast the little Cather spoons, then got in touch with Ray Donnersberger, at that time living in Chicago. Donnersberger is an intent expert who keeps hunting a new challenge, and he began breathing hard on the phone as soon as he learned the trip was to be investigative.

It developed that I had opened a Pandora's fly box because Ray tied flies and tested them until I needed sleep and began to wish the shad would go away. After he had found some flies that took fish regularly, he insisted on developing a fly of the same size that would catch no shad at all. This is the true scientific approach, but I tried to drop out after we began to score.

Some years later I got another angling tiger by the tail when I started Forrest Ware, a Florida fisheries biologist, into the flies-for-shad business. I told him where to go but he got lost and found a better place. He's caught a lot of shad and developed some fine flies.

Since a shad fly really copies nothing that swims, flies or walks, and since shad aren't supposed to feed after they begin their long trip upstream, most flies tied especially for shad are nameless. Almost anything gaudy and of the right size will work sometimes, but our most consistent winners follow a rather standard design now.

The body is tube Mylar, possibly with a shred of lead under it, and frequently there is a definite preference for one or the other color. There's a little hackle, generally white, yellow or orange, and a marabou tail in one of those colors. These components give you several combinations. Some good flies use red, but if I had to go with only one fly it would be a gold Mylar (or tinsel) body with white hackle and tail. When heavy hooks are used, there's no need for lead except in the swiftest and deepest water.

Thinking glitter was all we needed. I tried flies made of nothing but Mylar. They glittered all right but they didn't catch many fish, for me at least.

Go to the upper St. Johns, far up where the river is a web of channels with sod banks, a few tributary creeks and very few trees. Find a good curve where the dark current looks heavy, and while you make prospecting casts watch for a "washing" shad. The slow river and the occasional ghostly raft of floating hyacinths are silent but the shad make a sloshing sound when they roll or "wash." A small gar makes much the same sound so you have to watch pretty closely and detect the gar's head and tail swirls. When a small bass plops, the sound is completely different.

You can't walk to many of these places but a small flat-bottomed boat with motor is ideal, even though some of the best casting is from the sod banks or while wading. You can count on running aground, and it does little for your composure when the highway bridge from which you left is in plain sight while you lean on an oar or pushpole. Since the banks are unmarked by any kind of brush, a distant outboard boat appears to be running on dry ground, among groups of grazing cattle.

If you use a shooting head and monofilament running line on a middle-weight fly rod the way most of us do, you'll be happier wading into a few inches of water, even though there's a high and dry bank. When you wade, the monofilament feeds smoothly from the water instead of clutching grass and weeds as you cast. A whole sinking line works, too, unless you want extra distance.

In late winter and early spring, the best time, the bird life is almost overdone. Nearby herons and ibis make croaks and squawks you didn't think they were capable of, and ringnecks, teal and Florida mottled ducks

swing by at intervals. On some days there will be great flocks of white pelicans turning high in the sun or looking enormous as they come past with a watchful eye on fishermen. There are nearly always jacksnipe and coots.

Cast the fly across and perhaps a trifle upstream on a short leader and it drifts along the bottom, swinging below you. If the current is fairly swift in your bend you may not have to work the fly at all, but I generally retrieve it in foot-long pulls during the swing. There will be frequent pauses of the fly as it bumps along the bottom, and you'll set the hook frequently on a stubborn clam that clamps down on the intruder. There's not much vegetation on the best shad bottoms.

A shad strike here is dramatic only because you've built up anticipation. The line stops its downward travel and you set the hook tentatively, wondering about clams. Then the fish moves, usually starting slowly. With a trolled lure or in swift water the strike can be a jolt. Some of the runs are long and sometimes the fish jumps several times. Shad aren't noted for frantic fights but they never seem to quit entirely and just as he's almost within arm or net's reach he starts over again. The mouth is papery, and the longer he's on the more likely the hook will slip out.

Use of a landing net on shad is likely to develop into low comedy. It's embarrassing to hear a family feud erupt when one escapes from a wildly swung net aboard a trolling boat. The occupants, unaware that their voices carry over the motor noise, can sometimes scald the air. It is common to see two or three fishermen crowded against the gunwale of a tilted skiff and peering down into the depths with ready net while their shad jumps on the opposite side, unseen and unheard over the motor.

A flyfisherman who wants to keep his fish will be wise to use a net. St. Johns fish aren't big, a four-pounder being a good contest entry, and if you stick to fairly heavy leaders of around ten-pound test you can hoist a tired fish's head out of the water for the netting bit. Not the classic move but effective. Sometimes you can beach them. Grabbing one in your hand is an exercise in dexterity unless he's completely done in—and I never know when that is.

I've used an 8½-foot fly rod taking a No. 8 line, more than anything else. The leader is only about four or five feet long to keep the fly from swinging too shallow. If you want to be scientific, have flies of various weights, the heavier ones for faster current.

No one has said shad fishing is the most scientific angling art but the usual trolling combination of a small spoon or fly used as a dropper with a small jig or dart works at different speeds on different days. That's largely a matter of depth. Today's favorite color may be a dog tomorrow, but white and orange in various combinations are fairly reliable and so is yellow, whether trolled or cast. A favorite dart is white with a red head. The usual combination of two lures is called a shad rig, and can be bought already assembled at local shops.

Trollers generally do best with rather light spinning rods (they don't use fly rods for trolling much any more). The gentle nodding of the flexible tip seems to give the lure added appeal. Some trollers sit and pump their rods regularly; others just let the tips nod. The boat should go very slowly, generally about as slowly as the motor will idle, and depth is adjusted partly by line length. Seventy feet of line out is a pretty good start, but the fish aren't generally boat shy.

The soft spinning rod's second benefit is that it absorbs a shad strike without tearing the fragile mouth. Ten-pound line is satisfactory, about the only advantage of lighter material being faster sinking.

And now we can no longer avoid the supernatural. Tales of fishing luck and how one angler caught all of the fish while another caught none with the exact same outfit and method get pretty tiresome, but such things are unreasonably frequent with shad.

Last year I disembarked at a favorite sod bank with my wife, two fly rods and an ultralight spinning rig. An elderly lady, obviously dressed for flower gardening, was standing there holding a spinning rod as if preparing for bayonet drill. She deposited a jig and white fly in the water with a strident whoosh—25 feet out. She cranked in an astonished shad and I feared the fishing might be too easy for once. An hour later she had caught 11 shad and I hadn't had a strike on any of the superflies that had worked so well before. My wife announced she was going to try spinning, so she did—nothing, even when she imitated the rig the gardening lady used. The lady's male companion told me she had never gone fishing before. He wasn't catching anything either.

I have many more such stories, some of which have me as the hero, but suffice it to say that *unpredictability* is an overworked but accurate description of shad behavior. I have often seen two experienced fishermen exchange outfits while one continued to catch fish and the other caught nothing. A score of ten or 15 to nothing is routine. There are reasons, of course, but only shad know them. Shad are like that: favoring one angler's offerings to the total disdain of another's.

In a return to the real world I think it is wise to remember that the movement of shad is predominantly upstream for they are going to spawning areas from salt water. I have seen downstream fishermen in business while upstream fishermen caught nothing, and I have seen the downstream activity stop rather suddenly while the upstream folks got busy—obviously a bunch of fish being intercepted during their migration. If you see somebody into a fish I think you're better off above him than below him.

And what's the best way? Well, since it covers much more area, I consider trolling the most consistent method day in and day out, but when a caster gets a bunch of working fish located he'll make a big score faster than a troller.

Spinning or flycasting? I believe spinning most frequently catches more fish—but there are days when the flies are much better.

The American or white shad spawns in open water, generally over a firm bottom, the eggs being deposited and fertilized without a nest of any kind. Shad "washing" sometimes turns into darting displays on the surface and it is evidently part of the spawning routine. The shad is found up the

Atlantic shores from Florida to the St. Lawrence and probably the best-known sportfishing is in the New England rivers. The fish along the northern part of the range return from the sea to spawn more than once. The Florida fish characteristically spawn only once and then die. They do not run as large as in the northern range. Shad spend two to five years at sea and are sometimes found 100 miles out in blue water.

The best-known spot for St. Johns trollers is the Lemon Bluff area near Sanford, Florida, but I'd rather do my casting a little farther upstream. The multi-channeled Puzzle Lake area is also good. Trollers need more water for comfortable operations and bright days attract large flotillas near Lemon Bluff. The best fishing is usually from January 1 through March.

There's some commercial netting of shad far downstream but there are rigid restrictions, with those operations prohibited during most of the best of the season. Most of the commercially caught fish go north for sale. A shad is constructed largely of bones but they're a delicacy if properly prepared, and some who don't care for the fish eulogize the roe.

You could do a lot worse, and I'd rather you didn't call them stink salmon.

THE FINER POINTS OF PLAYING FISH

Lee Wulff

*A famous angler-teacher says that first you must
learn the rules . . . then you must learn when to
break them. (December 1978)*

IN MOST difficult endeavors the worthy participant should first learn
the rules, then learn when to break them. This is never more true than
when playing fish on light tackle. (Ordinary tackle becomes light tackle
when the fish you hook is bigger than you anticipated.)

The accepted rules are: keep the rod tip up; keep the line tight except
to give the fish slack when he jumps; keep the fish moving to tire him out;
and, finally, bring the fish to shallow water or surface for the capture by
netting, tailing, beaching, gaffing or whatever.

There are good reasons for all these rules. Keeping the rod tip up
means that the fish is working against a springy resistance, to prevent him
from getting a solid pressure that will break the line or leader. A tight line
keeps a steady pressure on the fish and thus tires him out. Giving slack
when the fish jumps keeps the line from coming tight with a solid jolt

against the tackle. If you stay downstream of the fish, it means that the fish is not only fighting the tackle but the speed of the current as well. Bringing the fish to shallow water moves him to a position where he can maneuver only laterally and cannot go *under* a net.

Some of the best examples of using these simple rules effectively used to occur at my salmon camps in Newfoundland. A fishing couple would arrive with a ten-year-old in tow, because he or she was not in summer camp and there was no other place for him or her to be. When the youngster began to get bored with the grown-up life-style of the camp and the lack of other youngsters on the scene, I'd suggest to one of the parents, "Would you like to have your son (or daughter) catch a salmon?"

Inasmuch as the parent had worked very hard to catch a salmon or two and considered this quite a tackle achievement, I'd usually get a look of surprise and then, "You're not kidding?"

When convinced that the opportunity was a real one, the parent would give up a rod in order to let the youngster fish.

The system I'd set up was simple. The guide would take the child out to the home pool in a canoe and have him cast as far as he could. He'd mark the line at that spot. Thus, with no loose line, and with the distance and direction of the casts determined, the fly would land in a small area consistently. Knowing just where the salmon were lying, the guide would then move the canoe until the fly was landing just in front of a salmon's nose.

Playing instructions had already been given to the youngster: "When a salmon takes the fly, lift the rod to vertical and hold it there. If the salmon pulls the rod down from the vertical take your hand off the reel handle and give the fish slack. When the reel stops running and you can get the rod straight up again, start to wind in. Wind in until the rod bends down. Then take your hand off the reel again and let the fish run."

This process was repeated again and again until the fish was tired. The fish was on a slack line most of the time, but since there were no snags in that pool no harm was done. Whenever the fish jumped he had slack line.

Eventually the salmon would tire. Guide and amateur angler would move to the shore, and the angler would continue as before. The guide would wade in and, when the time was right, net the salmon. Only if a youngster froze and held the reel tight against the line movement (or in case of a poor hook hold) was a fish lost. This shows how simple the playing of a fish can be when conditions are perfect.

Let's look at the rules more closely. The high rod does give a fine playing cushion, but when the fish pulls the line out at that high angle the drag of pulling the line through the guides is increased greatly. If a fish is being played on a very light leader, the extra drag of a high-held rod may be just enough to break it. If the angler wants to tire the fish quickly, he will want him to run far, expending maximum energy on the run. The high rod may slow the fish down and discourage the long, tiring drive. Pointing the rod at a running fish gives the least resistance and is the best procedure with light tackle.

It is worth considering here that success is determined by the length of time it takes to subdue a fish with given tackle. It's like driving a car. The driver in a race seeks the maximum speed he can make without losing control. Similarly, the angler wants to be able to exert the maximum safe pressure without breaking his gear. Those who are most skillful bring their fish in with a minimum of time—a special advantage if the fish is to be released. A quick capture will leave him with a reservoir of strength for speedy recuperation.

Slack is not the demon danger it is reputed to be when a fish is being played on a fly or a simple hook, because neither of them has any appreciable weight. They cannot be shaken free by the fish or rubbed off since they are on the *inside* of a fish's mouth. The fly or hook will only fall out if there has been so much hard pulling that it has worn a hole big enough for the hook to slide back out. It is something that rarely occurs until late in a fight and where hard, sudden pressures have been used.

I learned a lot about slack from photography. Before that I worried about it. Now I use slack to advantage against the fish.

In trying to get motion pictures of jumping Atlantic salmon, many years ago, I used to have a photographer sitting on the bank of the pool while I fished. He was supposed to be ready at all times, with the camera set properly for light and distance, to get the jumps whenever they might occur. He wasn't. Whenever I hooked a fish he seemed to be eating a chocolate bar or a sandwich, with his camera put down for just a moment; it was still set for sunshine even when a cloud came over the sun. The salmon when hooked would usually make several brilliant jumps before the cameraman could get into action. The result was that we got a lot of tired jumps when the salmon was weary, or far away after a long run.

In desperation I tried a wild idea. If I simply set the hook with a quick jab and then gave slack, I reasoned the salmon would think the bug he had taken had bitten him back and was hanging on the way sea lice do.

Accordingly, on the next rise I set the hook and immediately gave slack. As I had anticipated, the fish simply went back to his original position, which was where he wanted to be in the first place. Settled there, he felt no pressures or wild pulls, and the fly in his jaw did not seem to him to be a major catastrophe.

That gave me time to alert the photographer. Time for him to set aside his bottle of orange soda, check his camera for exposure and for the distance I indicated, and start it rolling at my command. Then when, on the suddenly tightened line, the fish felt the awful pressure and jumped, the camera got the quiet water first and then the fish coming up through it into a wild and desperate leap.

Once, many years later with an *American Sportsman* crew, I had a striped marlin hooked for five minutes while he paid no attention to the very light drag of my line as we followed just behind at exactly his speed. When the crew got the bugs out of their electrically driven cameras and sound equipment, I gave them the signal to roll and then by sharp pulls on the line signaled to the fish that he was in real trouble. That marlin then gave one of the most dramatic leaping sequences ever filmed.

After my first successful experience using slack right after the strike, I found that whenever I could give a fish slack (it isn't always possible in a fast flow with a bulky line) he'd start to look for a place to hold up and think it over. I've stopped steelhead in the middle of a downstream rush when I didn't think the McKenzie boat could keep up with them, and hundreds of other times I have used slack to help me control or play a fish.

I once hooked a tuna from the boat's tower and climbed down to the fighting chair with the 80-pound outfit in one hand and with just enough drag on the reel to keep the fish from overrunning till I could get to the chair and attach the harness. Meanwhile the crew was frantic and certain that the fish would be lost because there was no pressure on him.

There are some times when it's impossible to give fish slack, however. That's true when the fish is swimming fast enough to stay under tension from the drag of the line, like a salmon running downstream or a tuna that never stops but swims until he breaks free or dies.

Your playing strategy should be to get the first wildness out of the fish before he realizes he's in real trouble. I once stood by a friend who hooked an Atlantic salmon with a hard, heavy strike. The fish reacted by racing madly across the pool, skittering along the surface as he went, and ending up in the alder bushes on the far side. The pool was too deep to wade. The fish flopped around, snared the fly and leader in the alders, then flopped back into the water and swam away. The gentle strike, with a simple setting of the hook and then a relaxation of the pressure, would have been far less dramatic, but it probably would have saved the fish.

If you've set the hook, make sure your tackle is in order and your position good while you give slack, then play the fish on a very gentle pressure. He'll fuss a little and make a few short runs or easy leaps, but he won't give you the problems a completely fresh fish that's frantic with fear will give you. After that first short period of gentle playing, he'll be somewhat accustomed to the tackle and just a little out of breath. Then when you increase the pressure toward the tackle's maximum he won't be so surprised. He won't run or leap with maximum speed and wildness.

I remember a time when I'd just hooked a salmon and he made a magnificent leap before settling down in his lie again. I put on a moderate pressure and waited.

Seeing the bend in the rod the watcher said, "Is he well hooked?"

"Why don't you wade out and take a look," I suggested. "How the hell should I know?"

How does anyone know? He doesn't! Except in baitfishing where there's a certainty the hook has been taken deep.

How, then, should the angler play the fish? As if it were hooked lightly which it may be, or as if it were hooked well which it may not be? I choose the latter course, and for these reasons:

If I assume the hook hold is good and play the fish accordingly, I will use maximum tackle strength for each maneuver and bring the fish in as swiftly as possible. If I act as if the hook hold is not a good one and baby the fish, I will have him on much longer (perhaps needlessly) and may lose him simply because of the accidents that can happen in the longer time required. If the fish is poorly hooked, the chances are he'll be lost anyway. Only if I can see that the hook hold is poor when the fish comes close at the end of the fight do I become gentle where I could be strong. When a hook pulls out I do not fault myself. If I break a leader or line I do.

If you can bring a big fish in before he gets his second wind, you may save quite a bit of time. Some fish will fight with a frenzy that brings them to momentary exhaustion in a relatively short time. If they are not captured then, they get a second wind and can settle down to a long, dogged fight that can go on for a long time if the tackle is very light and conditions difficult.

I've found that a giant bluefin tuna on a long steady run takes a direction and holds it. I can tell when a captain is varying his course by watching the wake. If it varies from a straight line I know I'm going to have to vary my pressure downward while the boat seeks to line up with the fish again. The solution is to give the captain the proper direction when I can determine it, and let him take the course by compass or by a point on the horizon and hold it. Maximum pressure can then be held without reeling until the fish changes course.

Does that apply to flyfishing? It applies to sulking fish where the fish must hold his position. The idea is no line movement on the reel allows maximum pressure. It may not be apparent immediately but the effect on a fish can be devastating. Anglers who use the same light pressure on a sulking fish they'd use on one that was moving (a very common mistake) will find that it *doesn't* tire a fish. And they'll tell you sulking fish are invincible and must be moved by throwing stones at them or banging on the butt of the rod. Horsefeathers! Get a good position, put out a pound less than the awful pull it takes to break the same tackle when hooked to the back fence, and that fish will tire.

One of the best tricks in the book is to give slack when a fish swims into a snag. To try to hold him usually means broken tackle and a lost fish. If you let the fish swim into the snag and then give him only an occasional twitch or no pressure at all, sometimes he'll come out the same way he went in.

I remember a rainbow in the Red Rock River that headed for a snag and went right in under it, against the bank. He was on a long line, but I reeled in, wading close until I could see him flashing across the stream. After five minutes of coaxing, he came out to the deep water between us. The catch was that my line was still hooked around a strong, springy branch. I slacked off, waded to the tail of the pool where I could cross to the other side. Then I followed the line up to the snag, passed the rod through the place the fish had taken it and then, tightening up on the fish, soon captured and released him.

My longest time holding a fish steady was with an Atlantic salmon I hooked in the Humber. While I played him, a reel bolt came loose and I couldn't reel in or out. With the fish resting in the middle of the Sheldrake Pool, I tied the line to a yellow birch on shore, got into my car and drove five miles back to town to get another reel. When I came back the fish was still on. I put the new reel on the rod, tied the lines together and began to play the fish again. He had had a rest and gave me some fireworks, but 15 minutes later that 23-pounder was on the beach.

The time of the strike is one of the two most important times in playing a fish. When a fish is first hooked the angler's coordination must be at its peak. It is all too easy to hold the strike a fraction of a second too long. This lets a fish start to move at his fastest speed against a solid pressure. A quick pull is far better than a prolonged one. Several strikes, one after the other, tend to upset the fish, like digging spurs into a bronco. It's exciting but it certainly doesn't help in playing the fish.

The number of hook points to be set is important. *It takes more than twice the pull to set a double hook as a single of the same size.* This means that a double hook requires a heavier leader than does a single hook. Where there are trebles, it takes an even stronger strike. Doubles and trebles tend to give leverage with one hook working against another to tear the whole thing out.

The basic concepts of playing a fish are the same regardless of the tackle involved, but there are advantages and disadvantages to the various types. Long and limber fly rods give the best possible shock cushion, but there's a lot of resistance when the thick fly line must be pulled through the water. Fly rods have more guides than shorter plug spinning rods and thus generate more friction-drag when the line is pulled through them. The single-action reels used in most flyfishing are more difficult to reel swiftly than are the multiplying reels used in most casting and trolling. Getting to the right position quickly becomes more important then for a flyfisherman than for a troller or baitcaster, if he's fighting a fish of the same capability.

When it comes to following the rule and bringing a fish to shallow water for capture, the shore or wading fisherman has a better alternative —if he's able to use it. That is to capture the fish in deep water, say two or three feet, instead of six to eight inches. Look at it this way: a big fish is terrified of shallow water. He'll fight to the last of his strength to avoid being pulled into it. This takes time and, at any moment while the fish is in those desperate throes, an error or accident may free him.

The alternative is to wade out (or, if in a boat, work deep) holding the net steady at depth. The trick is to get the fish used to the net. All movements must be very slow and deliberate. The fish should think of your legs as immobile tree trunks and of the net and the rest of your body as something very slow moving and not dangerous. Then it can be coaxed or pulled gently into position.

A great deal of psychology is used in playing fish. In learning to make them act for movies, I had to learn how to trick them into swimming into areas where the cameras could get them. The cameraman cannot chase the fish and catch him in the camera's eye. The angler must make the fish *come to the camera*. Slight nuances of pressure and changes of direction of the pull can turn him. An illusion of escape and freedom may bring him to the right spot. Once you realize how fish react to pressure and angles you'll find places to use that knowledge.

Which side of the mouth did you hook your fish on? It's important to remember. The strategy is to play the fish right up to safe tackle strength on the side from which you hooked him and to relax the pressure a bit when playing him from the opposite side. Pulling the hook back against the way it went in, especially with long-shanked hooks, develops leverages that can free a hook in short order. Many a good fish has been lost because this back pressure worked a hole around the hook.

Tackle gives the angler a connection, no matter how delicate, with the fish he is playing. Through it he can read the fish's feelings and his capabilities. Sometimes I think I can almost feel their heartbeats and judge just how tired they are, how likely they are to run or jump and, if so, how far or how high. I know from where they derive their strength (some fish depend on speed, others on power) and I've learned to sense how they tire. If you can make a fish use his fins in an unusual manner, you can tire the muscles that move them.

If you can convince the fish you're playing that his cause is lost, he'll give up easily. When you've led him to believe he's about to be free and then he finds that he isn't, you can break his spirit. Fish behave differently. Each one is a separate problem. Then too, there is much difference in the capability of different anglers to play fish. But whatever your skill, to play each fish as perfectly as possible is both exciting and rewarding.

ODE TO OPENING DAY

Lionel Atwill

*A SPORTS AFIELD staffer reflects on the first
day of the season with humor and sympathy for all
those hapless participants. (February 1979)*

COME MARCH in New England the sun will rise one morning in a
cloudless sky and shine extra hard and bright. It will taunt the snow to
melt and the sap to run. It will make people shed their gloves and sweaters
and puffy down coats and say foolish things: "Well, it looks like winter's
finally over. I'm sure we're in for an early spring."

Twenty-four hours later that warming sun will probably hide behind
dun-colored clouds. The temperature will drop to its normal low. Snow
crystals will firm up. Sap will turn to viscous gum. People again will swaddle
themselves in feathers and wool and fall back into the rhythms of winter
—except for the trout fishermen.

For when the weather turns cold after that first day of March sun, the
juices of the trout fisherman will not gel like tree sap and rivulets of
snowmelt. The New England trout fisherman has spent too many winter
nights flipping through worn catalogs of rods and reels, vicariously battling
New Zealand rainbows or English chalk stream browns in the pages of

outdoor magazines, and daydreaming about last summer's battles—adding a few ounces to each fish, a few feet to each run, and a few trout to each memory of his fern-lined creel. When that first warm day of March arrives, the trout fisherman erupts with enthusiasm and never settles down.

He prowls the banks of favorite rivers, furtively looking for a mayfly hatch that never comes, and hikes into remote ponds still capped with hard, blue ice. He buys a license, ties flies, runs toothpaste through the action of his favorite spinning reel to hone the gears, perhaps raises worms in the basement, and waits.

He waits for opening day, which comes, like all great events, a day or two before anyone is ready for it. The flyfisherman has tied up 200 new flies but has forgotten to buy a license. The spinfisherman has sorted his lures and patched his net but has failed to check his line, which an attic mouse has patiently removed from its spool and meticulously—for a mouse—spun into a nylon nest. The baitfisherman has scouted his favorite water but has neglected to get any worms and discovers that his garden —his normal source of supply—is still locked in with ten inches of frost. Yet somehow a license is purchased, line untangled, and a worm obtained. The alarm is set for an unnatural hour. Almost all the gear the fisherman owns, including several recent purchases, is spread haphazardly through the living room. Then that day arrives.

The first day of deer season consistently yields the largest take. Duck season opens at sunrise to the sound of shotguns blasting and ducks hitting the water. Even upland bird hunters frequently come home with dinner in their game pockets their first day afield. But the opening day of trout season in New England is different. It is, for many fishermen, more ritual than anything else. The fishermen are ready but their quarry is not.

Water runs cold and roily or is choked with ice. Trout are sluggish, and few if any insects hatch on the surface to lure fish from their hideouts under stream banks, in deep cuts and behind submerged logs.

The trout fisherman, then, pays homage to better days ahead by torturing himself that first day. He endures cold weather, too many cups of coffee, snagged lines and leaky waders; but worse, he suffers from the delusion that he may really catch something—some people do, after all. Furthermore, he will go to his favorite spot, where last summer he saw a 19-inch brown sipping spinners, and discover that the pool is now a torrent of muddy water framed with the flotsam of winter. The pool he dreamt of does not even exist!

Still, he fishes. He fishes because it is the first day of a long, great season, perhaps a rewarding season that deserves tribute, and he fishes as much to honor the trout as to hook it. He fishes because he enjoys fishing perhaps as much as he enjoys catching fish. He fishes because he believes that by standing hip deep in turbulent, freezing water he can hasten spring. He fishes because trout fishing—even without trout—is just a bit better than doing anything else.

Some trout fishermen fish harder, although no more successfully, than others on opening day. Throughout New England trout season opens in early April. That is hardly spring (it is not even mud season), yet across those states lights in the houses of trout fishermen come on before dawn. All-night diners do a big business with eye-opening coffee, served to the endless patter of last season's fishing stories: "Last summer, I guess it was around the middle of July, I was down there on the Batten Kill at Johnson's Meadow working this ten-inch brookie, you know, over by that clump of grass; always half-a-dozen brookies over there. Anyway, I look down right off the bank, not ten feet from me, and see this brown holding behind this log. God, he was as big as a baseball bat!" The ten-inch brookie was probably six inches and the baseball bat most likely a smallish billy club, but just as fish grow from season to season, so, too, do fish stories. Both are natural processes without which fishing would grow stale from year to year.

Last year in one of those diners a friend of mine was downing his second cup of coffee before any other fishermen arrived. He told no fish stories, for he had no audience. Still, he was content, for he had a plan: let the others relive the heroics of last year; he would concentrate on catching fish this year, catching fish on opening day.

He knew of a pond in which lived many large trout. That pond was known to few anglers, and my friend schemed that if he got to that pond early, very early, way before first light, he would have the water and those large fish to himself.

So he left the diner, a half-finished cup of coffee, and a small pile of powdered sugar from a doughnut, around four in the morning. He drove far out of town and turned onto a dirt road still edged with high snowbanks. That dirt road took him to another dirt road, which took him to a third, and 100 yards off the shoulder of that road lay the pond.

It was a big pond but not big enough to be called a lake. Fed by cold springs and rimmed by alders, it was a perfect lair for trout. My friend prepared his gear by the headlight of his car and stumbled into the woods (for he had forgotten his flashlight), groping his way to the edge of the water. He took a cautious step into the water and through his waders felt the gentle nudge of ice against his shins. Patch ice, he thought, small chunks floating on the surface, and he cast his lure out into the blackness that was the pond.

He could feel when the lure dropped, and he began a slow retrieve. In 30 seconds his lure rattled against the end of his rod, so he cast again with more determination and retrieved again with more expectation of a solid hit by one of those trout.

My friend cast and retrieved for a good two hours, as he tells it (and he tells it with some reluctance), without even a bump to confirm that there were trout in the pond and that his plan to catch them was sound. And since he could see little more than his boots and his tackle, he did not even have the view of early spring to console him.

Of course, all that time he was casting to a frozen pond. The ice had broken up along the edge, but out in the middle, out where my friend could not see but where his lure landed every 30 seconds or so, the ice was several inches thick. I doubt if the trout beneath that ice were even bothered by the gentle thud of his lure.

Bad luck may plague the spinfisherman or worm dunker on opening

day, but the flyfisherman is cursed. He dreams of rising fish and clear water, of warm days and of clouds of mayflies and caddises choking the air. On the first day of the season, however, he faces muddied snowmelt, lethargic fish, no insects, and the boredom of dragging weighted nymphs or gaudy streamers through clouded holes in the hope of luring just one fish into a strike.

Opening day last year found me, fly rod in hand, on the edge of what I remembered as a small stream. The sun was low in the sky, but I could see well enough. Yet nothing looked familiar. There was no pocket water. The eddy I remembered behind a rock was not there—nor was the rock. I faced not a stream but a channeled flood.

Still I dragged nymphs and streamers through the water for two hours until ice built up in the guides of my rod and my fingers grew too cold to change flies. I quit, disheartened, but in the afternoon I joined two friends to canoe down a calm, remote stream pocketed with beaver pools. In the stream's quiet water we could see trout, not big fish but trout nonetheless. We cast the combined offerings of three fishing vests to them. We changed leaders and lines. We worked upstream and down. We cursed the fish, the weather, the brush that caught our backcasts, and our ineptitude. For all that, we were rewarded with a 30-minute snowfall and one brook trout small enough to spawn comfortably in a sardine can.

I drove home forlorn. I had observed the ritual of opening day, and for that I was glad; but I had been skunked, too, and for that I was humiliated and indignant. When I turned into my drive, I caught sight of a pair of waders still glistening with water hanging from a nail in my neighbor's garage. I backed into his yard and knocked on his door, hoping to find solace in commiserating with him, for this was opening day and certainly he had caught no fish. That was more a hope than a conclusion. My neighbor is a pretty good angler, a man who often catches trout. I wish him well, but . . .

"Come on in," he called out. "I'm back in the kitchen."

"Any luck?" I asked, as I walked through the dining room. That is the fisherman's obligatory greeting. It is not a question, really, especially if the angler being greeted happens to have caught more or larger fish than the greeter. As it developed, my neighbor had more to show me in the kitchen than a cheery hello. He had what all luckless anglers dread—fish.

"Well, I caught my limit this morning before eight," he answered, "but I let them go. So I went out about an hour ago and caught tomorrow's limit. Howdja do?" He was cleaning ten plump trout, stacking their slick bodies like cordwood on the counter next to the sink.

"I only went out for a few minutes this afternoon, right before it started to snow," I lied. "No luck."

"You want three or four of these?" he asked, waving the flaccid body of a 13-inch brown under my nose.

I could stand humiliation by the fish but not by a man who had caught them. "No thanks," I answered. "I'll probably go out this evening and pick up a few." Of course, I never did.

If there were 20,000 trout fishermen along the streams and ponds of New England on opening day last year, then there were 20,000 stories similar to mine. Perhaps fish figured into half of them. Still, those hapless, fishless trout fishermen will be out on those streams and ponds this year, certain that luck will be with them—or rather with *us*.

A FLY FOR ALL SEASONS

A.J. McClane

The nymph will catch fish every day of the year, in
the coldest or hottest weather, in calm water or
raging torrent, on top or down deep. (March 1979)

WHEN YOU live on a river, as I did for most of my life, you soon come to realize how inconsequential your fishing skills are compared to the survival skills of a wild trout. There was an undercut bank on the Beaverkill, near our cabin, that I was certain held an elderly brown with jaws like a nutcracker. For weeks I never even saw my fish, though I was on the water at all hours from late spring into autumn. A deeper, greenish pool above was calendar-cover beautiful and full of cooperative trout, but after the stream made its bend, and the current purled back under the hemlock roots and then spun away before dancing merrily over a pebbled riffle—that was the spot. I could smell it as sure as a coming rain in a dry summer. But the undercut was densely canopied by low-hanging boughs almost to water level, and the only way I could get a fly near those roots was by crawling on hands and knees and making a 30-foot cross-stream cast—usually with one elbow in the water.

It was a ridiculous performance, according to wife Patti, daughter

Susan, Arnold Gingrich, Bedell Smith, Bert Lahr and other critics who happened along. At one point I did consider cutting the boughs down, but that would be unfair to my spectral tenant. Four times out of ten I'd throw my backcast into a hemlock behind me and pop my leader. Three times out of ten I'd manage to get my fly caught in the opposite boughs on my forward cast. And when a cast did arrive on the water, only one or two ubiquitous flame-bellied brook trout, so abundant in these upper pools, would appear, making me even more aware of a greater presence.

In my daily elbow exercise I tried every kind of fly in the box. Not even a Muddler caused a stirring in the undercut. Toward the end of that season, when the water was quite low, I reverted to my Catskill boyhood and used a method one step above a wiggly garden worm. I attacked the problem from upstream with a small weighted nymph on a long, fine leader. I made a short cast and paid line out in the current, maneuvering the fly so that it drifted down into the hole to swim near the roots. Then I waited. Long minutes passed before I felt the tug, but instead of immediately boring back into his den, the trout came out, a sooty-black monster, probably momentarily blinded by sunlight. I splashed downstream, hoping to lead my prize away from the undercut. The fish helped by making one strong run, which left him belly-flopping in the riffle below—but this maneuver also snapped my tippet.

I have caught many trout greater in pounds than this fish measured in inches, and it would have been released in any event. The point of my story is that even the most sophisticated trout—and a brown of about 18 inches on the upper Beaverkill rates summa cum laude—can be taken on a nymph sooner or later. The versatility of this type of fly is remarkable.

There was another place downstream, a short deep run where the river spilled over barren bedrock in a foaming cascade; this was reliable for two or maybe three acrobatic eight-inch rainbows in the side pocket. But in that rushing water I was convinced no greater presence existed at all, unless it was ethereal. For some reason there was always an eerie golden light falling on that pool in the evening as though polarized through a stained-glass window. Nevertheless, it was a pretty spot in which to cast a fly while watching chipmunks scamper among the ferns. It was included in my daily schedule, which was less precise but as dedicated as any Swiss railroad's. (I can get sidetracked by a patch of wild strawberries.)

I must have fished the miniature cascade 90 times that season, from all angles with all kinds of flies. Even my rainbow friends were becoming reluctant, so I tried skimming a little gray caddis pupa over the surface to stir some interest. A darkly spotted brown came barreling out of the depths, and after a long seesawing contest of surging runs against my 6X tippet, he was measured against my rod butt—19½ inches. The nymph had been taken when fished like a dry fly.

Fishing with an artificial nymph is the basic method of trout angling. The nymph will catch fish 365 days of the year—not always the largest and not always the most, but it will take them consistently. Equally important is the *method* of nymphing because it teaches beginners everything they must know about trout habits and habitat. Nymph fishing can be successful in the coldest or hottest weather, in dead-calm water or a raging torrent, and from the surface to the very bottom of those secret places where great trout hide.

Nymph fishing is old and its development has quite a history, but it did not become popular in America until about 1930. In the half-century since, the totemization of G.E.M. Skues's *Minor Tactics of the Chalk Stream* has certainly inspired those who fish and those who write about it. For any angling writer, it is a rare privilege not only to describe his country and time but to give perspective to the sport. Skues succeeded in doing this, but in a strangely delayed way.

It's hard to believe now, but once upon a time nymph was a dirty word. In the formal establishment of 1910, Skues was considered a heretic "dabbler in unworthy excesses" by many of his peers. Gentlemen belonged to the Houghton Club, marinated their Stilton in 150-year-old port, and fished with floating patterns. It has never been clear to me why a fly that is sunken, presumably the inferior condition in which artificials originated in the first place, should become the villain in a morality play. Yet within my own lifetime I recall nearly being drummed out of the corps for casting a nymph on the hallowed waters of the Risle. This French chalk stream was still immune to Skues's development by July of 1948, though God knows it's only a verbal stone's throw across the Channel from Hampshire to Normandy. Yet the good word had not been passed.

I had caught and released three lovely trout that were obviously bulging in a slick run below the cider mill when our host, Edouard Vernes (who was flailing a dry fly upstream from me and catching nothing), came pounding down the bank and asked to see what manner of "bait" I was throwing into his river. He held my leader tippet between his fingers with a look of complete disdain and gurgled *nam-pff*! I thought he was going to have a stroke. If it hadn't been for an instant character reference from Charlie Ritz, who promised I would mend my ways, Vernes, a millionaire bank chairman who brooked no evil, probably would have snapped my 8½-foot CCF over his knee and sent me by square-wheeled tumbrel to the Bastille. The fact that I was demonstrating for Charlie how to fish a nymph was not mentioned until some years later in Ritz's book *A Fly Fisher's Life*. Even to think of teaching Charlie Ritz anything about trout was almost ludicrous, but my mentor himself had been insulated by the ground rules of chalk-stream society. Eventually Charlie met Frank Sawyer, the doyen of nymph artists, and became a fanatic on nymphing. I have never met Frank Sawyer, but I was flooded with letters from Charlie describing how Sawyer did this or Sawyer did that. It was as though he had translated the Dead Sea Scrolls.

I learned the fundamentals of nymphing back in the 1930s. The only popular American patterns, then purveyed by William Mills & Son, were the flat-bodied, lacquered creations of Edward Ringwood Hewitt—a design also claimed by John Alden Knight, although I can't imagine why. These nymphs came like licorice sticks in three color combinations: black with a gray belly, black with an orange belly, and black with a yellow belly. I seldom caught many trout with these, so, like everybody else who took fishing seriously, I tied my own.

Some idea of where the nymph existed by 1936 can be found in a little 55-page book, *Tying American Trout Lures*, by Reuben R. Cross. Rube, the Sage of Shin Creek, was a master craftsman, yet all he had to say about nymphs covered 4½ pages and concerned four patterns: the Guinea Nymph, the Black-and-White Nymph (grub), the Olive Wood-duck Nymph, and the Carrot-and-Black Nymph. Dan Todd, Ray Neidig, Mike Lorenz and quite a few other tiers in the Delaware Valley were experimenting with patterns.

Dan Todd was the Ulster & Delaware stationmaster in Margaretville. He amassed a considerable collection of trout foods preserved in formalin that he kept in his office. One morning a man named Olson (whom Dan detested for his murderous consistency in killing large quantities of trout with spoons and worms) saw a mason jar of pebble-type caddis cases sitting on his desk.

"What's them things?" Olson asked Todd.

Dan looked pained. "I just had an operation. Them's my kidney stones."

Olson stared closely at the jar. "God Almighty! No wonder you can't fish!"

I was fishing mostly on the East Branch of the Delaware in those days, places like Fuller's Flat and Keener's Flat, which by any standard were classic runs. A Catskill flat was often several miles long, containing more riffles and rapids than still water.

It was April of 1936 when I caught my first big trout. The weather was cold and snowy and the river was running high. I was fishing a home-tied nymph by casting upstream and letting it sink close to my bank—which was no trick with a waterlogged silk line. I caught quite a number of trout that morning before getting stuck in the bottom, and when that brown finally came thumping to life it was the biggest thrill a 14-year-old boy could ever have. The trout was too big for my landing net, and after getting the head stuck in its meshes I remember wrestling my prize into a snowbank. I walked home, feeling like one big goose pimple, by way of the lumberyard, the butcher shop, the drugstore, and the ill-named Palace Hotel, making sure everybody in town saw my fish. Dan Todd weighed it at the railroad station—7 pounds 2 ounces, not an adult trophy for the East Branch in those days, since fresh mounts in double figures to 15 pounds or more hung glassy-eyed on every saloon wall.

When I dressed the trout, some of the nymphs that filled its belly were still alive; its digestion rate had almost slowed to a halt in the near-freezing water. What fascinated me was the fact that the fish had continued to feed. Although big trout are often caught on bucktails or streamers, in *very* cold weather a nymph will outfish a minnow-like fly simply because the trout doesn't have to chase it through heavy currents. A nymph can be fished absolutely dead and catch fish, while a bucktail cannot; a nymph can also be fished alive when the accepted food form is otherwise dead. This is the ultimate conundrum.

I had some fabulous fishing in Montana last year during my annual fall trip. Western rivers are custom-made for the nymph artist, and some lakes produce big trout to no other method, except sporadically. Henry's Lake in Idaho is a classic example; here the trout gorge on green damselfly nymphs and also *Gammarus*, the so-called freshwater shrimp imitated by many nymph patterns. But the lake I have in mind is known for its voluminous minimayfly hatches where even the best dry-fly man can spook trout with a No. 22 on a 7X tippet. The naturals look like dandruff. There is some action at the beginning of an emergence, and you can hook three, maybe four, nice fish. But the real sport occurs when the gulpers (fish of four, five and six pounds) appear after rafts of spent mayflies are floating on the water. The fish cruise in a leisurely fashion, often porpoising in plain sight as they take ephemeral minutae out of the surface film. With countless thousands of naturals windrowed to a small area, the most perfect imitation is lost in sheer numbers.

After we spent a futile Montana morning casting at repetitive risers and hooking exactly three trout, Tom McNally provided the solution. McNally, who is an expert angler in every sense of the word and chronicles his adventures for the *Chicago Tribune*, learned nymphing fundamentals as a lad on the hard-fished streams of Maryland. He was also a pro boxer in his youth, and now shoots pool with Minnesota Fats, so he reacts to panic situations with sharply honed reflexes—in this case a No. 10 fuzzy-bodied brown nymph worked across the surface in a hand-twist retrieve. Absurd? Showing those trout something big and alive swimming through all those tiny inert mayflies commanded a gustatory response that had no equal.

The next morning we began hooking, with modest consistency, rainbows and browns in the 2½- to 4-pound class; these were hammered silver, deep-bodied, arrowheaded trout that leaped and rocketed off like bonefish. Many simply popped our tippets, and we lost several large ones in the lake's numerous weed beds. This method of outfoxing the gulpers was no fluke. Tom and I visited that lake regularly through September and into aspen-yellow October. On any morning when the water was mirror calm his method paid off.

I enjoy writing about the joys of nymph fishing. It reminds me of Rube Cross. When I mentioned his book earlier, I had to go scrambling through my library to check the title. I remembered the volume had a brown cover, but I had forgotton that he wrote an inscription inside, and that told me the year I caught my first big trout. I visited his hayloft shop the following winter to learn more about tying flies. A huge man, half poet, half mountain lion, he was generous to a fault. His dill-pickle-sized fingers spun the most beautiful flies I will ever see. But it's his inscription in my book that deserves to appear in print. The author remains anonymous, yet the words reflect to some degree the transcendental joy of angling:

> *To my young friend*
> *I dreamed,*
> *   that I again my native hills had found,*
> *the mossy rocks, the valley, and the*
> *   stream that used to hold me captive*
> *to its sound.*
> *   And that I was a boy again.*
> *   (Anon.)*
>
> *Reuben R. Cross*
> *Jan. 3, 1937*

McClane's Favorite Nymph Patterns

These are four old favorites that have taken many fine fish over the years. They suggest subaquatic food forms in general, and, except on those occasions when fish are truly selective, one or another will usually produce if worked at the right depth.

Strawman Nymph
Hook: Regular or 2XL in sizes to suit
Tail: A few strands of gray mallard or wood-duck flank
Body: Deer hair spun on hook thinly and clipped in a taper from tail to head, ribbed with pale yellow floss silk. May be tied without hackle or, if desired, a turn or two of partridge hackle may be added.

Hare's Ear Nymph
Hook: Regular shank, Sizes 6 to 16
Tail: Brown hackle
Body: Dubbed very rough with fur from European hare's ear, mixed with fur from the hare's face, ribbed with oval gold tinsel
Thorax: Tied very full with wing pad from gray goose or duck tied over
Legs: Dubbing from thorax picked out long and fuzzy; this represents the nymph legs.

Leadwinged Coachman Nymph
Hook: Sizes 6 to 12 2XL
Tail: Dark brown hackle fibers
Body: Bronze peacock herl ribbed with fine black silk
Hackle: Dark rusty brown
Wing pads: Small dark black duck upper wing covert feathers (cut to shape)
Head: Brown lacquer.

Iron Blue Nymph
Hook: Regular shank Sizes 14 to 16
Tail: Cream or gray hackle wisps
Body: Bluish muskrat fur ribbed with gold wire
Thorax: Bluish muskrat, no rib
Hackle: Grayish cream
Head: Clear lacquer over tying silk.

IN SEARCH OF THE 200-POUND TARPON

Stu Apte

The angler whose name is synonymous with tarpon
tells of the quest of quests. (May 1979)

IT WAS mid-May at the Riverside Villas in Homosassa Springs, Florida. The hot afternoon sun boiled down and ricocheted off the calm sea, creating an instant steam bath for the anglers, illuminating the five-foot-deep waters so that everything, from chunks of gaudy red sponge to six-foot-long tarpon, was plainly visible on the white sand bottom.

Easing through limpid waters at the head of its stalking column, the giant green-silver torpedo shape suddenly veered off toward a tiny, moving target. Instinct told the big fish the exact range and direction of its quarry, and in an eye blink it had slipped under the No. 5/0 streamer fly and daintily sipped it in.

Sixty-five feet away in a skiff not much larger than the giant tarpon, angler Joe Robinson felt a surge of adrenalin as he watched the fish take his fly. He saw the jaws close, hauled back on his rod, and struck the fish two, three, four times in quick succession. The battle was joined.

Instantly the big fish bent itself into a coil of fury and exploded through the gleaming surface, shaking its huge head and showering sea water for a dozen yards in all directions.

Robinson gasped. The towering fish blotted out a giant hunk of the horizon. "My God," he yelled, "that is one big fish!" It was so big that it scared him. He started to back off on the drag, then caught himself and decided to fight it the same way he had fought so many other tarpon before. He shouted to his guide, Dale Perez, "How big do you think it will go?" But there was no answer.

Behind him, Perez had already estimated the size of the fish to be larger than any ever caught with him on a fly rod. He would not call out the figures for fear of over-exciting the angler. Instead, he motioned in finger-numbers to Robinson's wife, Jackie, that it might be the big one. The *record*.

The world-record tarpon on a fly. But more than that. The legend. The four-minute mile. The moonshot of fishing. An almost mythical giant that awaits some flyfisherman, some day. A mammoth of a fish. It's hard to conceive of catching one on a fly rod, man's most graceful fishing stick, and 15-pound leader. A heroically proportioned, seven-foot-long scaled monster of 200 pounds. In tarpon fishing parlance, the Big Mamoo.

The fish—the 200-pound silver king—is pursued relentlessly by two dozen or so dedicated angling fanatics. It is coveted by them more than anything else in the world. This elite corps of experts annually spends an outlandish amount of time, money and effort to conquer the 200-pounder. They journey to the Florida Keys and Homosassa each spring and summer, following their obsession of perhaps getting a glimpse of the fish that, like Ahab's white whale, stirs their blood and holds them ever in its grasp. Their goal: Get a hook into the legend before someone else does.

Each of these men has seen fish he believes would reach the mythical 200-pound mark. A number of them have had hookups only to lose the tarpon at the last moment, through snapped lines, broken rods, missed gaffs or violent leaps. And each has his story to tell of catches, records, misses, the fun and frenzy of pursuing the monster with rod, reel and calculator. And the stories will continue as long as the quest for the biggest tarpon goes on. For these are totally dedicated men who will not stop until their goal has been realized.

Joe Robinson, a fisherman for 30 years, never considered he would actually catch a world-record fish, until he saw the monster at Homosassa. "It was the first fish in the line—in a long single file—and I cast about 75 feet to it, with a cockroach-pattern fly made out of grizzly saddle hackle and brown bucktail. I let the fly sink for just a moment, stripped it twice, and the fish came up like a trout and sipped it down. An unbelievable take. Not with a big surge, or a wild gush, but like a trout taking a nymph."

The explosion that followed had guides in other boats screaming with delight and encouragement. The tarpon jumped, head-shook, crashed down, and jumped again, the picturebook display expected of a world-record tarpon. Robinson played it perfectly, bowing to the fish each time it soared from the water, winding madly each time it gave him some slack, painfully slowing the line with his fingers when the fish ran. Then it was over. He had won.

"The overall fight was 45 minutes," Robinson said. "We probably could have shortened that by about ten minutes if we had used a body gaff, but we elected to use a lip (release) gaff instead, just in case the fish wasn't as big as it appeared in the water."

They pinned the giant to the side of the boat, and brought out their tapes and calculators, tools that record seekers rely on to estimate the true size before killing a precious and respected foe. The fish measured just short of seven feet, and had a girth of just under four feet. It was a new record for 15-pound-class fly-rod tippet at an even 180 pounds. A good fish, but not quite the *Big Mamoo*.

"I think a lot of people make mistakes in going after only records," Robinson said. "I get a kick out of just catching them, just fishing for them. The record is a dream that somebody else can have."

Other members of the giant-hunting fraternity will stop at nothing less than the record. Jimmy Lopez is one such angler. He has been flyfishing for 25 years and has landed a number of big fish, including the one-time 15-pound-class fly-rod record of 162 pounds. He missed a bigger fish when it almost drowned his guide.

"We were right off the pipe channel at Man-O-War Key when I hooked the fish. Fought it for I guess 50 minutes and brought it to gaff," Lopez told me.

This tarpon was not yet ready to be mounted, however. When guide Clarence Lowe plunged the gaff into its side, it lurched straight down toward bottom. Lowe is a big man who weighs about 240 pounds, but the pull of the tarpon was irresistible. In seconds Lowe was overboard. He had to let go, and the tarpon escaped.

"That fish was the biggest I've had that close to the gaff," Lopez said. "I don't know how big it was, but it must have been over 180 pounds."

Billy Pate, a renowned angler who fishes "70 days a year for tarpon," and spends "about $12,000 a year" in his search for the biggest tarpon, has caught almost every species of billfish on a fly rod. In his 30 years of flyfishing he figures he has hooked at least three monsters in the 200-pound class. He hooked two of them in one hectic day.

"I had one on 12-pound tippet that jumped twice real close to the boat, and immediately came unstuck," he said. "Shortly afterward I was blind casting when I hooked up with another. That one was on 10-pound tippet! I followed it over the channel for an hour and a half and finally put too much pressure on it and broke it off." That, however, was not Pate's most memorable fight. One lasted all day and into the night.

"The battle took place at Homosassa," Pate said. "It took us north of the Bird Islands, around Black Rock, and finally right to the mouth of the Homosassa River. We hooked the fish at 7:30 in the morning, and fought it all day. Every time I would get it close to the boat, the guide, Hank Brown, would stop the engine and come forward to pick up the gaff. I could never get the fish closer to the boat than two feet away, however. With 10-pound tippet, there was just so much pressure I could put on it. We fought that tarpon all day, until 8 p.m., when we finally ran out of gas. The fish broke off."

Expert anglers believe that the Homosassa tarpon is a different species from that found in the Keys and Central America. It is shorter, with a smaller head and much larger girth. In the spring, the tarpon run in the Homosassa River watershed contains more large fish per school than any

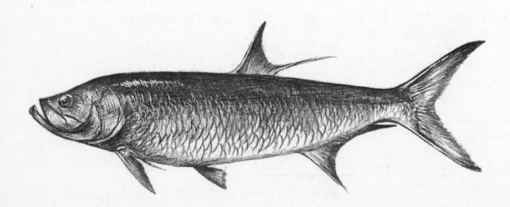

other run. Most members of the angling fraternity agree that the legend will be caught from these waters.

Eddie Wightman, a well-known Keys guide, thinks the different shape of the Homosassa tarpon might be a result of circumstances. "I have no idea if they are a different species. They're stockier, but that may just be a feeding situation. I haven't heard any biologist say they are different."

Wightman has seen his share of giants, at least one of which he estimated would eclipse current ideas of "bigness."

"The biggest tarpon I've ever seen was when I was in a helicopter flying over Homosassa. The fish was so huge that it looked like a manatee; I guessed it weighed more than 300 pounds. It was lying like a queen bee in the center of a daisy chain, the ritual mating circle of the tarpon.

"After seeing that monster, I've made a point of having my angler throw his first cast right into the middle of a school of tarpon. The big one is so used to being protected that it will usually eat anything it can catch."

It was while fishing with Wightman that Carl Navarre caught a 165-pound tarpon on 12-pound-test tippet, which would have beaten my current 154-pound record. Navarre fought the fish for 21 minutes before bringing it to gaff. The silver king jumped only twice, ran out all of his backing, then turned abruptly and came back toward the boat. Navarre's rod broke before they could gaff the fish, which consequently was disqualified from record consideration.

Like other anglers, I, too, have had luck abandon me at the most inopportune time. I've had the *Big Mamoo* on only once during my fishing career.

It was one of the longest fights I've ever had with a giant tarpon. The battle lasted 50 minutes, and occurred off Loggerhead Key, a tarpon hot spot. My guide was new at tarpon fishing and did not understand the mechanics of boat poling, or body gaffing big fish. My friend Frank Moss was along too.

The big tarpon snatched up my red-orange streamer fly and I zapped it with the 4/0 hook. It was a huge fish, and I was certain it would top 200 pounds. After fighting the fish to a standstill in under an hour, I had my leader in and was ready for my guide to gaff the fish. He picked up my standard eight-foot-long tarpon gaff, made a stab at the monster, and missed it. In the same swipe he snapped off my leader, releasing the fish. It sank slowly away as I sank slowly to the bottom of the boat, hurting inside and out. But fate still had its fickle finger waiting for me that day. I rerigged my tackle, and soon hooked another tarpon. The fish jumped immediately, and I thought it would only weigh around 100 pounds. Within 15 minutes I had the fish ready to gaff, but suddenly the pressure of the fight became too much for my rod handle. It was an experimental model that gave way at a glued joint and came apart in my hands, making the catch ineligible for record. The tarpon weighed 151¼ pounds, just over the then-existing record (also mine). It looked to be only half the size of the first fish that day, so I'm certain the larger one was well over 200 pounds.

The strain put on equipment is no less than the strain put on anglers who fight fish so large.

One year, Capt. Hal Chittum was guiding at Homosassa when he gaffed a fish larger than himself. The fish, it turned out, wasn't ready to give up the ghost. Chittum was dragged over the side, still holding the gaff, and dragged more than 20 feet across the rocky bottom before he finally let go. Hal is a husky young man—six feet six inches tall and 235 pounds—but the fish was stronger. Wearing only shorts and shirt, Hal was cut and bleeding as he climbed back in the boat. The gaff, its eight-foot-long handle barely longer than the fish, trailed as the monster, still hooked, headed for a shallow sandbar. The fish finally broke free when it wrapped the leader butt section around its tail and snapped the tippet in one slashing, powerful leap.

Another tarpon fisherman almost drowned when the hook, still imbedded in a live tarpon's mouth, snagged his hand. The tarpon shook and swam away, dragging the struggling angler with it. He was found hours later, barely alive, beached on a shallow sandbar and still attached to a very spent fish.

Other anglers have been injured when large tarpon have suddenly jumped into the boat with them. A 100-pound-plus tarpon can make a shambles of a cockpit in a hurry.

Most tarpon skiffs are in the 16- to 18-foot range, and have casting platforms to allow the angler to view the surrounding waters and cast from a higher point. The boats have big outboards for traveling to the fishing grounds, and either 18-foot pushpoles or electric trolling motors for movement in the shallows. Tarpon in shallow water are extremely sensitive to motor noises and will spook if an outboard is driven within a quarter mile. Knowledgeable anglers shut down at least that far out, and become incensed when a careless fisherman comes charging into the fishing grounds under power.

An electric motor doesn't spook the fish, however. When used in conjunction with a pushpole, it is ideal for following a running fish. If the fish continues to run, though, there may be no choice but to fire up the outboard, since it is almost impossible to turn a strong fish with the light leader tippet. Billy Pate uses two trolling motors, almost to the exclusion of the pushpole.

Tackle used by most experts is similar in quality and performance, if not brand name. Most use a nine-foot graphite or glass saltwater fly rod; either a positive retrieve or anti-reverse single-action saltwater reel with a capacity for several hundred yards of backing, and 80 to 90 feet of intermediate slow-sinking flyline or a 30-foot shooting head. While I prefer a No. 4/0 hook on most tarpon flies, some anglers use a No. 5/0. Some go as small as a No. 2/0. According to Pate, "You get better penetration with the smaller hook." He uses small hooks even when he's using 15-pound tippet. All hooks are carefully triangulated with a pocket file for extra sharpness.

The flies vary, from red-orange five-inch streamers in the Florida backcountry, to blue saddle-hackle streamers on the "outside" waters of the Atlantic, to the cockroach pattern used by Joe Robinson to take his 180-pound record.

The gaff is one of the most important items in the giant tarpon arsenal. It is usually an eight-foot long-handled kill gaff with a four- or five-inch bight, triangulated to a needle point with three cutting edges. A smaller gaff simply won't handle the giants. A lip, or release, gaff is also carried by most anglers, but the fish must be quite tired to be landed by this small one-hand gaff.

Despite all the special equipment and effort used by this fly-rod fraternity of giant tarpon hunters, not one of the anglers will say he actually expects to be the one to make the ultimate score. Many fear a rank novice will be the lucky person, but most believe that if there is any poetic justice it will be one of those who has invested a substantial chunk of time, money and sweat into the noble quest who will reap the reward.

The record has been broken several times in the past few years. In the 15-pound tippet class, it has been held by: Jimmy Lopez—162; Dr. Charles Oyer—170; Tom Evans—177; and now Joe Robinson—180 pounds.

The record could fall again this spring—perhaps by one pound, perhaps by 20. It all depends on lady luck. The giant is out there.

The Rules of the Game

The 200-pound figure is, of course, a manmade goal, just as the four-minute mile once represented a plateau of achievement. Not too many years ago, in fact, a 100-pound tarpon on a fly rod was considered a near-impossible feat. Then in 1957 Jerry Coughlin boated a 135-pound silver king and thereby established a new goal to shoot for. Perhaps, when the 200-pound mark is surpassed, the 300-pound tarpon will be the new moonshot. Tarpon records, like all man's measures, are made to be broken. That may be the key to the angler's fascination.

The flimsiest fly-rod category—6-pound class—shows an 82½-pound record, one that I caught two years ago with Capt. Hal Chittum. Because 6-pound tippet is so light, that mark may stand for a long time.

The 10-pound tippet record, held by Billy Pate, stands at 105 pounds. That could be knocked off soon, as 10-pound tippet gives the angler a better chance of landing a big fish.

The 12-pound mark is 154 pounds. I have held that one since 1971, at three pounds over the 151-pound mark I established in 1967.

The 15-pound tippet, naturally, gives the fly-rodder the best shot at a heavy fish. Normally a ten-to-one ratio of fish weight over tackle is considered an optimum challenge, so that anything heavier than 150 pounds is really pushing the odds. In that context, Joe Robinson's 180-pounder on 15-pound-test tippet really comes into focus, giving some idea of what it will take to boat a 200-pound silver king on a fly rod.

We know that the 200-pounders are out there, because a number of them have been caught on conventional tackle with heavy lines. The all-tackle world-record tarpon, taken on 30-pound-test line, weighed 283 pounds. That one was caught at Lake Maracaibo, Venezuela, in 1965. The largest tarpon ever taken in U.S. waters weighed 243 pounds. That one was caught on 20-pound-test line off Key West in 1975.

But fly-rodding is a special challenge, one that requires a lot of teamwork between the angler and boatman, and one that requires strict adherence to the rules. To qualify for a saltwater fly-rod-record category, you must use a fly rod and a fly made of material that can be false-cast and presented to the fish in the orthodox flyfishing manner. This prevents somebody from using a lure that can be jigged or just dangled in the current. The tackle qualification allows as much backing as your reel can hold, plus the fly line. But the rules also state that the reel must be a single-action type. This limits the gear ratio to a one-to-one retrieve, unlike conventional or spinning reels with a four- or five-to-one ratio. The weak point in the chain is the tippet. It must be a minimum of 12 inches long, and cannot exceed the breaking strength of the category. A 10-pound tippet, for example, must break at less than ten pounds of dead weight. At the end of the leader-chain is the trace, a heavy shock leader that is usually 60- to 100-pound-test mono. Heavy trace leader was not always used and, when it became legal, it changed the future of saltwater flyfishing.

Before trace was allowed, the tippet-weight leader had to be used all the way to the fly. The tarpon's ability to cut through the tippet made catching almost any tarpon extremely difficult. Even 10-pound mono is no match for the abrasive mouth of the silver king. The heavy trace gives the angler a break, but the 12-inch tippet keeps him honest.

The 200-pound mark might never be reached, but it is almost inevitable that it will be. We know that the big ones are there, and several of us have had them on. To the dyed-in-the-wool fly-rod tarpon hunter, it is only a matter of time. Now the big question is, who will be first?

BEING UNCOOL IN A COLD STREAM

Thomas McIntyre

SPORTS AFIELD's hunting editor once labeled
flyfishing the epitome of fraudulent sport. He now
knows better. (January 1980)

THINGS happened this way: I never got around to being cool. While many members of my generation have scored extravagant victories in that field, I remain irreparably uncool—taking matters entirely too seriously. I am openly hostile to purveyors of popular claptrap. I am notorious for taking unenlightened stands, once going so far as to threaten a blithering Trotskyite with bodily harm after his dismissal of Ernest Hemingway's oeuvre—including my very favorite story, *A Day's Wait*—as so much "bourgeois apologia." But what I am most uncool about is when someone tells me that sport (hunting and fishing) is a pastime.

There has long existed for me a wide gulf between sport and pastime. Three-putting the ninth hole or sailing a Frisbee at the seaside are pastimes. True sport, on the other hand, involves the qualities of alertness, homage, and tragedy that the late Spanish philosopher José Ortega y Gasset points out in his meditations. Above all, though, sport is authentic; and its authenticity is derived from the fact that it is about killing and eating animals. It is serious business.

Any taking to the wild involves for me this authenticity of trying to kill and eat something. Other, cool ventures (hiking for hiking's sake, birding, hunting with a camera) are only cheats and subliminal gestures of the real thing. Even the wild itself can be compromised thus: take a portion of it, ban the traditional killing and eating of animals on it, lard the Byzantine regulations for its use with generous quantities of Ecoschmaltz (a state of mind—according to a subsistence urban poacher I know who regularly dines on bread-fattened city-park ducks—that holds that the mother lion on the African plain must guard her babies the way Mutual of Omaha guards your loved ones), and what you will have will no longer be the wild, but some acreage operating on about the same natural order as Fantasyland. Once included in this conceit of mine were all national parks and catch-and-release stretches of trout water.

This brings me at long last to flyfishermen. What with their rickety tackle, bizarre garb, entomological display cases of hand-tied imitations, their engaging in a so-called "blameless" pastime, and their supposed pious horror at killing a fish, I thought—prowling around the way I was, as sanguinary and spooky as *Beowulf's* Grendel—they were perfect embodiments of all that was unauthentic, pantywaist and cool. I had no intention of becoming one of their number.

Then one evening on a rumbling stretch of the Chilcotin River in British Columbia, I saw a lone man flyfishing. It was water for a wet fly, I have since learned, but he had only an Adams and an old rod to present it to the opalescent water with; and that was precisely what he was doing, standing on two slick stones, shod in battered sneakers and rolled-up Levi's, with a coil of orange floating line clamped between his lips. On the opposite bank a vast herd of California bighorns was bedding down contentedly. Feeding night-hawks seemed to swirl in his hair and, with each rolling, fluid, heroic cast he made, I knew I was getting an eyeful. An eyeful of what I could not say, except that it was an act of uncompromising beauty—a beauty defying suspicion. As beautiful as lonesomeness. And he never even got a rise.

So, with my cherished bigotry shot all to pieces, I decided I was going to have to look into this matter.

The first thing I discovered was that not one of my acquaintances knew the first thing about flyfishing. I did, however, find a dusty, nine-foot

Tonkin canepole in the garage—buried behind old goose dekes and surplus British 303 ammo boxes—put there by whomever had bought it and on his own had learned how not to use it; and on my own I diligently learned how not to use it too. There followed a certain period of languishment.

Finally, despite the shameless way I had spoken against them as being unauthentic and cool, I was as surprised as anyone to find myself on the way to flyfish in the catch-and-release waters of Yellowstone Park. To make matters worse, I stopped off at the Continental Divide and the National Headquarters of the Fenwick Institute of Fly Fishing (I could not have made up such a name) and joined a class of a dozen MDs and a retired rural mail carrier from Idaho—all eager to be taught the art. I felt like I had sold out.

For two days under a September Montana sky littered with honkers, under a relentless Jack Daniel's headache, and under the tutelage of Mr. Frank Gray, I grudgingly learned to rollcast, pick up and lay down, falsecast, shoot line, single-haul, double-haul, mend line, snap flies off the 6X tippet with a sound pistol fire, and gawk at a jaded casting-pond cutthroat rising to my hookless practice fly and running a good two feet before breaking off. On the third day I went fishing.

Buffalo Ford on the Yellowstone was aptly named. In the morning there was the rich smell of sulphur in the air, the bugling of an elk some-where in the timber, and a gigantic bull buffalo smack in the middle of the trail. We detoured a respectable distance around him to get to the river.

Once on the bank, we stretched the memories out of our leaders, tied on and dressed our flies, and waded in over the stony bottom with our rickety tackle and bizarre garb—the icy water almost reaching the stainless-steel hemostats clipped to our vests. My waders wrapped tight and cold around my legs, and I had the eerie sensation that I was turning into an aqueous solution. We came to a riffle, and in bad light and wind Frank Gray put me on my first native cutthroat.

The fish appeared as a drifting brown smudge in the swift water, and I wanted it to be mine. Frank maneuvered me into position, explained again how to present a fly, and then watched me cast the Royal Wulff over the trout. There was no hatch on—the big ones of mayflies and caddisflies and salmonflies all having come and gone—and the trout were nymphing on bottom. But I wanted this trout on a dry fly and was determined to take him no other way. After about an hour of serving up the imitation to that cutthroat, and every other cutthroat in sight, I cast the fly over the riffle for an untold time and dumbly watched it drift into invisibility in the lambent glare coming off the moving water. This time, however, Frank Gray took in a lungful of air and asked me something to the effect of, "Why in the hell don't you hit him?"

To be honest, I hadn't given it much thought; but, while answering "Huh?", I did manage to lift the rod tip. The cutthroat leapt into the air. The combat, witnessed by Frank and two interested ravens the size of mopeds, lasted four glorious minutes while the trout turned every which way but loose. He fought wonderfully, and when I brought him to hand I found he was 14 inches of foul-hooked fish. I had reacted too slowly and had snagged him behind the gill. Promising myself to do better next time, I carefully unhooked the cutthroat and sent him on his way.

I'll admit it: Stalking trout with a fly rod is as authentic and uncool a sport as any I have ever practiced—and possibly more so. (You knew this, I know, but please recall that I did not.) In trailing them you experience the same Paleolithic thrill of trailing big game—and the same essential fear of spooking them. There is in the strike the mortal perfection of hitting a flushed pheasant with the first barrel. Casting a fly with grace requires the touch of a matador presenting a series of veronicas with the cape; and, similarly, no toro bravo ever charged more courageously and truly than a rising cutthroat. All right—there simply is *no* sport I can think of to compare with stalking a cutthroat: Its proportions are *that* mythic. Nor, as I've come to understand, is releasing a captured trout the self-congratulatory act of charity I once impugned it to be. Hemingway said some place in his oeuvre that, because we assumed a godlike stance not in keeping with the humility demanded of the pious, it was a pagan act to take an animal's life. How much more pagan and godlike—even egomaniacal—then, must it be to *grant* an animal his life? Now there is a matter more than serious enough for me.

I landed four cutthroats that day, fought another to a draw ("long-line release," Frank Gray termed it) and, moving downstream, struck and took the hook away from at least six more before finding that the hook point had broken off somewhere upriver. But it was still a fine day in the wild, and I would exchange it for no other. (Trout angling does that to your writing.)

When we came back up to the road from the river, I looked across to the soft yellow hillside and saw something that sent all my hard-won new notions up in a puff of smoke.

The bull buffalo we had had what seemed the common sense to detour around in the morning was now lying comfortably in the grass. Around him, at no more than two yards distance, was a semicircle of tourists armed with Instamatics. There were turret-lathe operators, federal magistrates, mothers with babes in arms, Little Leaguers, Social Security recipients, punk rock artistes, cocktail waitresses, professors of baroque architecture and born-again Baptists. Not one knew buffalo from Shinola, and they were all closing in for better camera angles.

I felt sick. It was from the despair that all cynics (who are no more than disappointed romantics) must pay for seeing the general populace once again live up (down?) to its ghastly expectations. Desperately hoping it was all some kind of an illusion, I asked one of the guides if by any chance he knew what they were up to.

No, he answered, and he doubted they did either. The last time a crowd had gathered around a bull buffalo in the park, he told me somewhat wistfully, the crowd's resident naturalist had decided to position the bull for a standing shot and, with a wink to the little women, had planted his toe on the furry rump. Had to use blotter paper to collect enough of him to hold services over, the guide said.

I was clenching my teeth—not for the crowd but for the buffalo. Without knowing it, he was performing for these cretins like something out of Ringling's. Forty taxpayers crowded around a ton of brute potential energy and figured he was some sort of natural history exhibit—a show-piece—no more lethal than a guernsey. "The buffalo are tame as cattle," 40 postcards would say later in the afternoon. Was that, then, all the park was too—a postcard attraction? And had those native cutthroat in that catch-and-release stretch of river merely been "performing" for me—pretending to be fighting for their lives?

I stood there, cooking in my waders, my new three-ounce rod feeling like eight and a half feet of lead pipe, and wondered how the park officials kept the generators and cables and tracks that everything ran on so ingeniously hidden. The mob on the hillside, by denying the buffalo the respect due his true ferocity, was making a mockery of the animal that once owned the Plains. And they were getting away with it, too. That was the worst thing. It made the buffalo, the park and everything connected with it look as much like imitations as the hand-tied flies in my plastic box.

And then a shirtless rock 'n' roller, the quintessential cool dude with orange shorts and a $10 plastic camera, squatted two feet from the bull's muzzle to snap his photo. The bull stared at him, chewing a wad of prairie grass, and thought, "This has gone far enough." He chewed a few seconds more and then sprang liquidly to his hooves without preamble. He swished his tail meaningfully and lowered his magnificent head at the defective—who refused to budge even then and just went on blithely exposing film. The buffalo swallowed his cud and charged.

The orange-togged imbecile reacted instinctively—for once—and threw himself backward as the buffalo's shaggy face thundered over him in a blur. Then he was on his feet and passing everyone in sight as there was a general stampede down the hill to the tinted glass safety of the Detroit products. The buffalo halted two steps beyond where he had routed them and turned to watch their flight. Then he ambled off into the trees, exuding noblesse oblige. He had just thrown one back.

A loony angler, who until a few days before hadn't known a nail knot from a granny, began to applaud. He applauded because he now knew that that buffalo *was* authentic and wild; that the park, despite the inherent venality of such a place, was yet an authentic and wild piece of ground; and that those native cutthroats, who would never see a blanched almond slice or a drop of meuniére butter, were something authentic and wild too. He also knew now that when you least expected it, the unexpected went pinging around you like wasps in a jar—and that it was the constant droning of the expected that cooled you. He knew now that that was something he did not have to be.

If it were possible to find the unexpected when armed only with a fly rod, he thought, then the potential for authenticity in this far from best of all possible worlds might very well be limitless.

TERRESTRIAL TIME

Art Lee

Every angler should have the chance to slap a
hopper imitation on the nose of a big trout and to
experience that eternity before the eruption.
(August 1980)

EVERY year in late August or early September there's a single day—or
more precisely a single night—when New York's Beaverkill is revived from
the summer doldrums. One morning without warning you awaken to find
your house chilly, and you know that during the night the oppressive heat
and humidity that were glued to the valley have been crowded out by the
cool, dry air that will keep the river in good condition through the last
days of fall.

Nobody can predict when the pivotal time is coming, and that is the
real beauty of it for those who live with the river and experience all its
changes. A phenomenon rather than an event, the day isn't like an Opening
Day that may prove disappointing when it finally arrives. Instead, the
significance of the river's day of recovery is similar to the one each winter
when the ice goes out, when you are finally reassured that there are in fact

bright days beyond the bleak ones that have dominated your life and your actions for so many months.

When you get up early that chilly morning and go out to scout the river, you can spot the change with ease. Although the water won't be any higher than the day before, and although the pools and pockets still appear cramped between skeletal stones, where the surface had been rooted in feverish heat just yesterday, the length and breadth of the river will seem somehow comfortable as it passes under a gauze of mist. Where a strange and deathly stillness had gripped the scene the day before, you will now spot renewed movement everywhere. Scores of trout will abandon the shade and spring holes and begin pulling at the surface with a nonchalance that belies the degree of privation that had been their burden just 24 hours ago. Streamside foliage will be dewy but otherwise unchanged, and yet you can be sure that soon the coldness of the nights will touch all the grasses, bushes and trees, leaving behind just a hint of the splendid colors that will explode across the landscape with the first full-blown frost.

This day marks the beginning of a second trout fishing season, an entirely different sort of season than the one in spring for which Catskill streams are best known. Although some aquatic insect hatches will occur, they will never be as beefy or dependable as the profusion of mayflies and caddis that emerged from April through June. Fishermen devoted solely to free-rising trout, fish working only on hatches or spinner falls, may dismiss the performance of these second-season streamborn insects as "sporadic," angling jargon for third-rate; and while this assessment may be accurate enough in light of their criteria, it really says little about what the second season holds in store. In fact, during the period after the water cools off, the business of mayflies and caddis should hardly matter to you at all. What does matter is that another order of insects has come to the fore with a buzz, hop, wiggle or crawl. This second season, you see, is terrestrial time.

Terrestrial insects include many hundreds of species that inhabit only land throughout their life cycles. In late summer the banks of the Beaverkill, as well as those of most other waters, are flush with crickets, ants, bees, moths, grasshoppers, inchworms, caterpillars, spiders and beetles in seemingly endless sizes and descriptions, and while few if any take to the water on purpose, those that end up there usually don't get enough time to reconsider their fatal mistake. For most trout, terrestrials are a favorite meal.

There are good and bad years for terrestrial insect crops, just as mayfly and caddis populations are subject to periodic booms and busts. While aquatic insect larvae tend to mature during periods ideal for angling, however, terrestrials, particularly beetles, hoppers and crickets, generally flourish during the most oppressive times of summer. Even as the heat dehydrates the land, you will see them in ever-increasing numbers, most getting by nicely on microscopic droplets of dew. Some may even be found on the banks of receding rivers and streams, claiming rocky wastes that lie underwater at fuller times of year. Tufts of ripening grass that sprout on gravel bars away from the flow become luscious little Edens. There the essentials of life, nourished by water retained in the sand, support whole colonies of terrestrials; and unless a bird suddenly swoops down to pluck one, or the runoff from a violent summer shower sweeps them all away, leaving behind only the grass bending in the current, the insects live on easily and entirely unaware of their tenuous grip on life.

Of all terrestrials, my favorites have always been the grasshoppers—not so much because I believe trout like them best as because they bring back cherished memories of the Pulver Station, the Green River and Little Indian Creek, virtually unknown small streams that my father and I used to fish. I remember Pop used to fix me up with a quart mayonnaise jar by punching air holes in the lid and attaching a stick to it. In the morning, when the dew had burned off, he'd send me to a field down the road to catch fresh hoppers for our afternoon's fishing. On my way I'd stop at a gate to feed sugar cubes or carrots to Tilly and Daisy, great palomino draught horses belonging to the Lamoree farm. Sometimes Will Lamoree would be standing at the gate, and he'd bend at the waist and cup a stone-deaf ear to try to hear about whatever local goings-on I had picked up at the breakfast table.

"Slim Pultz saw an 8-tiner in the Canaan Center swamp," I'd shout, and the old man would nod tentatively.

"Ain't got no use for diners, myself," he would say, reaching over and ruffing my hair with a huge, calloused hand. "When's Bob Dayton coming up?"

"Tomorrow," I'd shout.

"Didn't get ya," he'd say.

"To-mor-row," I'd shout again, and Will would nod with a look that told me he'd find out from his wife, Florence, after she'd browbeaten him into putting on his hearing aid.

Then I'd shout, "Good-bye" and wave to be sure he understood, and pausing long enough to let him ruff my hair again, I'd scurry along toward the scent of timothy and bromegrass, alfalfa and clover.

I haven't fished with live grasshoppers since I first learned that imposters fashioned of fur, feathers and hair work almost as well and survive a lot longer with nothing to eat. (I have to admit, though, that even now I can't resist the urge for an occasional grasshopper hunt.)

I've never understood why the Beaverkill isn't busier during the second season, because heaven knows it's busy enough for three streams during the eight weeks or so of the first one. Perhaps a lot of fishermen can't reverse the negative inertia that inevitably sets in with the onset of the doldrums, or maybe word of the river's turnabout doesn't make it down to New York City and Westchester County and the New Jersey suburbs before most sporting minds have turned from trout to pheasant, grouse, waterfowl and white-tailed deer. But why complain? After all, to have a river, any river, virtually to yourself day after day in times like these should surely be savored as a lingering, pleasant dream. It's just that when the river is the Beaverkill, I can't avoid a feeling that all the privacy is somehow scandalous, like gorging yourself on squab or lobster while good friends are home eating hamburgers and french fries.

Everyone ought to experience a reborn river, be it the Beaverkill or any other one. Nobody should be denied the clean, bright days, bracketed by frosty mornings and evenings. Everybody should see the pools afire with reflections of the hills, should walk the riverbanks all glowing with waves of goldenrod and wildflowers stirred by cool breezes. Nor should a single angler miss the echoes of chainsaws working the mountainsides or the geometric formations of geese traveling high overhead or the arrival of the naive little grosbeaks about the time when mergansers reared on the river are ready to take off and fly south.

You have to see the great swarms of flying ants that are born near the river almost daily, the spiders and inchworms dangling temptingly from gossamer threads just over the water, the balls of tiny diptera, countless millions of them, rolling along as if all of one body beneath the branches of overhanging trees. Every angler should know the sipping rise of a trout to a perfectly placed ant, the charge of a well-set hook and the agony of leaving your tiny fly behind after breaking a fragile tippet. Each fisherman should have the chance to slap a hairy hopper imitation on the nose of a big trout and to wait the eternity of a second or two for the eruption that flings the surface in all directions.

But, most of all, nobody should pass up seeing the trout themselves. Firm and strong again in anticipation of forthcoming migrations upriver, their sides blush with blotches of red and orange that testify to their growing ardor. The jaws of the males are hard and angular like young studs ready to fight for love, while the bodies of the females ripen full and rounded, bursting with the stuff of new life.

I never kill a trout at this time of year, not even to complement messes of shaggy mane mushrooms my wife, Kris, and I pick from around rotting wood in the lots adjacent to our home. It is enough to have fooled the trout, to have hooked them on ants, hoppers or beetles, and to have fought them to your net where their eyes, those expectant but nevertheless undefeated eyes, tell you you cannot kill them, not when there still remains so much for them to do.

Terrestrial Tips

Although aquatic insects have long dominated the philosophy of flyfishing for trout, anglers are now beginning to appreciate the role terrestrials can play in making the experience complete. Some even believe that terrestrials are more interesting to tie and fish, likely because the appearances and habits of these insects are more varied than those of their streamborn counterparts.

While space does not permit a complete listing of the innumerable landborn insects and their appropriate imitations, it's safe to say that the following three types have proved consistently reliable.

Ants—Trout have a particular fondness for ants, probably because they are both prolific and hardy; that is, there are lots of ants available despite extremes of weather. Look under stones along a streambank, soon after the snow melts off, for example, and you'll find ants busy at work. They will still be at it during the final days before snow comes again.

Ant imitations can be dressed in many styles, most of which are available from retail tiers. The two most popular shades among experienced flyfishermen are black and cinnamon, probably because these are the colors of the most abundant species in nature. To tie an effective ant is as simple as winding a small ball of black fur or polydubbing near the rear of a hook, followed by a couple of turns of black hackle, clipped top and bottom, in the center, and then a second, slightly smaller ball of dubbing near the hook eye. These ants can be greased for dry-fly fishing or left untreated to absorb water for wet-fly fishing.

Ants are effective throughout the season, though periods outside major emergences of other insects understandably have the edge. Ant imitations are best presented to trout near streambanks, but fishing ants in center stream can also pay off. Being poor swimmers, ants are carried by the whims of currents and may be encountered by trout virtually anywhere the water goes.

The dead drift is unquestionably the most effective method for fishing ants dry. When several dead drift presentations fail to induce a rise, however, a slight twitch can sometimes awaken the quarry. When resorting to the twitch, remember to transmit the action only to the fly. If the tippet is allowed to disturb the surface, even the most unsophisticated trout is apt to be put down.

Ants fished wet are also most effective on the dead drift, as they imitate helpless insects that have been swamped by the currents. When fished below the surface, ants tend to be most useful in broken water where naturals are likely to be overcome by water turbulence.

Although large ants (up to No. 10 hooks) are common, trout seem to favor smaller imitations (Sizes 16 to 22), perhaps because smaller imitations can't be given critical inspection by the fish. The best condition in which to fish them is during a wind that's apt to blow significant numbers of naturals from the banks onto the water.

Hoppers—The availability of grasshoppers to trout varies widely by region, and anglers can help themselves by pinpointing optimum hopper periods in the areas they intend to fish. Dozens of hopper imitations are currently popular, the best two probably being the Letort Hopper and Dave's Hopper.

Both are made of buoyant deer hair, are reasonably easy to dress, and can be bought in a wide range of sizes from most tackleshops.

Hopper imitations are best fished near spots where naturals fall into the water. A typical location would be a run six to ten feet out from shore along a stream with grassy banks. Hoppers are usually fished like dry flies; that is, dead drift across stream, across and slightly upstream, or on a loose line across and downstream. While leading fish by several feet can work well, you do even better by dropping your hopper either a few inches upstream of a feeding station or right over a trout's nose. It's important to provide for long downstream drifts with such presentations, as trout often turn and follow hoppers 15 feet before taking them.

Imitation hoppers sometimes undergo careful scrutiny by trout, and the angler must consider the pros and cons before deciding to enhance the action of his fly by moving it in any way. Take extreme care to avoid leader drag that may put trout down. Toward that end, the smallest possible tippet diameter is recommended.

Beetles—Hundreds of species of bugs comprise the beetle category. Perhaps the best-known beetle fly pattern is the Jassid, which unfortunately is tied with a jungle cock wing. Because jungle cock cannot be imported and existing supplies are virtually exhausted, the Jassid has become all but impossible to tie commercially. Excellent substitute patterns are available, however, with equally attractive wings fashioned from ruffed grouse or hen pheasant feathers. These alternatives work no less well than the originals, and perhaps even better in large sizes.

Walt Dette of Roscoe, New York, has featured a beetle pattern that has proved effective across the country for 40 years. The fly is begun by tying in a clump of deer hair, dyed brown or black, just forward of the bend of the hook. Peacock herl is wound as a body, and the deer hair is then drawn over the top of the body to form a cased wing. Excess deer hair is clipped square near the hook eye to represent a head, and the top of the wing is lacquered for gloss and durability.

Beetle imitations will take trout throughout the season, though periods when naturals are plentiful should prove best. Because most beetles can fly, it's not necessary for imitations to be fished on any particular part of a stream. If given just one cast, however, I would probably place the beetle in a small side eddy under an overhanging tree where beetles congregate. Beetles are best fished dry, but permitting them to sink as if overcome by currents also works well. A floating beetle's silhouette is very important, and anglers must be sure their flies float low on the surface, preferably with only the cased wing out of the surface film. Initial presentations should be dead drift, leading trout by several feet. If that technique fails, try progressively shorter leads until, finally, the beetle is slapped right on the trout's nose. Twitching the rod tip should be employed only as a last resort.

40

THE EVERYDAY LETORT

Harrison O'Connor

*The skittery trout in this spring creek can humble
the most experienced anglers. (March 1981)*

OBSERVE the usual feeding behavior: the long, staring pause before the convulsive, lurching gulp and angry chomping of jaws and spitting up of gelatinous algae. Presented with an unusual food item, they feel the nervous energy of indecision. One cannot but notice the irritability expressed by the ticking motion of the head. "Should I? No, no!" is clearly spoken by those mute lips. Their initiative so often punished, they fret decisions; taught by fear, they adhere to a regimen. When not withdrawn to dark rooms, they may wander up at any hour to appease appetites dulled but comforted by a repetitious diet. "A cress bug is a cress bug," say the grim brown trout of Pennsylvania's Letort Creek.

   I fish the Letort 20 weekends a year. Every month of the calendar, knee-deep in muck or in snow, I stalk these coffee-and-cream-colored browns. Not every newcomer finds the Letort exciting to the eye, however. I have been told, somewhat huffily, that "I like to fish under the hemlocks," and I have wanted to reply, "I don't fish for scenery." That is not true, though. From the first day I have loved the derelict appearance of this spring run.

I was initially struck by the dark, secretive pulsing of the limestone-green flow, not realizing that the mysterious appearance was a lack of reflected light off a gravel bottom. There is no gravel, not even where a chute cuts deeply through the many feet of muck that years of weed growth and subsequent siltation have accumulated. I yanked up handfuls of cress and immediately felt the skin-crawling presence of hundreds of sow bugs and shrimp. I stooped my head low over shallow water and saw a scudopolis: Every inch of bottom was alive with the slow motion of cress bugs. Then I went looking for the rising trout for which the Letort is famous.

One walks through swampy meadows, through pasture luxuriant if rank with weed, through long, tree-darkened stretches of stream, all the while listening to the roar of an interstate highway, the sirens of a fire department, the takeoffs and landings of small aircraft, the buzzing of lawnmowers, the voices of neighbors calling over fences, and the sudden roar of approval from a nearby baseball park.

Unmoved by the clamor, the eye sees only the utterly calm and silently flowing spring water and, now and again, a trout. The fishing is seldom good enough to become all-encompassing, but the remarkable stealth of the trout insists that the eye remain sharp. This trespassing into the business of trout through the backyards of men makes me feel like a ghost. Clearheaded, smoothly flowing, exactly on edge between two species, I am neither reminded of responsibility (unless a small child cries when I suddenly feel dreary) nor committed to action. Instead, I am poised. Poised for hours, a wonderful state of mind.

Since regulations permit the killing of one trophy fish over 20 inches, one easily becomes obsessed with wanting to see such a fish. I supposed daybreak to be my best chance.

Many has been the dawn when I arrived to see every trout in the stream, or so it seemed, actively rooting, their tails flapping in the air as they darted forward to gulp a shrimp, a feeding tempo as regular as a rise to a good hatch. Relaxed by the night, the fish had worked themselves up to this accelerated feeding. The tempo of their tailing was the measure of their confidence. The fisherman hopes to match the rhythm of his casting to the fish's impulse to feed. The faster the trout tails, the easier it is to slip him a fraud.

Those mornings taught me where to look when the stream appears dead, as it usually does. The rooters—trout ranging in size from 13 to 16 inches, with a few up to 18 inches long—rise up out of the green holes, slither across the water-skimmed banks of mud and submerged cress, and make their way into narrow, silt-bottomed sloughs between the cress beds or between the cress and the grassy bank, wherever little current flows.

If I positioned myself to polarize the glare on the water, I could see trout hovering in inches of water in these alleys. They seemed in a stupor, barely finning in the slack current, but occasionally one tipped down and scooped a scud off bottom, the tail barely wrinkling the surface, the mouth flashing white.

I cannot say how many days I walked along the Letort looking for rising trout, all the way presented with the challenge of rooting trout. Seldom did I meet another fisherman, although just a few miles away there are limestone streams so flogged by flyfishermen that the trout tolerate anglers rollcasting line across their backs. I finally asked myself, can it be that the Letort, inspiration for *A Modern Dry Fly Code*, *In the Ring of the Rinse* and *Rising Trout*, hosts a population of brown trout that prefer rooting to rising? Had I thought more carefully about the stream's apparent lack of popularity, I should have guessed that the Letort does not offer the predictable hatch action that most flyfishermen seek. One expert trout fisherman told me the Letort was finished. Yet my eyes saw that the stream was overloaded with constantly feeding, one-and-a-half-pound trout. It is the tempo and style of the feeding that has turned everyone off.

From time to time during the heat of the day, I did see midstream rise forms. But experience taught me that these free risers, usually holding in the main current at the tail end of the holes, are nearly always trout under 12 inches in length. The bigger fish, when they rise, need to feel disguised. They typically choose stations out of the current, under an overhanging tussock of grass or beneath a low bridge.

On the Letort, the size of the fish governs its feeding habits in this way: the "yearlings" rush here and there in the pools and show a preference for food on the surface; but once a trout grows to 13 inches, he chooses a much more energy-efficient feeding station in the shallows. But so extremely self-conscious does he feel, holding in half a foot of water, and so vulnerable, having wiggled across broad mud banks to a position many feet away from his hiding hole, that he depends for his safety upon minimal movement. Though grasshoppers sail in the meadows and beetles hang in the bushes and the yearlings blip-blip in the pools, most days he deliberately roots scuds. Those trout able to grow over 18 inches long at this point quit the shallows, at least during the day. They are large enough to feed on the ample supply of crawfish that begin to move with darkness.

Observe the typical Letort trout, a fat 15-incher. When he first arrives on station, at the tail end of a shallow trough of slow water, he does not move at all for quite some time. Barely finning, he seems to stare straight ahead. Like a groundhog that first rears to scan a memorized view before feeding, this trout watches his limited horizon for movement.

At last he carefully tips down and scoops up a cress bug, an action as subtle as a quick discard from an expressionless card player. So begins the listless tailing that does not mark the surface except for the occasional wrinkle. The fish is well aware that eagerness gives away his game.

After a period of successful, unmolested feeding, he begins to work a beat. Now the trout darts forward two feet to intercept a shrimp—no cress bug requires such effort. Chomping his mouth, settling back away from the puff of disturbed mud, he watches the edge of the cress for another victim, then darts forward again, and so progresses up the alley.

Finally he turns, swims back to the beginning of the beat, and after another period of watchful waiting, resumes the patrol. That his tail now regularly breaks the surface at the moment of interception indicates the fish has slightly relaxed, though certainly the tempo of the tailing is not as accelerated as during the dawn sprees. By bright of day the trout keeps up his guard with intervals of watchful immobility, a habit that is rewarded when unobservant anglers walk by on the banks; for the more times the fish routinely scoots to the safety of his green hole, the surer of his shallow feeding station he becomes.

The really good rooting trout, one that's 17 or 18 inches long, tails at a rate that is less regular and even-spaced. Halfway up the beat, he turns and scoots out into the pool, reappears one minute later at the starting position, picks up one or two cress bugs, then swims up the alley and enters a pocket of backwater, there to linger and stare. This whimsical pattern, rooting interrupted with scoots of nervous swimming, suggests the trout knows that the more unpredictably he feeds, the less vulnerable he is to being tricked by a properly pitched fly.

Later, during the terrestrial part of the day, the occasionally grubbing trout is observed ticking with nervous hesitation and excitement when a wriggling ant passes overhead. How he relishes the sharp taste of ant! But after hours of disciplined tailing, how loath he feels to make a move so bold as a rise, an action that recalls the hook's sting from yearling days.

Eventually, the trout does rise. He completes the action with an alarmed scoot forward, just as if he had felt the hook, a nervous response telling of the fish's experience. Then he settles into a pattern of rooting interspersed with a few daring rises. I have hidden in the bushes and watched a trout gulp down a couple of cress bugs almost angrily, then rise carefully for a floating insect, then root again.

It has been my observation that such a trout, when presented with a floating artificial, is far more selective—concentrating his mental energies on making the decision to rise—than when he is offered a sinking fly that reaches his depth. The opposite should be true—in the slow current, the fish can take a better look at the wet fly. Yet I have taken Letort browns with pink maggots, nothing more than a wide-gapped hook wrapped in pink floss ribbed with copper wire, a quick-sinking fly that cannot resemble either a cress bug or a shrimp. I believe the fly simply slipped up on the trout, triggering the go-ahead response from a fish that has spent hours maintaining his invisibility by careful rooting. The floating artificial excites him, concentrates his mental powers; but it asks him to break out of that comforting groove of rooting, which lets the trout feel most secure since the cress bugs are always there. The sunken fly asks only that he open his mouth.

It's possible that this same trout, with growing confidence, warming water temperature and an abundance of surface food, may slip into the groove of rising. If so, he is usually an easier fish to catch because he is so much more interested in the menu than the listless rooter. On those rare days when I have found the fish committed to surface feeding, I have had my best scores. But if something should frighten this rising fish, he will scoot for his dark hole; when he resumes feeding, he will again root up his confidence before rising.

The angler cannot always expect to find rising trout, even during the prime terrestrial hours of late season. Rather, he will encounter fish displaying varying degrees of self-confidence. That one over there, caught just this morning, fins sullenly. Another has chosen a feeding station where he is regularly flushed by passing anglers, or even couples out for a walk along the railroad tracks. Out of nervous habit, he tails, scoots out into the pool, then returns to root again. A third trout rises steadily in the middle of a brushpile where the angler's fly rarely interrupts his concentration on choice food.

The Letort fisherman must observe each trout, not merely to see whether he is rising or rooting, but to determine at which tempo, and how voraciously. Then match the hatch if you will but, more important, match the mood. The choice of fly is more psychological than entomological. For instance:

On the inside bank of a bend in the stream, a gentle rise form disturbs the slack water—a welcome sight for the fisherman frustrated by a morning of rooters. I move into position where I can watch the fish. Ah, the trout dips forward, tail barely wrinkling the surface. Moments later, something passes over his head and the fish twitches. Does he want to rise? Is he afraid to rise? He is not tailing vigorously, not in that groove of rooting. Apparently he hasn't been feeding steadily on terrestrials either; he clearly lacks confidence. He looks like a trout in a "normal" stream that is waiting for a hatch. I believe this fish is waiting on his nerve.

At last he eases up and sips something off the surface. Then he roots, once, twice. I see all the signs of caution in a fish that has not been at his station for a long time. Because of his reluctance to show himself, I choose not to offer a dry fly. I ponder my flybox.

If I select a wet fly tied on a No. 24 to No. 28 hook—say a floating mayfly nymph or midge pupa—I won't have the necessary sink rate and the trout must still rise. A fly as large as a No. 16 could easily frighten this fish, he that fins suspiciously in the slackest of currents. Why not make the obvious choice and pitch him a small cress bug? Instead, my fingers pinch a No. 20 lacquered black ant out of the box. This fly will sink quickly and may stimulate the fish to move for his food. To interest a fish in a cress bug, the presentation must be perfect. But for an ant, the trout perhaps will move a foot. The sinking ant tempts him with, "Here's one you don't have to rise for."

I have since had my good dry fly days: "June 4—sulphur action"; "August 21—unbelievable heat and humidity, with the fish picking up terrestrials all afternoon"; "October 7—a sudden flying ant hatch." Such days are rare. So is the morning when you arrive expecting to stalk rooters, immediately see a rise form, and say to yourself *Now* the floating ant will do its work." Uncommon are those dawn sprees when every fish in the stream is tailing, not merely greedily, but euphorically (though mornings in May are a good time to anticipate such action, which will last until 11:00 a.m.). And if you fish the stream persistently, you will discover the free-rising, mature trout of late season that has made the Letort famous—this trout, having found a station that is either inaccessible to most angling or so hidden from the angler's eye, has developed the confidence to think only about preferred food. But it is the rooting trout on which the Letort fisherman must depend for day-in, day-out sport. It has always been that way.

Any organized description by me on how to catch these rooters would be a lie. In fact, I am still working on the basic pieces of the puzzle. I can say this, however: Of any spring creek I have fished, the Letort offers the finest finishing course on the problems of approaching skittery trout.

Lying in bathtub-sized puddles of open water in the cress, able to feed merely by tipping forward, these trout concentrate their full attention on the fisherman. They come to depend upon his habit of wearing bright clothes, of following paths beside the stream, of moving steadily, of casting repetitiously, and of preferring certain flies. I have a friend who liked to wear a dapper, white fishing vest. How the stream punished him!

My biggest mistake may be that I like to creep close to a trout to see every flicker of fin. I often take one step too many. Perhaps, unconsciously, I recall those days when a fine rain, not really a rain at all, pinpricks the surface, when a fisherman can almost walk the fly into the mouth of an unsuspecting fish. The close-stalking game seems to depend upon the lighting. Certainly the fish are more relaxed on overcast days, feed more regularly, and therefore are more easily caught. Yet there is a particularly penetrating brightness under a certain dark sky that, though it gives excellent visibility to the angler, also allows the trout to see backwards an extra 15 feet.

Most of the rooters I have caught were taken from the near bank, where I was able to stalk within 40 feet. Total passivity is the sign of a wary fish. By crouching close behind such a fish, within "pitching range," I can choose the best moment to cast, just when the trout lets down his guard and activates his hunting instincts. My first throw is usually off. Or else the fish tails just as I start casting. In either case, I wait until the fish is again preoccupied before I lift my line off the water—an action that frequently disturbs the cress, signaling the alert trout to freeze up and wait for further evidence.

At this close range, one can actually sense the fish's mood in order to know how long to wait before casting again. If the trout's head turns toward the fly, then back, then toward the fly again, in slight but sudden movements—he seems to be ticking with indecision—then the fly is right or nearly so; but for the moment, for reasons of drag or something else, it is wrong. If the same fly is immediately pitched back above the aroused fish, even if the throw is drag-free and on target, the trout will not budge. Once disturbed by doubt, these fish habitually settle into a well-rehearsed groove of slow-finning, watchful passivity.

If a too-eager fisherman persists by casting, the fish will simply stare at the fly, and stare, and stare, though each presentation swims the fly within inches of his snout. Finally, the trout will unlock his hold in the feeble current and begin drifting. Ever so deliberately, he will back down the alley, then suddenly turn and scoot out into the deep (all this only if the presentation is not frightening, for any big mistake on the part of the angler immediately results in a scooting fish). Now, whenever I see that fixed, bug-eyed staring at a fly, or notice a fish drift tentatively backwards, I rest the trout for a good ten minutes.

When a Letort brown likes a floating fly, he quivers with excitement. A good sunken fly he simply gulps. I believe a flytier has to exercise more skill dressing a floater than a sinker. As to what makes a good fly for this stream, the obvious answer is one that is black. The starling-hackled midge, the ant, the cricket and the sculpin, all tied in black, are a range of flies that will move these browns. Productive dry flies are: a No. 24 Adams, a No. 24 black Humpy, a No. 16 house fly, a No. 16 black ant and a No. 24 flying ant. Actually, an angler fishing the Letort in September and October could also do well with odd, low-profile dries that float in the film.

Most days, however, the choice of flies is all too simple: a small fly that sinks promptly. A cress bug, a black, lacquered ant, the same sinking ant with a red floss tail, a maggot tied with black, white or pink floss, a fat hare's ear, a fore-and-aft hackled peacock, in fact any quick-sinking buggy fly will catch rooters. I have not found a good shrimp pattern.

The ploppy sound of a chunky No. 20 wet fly must ring a familiar bell with these fish. Time and time again I have made a poor cast, plopping such a fly to the side and behind a fish, only to see him turn promptly and sometimes take. Though he is rooting, he hears the terrestrial plop, turns involuntarily, sees a fly sinking at a natural speed, and takes because he does not have to think about rising.

When casting to a tailing fish, I sometimes can see the sunken, drifting fly—that is how close this game may be played. If I cannot see the fly, I watch for any sudden movement of the trout's head in order to know when to strike. Now and again I make a perfect cast and the fly floats right into the fish's mouth. I see that suddenly irritable headshaking, the gill flaps fluttering as the trout tries to rid himself of the sticky, offset hook. I lift deliberately to feel him. So light is the strike·that the fish is not certain what has happened—feeling no resistance (I instantly drop the rod tip to horizontal), he does not boil away for the deep, but scoots forward two feet, then fins nervously, waiting and watching. The fish is hooked and he doesn't even know the battle has begun. Rod pointed straight at the fish, I reel up the extra flyline, then lift to start that panicked, swooshing scoot for the deep hole. For me, that is *the* moment in fishing, not the landing of a played-out fish.

41

TROUT OF THE SMOKIES

Dave Bowring

These pristine streams that stair-step out of the Tennessee mountains provide fast fishing in an isolated environment. (April 1982)

IT FALLS down the mountain as if in a hurry to be someplace else, this Little River. Clear and cold and full of whitewater flumes choked between house-sized boulders and rocky shorelines, the river winds quickly to a lower elevation in the hardwood-cloaked mountains of Tennessee. Trout-rich pockets lie between the white fans of aerated current, but don't let their appearance fool you. The slippery bottom and deceiving water depth have dumped more anglers than you might imagine.

The flats of slick water are what you should really be watching. These stretches begin to show life along about 2 in the afternoon. No great thrashing of fish, of course—these are wild trout and wary in their lifestyle. But they show themselves nonetheless when the mayflies and stoneflies begin to hatch and lift off the surface in their erratic, up-and-down flights. One smallish stonefly is slow to escape the surface film and it disappears in a foot-wide swirl left by a ten-inch brown trout. Under the overhanging beech limb, a larger rainbow works steadily as egg-heavy mayflies dip and tap the stream in a rite of reproduction. This is not hard work for the trout. The insects touch the slack water with their abdomens, and the trout needs only move side to side, forward or back, a few inches to eat its fill. The swirls left by its feeding move slowly downstream in the slack sidewater, broadening and finally disappearing where the river narrows and hurries into riffles.

"Ah, will you just look at those rises!" remarked Gary McCown as we half-slid down the loose-shale walls of the river's little canyon. With one hand holding him in place, he pointed with the other. I followed his gaze and for the first time saw that fish were rising all over the nearest slick.

"Dry-fly time," I said as I grabbed a protruding cluster of roots to keep from sliding all the way to the water.

"Best time of the day," Gary responded as his wadered feet reached the relatively level ground at water's edge. "I fished this stretch a week ago and must have caught 20 trout between 2 o'clock and dark. There were feeding fish *all over* the place."

The stream we were about to fish, the Little River, is never stocked but has a healthy population of rainbow and brown trout. Its entire length is within the boundaries of the Great Smoky Mountains National Park and, like all 600 stream-miles inside the Park's boundaries, is full of some of the richest trout habitat I've ever seen. And although the Little flows alongside Route 73, it is unusual to see many other fishermen there. Visit the stream on a weekend and you may note a handful of anglers scattered here and there. Delay that visit until after 3:00 p.m. on any Sunday, and you'll have the entire stream virtually to yourself. Wait until a weekday, and you'll probably be the only rod on the water.

The fishing is as good as the river is uncrowded. The water contains rainbows that average ten inches long and, better yet, brown trout that have been known to weigh more than six pounds. The average is less than a third of that, but 17-inch browns are caught with regularity. These are holdover fish that have responded well to the Little's varied menu of insect life and its oxygen-rich waters. One angler I met astream told of a 22-inch brownie he'd taken the week before on a tiny dry fly: "It was my best fish in a long time and, against my better judgment, I creeled it so I could put it on my wall," he said. "It's a shame to kill a beautiful fish such as that, but it was something I wanted to remember forever."

Gary McCown, my fishing companion for the day, is a dentist from nearby Loudon, Tennessee. He's also state director of Trout Unlimited, which has helped the National Park Service (NPS) design the far-sighted fishing regulations for the area. Gary is an accomplished flyfisherman who is worth listening to.

"Early in the day I might try a nymph, say a Tellico on a No. 10 hook with added weight, or maybe a Gold-Ribbed Hare's Ear," he explained as we rigged up. "In early afternoon, when the mayflies and stoneflies start coming off the water, I'll go to a Thunderhead, a Trude or an Elkhair Caddis. These patterns usually catch fish until about half an hour before dark, and then I'll switch to a pair of wet flies, one light and one dark, fished on a dropper. That's a killer in late evening."

At the moment it was early afternoon, and trout were rising wherever the rapids gave way to pockets of slick water. Some of these pockets were long and broad, while others were bathtub-sized, tucked away in a stair-step pattern where the river fell down the slopes. "Find a bit of smooth water and you'll find trout," Gary advised me. A bit of experimentation proved him correct.

Gary moved off downstream, intending to fish his way back up, so I turned into the current in order to fish my large dry fly upstream. I shook out a working line over the tree-shaded slick, all the while looking for rising fish. A small dimple only a rod's length away caught my eye, but I ignored it as the fish was obviously small. I stepped upstream, slipped momentarily on a bottom rock the size of a bowling ball, and then spotted another riser.

This fish looked better to me, judging by the rings it left in the film, and was taking what appeared to be mayflies from a stretch of water flowing beneath an overhanging tree limb. I dropped my rod tip from vertical to nearly horizontal and snaked a cast upstream from the rise. The little dry plopped lightly on the river and began its drift back to the foot of the slick. The fly entered a tiny eddy and had just slid into the fast water when the fish rose and took. The movement hardly dimpled the water. I tightened into the trout, feeling its first tentative tug followed by a more urgent pulling that culminated in a half-jump beneath the tree limb. One quick look was all I needed to tell me it was a rainbow. The trout jumped twice more, and then turned cross-current and ran just under the surface against the light pull of my rod.

Tiring, the fish came easily to me and, taking a tip from Gary on how to release a trout without touching it, I clamped the head of the fly in a pair of hemostats. I paused only long enough to admire the beauty of the ten-inch fish. The rainbow wore the dark, heavy spots of its species over a wide crimson band of color from cheek to caudal fin. Its head was small in proportion to its body, marking a fish that enjoyed plentiful food and fast growth. Then, with one sharp twist of the hook shank in my hemostats, I pulled the fly out of the fish's mouth and set it free. I stood up, blew on the fly to dry it, and began looking for another target.

I could see no more risers within casting distance, so I moved to the foot of a channel of rolling, heavy water that fell from rocky shelves punctuating the course of the stream. The whitewater revealed no fish, but I thought I might be able to entice a trout with a nymph. I broke off the dry and replaced it with a weighted nymph of no particular classification; the body was of olive grizzled material with a forked hackle tail. I chose it because it would sink quickly and would scrape bottom, even in fast current.

The fly was dropped (I have a hard time *presenting* a weighted pattern; it usually just *drops*) at the foot of the whitewater, and it pulled the leader down with it as its lead-wrapped shank reached for bottom. The fly was carried quickly back to me in the fast water and I picked up and cast again, this time just off the main churning of the rolling water. In mid-drift, the fly stopped abruptly. I yanked line back through the guides, whipped the rod up, and a dandy brown came up through all that moving water. Thrashing against the prick of the hook, it started a downstream run that nearly took it between my legs. The fish used all of the river's considerable current against the rod, flashing from one bank to the other, dodging on the far side of midstream rocks, threatening to gain the next set of stair-step riffles and freedom. Rod pressure won out, however, and I soon eased 15 inches of bronze trout up onto a sandbar. The trout's jaws were creamy white and showed the beginnings of a kype. The head and dorsal area were a deep golden color that faded into white on the belly, and all over were the black, blue and red spots typical of a wild brown trout. I could have killed that fish—it was well over the stream's minimum length of 12 inches—but instead I flicked the hook free and eased it back into the river where it finned once and then was gone.

The following morning Gary suggested we fish Abram's Creek, another premier trout river in the area. A short drive took us to Cades Cove, a combination campground and trailhead, the trail following the course of Abram's Creek some 25 stream miles to Chilhowee Lake far down the mountain. The morning was sunny, the air was clear, and even the area's wildlife seemed stimulated. A whitetail buck, his developing antlers still in the brown velvet of May, ambled through an open woodlot. A wild turkey, its rufous head and neck plain above tall green grasses, ran across a wide field and disappeared into the woods. A red-tailed hawk dived and swooped but could not shake its unwelcome retinue of songbirds close behind.

Abram's is another freestone river flowing entirely within park boundaries. Its upper reaches—nearest easy auto access to Cades Cove—serve as a nursery for rainbow trout, which move upstream to spawn in spring before migrating downriver to deeper pools for the rest of the year. It's wise, therefore, to walk a couple of miles downstream to where the larger trout are found. This can be done by means of the good-quality dirt hiking trail that parallels the creek all the way to Cades Falls and beyond. The trail lifts and falls over two low mountains enroute to the big rainbows, but the hike is worth it.

Abram's Creek is another stair-step arrangement. The little watercourse flows on the same level for up to 30 yards before quickening again, all slick and smooth over bottom rocks turned light brown by the moss and their veil of current. Some of the pools are much smaller, however, yet all of them seemed to hold at least a few rainbows. At the end of every pool come the rocky steps, sedimentary layers of limestone arranged in descending order over which the river splashes and sparkles. The air above the river, turned dark and shady by overhanging woods, is silently alive with aquatic insects—mayflies, stoneflies, caddisflies—that bring trout to the top and make an angler's heart skip a beat.

This was the way it was when Gary McCown and I found it early that May morning. The insects were just beginning to hatch and the tempo of our fishing matched the acceleration of the hatch. We would hike downstream for perhaps 100 yards, enter the rise-dimpled river, and fish our way back up. By midafternoon we had caught and released an estimated 30 trout between us. None met the creek's 12-inch minimum size limit, but all were wild stream-bred fish.

There are dozens of other streams of various sizes in this vast park straddling the Tennessee-North Carolina line. Some of them hold native brook trout that are conjectured to be a distant subspecies and, for this reason, must be returned unharmed to the water. All of the rivers and brooks contain good numbers of native-born browns and rainbows—enough to keep me coming back to this area for many a spring to come.

MAYFLY ARTISTRY

Jay Cassell

SPORTS AFIELD's senior editor knows these insects as objects of beauty, imitation and predation—the very foundation of flyfishing. (May 1982)

PICTURE the scene. You are wading slowly through a long riffle, being careful not to slip on one of the many algae-covered rocks. Ahead of you, above the fast water, is a wide pool. You've picked up a few fish earlier this spring afternoon, but now you're excited. Why? Because the tail of the pool is pockmarked with rises, some of them obviously made by large trout. The rises seem to be spaced at regular intervals, too, which means your chances of hooking a fish or two are good.

As you watch, you can see why the trout are so active. A hatch is beginning to come off. You observe the water nearby, straining your eyes to find an insect. There! A dark-colored form pops through the surface film, rests for a split-second, and then is airborne. Its steady flight betrays it as a mayfly. You dig into one of your flyboxes and start to search just as one lands on your arm. You grab it. Close inspection reveals it to be fairly large, with dun-colored wings, three needle-like tails and an almost reddish body. A type of Hendrickson, no doubt. You dig back into the box, find a No. 14 Hendrickson imitation, tie it onto your 5X leader with an improved clinch knot, and move slowly toward casting range. On your first cast, you hook a plump, 15-inch brown trout.

Flyfishermen love hatches. A good angler can pick up the occasional fish throughout the day, but the hatch is when the really hot fishing takes place. Now the large trout finally come to the surface to feed, moving up from bottom to slurp away at the tidbits that float overhead. Imitate that insect—from proper presentation to drag-free float—and you stand a good chance of catching that fish. But make one mistake—a splashy cast or a poorly tied fly—and chances are you won't have anything to boast about.

Flyfishing is a scientific art, shared by entomologist and romantic alike. You can go astream and spend all your time concentrating on your quarry, gleaning information from the insect hatches to help you succeed in your quest. Or, you can wade into the water and, while casting haphazardly, simply soak in your surroundings and be thankful for another glorious day afield. Most of us are somewhere in between these extremes, though we are all linked together by our predatory instinct to catch fish. So, too, is the trout a predator—not just of mayflies, but of caddisflies, terrestrials, stoneflies and other fish.

The next time you're out fishing, take a few moments to observe one of the objects of the trout's predation—the adult mayfly. This fascinating insect is a prime item on the trout's menu and a beautiful creation with no two exactly alike.

The adult mayfly actually lives a very short life—often no more than a day or two. Most of its life is spent underwater as a nymph. It all begins when eggs are deposited in the stream. In some species (there are over 600 species in North America), the female drops down to the surface and forces the eggs from her body. Other females crawl into the stream and lay their eggs right on a rock on bottom. In most species, the eggs hatch after a month and the newly hatched nymphs disperse to a preferred part of the stream. They feed on decomposing plant material or minute algae and go through a succession of molts, throwing off their outside skeletons as they outgrow them. When they near maturity, some species migrate to parts of the stream preferred for emergence.

Emergence differs among species, but in most the nymph either floats or swims to the surface where it struggles to shuck its husk. After it transforms into the first winged stage—called a dun—it flies slowly and steadily to vegetation on the bank. There it rests overnight and readies itself for its transformation into a second winged stage, called the spinner. For most species, the next day is the most critical in its life. On this day the females fly into great swarms of males, mate, and lay the eggs soon afterward. Neither the male or female of most species feed as adults since that stage of life is totally dedicated to procreation. The males in the swarms soon exhaust themselves and join the egg-laying females in death on the water's surface.

Mayfly adults provide a lesson in life. In no other insect is the adult stage so brief and with such singular purpose. We must appreciate its qualities as we might a sunset, for too quickly it will be gone. And we must appreciate, also, that a whole sport has grown up around it.

BASS BUG TRADITION

Jim Dean

We can all thank Matthew H. Hodgson for helping keep this rich sporting heritage alive and flourishing. (June 1982)

SOMEDAY bass fishermen may reflect nostalgically on the era of grape-flavored plastic worms, depthfinders and foot-controlled electric motors, but that is admittedly a bit hard to imagine. Perhaps that's because bass fishing—unlike trout fishing—has not yet attracted a great body of tradition. Although a few fishermen collect old wooden plugs, early rods and casting reels, bass fishing has spawned little else in the way of romance.

Despite this, the modern flyfisherman who double-hauls a cork-bodied bass bug on a largemouth-infested millpond is actually following a rich tradition—even if he doesn't know it. Likewise, so is the angler who seeks smallmouth bass on a deerhair bug in a river or lake.

The bug you knot to your leader may trace its origins to the turn of the century. That old, paint-cracked popper could have been made by Ernest H. Peckinpaugh, who is thought to have originated the cork bug. Your deerhair bug may be a direct descendant of the pattern popularized decades ago by Dr. James A. Henshall, the acknowledged father of bass fishing. The color patterns of some of your favorite bugs may carry the names of well-known earlier Americans such as writer Zane Grey, humorist Irvin S. Cobb or conservationist Gifford Pinchot. Regardless of their origins, the best of these old patterns work as well as they ever did. And if you like the notion of catching a bass on a bit of history, you can thank Matthew Hodgson for the opportunity.

When Matt and I first fished together several years ago, he handed me a large box and sat back to await the reaction he has since come to expect. Inside were dozens of bass bugs tied with deer hair, cork and other materials, each a precise replica of a classic floating pattern. Some were similar to those in my own box, but many were totally new to me despite the fact that they were based on designs that might be 75 years old. I was justifiably impressed.

"Each bug is as accurate to the original as I can make it," Matt explained to me. "And that wasn't easy, because you'd be surprised how little has ever been written about the history of bass bugs or flyfishing for bass. Many knowledgeable fishermen don't even know who originated the various types. I've researched the patterns in old magazines, catalogs and books where possible, and have even written and talked to surviving old-time tiers and manufacturers. I suspect much of what I've learned could easily have been lost in the next few years because some of my sources have been hard to locate. I'm not aware that anyone has ever systematically tried to gather it all together, but it's been a rewarding pursuit. Of course, the most fun has been reconstructing the replicas and fishing with them."

As we cast Matt's bugs on that sultry afternoon, he told me the history of many of them. I don't remember if we caught many bass, but I do know that each fish we boated had something special about it. It was somewhat similar to fishing Theodore Gordon's Catskill rivers with his classic Quill Gordon, although this time the friendly ghosts were Henshall, Peckinpaugh, Adams, Dilg and others.

According to Matt, the heyday of topwater bass bugging began shortly after the turn of the century and lasted until the early 1950s. During that period a bass fisherman was more apt to use a flyrod than he is today. Spinning came later on, and the average bass fisherman considered his long flyrod a practical companion for his short steel plugcasting outfit. Yet even then, improvements in casting tackle and the new spinning reels were making inroads into the sport. A less obvious, but highly significant, reason for the decline in bass bugging is the fact that virtually all bass bugs were, and are, made by hand.

"Not only must they be handmade, but many patterns also take far more time to construct or tie than trout flies," Matt says, "In the 1920s and 30s, labor was cheap and many individuals and manufacturers were able to offer a wide variety of bugs. Even so, the bugs were never inexpensive. Forty years ago, in the era of dollar steaks and nickel beers, such leading manufacturers as Peckinpaugh, Heddon and Weber were getting 50 cents for a bug. After World War II, rising labor costs drove virtually every quality bug off the market. Instead of an expanding interest and availability of patterns, as in the case with trout flies, the bass bug business dried up. Only in the past few years have tiers such as Dave Whitlock come forth with new patterns."

The origin of the floating bass bug will probably always be obscure. Some believe they simply evolved from the large, colorful wet flies that were in use back then. Henshall, author of the popular *Book of The Black Bass*, wrote in one of the later editions that he believed the first floating deerhair bugs were variations of the old Florida bob, which was nothing more than a treble hook heavily dressed with bucktail and bushy hackle. These lures were fished from a short line on a long jigger-pole. Naturalist William Bartram described them as early as 1764. The first deerhair bass bug Henshall ever saw was given to him in 1893 by M.D. Butler of Indianapolis, Indiana, and such bugs had rapidly gained in popularity by the turn of the century.

Henshall liked them and hoped that bass bugging would become so popular that it might replace the growing interest in plugcasting. Ironically, the father of bass fishing detested artificial plugs and short casting rods. "It is," he wrote, "a consummation devoutly to be wished that the comely bass bug used with the flyrod may eventually supersede and supplant the casting stick and the murderous plug."

Despite the effectiveness of deerhair bugs, they did present some problems. The heavy silk lines in use at that time tended to sink quickly when worked, dragging the absorbent bug underwater even though both line and bug had been thoroughly greased. Matt is convinced that this led to the development of the cork-bodied bug, as such bugs continued to float even when the line sank.

The origin of the cork-bodied bug is almost as obscure as that of the deerhair bug, and it is certainly more controversial. Ernest H. Peckinpaugh of Chattanooga, Tennessee, may have originated the first cork bugs prior to 1910, but he's not the only one who might be due the credit. Henshall believed Louis Adams, a New Yorker who was also a Maine guide, developed the first cork-bodied bass bugs. Adams apparently gave some of his bugs to B.F. Wilder as early as 1911. Wilder, who was editor of Butterick's *Pattern Magazine* and an avid angler and flytier, improved Adams's bugs and used them in 1912. Chicago newsman and outdoor writer, Will Dilg, also credited Adams. Indeed, both Wilder and Dilg could accurately lay some claim to the development and popularization of such bugs.

To add to the confusion, Peckinpaugh also recalled giving Wilder some of his early bugs. Before his death in 1947, Peckinpaugh described in a letter how he had developed a double-hooked, cork-bodied bream bug for late afternoon and night fishing. Around 1910 he discovered that bass would also strike these bugs, and he began making larger versions— still with double hooks, since he had found no way to secure a single hook firmly in the cork.

Peckinpaugh began making these bugs for sale sometime after 1910, and tourists passing through Chattanooga enroute to Florida bought many of them and spread the word. As his Night Bugs (as he called them) became more popular, they were offered in the Hildebrandt Company catalog about 1913. After 1914, when the English double hooks became unavailable, Peckinpaugh switched to single hooks and found a way to secure them in the cork bodies. He eventually gave some of these bugs to Wilder, who in turn passed some along to Dilg. Working with champion caster Cal McCarthy of Chicago, Dilg developed a series of patterns which became known as Mississippi bass bugs.

"To Will Dilg," wrote Peckinpaugh, "should go the credit for popularizing the cork-bodied bug, as it was due almost entirely to his writing about them in the magazines that made them accepted."

If Peckinpaugh's memory served him correctly, his graciousness may have been misplaced. Both Dilg and Wilder did write articles about the bugs, but neither gave credit to Peckinpaugh for the idea. In one of his articles for the now-defunct *Outers' Recreation* magazine, Dilg wrote that ". . . Wilder found Mr. Adams using these bugs on the Belgrade Lakes in Maine. Mr. Wilder greatly improved them and during the winter of 1915, I met him at Long Key, Florida. He told me about this wonderful lure, and soon after I returned to Chicago he tied a few and sent them to me with his compliments. The Wilder bug has a cork body and feather wings. It has no tail. I tried out these bugs on the upper Mississippi and had some wonderful fishing—one evening, on a Wilder bug, I took seven bass of an average weight of four pounds. In 1916, I saw the necessity of standardizing a few patterns. Therefore, one day I gave a luncheon at the Chicago Athletic

Club and invited some of Chicago's expert fishermen and professional flytiers. At this luncheon, we adopted 12 patterns and named them."

Some provocative questions arise. What bass bugs did Wilder give Dilg after they supposedly met in 1915? Were they improvements on Adam's design, or Peckinpaugh's bugs, and who gave them to Wilder first? Was Peckinpaugh simply mistaken in thinking that his bugs had been used as the models? Did the developing friendship between Wilder and Dilg spawn some unsavory collusion, or was it just good business and recognized as such even by Peckinpaugh? Was Adams the innovator after all? Perhaps we will never know, especially since Peckinpaugh apparently did not make note of the year he gave Wilder his bugs and never seemed to hold any grudge. Indeed, the true originator of cork-bodied bass bugs may be someone who is now totally forgotten. It's quite possible that such bugs were developed almost simultaneously by several people.

Whatever the case, Peckinpaugh included the line of 12 standardized Mississippi bass bugs patterns in his catalog for many years thereafter, and so did other manufacturers. In the meantime, Wilder designed a series of round-nosed, cork-bodied bass bugs that he introduced in 1922 in an article he wrote for *Outers' Recreation*. These excellent bugs were designed to imitate an injured minnow quivering on the surface. Wilder called them feather minnows, but when Heddon began producing a line of these bugs it is not surprising that they were advertised as Wilder-Dilg feather minnows. And Peckinpaugh—bless his unjealous or businesslike heart—soon added these lures to his own catalog.

Floating bass bugs were quite popular by the early 1920s, and even Henshall developed a series of standard deerhair patterns that were produced by Weber. Henshall may only have lent his prominent name to Weber's enterprise, but when the first patriotic red-white-and-blue pattern failed to catch fish, he insisted on replacing it with a yellow-and-black bug.

It was about this time that the first true poppers—bugs with cupped faces—appeared, and they were well-received almost immediately. Again, Peckinpaugh is thought to have invented the style. Throughout the 1930s and 40s tackleshops carried many such innovative bass bugs, most of which have since passed into history. While the names of many of these bugs will bring back fond memories for older anglers, there are far too many to mention. Some, however, can't be overlooked.

Among the best-known bugs of this era was the Jack's Bass Houn', manufactured by the Marathon Bait Company of Wausau, Wisconsin. Though difficult to cast because of its spread deerhair wings, it was deadly on largemouths. Another famous bug was the Calmac bass bug or moth, which was patterned after the Mississippi bass bug and named for Cal McCarthy. South Bend sold thousands of them. Deerhair mice and frogs enjoyed considerable success and were manufactured by many companies. Perhaps the most artistic deerhair frogs were tied by Joe Messinger of Morgantown, West Virginia, and sold through Abercrombie & Fitch in New York. Messinger's frogs, with formed and painted eyes, are true marvels of the craft.

John Alden Knight, best known for his Solunar Tables, developed what he considered to be the perfect cork bug. Called the Mystery bug, it had a round body and trailing wings and tail. It was easy to cast, yet bulky enough to appeal to big fish.

Tom Loving was another important figure in the development of classic patterns. Loving designed the Gerbubble bug, a large popper with a hackle-fringed border. The Gerbubble bug was a favorite of Joe Brooks, one of the best liked and most influential outdoor writers until his death in 1971. Brooks considered the Gerbubble bug the best all-round choice for largemouth bass, and he used it extensively in Back Bay, Virginia, and Currituck Sound, North Carolina. He also helped popularize another of Loving's creations, the Marsh Hare, which was a palmered fly designed to imitate a baby muskrat.

Some of Brooks's angling buddies from Richmond, Virginia, originated one of the oddest, and certainly the largest, of all bass bugs during the 1930s. Called The Thing or the Richmond bug, it was a massive cork popper with five three-inch-long moose-mane wings or tails. Casting it is akin to throwing an anchor, but it will wake up the lunkers. Another oddity is the Angler's Roost Upright or Mistake, a bug with upright wings attached to either a deerhair or cork body. It was conceived by Bob Bigelow and sold through Jim Deren's Angler's Roost shop in New York City.

Of all the deerhair bugs, perhaps the best is a simple design by H.G. Tapply, a New Englander who for many years has written Tap's Tips. Tapply's versatile bug is easy to cast and can be fished as a quiet moth or a noisy popper. Its flat face creates just enough of a soft pop to attract a bass without frightening him.

Though it's unlikely that top-quality commercial bass bugs will ever be as available as they were in the period through World War II, bass bugging is far from dead. The development of graphite and boron flyrods and better flylines and leaders has helped, and there seems to be a growing interest in tying bass bugs. There are even a few good bug patterns available through reputable mail-order houses, although over-the-counter bugs are usually poorly designed and constructed.

While the bass bug enthusiast will no doubt always be a somewhat solitary soul, it is this kind of angler who will probably find his sport enriched by an infusion of long-awaited tradition. Like Matt Hodgson, he will construct and cast his bugs on those quiet ponds, lakes and rivers bypassed by the growing hordes, and his pleasure will be in knowing that he can catch bass using a method and lure that closely trace their lineage to an earlier time. That kind of romanticism has always been a part of trout fishing. Why should it be any less appealing to those who seek the black bass?

MIDSTREAM CRISIS

Lamar Underwood

*SPORTS AFIELD's former editor wonders, who
the hell shot his ducks? And, his more immediate
problem, what to do about those trout?
(February 1983)*

AS THE YEAR began, I decided to embrace the advice of my friend
Sparse Grey Hackle, who told me: "Let the wolf out!" He was dead right.
It was the only way to go. No more Mister Nice Guy!

My New Year's resolution was a notice served on all creatures, great
and small, that in the open seasons ahead I was going to fill my hand. I
was fed up with two-trout days, three-bass weekends, and no-deer vacations.
I'd had it with calling to bird dogs that wouldn't stand still and turkeys
that would (two ridges away!). I didn't want to see another pheasant getting
up 200 yards away down a corn row or another bay full of ducks and geese
rafted up and preening their feathers under skies that had flown in from
Palm Springs.

Government wags told me that in the previous season some 2.5 million
hunters had shot 12 million ducks. The calculator that lives beside my

checkbook told me that works out to five or six ducks per hunter. I didn't get any five ducks! Who the hell shot my ducks?

All-around, the previous year had not just been bad; it had been a disaster. I zigged when they zagged. The northeasters and I booked into the same places at the same times. I frightened the spots off brown trout while bass slept through my offerings. The deer left the mountain country I hunt; but those from the woods alongside my house found my tulips and peas in the spring, then shredded two young pines during rub-time in the fall. Plenty of geese crossed the pit blinds I hunkered in all season, but they were so high they were a menace to aviation—and they held express tickets.

My dismal performances afield forced me to face what the late John Foster Dulles called "an agonizing reappraisal." Clearly, my tactics were lousy; my timing stank; my equipment belonged in a museum.

I knew better than to seek some all-embracing formula as my game plan. Each subject would have to be tackled separately, tactics and gear made precise. The geese, I felt, would be the simplest problem to deal with. I began squirreling away the bucks to purchase a 10-gauge magnum automatic, with which I intended to wreak havoc on the Eastern Shore. My more-immediate problem—and infinitely more complex—was what to do about those trout.

Since the Romans knew nothing about split-cane rods and matching the hatch, they invented a calendar that starts the new year off from the pit of winter. For me and millions of other fishermen the real new year begins on the opening day of trout season. My usual opening-day scenario looked like this:

An already-pudgy figure, bulked further by enough clothes to outfit the Klondike gold rush, stands hip-deep in a flow of black water torn into sudsy rips by protruding rocks and bearing of the countryside what the winter snows have been holding in storage: sticks, leaves, tires, a bloated cat, the occasional beer can. Overhead the sky is a glowering mass of putty, against which the bare branches of the trees snap and creak with iron-hard stiffness as blasts of wind arrive from Siberia. For hours our man alternates making casts, peering intently at the jaunty little flies that ride the current like miniature galleons, and fumbling stiff fingers through his flybox in search of new offerings. To find a greater fool, you would have to look inside an icefishing shanty.

The bottom of a trout stream is its food factory, and on this day it will not be violated by anything except the soles of el piscator's waders.

Although he will soon abandon his dry flies (how quickly the credo fades: "I'd rather catch one on top than five down deep"), our man will make only tentative probes into the depths. His wet flies, streamers and nymphs will sweep harmlessly over the heads of the stone-hugging trout. Troutless by 3 o'clock, he will seek the solace of the ledge where fire, firewater and kindred snake-bit companions will be waiting with tales of woe and livers in various stages of distress.

Long before opening day dawned last season, I was determined to never again be a part of this demented tableau.

For weeks I hit the books with an intensity seldom mounted in my professional life. Schwiebert, Whitlock, Marinaro, Swisher-Richards, Gucci-Nastasi—the great masters of flyfishing for trout were devoured. Their instruction manifested itself in a barrage of catalogs and small packages of flies arriving daily from every corner of troutdom. My wading vest bulged with trinkets. Latin names of bugs came trippingly off the tongue.

Opening day. I stood thigh-deep at the head of a pool of black water, frigid and swollen with runoff. Coming to the stream, I had received the usual assortment of reports that the fish were in a coma. The voice on the car radio had said something about snow. None of these things intimidated me at all. This year I was ready.

To meet this early and elemental trouting condition, I pried open a box of nymphs. These were not ordinary nymphs, but masterpieces of illusion—caterpillar-like, hairy-leggy-juicy-looking. Each was weighted with enough piano wire to outfit a Steinway. Never mind that they would hit the water with the finesse of a slamdunk. They would go down, my friend, down, down to the very noses of those frozen wisenheimers. I would fish these creations with a leader hacked to three feet. (Long leaders, I had learned, rise in the pushing and swelling of the current.) The whole outfit would ride down with a high-density sinking line topped by a fluorescent strike indicator to tell me when I had a customer.

You don't cast such a rig. What you do is sort of heave the whole mess out and to one side, paying close attention that a hook in the ear is not the immediate result of the effort.

I watched the curls of line and leader straighten downstream toward a boulder that slashed the smooth flow. I tried to form a mental image of what the nymph was doing—sinking, tumbling, ticking over rocks. The line straightened past the boulder. I paid out three more long pulls from the reel, watching the strike indicator bob on downstream. Suddenly I thought I saw it dart forward. I came back with rod and line and felt the weight of a trout. As the brown—a lovely 15-incher—darted and splashed on the way to the net, my elation soared. My patience and virtue and hard study were to be rewarded. The masters of the game were indeed wise and learned men.

After that, you can imagine my hearthammering excitement when the next 30 minutes yielded two more fish, about the same size as the first.

Then the devil sent his disciples to descend upon me, like a plague of locusts. First one, then two, then three other anglers were crowding into my stretch of water. Not one asked what I was using. They simply assumed I had found "The Place."

Never mind, I told myself. You can afford to be generous. I waded from the stream and pointed up toward uninhabited water. In a few minutes I was sloshing, much too fast, through a bouldery run of pocket water when I felt my right foot sliding down an eel-slick ledge. I lurched hard to the left, but that leg would not bear the burden. I went down into the water on my back with a teeth-jarring crash. Totally submerged for a second, I stood up and cursed my luck and the worn felt soles of my waders. I was drenched, achingly cold, and clearly out of action for the rest of the day.

As I waded to the edge of the stream, I discovered another result of my accident with dramatic suddeness. As I made a little sideways move with my left leg to step around a rock, I felt a nauseating wave of pain. I did not want to feel such a shock again, ever, so now I picked my way gingerly along, trying to protect the knee.

Yuk! Yuk! See the man all soaking wet and limping toward his car. Fat-ass must've fallen in. Yuk! Yuk!

A prominent physician whom I trust sentenced the knee to six weeks of healing. Because I could not wade the stream, I could not fish for trout. The great fly hatches of early spring for which I had prepared myself so diligently came and went: the Blue Quills, the Hendricksons, the Grannon caddis, the March Browns.

My mood was foul and depressed. Without my jogging program, with which I had successfully been losing weight, I quickly regained ten pounds. Going to work in New York on the train one day I was struck by a thought as morbid as any I've ever had: The obituary page of *The New York Times* named very few males in their 90s. No, the ages of the boys getting their names in the paper were in the 70s and 80s. At age 45 I had the startling realization that in all likelihood I was more than halfway to the barn. Life begins at 80? Give me a break!

Okay, my somber mood told me, so you've lost some of your good moves and speed. You can't hit a 60-yard mallard or sink a three-foot putt. On the tennis court children who can't get into an R-rated film have you gasping like a beached whale. The guide can show you a tarpon at 60 feet, and you may or may not be able to get the fly to it (probably not, given any kind of wind). But relax, buster. For the years have given you wisdom. Look at what you did with those opening-day trout!

I was still clinging to this slightly uplifting notion when I finally got back to the river in late May. One of the year's best hatches remained. According to the grapevine, the sulphurs had arrived in tentative numbers two days earlier, and all signs pointed to their major emergence late that evening.

The hatch of *Ephemerella dorothea*, which goes on with diminishing consistency for about six weeks on good eastern streams, ranks as a favorite because it stirs smart, selfrespecting trout into an unusual orgy of gluttony. Unlike some mayfly hatches, which deliver more sizzle than steak, the appearance of the No. 16 yellow-and-dun flies in the last hour before darkness produces fishing so fast and exciting that it is the stuff for cool hands and stout hearts.

My favorite slick-water was flat empty that evening. My recent misfortune was all forgotten as I waded into position and made a few desultory casts while waiting for the hatch to begin. The air was heavy with humidity, and low clouds on the ridges promised that darkness would come early and perhaps a thunderstorm with it.

The time that passed seemed interminable. Nothing came off the darkening water, not even caddis. A kingfisher flew upstream, scolding my presence. I heard a great horned owl up on the mountain and an answering cry from nearby. Then I saw the first delicate yellow mayfly climbing steeply toward the trees. In a few moments there was another, then another, and then I actually saw one in the instant it left the water—and beyond it the swirl of a trout.

My line arched through the growing dusk. I saw my artificial Sulphur begin its jaunty ride down the feeding lane where the trout had swirled. It floated on downstream unharmed. There were other rises all over the pool now—not splashy waterthrowing slaps, but subtle bulges and swirls.

I really started worrying when my bogus Sulphur made three more rides through the melee without interesting a trout. What was wrong? The fly? The leader? My thoughts screamed as I watched the hatch and rises go on: You've been out of action so long you don't know what you're doing!

In the middle of this burst of selfcondemnation I saw something—flashes of darting trout just beneath the surface. That was it! The trout were not taking the surface duns! They were nymphing, gulping the insects as they rose to the surface and in the film as they emerged into winged shape.

I was prepared for this, but my hands trembled as I opened the flybox and got out a floating nymph. The light was going fast, but I managed to tie on the fly without digging out my night light. In my excitement, however, I dropped my reading half-glasses into the stream. Klutz! Fool! I should have had them on a cord around my neck.

No matter. I had the right ammo now, and the fish were still going strong as I roll-cast the nymph to the top of the pool. Instantly a trout was on, and I felt a flush of ultimate satisfaction.

The fish was a strong pulsating weight as it struggled upstream for a few seconds. Then the line went slack as the trout bolted downstream almost past my legs, a momentary shadow that caused me to gasp: I was into my largest trout ever.

The reel screamed appropriately as the fish bolted downstream. He reached the lip of the falls that terminated the pool and turned to face the current. The steady pressure on the 5X felt unbelievable. I had the feeling of the fish backing up, backing to the edge of the tumbling water. He was going to be washed over the lip! I had to do something! I palmed the flange of the reel, increasing the drag, and thereby succeeded in instantly breaking off the trout as surely as though I'd been trying to.

I reeled in the sickeningly slack line and looked at the 5X tippet. So many trout were still taking the sulphur nymphs all over the pool that the excitement smothered the loss of the big fish. I quickly had another floating nymph out, ready to tie on. I felt my shirt pocket for my reading glasses and remembered where they had gone. I held the fly at arm's length against the gloom of the darkening sky. No way. I could not thread the eye of the hook in that dimness.

No problem. My night light had a magnifying glass that fit over the top of the light. No sweat, just stay cool.

I was deeply aware of the rises continuing all over the pool as I pulled the light out and draped its cord around my neck. I felt deeper into the pocket for the magnifying glass. It wasn't there! I flipped the switch on the light. Nothing! *Click, click. Click, click.* Still nothing! Okay, the batteries are dead. You're on your own. Now just hold the fly very still against what is left of the sky and tie it on.

My panic rose as I tried unsuccessfully to tie on the No. 16 Sulphur.

I tried a No. 14. It would not go. In a final burst of madness and inspiration, I dug out a No. 10 Blonde Wulff, the biggest fly in my vest. Maybe it would work on these feeding fish.

Perhaps it would have. I don't know. I never got the Wulff tied on. My vision is 20/20, but at age 45 I could not see close up well enough to tie on a fly and resume fishing a hatch that I had waited for all winter.

I reeled in slowly, felt the end of the leader reach the reel, then broke down my rod. The splashes of feeding trout popped out from the darkness. I could not see the rises now, but they were distinctive above the murmur the current made as it tailed from the pool downstream.

Slowly the disappointment drained away. The easy moves, the good speed. Going, going with the years. Yet it was true: you were wiser, vastly richer in the things you knew. Such as realizing right now that what made fishing so great was that on any given outing, things could happen that you would remember all of your days. Few other times in life could offer that.

That is the easy part of change—the knowing, the feeling. The other side is that you have left something precious behind—something you had used up and would have to go on without.

Flashes of lightning came across the ridgetop, then the roll of advancing thunder. The feeding grew quieter, then died out completely. The bursts of lightning helped me find my way up the hillside to the lane that led back to the car.

I did not know if I had reached the end of something or the beginning.

The wind blew on the high ridges, gusting along the slopes, coming down to the river.

SEX AND THE SINGLE FISHERMAN

Paul Quinnett

*He taught her about flies. She coached him on
kissing. It was as perfect as a rise on Simpson's
Glide. (July 1983)*

NOT LONG ago a young flyfisherman asked me if I thought it a good and novel idea to invite a girl to go fishing with him. I told him it was a fine idea, if hardly novel. Then I queried him as to whether his plans for the young girl were honorable.

"Oh, yes, sir," he replied. "They are! They are! I'm taking her to Kelly Creek."

Thus reassured (Kelly Creek is the best cutthroat stream in northern Idaho), I gave him my blessing.

Many outdoorsmen are of the opinion that our young friend here is wrongheaded, that sex and fishing do not go together. This notion is primitive in the extreme, even sexist. In fact, there is nothing I can think of that goes together better than sex and fishing, unless it is sex and hunting.

I got my start with sex and fishing in 1956, back in the days before much was known about sex. All my fishing pals seemed to know a great deal about the new fiberglass flyrods, but no one seemed the least bit knowledgeable about sex. I would have to learn the hard way—directly from a girl. As I gradually got enough courage to act, I realized that asking a girl for a date (even to go fishing) was considerably more difficult than tying a full Royal Coachman on a No. 20 hook.

Veda Wingate was one year my senior and possessed several fine qualities, among which was the important fact that she hardly ever turned down a date. And then there were those promising rumors that she knew about kissing. Best of all, she went out with boys who, because of insufficient means, were forced to borrow their father's car in order to take a girl out. I called her. She said yes, and I quickly tied up a dozen caddis.

As the day of the date with Veda neared and as a probable result of the anguish and mental torture any young man suffers prior to such a first adventure, a pimple about the size of a grapefruit appeared on my left cheek. No amount of doctoring brought any relief. Mother assured me it was only a tiny blemish and daubed it with some makeup. The result: a powdered golf ball. If the fishing was slow, I'd have to kiss left to right.

My father wasn't much of a rake in those days, and his taste in cars ran to gray-green, four-door Buicks. Hardly suitable wheels—I'd wear sunglasses to avoid recognition by my peers. And since we were headed for Lytle Creek where one could encounter the odd rattlesnake, I strapped on my 22 pistol.

An hour before daylight I wheeled up, parked and approached Veda's house.

"Your date," gasped Mrs. Wingate in a halfscream, "is here!"

As a member of the duck tail and pomade fraternity of the 50s, I had come to expect some register of alarm from adults. I guessed it was probably the powdered golf ball and the dark glasses (I'd forgotten to remove these) that caused her to sag against the doorjamb.

I was wrong. It was the pistol. "My god, Harry," I overheard her whisper to her husband, "he's taking her on a holdup."

Mr. Wingate, a steel worker of towering proportions, did an admirable job of grilling me as to my intentions while I waited for Veda to come downstairs. I gathered he was not a fisherman and remember mumbling something inane and highly improbable about attending Harvard after graduation to which Mr. Wingate, apparently unconvinced, cracked his knuckles.

"Daddy liked you," Veda said, as she slid into the seat next to me.

"He never said a word," I said. "How could you tell?"

"He didn't threaten to break both your arms if you kissed me. Daddy always says that."

Greatly relieved, I studied Veda's face in the soft light. She had dark eyes, terrific teeth and a pair of lips that caused me to slam the Buick into reverse and bounce it off her father's Ford.

Pressing the speed limit and mindful of any Fords slipping up behind me, I soon learned that Veda was a painfully thoughtful girl. She said nothing about the golf ball or the sunglasses or that I seemed preoccupied with my rearview mirror. She even kept silent as I sideswiped a parked Nash Rambler, the immediate result of her placing her hand on the inside of my thigh.

Once out on the open road, I began to relax. For a teenager I was quite eloquent, and during the next hour I regaled Veda with all the fishing yarns and stories I could cram into four complete sentences.

"Why, it's lovely," Veda remarked when at last we arrived at Simpson's Glide, the spot where I had planned to show Veda the ropes and maybe even teach her the rollcast. "But, gee, it looks cold outside," she went on. "Can't we sit here for a little while and keep each other warm?"

Unprepared as I was for this open invitation to romance, I made my first move—quickly and without hesitation.

It wasn't the loud slap I delivered to her forehead with the back of my hand as I blithely slipped my arm around her shoulders, so much as it was the can of worms I dumped into her hair that unsettled me. But Veda was a class date—she kept her screaming to a minimum and said not a single word about why a flyfisherman had worms in his possession in the first place.

Once the worms were recaptured and my arm was securely around Veda, I spent the next 40 minutes ignoring the obvious signs of interrupted blood flow in my right arm. I might well have lost the limb altogether had Veda not remarked that my brow was covered with perspiration.

"Does your arm hurt?" she asked.

"Of course not. Probably my malaria acting up," I replied. And it was true. My arm didn't hurt. The searing pain had passed 20 minutes earlier. I was, in point of fact, somewhere near the gates of heaven; my arm around a beautiful girl and a rise just beginning on Simpson's Glide. What did it matter if my casting arm might have to be amputated?

At about this juncture, Veda reached up with her hand and locked my now-defunct fingers in hers.

"Why, your hand is icy!" she said. And with that cogent medical observation, she whipped my now wooden arm up over her head in one swift movement and brought the remains to rest in her lap where she began to rub it with great vigor. This caused me some minor discomfort. I passed out.

When I came to, Veda was snuggled down against my fishing vest playing with my nymphs. I had learned my first lesson about sex and fishing: never cast your arm where you can't make an easy retrieve.

Meanwhile, a nice hatch was underway on the stream. And while I studied the rising trout, Veda lifted her sweet face to mine, looked deep into my still shaded eyes, closed hers and spread her lips slightly. At the time I thought she meant to comment on the rise but didn't know what to say. After all the girl was a beginner and knew nothing about caddis hatches and such.

When at last the trout were slapping insects with a fury up and down Simpson's Glide, I was overpowered by two great urges—one of which was to lay a fly on that busy water. I made my second move.

Moistening my lips (this was the extent of my knowledge about sex), I launched a kiss. Veda responded beautifully, making a midflight correction on her own which permitted me to land within an inch of the target, albeit an inch high. I had learned my second lesson about sex and fishing: you close your eyes *after* you lock lips.

Then we got to fishing. I explained all the details: floating lines, tippets, dry flies, wet flies and how, when and where these don't work. It was at least the finest day I had ever spent on a trout stream, although I regretted how little close-in coaching Veda required to master a decent backcast. She was so good that all the worms survived the day.

Then, suddenly, the hatch and the day ended. Still a neophyte about fishing and sex, I took this as a signal to return the girl to her home where, without warning, Veda swept me into her more experienced arms and kissed me full on the lips, right there on the front porch in broad daylight.

I don't know how long that kiss lasted, but it buckled my knees and, somewhat unfortunately, caused a No. 6 streamer hanging from my vest to snag her angora sweater precisely at the bustline, bringing about a most pleasant intimacy.

While Veda chuckled and whispered sweet nothings, I immediately set to work to remove the fly. I was busy with both hands when the door behind us suddenly swung open.

I don't recall Mr. Wingate's opening remarks, but I do remember deciding that trying to extricate the streamer (even though it was a favorite pattern) from Veda's sweater seemed an awful waste of time, so bidding a hasty farewell, I started down the steps, trailing a length of leader from my heart to hers.

Like a big fish on a hard run, the leader snapped as I cleared the porch. It is surprising how little strength there is in a six-pound tippet when a young lady's father has spied you with both hands in the vicinity of his daughter's bosom, or how fast a pair of recently buckled knees can carry a properly motivated young man.

Gaining speed, I stumbled through a privet hedge, piled into the Buick and, hitting the wrong gear, slammed Dad's car into Mr. Wingate's Ford (which balanced off a fresh dent in the opposite fender) and started for home, leaving what we used to call a "patch" of black rubber down the entire length of Elm Street between Sixth and Seventh avenues.

Years later in college I met a girl who knew all about flyfishing. She had a terrific backcast. She dressed her own lines. And then, one slow day on the Logan River as we worked out our relationship, a Muddler Minnow from her vest snagged in my shirt. Unable to get free, I married her.

FALL RIVER TROUT

Peter Kaminsky

Brimful with native fish, this creek, born of 1000
springs, offers flyfishing supreme. (August 1983)

BEFORE he found paradise, Dennis Swope worked for the Safeway in San Francisco. He took up flyfishing as a release, and on weekends would pile into his pickup truck and drive hell bent for leather until he hit some good fishing water.

One such Friday brought him to the river just as the sun was leaving the water. The caddis had begun to pop and the trout were making splashy rises. Swope rigged up, sailed a little yellow fly to a likely spot and hooked a fat rainbow.

He headed straight for the local Safeway and got a transfer.

Dennis Swope knows where he wants to be: in northeast California, close by the wild fish of Hat Creek and the Fall River, two of the richest trout streams in the nation.

If you drift down a mile of the Fall, casting as you go, your fly will pass 3500 trout. You may not catch 3500 fish. You may not catch any. Just like everywhere else, you have to know what you're doing. You have to learn special techniques, the cycles of insect life, the rhythm of the seasons, days, wind and weather. Get to know the river, though, and you should take your share of trout.

The setting is a wide valley guarded by a ring of mountains, most of them volcanic. Mt. Lassen is on one side and Mt. Shasta, more distant, rises on the other. Even in high summer their peaks are topped with snow. Closer in, Soldier Mountain watches over the river. Keep your eyes on Soldier, as it'll tell you if the weather is fixing to do anything unpleasant. Soldier Mountain is well named. Most of the time it will keep the enemy out. It takes a lot of rain to get past it. But when the clouds hang low, obscuring the summit, you have to decide if fishing is worth getting soaked to the bone.

The valley, flat as a table, sits on a bed of lava. Alluvial soil covers the lava. Marsh grass and tule reeds provide most of the vegetation, with an occasional tree to break up the vista. There are ducks and geese, coots, herons, eagles, ospreys, muskrats and deer.

And then there's the river. It starts as snow on the mountaintops, melting and seeping down through limestone and lava, collecting underground, flowing toward the valley floor through a series of natural tunnels and tubes in the volcanic rock. At places these tubes ascend to the surface, bubbling up as springs. The Fall River is born of 1000 such springs. It is slow moving, nutrient rich and full of life.

There is a providential impurity in the water that prevents the stocking of foreign strains of rainbow trout. A few browns have found their way into the system, but they comprise barely 5 percent of the population. When you catch a Fall River rainbow, you know that he comes from untold generations of native fish. You know, by looking at him, that he is well-fed and strong. You know, if someone tells you, that he'll grow about three inches a year. And lastly you know, if you release him, that he (or she) has a chance to grow to four or five pounds—and that is a lot of wildness to have on the end of the line.

Indians lived here first. Called the Achuwami, they hunted deer with bow and arrow. They didn't really *hunt* ducks, however. You could say they tricked them instead by stretching a line across the river, affixing a series of nooses to the line. When waterfowl arrived, the waiting Achuwami stood up and raised a terrible commotion. The ducks, taken aback, would start their running flapping takeoff, unmindful of the nooses in their way, and *thunk*! They'd hang themselves and the Achuwami lynch mob, feeling no pangs of duckocide, went home with dinner.

When they tired of duck, the Achuwami would capture trout in their fish traps. If they felt energetic, they could always stroll downstream and spear a few salmon. All in all, life was pretty sweet in the Fall River Valley. The trouble started when the white folks settled in. There was bloodshed. The records tell of a "massacree" here, an ambush there, of burnings, beatings, rapes and looting, of young children who went berry-picking and never returned.

The settlers put up a fort. The government sent in the cavalry. The cavalry chased the Indians all around the lava beds, and in the end peace came to the valley. The settlers kept the lion's share and the Indians were given their allotments, which they hold to this day.

Having fought so long and hard, having lived in the shadow of death and danger for so many years, the landowners felt very strongly about the sacred rights of private property. Their barbed-wire fences extended across the river. If you wanted to fish the Fall, you had to know somebody.

Or you needed a pair of wire cutters. In 1969 a certain Judge Barr, from Yreka, slipped his boat into the river and proceeded to cut every piece of wire he found, or so the story goes. More than one righteous rancher stood and glowered on the riverbank, shotgun held at port arms. But Judge Barr must have said something such as, "Look fellas, this here is a boat that I'm floating the river on, right?"

When a man in a boat makes that kind of statement, there's no denying it.

"Okay," he reasoned, "so if I'm making my way down the river in a boat, I'd say that you could make a pretty airtight case for this being a navigable river."

Again, the judge's logic was compelling.

He continued: "Then this is and always has been a navigable waterway, and you boys are blocking a navigable waterway and that's against the law. So, if you'll pardon me, I'm just going to get on with my snipping because it's my civic duty and when I'm done, I believe I'll catch a few Fall River trout and fry them up for dinner. Be seein' ya."

Well, the farmers and the retired gentlemen ranchers and sportsmen were none too happy about this country lawyer and his fast talk. They didn't care much for his wire cutters, either, so everyone went to court. The judge had the locals dead to rights. The river was opened to the public.

That could have been the end of the great fishing on the Fall. Just picture it. Word gets out about this rich man's preserve that's full of big rainbows. The weekend rolls around and 200 trailers pull up with their boats and their 40-horse engines and they start tearing up and down the river, cleaning up on nightcrawlers and trolled lures.

Don't get me wrong, there's not a thing in the world wrong with big engines, nightcrawlers or trolled lures. But not on the Fall. It's a very special little creek that wants to be handled with care. Cal Trout, an excellent organization, has led the fight to preserve this fishery. The group succeeded in lowering the limit to two fish per day. And it pushed for, and won, the Wild Trout Program that forsakes stocking and calls for stream management on a natural-reproduction basis.

Gasoline engines are also outlawed on the upper river, although electric motors are okay. Electrics are slow and limited in range, requiring deliberate fishing rather than helter-skelter running after honeyholes. Wading is prohibited, and that saves a lot of wear and tear on the fragile river-bottom. Bank fishing is out of the question because the landowners still hold title to the riverbanks and there's nothing the courts can (or should) do about that.

So you put your craft in at one of two public access points and you're ready to fish. If you are there at the right time of year, it is possible to catch fish all day and into the night.

We arrived quite early on our first day at the river. There had been a good insect hatch the day before and we were there to fish the spinner fall, according to the time-proved local style that goes something like the following:

You maneuver the boat into position about 50 or 60 feet above the riseform. Although there is food all over the surface, you will usually find fish near weedbeds. These waving stands of aquatic grass, full of insect life, are the breadbasket of the river. The surface food is an extra treat, but one that rarely fails to attract trout.

You will have picked out a big fish, having remembered that quite often the biggest guys are the gentlest and most rhythmic sippers.

Preparatory to your first cast, you strip out 40 or 50 feet of line. Next you cast out about 20 feet of line. Don't worry that your fly is still 30 feet from your fish. All you're doing here is placing the fly *precisely* in the feeding lane.

Lift your rod tip to straighten out the line and leader. This will ensure that the fly is the first piece of tackle to pass into the trout's window of vision.

Okay. You're ready for your first pass. Using an up-and-down motion, you feed line through the guides. You kind of toss the line out on the upswing. The proper motion reminds me of the way some basketball players shoot underhand foul shots. It's a two-handed operation—tossing line with the rod hand, feeding it with your free hand. All you want to do is to keep up with the speed of the current while maintaining contact with the fly so that you are set to strike when the fish takes.

I practiced until I got the hang of it and set my fly down in the middle of a large group of spinners. My partner, Mike, advised that this was exactly wrong.

"Think about it," Mike said. "If there are 100 flies going by together and yours is among them, those aren't very good betting odds, especially when yours is the only phony in the pack.

"What you want to do is false cast until there's some space between groups of flies. Hit that spot and start drifting. If you're in his feeding lane, he'll take."

I did as I was told. So did the fish. Somehow we didn't connect. It takes some practice to pick your fly out of the surface glare. When you do, it's incredibly exciting because you know just where the fish is so that you get those long moments of expectation as the fly passes over the mark. It's somewhat like hunting, when you know a bird is going to flush and you know you're going to have to react. That moment is one of the great thrills in sport. If you can't see what's happening, however, you're out of luck. You strike, as I did, when there's no fish, and you fail to strike when a fish takes. You just have to stay with it until you get it.

Then the wind started to blow. It comes up strong at some point every day during summer, and there's nothing you can do but find yourself a lee or wrap it up until afternoon.

We wrapped.

Back at Lava Creek Lodge, the barometer told a tale of woe. We mixed up some hot cocoa, poured in a couple of fingers of Amaretto and topped it with whipped cream. It went down nice. We sat in a row at the bar, hands on our chins, elbows on the counter. We stared out at Soldier Mountain. It was wreathed, funereally, in rain, fog, mist, wind and more rain.

Next morning I went out with Carl Jaeger, a two-year veteran on the Fall, 12 years in the service of trout fishing: Montana, Wyoming, Colorado, Idaho, Ohio. He's a guide in summer, a tier of flies in winter.

We made our way upstream. Carl was confident that we would find some dry-fly action, but the fish were of a different mind. Undaunted, Carl resorted to a technique called indicator fishing. A dry-fly purist would in all probability call it nymphing with a bobber.

To fish the indicator, you tie a nymph onto two feet of tippet. Take some day-glo poly-yarn and clinch knot it to the juncture of leader and tippet. Then trim the yarn until it's the size of a healthy spitball. Cast downstream. *Watch the indicator.* The take is gentle, requiring a quick response.

It's an awfully good method when there is no sign of surface activity. It also works when the fish are taking nymphs just under the surface.

We caught a few fish. An osprey roared down, and some redwings chased her. She made another pass and took a fat fish. We floated past some Indians. One of them chanted: a magical moment until he tired and flicked on the stereo . . . Led Zeppelin. A jet fighter dove over Broken Mountain, flying so low he could have singed our eyebrows as he streaked across the valley. The rain clouds gathered.

When we reached the lodge, the clouds had built to a full-out storm. My heart nearly broke. Dennis Swope had stopped in to take me down to fish the Hex hatch. Hex stands for *Hexagenia limbata*, a humongous mayfly that comes off at dark. They say if you're ever going to catch a big fish on a dry fly, it will be at Hex time.

You do need a little cooperation from the elements, and right about then Nature was throwing a temper tantrum. We sat around the fire, convincing ourselves that it beat working—but every so often one of us got unconvinced. We took turns pacing, tapping the barometer, staring outside.

And then we saw a rainbow arching across the sky, rising from the lower river. We took it for a sign and a promise, like God gave to Noah.

We arrived in time to watch the clouds and rain roll back in.

"What the hell," said Dennis. "Let's fish!"

"What the hell," I agreed.

The Hex hatch never did come off, so we tied on some Zug bugs and fished them down and across, the old-fashioned way. I took a nice fish. He jumped twice. It felt terrific.

SIGN OF THE FISHES

Ted Kerasote

*During your time on earth, you shouldn't be afraid
to do something that's not in the exact path you
originally chose, especially if it involves a lot of
fishing, advises this SPORTS AFIELD sage.
(November 1983)*

I WAS BORN under the sign of the fishes and have spent some years searching the earth for them. Pisces is a constellation of both hemispheres, but its stars, the two leaping fishes, happen to point south. It seemed that when I caught a glimpse of them through the clouds hanging over my northern home, they prophesied the way in which I had to go.

Junin de los Andes lies at the base of the cordillera in the Lake District of Argentina. All of its dirt streets eventually meet on a square filled with pine trees and a large gazebo. Land Rovers cough on the streets, kicking up stones and dust. From the open doors of restaurants the sounds of fast guitars and the voices of singing gauchos leap, punctuating the cool autumn air.

On the edge of town flows the Rio Chimehuin. Willows and cow pastures border it, and in the meadows tall chestnut horses gaze sagaciously.

327

The Hosteria Chimehuin also edges the riverbank and sometimes, on a March afternoon, I would walk through the courtyard and into the snug dining room. A fire would be turning to white ash in the hearth, and the girl servant, her straw-colored hair pulled back like the wickers of a cottage broom, would be finished with most of her lunchtime chores.

She often made me a double espresso and put a cake on the table with it. She said the cake was a *regalito*, a little gift, and charged me the cost of our conversation for the coffee, though out of habit she stood while we talked. We discussed Mendoza, where she had been born and I had climbed; and Junin, where she had come to start a new life and I had come to hike and to fish for trout.

Behind our table hung photographs of the renowned fishermen who had stayed at the Hosteria. Among the anglers pictured were Charlie Ritz and Joe Brooks and Al McClane. Their smiles were as large as the ten-kilo trout they held.

The straw-haired girl poured me another cup of coffee, that particular afternoon, and wished me luck for the evening's fishing. She used to worry about my sleeping under the sky and wading the river in only shorts, worried that I might catch cold. She told me, "Someday I hope you are rich. Then you will return and take a room at the Hosteria."

In the late afternoon I worked up the river, the valley wide and filled with sun. I cast as I went, concentrating on my style: stiff wrist, stop the rod at 1 o'clock, wait until the line unrolls, drive forward smoothly. Fly-fishing is the most difficult angling technique to master, requiring strict attention to subtle details. When done correctly—the angler exerting just the right amount of applied force—even the longest cast appears to have been accomplished without expenditure of energy.

I soon began to see enticing pools upriver, and instead of stalking them properly I tried to double haul. Rather than reaching the desired distances, however, my line began to collapse in a tangle; I snapped off a fly; and on the next cast I snagged myself in the back of the ear. This was nothing new. When I had begun to flyfish I had expected immediate proficiency, was quickly disappointed with my inability to cast elegantly, and like many of us when faced with something difficult, chose an easier course: I was lured away by spinning and baitcasting, each of which promised long casts and more fish in the short run.

Despite my lack of discipline, I had never completely given up flyfishing. It was too intriguing, too graceful a sport to abandon; and, I must admit, any time I chose a flyrod for an outing it transformed the most ordinary stream into a wild river.

I continued up the Chimehuin and, climbing back into the front range of the Andes, where the river narrowed, I spotted some promising water. I kept my casts short and neat, let the streamer flash through green chutes, and as my line straightened they hit. One was better than three pounds. Then, just as the sun was a half circle above the mountains, the rod jerked in my hands. A large silver fish leapt from the stream, hit the water and fled. I ran after him, along the rocky bank, the tiny reel protesting. Upside down, suspended against the sun, the trout leapt again, and my fly came back to me, lazily, through the twilight.

I walked to the road and started hiking toward Junin. A hitchhiker was standing at a crossroads and we greeted each other. He was French, almost 50 years old by the wrinkles around his eyes, much younger in his smile, dressed in corduroy slacks and a neat white shirt. A small knapsack leaned against his leg. We exchanged pleasantries awhile, then retired to the cafe for a beer.

The French hitchhiker told me that he had been a math teacher in North Africa for 17 years. He had recently come to South America and was presently living in Buenos Aires. However, he made it clear that he no longer worked at teaching.

"What work do you do?" I asked, being polite.

He held out his hitchhiker's thumb. "My work," he said. He had been to Tierra del Fuego and back and planned to go to Venezuela. He worked mostly all the time now, he told me, and asked me, moving his head in the direction of my rod, if my work went well. "The work goes very well," I said, and I described the trout I had released and the one I had lost. We clinked glasses.

In the morning I sat by the Rio Chimehuin, ate my breakfast and tied some new leaders. The sun was warm upon me and sparkled on the rapids. Behind me the pastures awoke with hazy yawns. I ate an apple, sliced and dipped in wheat germ, and some Gouda that was still cold from the night. Then I drank a cup of black coffee cooked on my small stove. This was my standard breakfast and I always enjoyed it—the freshness of the apple contrasted with the milkiness of the cheese, the astringency of the coffee washing it all down.

When finished, I slung my pack on and started out of town toward the crossroads. I was planning to hitch to the Rio Malleo and then walk along it to its confluence with the Rio Aluminé. I had read in the Hosteria's copy of *McClane's Fishing Encyclopedia* that at this confluence, far from any road, was a large pool where possibly the largest brown trout of Argentina lived.

The air was cool, and the mountains were feathered with their first snow. Behind the foothills rose the Volcan Lanin, a white 13,000-foot tetrahedron that I had climbed with two friends just a week before. The morning dawned in my lungs. It was a good day to be alive.

By midday it wasn't. It was cold, it was windy, and only three cars had passed. I had my usual 2 o'clock falling out with South America.

It was apparent, however, that more traffic was going in the opposite direction. I dug out my road map and saw that the Chimehuin, which I was standing near, also met the Aluminé, south of the Malleo. Surely there would be a great confluence and large trout there. I could also see that the road I was on would leave me about a day's walk from this confluence. Cursing McClane for having biased me, wishing I had something besides a Texaco road map for my hike, feeling indecisive, I walked to the other side of the road.

After a few hours an old Falcon compact came along. As it went by, the two men inside gestured to their overloaded backseat. I threw them a pleading wave; they slowed and returned.

I saw fishing rod cases in the rear window and, when the passenger opened the door, two elderly men. Both had stiff, short mustaches, the kind worn by British diplomats and field marshals during the '30s. We began to speak Spanish, but soon fell into English.

"You looked so terribly disappointed," the driver said as I made room for myself on the rear seat, "we had to stop." He wore a sea-blue sweater and smoked a high-bowled, stodgy pipe. His eyes were like the diamonds in a curling wave and his hair was a tangle of clouds. He was thickset beneath his sweater, and the backs of his hands were freckled. I thought to myself that he looked like a sea captain.

The other man was slightly built, and though he had obviously been fishing most of the day, his khaki shirt was impeccably clean. Below his curving Arabic nose and soft yellow eyes was a blond version of the driver's white mustache.

The dashboard was covered with maps, tobacco pouches, loose cigarettes and a shapeless woolen cap. Big trout flies—Muddler Minnows, marabous—were hooked into its brim. Mackinaws were piled on the seat, and on top of them was a picnic basket stuffed with gloves, a thermos, a pint of whiskey and the remains of a chicken.

The driver must have caught my glance, for he told me to take some whiskey. After we had a round, we began to talk about the fishing, but hardly had I said a sentence when the driver interrupted with, "Caught an eight-pound brown this morning. By a friend's house, private grounds, lovely fish. On a black fly. Lovely fish. He—*augh, augh, acha, uhaa!* . . . never smoke, my lad, never." He rolled down the window and spat. His friend, after the driver had regained his composure and returned his concentration to the road, added, "Yes. A lovely fish."

Their English was so faultless that I remarked on it and the driver explained, "When I was in the Argentine Embassy in London I met a girl to whom I became engaged, and later married, by the way. She would invite me to dinner and her father spoke horrible Spanish, so they would always talk English around the dinner table. My English was as wretched as her father's Spanish, so I bought myself Fowler's grammar book. I think it was my discipline that won her heart. You know the English."

I mentioned that I did, having gone to the university in London. He asked in what had I read. I answered literature and philosophy. Like a knee jerk the two men replied, "Better than engineering."

Then the driver asked, "What work do you do now?"

I said, "I fish."

He asked if I had ever heard of Joe Brooks. I replied yes, and he recounted how he and Brooks and Curt Gowdy had made a 90-minute program at Lake General Paz. "For the ABC television network. We were trying to break the world record for brook trout but, alas, we failed. I think the days of the glorious fish are gone."

His tone of dismay moved me to ask how the fishing compared to that of, say, 30 years ago, and he said, "You're too late, my boy. The Spooner Rooners have killed it. Blast the bastards! With their treble hooks everywhere."

"Why do you say that?"

"I've lived on Lago Traful for years and they've killed it, those grapplers."

"But people tell me it still has good trolling."

He began to scratch his chest, saying, "I get itchy when I hear that word. Trolling!" He twitched his shoulders convulsively. "Can't stand it. Only time I do it is when the wife asks for a fish for dinner, and then I troll with a fly. I did an experiment once with a grandson. He used a streamer fly, I a spoon of *nácar*; how you say?"

"Mother of pearl," I supplied.

"Yes, mother of pearl. And he outfished me ten to one."

The driver had begun to rub his knee while we were talking. Suddenly he cried, "Damn rheumatism! Holding down the accelerator aggravates it. Used to wade streams like you, in shorts, and now I'm paying for it. You'll pay for it too, but you don't think of that now. One never does. This is the highest mesa around," he interrupted himself as we reached the top of our climb. "A magnificent view of the country."

We gazed across the *llanura*, the yellow plains of Argentina, to the Andes and the purple western sky. The car rolled into the valley of the Chimehuin; the mountains were lost to sight. We began to talk of the country: of Argentina, its political troubles, its people. I remarked that it was unfortunate that the gaucho was disappearing, taking with him the romance of the pampa.

"Oho, but you're wrong," the driver said, shaking his head. "He's still here and as proud and honest as ever. And thank God we have him! When he goes, the shambles will be complete. One thing you should know, for it might be useful, and it will tell you something of his character. You should never hail a gaucho, for is that any way to call a man, as if yelling at a dog? You must walk up to him, and talk to him, and he will respect you for it. And if approaching his house, never gallop up, but walk your horse the last 200 meters. Do you know why? . . . I didn't think so. To allow his women to dress their hair, which is only civilized. They have some fine customs."

We watched the river wind by our left side. It wound under red cliffs, under banks dense with pine, the river aquamarine through poplars turning gold with autumn. The driver remarked on this—the color of the poplars—and how it was sad that the fishing in the Chimehuin was "washed up" and I had missed it. His friend disagreed, saying that I was hiking to a rarely fished section of the river. But the driver didn't answer and they left it at that.

As we drove along I began to hope that the driver would invite me to his house on Lago Traful. I wanted to fish with him, to talk into the night. I wanted a roof over my head and a bed to sleep in.

But we parted when we reached the crossroads—they south to Traful, I to walk the Chimehuin. We exchanged names. The driver's was Tito and his friend's Poncho. Tito said it was too bad I couldn't come along to the next junction, for he knew of an excellent café there, and we could have had a double espresso and a ham and cheese sandwich, which they made very well.

"But of course," he added, as he slowed to let me out, "you must go on. It's your time to be keen."

Dusk found me along the river, and I missed the only strike I had. The night fell and the mesas were transformed into dark rectangles beneath the stars. I spread my tarp against the wind, ate some pea soup and a small can of sardines, and drank a cup of tea. The river talked of the mountains it had recently lived in, and the wind of snow and far spaces.

I awoke to a morning that was tungsten blue; and it happened, by coincidence or portent, to be my birthday—sign of the fishes. I wondered how to recognize it. Finally I said, "Good fishing, Señor." I tied on a yellow bucktail, put on damp shorts and entered the pool below my camp. The water was numbing.

The wind, being still, allowed me to make a few lovely casts, the long S of green line tight and singing. As the freezing water pulled at my thighs and sprayed my arms, I thought of the people close to me—the people who would think of me on my birthday and probably wouldn't understand how happy I was. My rod tightened at the strike, and my leader parted.

I ate breakfast, broke camp and made off downstream. The sun grew hot over the sandy pampa clumped with grass, but I continued on for ten or 12 kilometers. I passed several small herds of cattle, a few flocks of sheep, and a gaggle of brant that rose like a white blanket before me. Jack-rabbits sprang from beneath my feet and jigged laconically away. Mostly I passed crumbling bones and parched rock, a few bloody bird feathers and sunning lizards. The sound of the river to my left was reassuring. I knew that so long as I continued downstream, I'd eventually reach the Aluminé.

When the sun crossed my meridian I angled back to the water, took off my boots, hung my feet in a pool and had lunch—salami, a piece of brie-like cheese, a slice of onion, and some biscuits and a square of chocolate for dessert. The chocolate was the only sweet I carried, and because it was the only one, a dessert of it was sweet indeed.

I continued to hike, with the pack, after all those months-upon-moun-tain-months, simply there and heavy. Although I was enjoying the starkly yellow, sparse green land, I became lonely—for the friends I had climbed with, for someone like Tito to fish with, for my solitary way across the arid mesa country. The face of a woman I had left forever crept into my mind, and my walk to the confluence became purposeless.

I felt the pang, its rending a reward, and I thought, it's been a long solitary time southward, this 15-month cleansing, this experiment in using time differently. I'm happy with it, and when I've gone far enough I'll return and see the people that often live in my thoughts: Parker, my university friend, with whom I've hunted many woods; my brother P.V., with whom I grew among the fish of the North and who's my companion on the sea —the two men who've never forgotten the times we spent together, and of course the rest of the family, who by separation have become dear.

And then I thought, perhaps it's all about this: Each of us is given some 70 years, a decent amount of time and such a niggardly small gift when you have the eyes to see the gifts you must leave. In that time you shouldn't be afraid to take out a year or even more to do something not in the straight path you originally chose. You shouldn't be afraid to watch the turning of stars and clouds and strange peoples, for although family, country and abiding loves will never afterwards be holy, they will have become tender and subtle in unimagined ways.

Understanding this for the first time, not in my head but as miles beneath my feet, I knew what could not be avoided: to work and to sweat, to be in pain of body, mind and heart, would be the only way a goal could become sweet. "So walk hard my friend," I told myself, "walk hard and grin when it hurts even to cry, when you crave to lie and sleep, for there'll be nothing but the long sleep afterwards."

During the remainder of the afternoon I hiked over desolate mesas without catching sight of the river. Behind me were the Andes—gray, stern, snowcapped—and around me nothing but yellow burnt hills, sage grass, the skeleton of a sheep. I ran out of water; a lone hawk circled in the sky; I felt alone.

I climbed a mesa and came in view of the river again. Willows lined the banks; glittering water interlaced the sandbars; a row of poplars marched up a hillside. The distant mountains shimmered in the heat waves. A slight breeze moved the grass; the flies buzzed—life was close. My head began to pound: death seemed close as well, and precious, and as unimportant as my old age.

Across the valley, downstream from where I stood, another large river joined the Chimehuin. I was sure it was the Aluminé, and that this was the *confluencia* I had been hiking to.

I reached the other side of the river by fording, and I was glad that I had had the foresight to cut a wading staff. I would have been washed away if I hadn't.

I made camp, drank the sweet river water, bathed and lay in the sun. Then I waded into the water, and with a fly tied in New Hampshire, I cast into the eddies. Suddenly a rainbow vaulted into the air as if to take a look at the upper world, but he was at the end of my line.

I caught another and lost some, then hooked a large brown trout that fought powerfully. I brought the fish to shore, looked once at his orange flanks, and decided to return him. The sun was going down, the mesas were carmine, and I was pleased.

Gathering some dead willow branches, I lit a fire and then sat down. The river rushed deep and strong behind the flames and there was not another light in the valley of the Chimehuin. The stars shone brightly in the heaven and I could see the Milky Way and the Pleiades.

I ate a can of meat fried in butter and the rest of my chocolate bar, then some biscuits. The chocolate was bittersweet and cut the tongue, while the biscuits had a bland vanilla taste. Together they were outstanding. I had planned on saving them for the following day, but it was my birthday and birthdays do not come every day.

I gazed at Crux, which is the cross of the southern sky, and after a while took out my pad and began to write of the trout and of my stay in the Lake District. It was soon time to tie new leaders and to see what flies I had left. It had been time to do that some time ago, but of all things I love I love this the most, the casting of words in the rivers of my days.

As I slipped into my sleeping bag, the night's cool air was rare and I felt graceful. I was alone and silent along the sound of the water, at ease in the creation, having come a long way to this confluence, my rivers wide and tender for their journey's rigor.

FOLKTALES AND THE TRUTH ABOUT TROUT FISHING

Anthony Acerrano

In the world of angling, which is more powerful, legend or fact, wonders our popular SPORTS AFIELD fishing editor? (January 1986)

"I saw a trout that I have known for a long time. . . . He is many years old and weighs many pounds and moves slowly with wisdom."
—Richard Brautigan

BRAUTIGAN'S words are not the beginning of a fishing tale, but are plucked from the midst of one of the author's more inscrutable 1960's allegories. This unintentional deception is familiar to those who, anticipating hard angling information, opened a copy of *Trout Fishing In America* and peered bemusedly into the lyric babble of its pages—an image that must have delighted Brautigan to no end.

But for all of the author's literary iconoclasm, he unwittingly perpetuated one of the mustier cliches of fishing literature, and of flyfishing literature in particular: that of the singularly old and large trout, heavy with pounds and wisdom, who has taken up lodging in a certain pool, under a specific logjam or behind an invariable boulder. Here this ancient creature resides as the calendar pages fall and the years glide by. The fish—usually named Old Leopard Spots or Old Grandpaw or Old Something—becomes a perennial quarry and a kind of dear friend, to the point where the fish allegedly *recognizes* the angler, or his hooked offering, on sight. Time after time Old Something rises up and studies the fly laid so perfectly at his disposal, and the fisherman's breath stops and his heart pounds. At the last minute, of course, O.S. wrinkles his nose at the obviousness and coarseness of the whole situation and turns away, lifting his large forked tail clear of the water in a gesture of farewell and contempt, sinking back to his home under the logjam or behind the boulder, leaving the angler shaky and weak-kneed. Still, he must smile in admiration for such a game rival. Later, at home, he tells his wife: "Oh, that Old Something, he outwitted me again!" and his wife, looking at him appraisingly, finds this easy to believe.

After enough years of this matching of wits, the angler through sheer skill and presentational ingenuity, manages to fool Old Something and hook him good. O.S., in shock and outrage, tears and foams and leaps in a way that would shame a 100-pound tarpon, until the web-thin leader pops like a cap gun and the fish is gone. The angler reels in his slack line sadly and goes home, where his unsympathetic wife makes him mow the lawn and put up storm windows.

By now enough years have passed to equal the life expectancy of a dozen trout, but still O.S. lurks beneath the same logjam, or behind the same boulder. Miraculously, in all this time no one has channelized the stream for irrigation purposes, no one has drained the pool to make room for a supermarket parking lot, no progressive upstart has turned the lovely banks into a subdivision. Equally amazing, the angler has not been forced to relocate because of a job change, nor has he been fired because of his obsession with what the rest of the world calls "a silly fish." And his wife has not left him for someone richer, better-looking or more witful.

One day the angler creeps up to the pool he has come to know so well, to the logjam (or boulder) he has beat to particles with his flyline over the years. He sits and studies the water, a keen glint in his eyes. He has come up with a trick, an ingenious ploy, that simply cannot fail.

While the angler is preparing his deadly presentation, his last-ditch attempt to bring O.S. to creel, it is easy to imagine O.S. down there in the crystalline depths of the pool, under the logjam (or behind the boulder), resting buoyantly in the cold aqueous world, finning a little to hold his place, watching out of the corner of his eyes as bits of flotsam come gliding by in the current. A yellow birch leaf twirls by in slow motion; next comes a short stick that looks almost like a caddis casing, so bumpy and gnarled is it; and then a sculpin, so plump and fat and *zip*—so tasty.

With the sculpin digesting nicely, O.S. lets his sage mind roam. He wonders when he will see his old rival the angler again. He thinks of him fondly, in initials, as Old S.O.B. Grudgingly he must admire the tenacity, if not the wit, of this angler who keeps coming back. Certainly his presentations are crude and even offensive, but it is good fun to tease him and give him the tail every now and then. Ah, here comes another sculpin darting along the edge of the logjam (or behind the boulder). One little flick out there and—*gaaaagh!*

When the angler sees O.S. hit his sculpin fly, he bursts into a big grin and yells out: "I got you now, you old fox!" and a tremendous pool-churning fight is underway, a battle of Homeric proportions.

Eventually, after an hour or so, the trout of many pounds and much wisdom is beaten and drawn toward the net. The fisherman looks into the eyes of his opponent and sees sadness and disillusionment where once was confidence and sagacity, and his joy drains from him and his victory is hollow. He pulls the huge, heavy length of O.S. from the water, and the fish gapes and pants. The angler hesitates only a moment. He looks the fish in the eye and says, "Well, I finally showed you who's smarter. But I just can't do it." He removes the hook and slips O.S. back into the water. O.S. hovers there a second in disbelief, then he understands and zooms off. He considers giving the angler the tail, just for the hell of it, but things have changed now. He fins feebly down to his home under the logjam (or behind the boulder) and rests.

The angler goes home and doesn't say anything. His wife looks at him and says, "I bet that Old Something outwitted you again, didn't he?" And the angler smiles cryptically and nods. "Yeah," he says, "that Old Something, he's some kind of fish," and the story ends and no one is surprised and everyone is happy.

This nearly epic folktale of troutfishing has been around for at least two centuries, in slightly varying versions, and recent printed evidence indicates that it's still alive and well today. Let us admit that the tale does ring with a certain nostalgic appeal.

Perhaps it's nostalgia, or a childlike urge toward fantasy, that keeps the folktale alive in modern angling literature. And maybe this is also why each time it appears I find myself going along with it, like a film buff who has seen an old and sappy picture over and over but who still sits through for the ending. There is a comfort, a reassurance, in the known and predictable thing.

But one day not too long ago, made grumpy by the inexplicable processes of biology and psychology, I stopped reading halfway through yet another Old Something epic and impulsively hurled the magazine across the room, where it splattered against the wall, frightening the sleeping cat into rather startling gymnasitc reactions.

"Why?" I asked outloud, possibly to the cat's tail as it whisked around the corner and out of sight. "Why hasn't this ever happened to *me*?" The implausibility of the whole thing struck me: this was all a fake, a piscatorial Easter Bunny. In years of devoted trout fishing I'd never experienced anything close to what was put down in these fairytales. Was it me, or was it some essential untruth in the story?

Now it is well enough known that angling is not a subject steeped in Truth. Indeed, I've learned that there is only one truth you can depend on in the world of fishing: *Everybody lies.*

Given this propensity to alter reality in a self-serving way, it's not hard to find the origin and maintenance of the Old Something myth. But sitting in private and having, therefore, no need to lie to anyone, I had to admit the blunt fact that *I* at least had never had an extended "matching of wits" with a particular fish; certainly not anything that lasted more than a day or possibly two. In all honesty, my encounters with individual trout seldom exceed a half-hour.

Maybe my experiences are a product of my own faults. I've never been an Ahab for trout. No one particular fish has ever seemed crucial to the fulfillment of my destiny. Beyond that, I've always been suspicious of those who make a big deal out of "outwitting" a trout, a creature whose cranial capacity is approximately the size of a thimble. Those fish I have caught were invariably beautiful, lovely children of nature; but if you look deep into their eyes you will find neither wisdom nor wit, but only blank, monofocused vacuity and a certain urgency to get back to the water.

Even so, you would think that in 15 years of devoted angling I would have encountered at least one Old Something, somewhere. Not necessarily a trout with deep, serious eyes and the mind of George Bernard Shaw— not necessarily a fish who knew me well enough to wave a fin at my arrival—but simply a large, wary trout that could be depended upon to appear in the same place day after day, month after month, year after year; a fish that for some reason I couldn't catch no matter what I tried.

More importantly, I'd like to find the place where all of this could happen, where I would have that trout and its pool all to myself as the decades rolled by, a place where nobody would come in and wreck things. I've never seen such a place in real life, but it would be nice if it existed, somewhere, somehow.

All of this cogitation makes me think about the streams I *do* know, with real water and real trout. I know some pretty good ones too. One, in fact, in Montana, that biologists say has a four-pound brown every 30 feet. It boggles the mind—a potential Old Something every 30 feet! I've had good times on that stream, and then I've had times when the place seemed cleaned out of anything over 10 inches.

There was one day, though, in July. I had the whole river to myself, not another fisherman in sight. A storm was coming in, turning the sky the color of Concord grapes. The cottonwoods had their leaves laid back so that the undersides shone silvery-green, and the air felt heavy enough to hold in your hands. The fish started to go crazy, smashing my little Muddler as though they were angry at it. Good fish too, browns in the two and three pound range, brawlers, leapers even. Every other cast brought a fish, and the rod seemed continously bowed and dancing. I came to a thick gnarl of submerged roots and dropped the Muddler with a *plap*, deep into the tangle. A large brown rose to it and slashed, missing the fly. I cast again to the same place and saw the fish nose up and then sink back again. "Garr!" I said, or something to that effect, and cast again.

The sky was rumbling now, grapey-black, and once more I smacked the Muddler down and wiggled the rod tip, making the fly twitch and jerk just below the surface. There was a brown streak, and the fish hit, then ran. The weight against the rod made me caution myself: "This is a good one; *don't blow it.*" I whooped after another hard run and worked the fish away from a root tangle, bringing him out where he again took off downstream. The clouds boomed. Incongruously, a sudden shaft of sunlight softened the whole scene in a magic glow. I kept steady pressure on the line and eased the fish in, until its head was above water and I could see the Muddler's gold tinsel shank sparkle in the fish's jaw.

In the net the trout was long and thick and beautiful. The magic light turned him a coppery, gleaming brown; the spots on his sides were iridescent. Quickly I removed the hook with a twist. This one was well over four pounds, maybe edging five. I sunk him into the water and peeled back the webbing of net. His gills worked and I reached down and grasped the meat of his tail, cold and slippery-smooth, and waggled him gently. Then he tugged and spurted away, and the thunder in the sky told me it was time to go home. I left, knowing I'd experienced something true—the real thing, something beyond the mere stuff of folktales.

CELEBRATION OF SPRING

Jerome B. Robinson

*SPORTS AFIELD's gundog editor discovers that
the two oldtimers had it right, it's not how the
fishing is at any given moment, but the
accumulation of a lifetime of experiences that
counts. (March 1986)*

ON THE shore of Lake Seboomook in the Penobscot headwaters deep
in the woods of Maine, two old men were boiling a pot of coffee over a
little hardwood fire when we came by.

"Come in and have a cup," they hailed us when we asked about the
fishing. "Fishin's jest what we was talkin' 'bout."

We went over and had a cup and then another, for the coffee was
wonderful stuff, boiled with eggshells in it to make the grounds settle. It
wasn't so strong as it was rich, but the conversation that came with it was
richer still.

"John, you 'member the time we wuz up to"—then he'd name some
unpronounceable Indian-named lake—"and we hit the salmon jest right.
Hell, you couldn't troll 100 yards without a strike, and they wuz good

ones. Four pounds, a lot of 'em. A Grey Ghost streamer didn't have a chance in that water."

Then old John would come back. "Yep, I remember that toime. When we wuz done we paddled on down"—then he'd name another unpronounceable lake—"and you caught a square-tail trout big as the blade on that canoe paddle."

For the rest of that windy, rainy afternoon we sat and listened to those two old men. Their conversation drifted from lake to lake and down through the connecting streams that held whole watersheds together. Over the years this pair had paddled and camped and fished the headwaters of every major river system in Maine. They carried mental maps of how the water flowed and where the fish had been found in lakes and streams that spanned the whole top half of Maine.

They were fine-looking old birds, too, with stagged-off pants and plaid wool shirts that carried the scent of many campfires. Their old felt hats were not "decorated" with flies, but each held a couple of old favorites. Their canoe was a 20-footer with varnished cedar ribs that glowed with the patina of age and careful use. There was no outboard motor, just two old hand-carved paddles, and propped against the center thwart were a pair of pack baskets in which their fishing gear and coffee pot were carried.

When the wind died, they were ready to go.

"There's 10,000 square miles of woods and lakes and rivers to see in the state o'Maine," one of the old fellows told me that day. "Try to get to all of them. It'll make you a lifetime of memories. . . ."

That was more than 20 years ago, and I've been trying ever since. Each winter I get thinking about those two old men and all the places they had fished from ice-out right on through until bird season, and I can't wait to hear that the lakes are unlocked and it's time to go.

To anyone who fishes in Maine's north woods for landlocked salmon, brook trout or togue (as lake trout are called in Maine), ice-out holds the kind of magical excitement that Christmas does for kids. This is the true opening day, when another fishing season begins. For when the ice goes out, fish that have been locked beneath the surface all winter come to the top to cavort in the oxygen-charged water beneath the wind-driven waves. It is a time when salmon and trout will hit streamer flies trolled right on the surface. At ice-out smelt come in from the depths of the lakes to run at night up feeder streams to spawn; and trout and salmon gather at the

stream mouths each morning to feed upon the little fish as they pour back into the lake.

For a few days after ice-out there is a flurry of excellent fishing when the best salmon and trout of the year are taken. And even though it's May, the weather is usually cold and rainy with frost at night (ice-out in the north country occurs on the average about May 8).

Bud Wilcox, the flytier from Rangeley, Maine, is the best ice-out fisherman I know. Bud goes in over rotting snowdrifts and gets his canoe in the water at the crack of dawn. He paddles to the mouth of a brook where smelt are running and anchors about 100 yards offshore in 15 to 20 feet of water.

"You don't want to fish right up in the mouth," he says. "The smaller trout will be up in there, but the bigger fish lie offshore in deeper water, where there's less competition."

For this kind of fishing Bud invented the Kennebago Smelt, one of the most effective smelt flies ever tied. He uses a sinking line, casts out toward the smelt brook, then counts off 60 seconds while the line sinks before starting to steadily strip in the line.

"Always look behind the fly before you take it out of the water to make another cast," Bud warns. "More often than you think, there'll be a big fish following the fly. If one is there, leave the fly in the water and twitch it around the canoe or make just a short roll cast and bring it by him again. I hook a lot of big fish right beside the canoe."

I have fished with Bud when he took five brook trout over two pounds apiece in two mornings just after ice-out.

The best days for trolling for salmon are those that are overcast with a brisk chop aerating the water. Then the salmon will be on top, and any number of smelt fly patterns will take them. You tie on 20 feet or more of 6- or 8-pound-test monofilament leader and troll with a flyrod. Floating lines, sinking-tip lines and high-density sinking lines are all used successfully.

In the old days men trolled from canoes paddled by guides or companions, but today we do it with small outboards run at a brisk walking speed.

"Most people troll too slowly," my friend Al Diem insists. "If a fish wants a fly, he'll catch it even if you're moving fast. If you're trolling slowly, the fish doesn't have to make up his mind as quickly, and it often loses interest." Not everyone agrees with this theory. We ran into one old-timer who watched Al and me zooming up and down the lake and shook his head in dismay.

Later he told us, "I couldn't tell if you fellas was towin' a fly or a water-skier."

But there was a reason for trolling fast that day. It was just after ice-out, and we had rushed over to Maine in the middle of the night to fish the West Branch of the Penobscot, but when we arrived at daylight we found the river flooded over its banks.

So we made a U-turn and roared all the way back across northern New England to get Al's boat in Vermont and go fishing in Lake Memphremagog. It was almost dark when we launched, and we were frustrated, having driven for 14 hours and not fished yet, so Al was trolling fast. And, by God, we hooked three nice salmon before darkness fell, and showed up at his house in time for dinner. That's how the fast-trolling theory was born—out of frustration, not by analysis, but it seems to work.

At times you've just got to go fishing, and ice-out is one of those times. But a month later the weather is better and the finest fishing of the year takes place.

"Come when the alder leaves are the size of mouse ears," an old Maine fisherman once advised me. But when I've called ahead to check on the progress of the alder leaves, I've always felt a little silly using the mouse ear reference.

"How big are the alder leaves?" I ask.

"Whut?" comes the Maine voice at the other end of the wire.

"The alder leaves. Would you say they're approaching the size of mouse ears?"

"Depends on the size of the mouse. . . ."

But there was a time when Sherry and I were up in the Allagash and the alder leaves *were* just the size of mouse ears. It was Memorial Day weekend, and the insect hatches were just beginning to come off along the lakeshores every afternoon. We could paddle out from any campsite in the evening and take plucky foot-long brookies on dry flies with ease.

One afternoon just after a thunderstorm we paddled up into a beaver flowage at the mouth of a tributary stream, and trout were rising everywhere. Using Grey Wulff dries, we took two trout that both measured exactly 17 inches.

I thought I knew the secret then and marked that place down as a sure thing for Memorial Day weekend. Years later I returned with a gang of fishing friends, and we launched a four-day assault. The resident forest ranger told us that the fishing had been outstanding until a few days before we arrived. He said the party that had just left our campsite had hooked and released numerous brook trout up to 3½ pounds and togue up to 12.

"They really had the switch turned on all last week," he said, beaming.

Well, they really had the switch shut off while we were there. We had to scratch to get enough nine-inch brookies to make one supper; and as for togue, we would have struck out altogether had it not been for a three-pound fish that came out of nowhere and hit a Rapala that my 10-year-old son, Matt, was trolling on top at high noon.

We fished the brooks, we applied the Bud Wilcox method off the mouth of smelt brooks at dawn, we cast flies along shore when the wind died at evening, and we dragged lures at various depths for togue.

Jim Henry was there in full high-tech regalia, too. He had fitted his 21-foot Mad River Kevlar Grand Laker canoe with a pair of downriggers and planing boards and Lowrance's latest electronic depthrecorder. He could troll at any depth and cover an area out to 150 feet on either side of his canoe, and he could show you every fish he passed over on his graph printout.

The forest ranger hadn't seen planing boards before and questioned why anyone needed them.

"I can troll a shoreline while keeping the canoe out in the deep water," Jim explained. "Or if a fish is shy of the motor I can be trolling lures up to 150 feet out to the sides."

The ranger looked over the planing boards some more, and then he said, "I guess there's no regulations against using them things, long as you don't have anybody ridin' on 'em."

Two days later he stopped by again to see how we were doing.

"Gettin' skunked," Jim said.

The ranger looked at all that high-tech equipment and smiled. "I'll see if I can get you one," he said.

That evening he went out in his big canoe and trolled slowly up and down in front of his cabin with a live smelt and a wire line, the way they've done it in Maine for 100 years. At dark he came into our firelight bearing an 11-pound togue.

"Thought this might feed your bunch," he said. "It's a little too big for Norma and me. . . ."

Well, that fish sure threw us into a tailspin. We had been planning to move on down to Lake Chesuncook and try for salmon, but as we ate that beautiful orange-fleshed lake trout—filleted, skinned, cut into portions, floured and seasoned, and then cooked golden brown in a skillet—we decided to stay another day and fish the way the ranger did it.

One day more stretched out to two, and at the end of it, when we finally threw in the towel and left, the score was ranger, seven fish over five pounds; our gang, zip.

I remember another spring when we had *the word* from another old character who claimed to have the secret for taking togue in the Allagash. He said the date was precisely May 17, regardless of the weather or the size of alder leaves.

All you did was hike in for three miles over the worst carry in Maine, set up camp at a spot marked on the map, and catch a mess of chubs on flies. Then you hooked a chub lightly under the dorsal fin, added weight, and sunk him to bottom in 30 feet of water off the ledge that stuck out from the campsite.

"The chub will never hit bottom," he said. "A togue will take it every time."

So on May 15 we were there, two days early. We set up camp, caught some chubs, and started fishing. That night we ate chubs for supper. Next day we fished from dawn till dark. Caught plenty of chubs and kept them alive in the coffee pot. We hooked them lightly under the dorsal fin, weighted them, and pitched them off the only ledge there was. They made it to the bottom without being intercepted and stayed down there until they drowned. We never got a strike. Supper was chubs again.

Next day, on the 17th, the old man arrived.

"Let's see 'em," he said, rubbing his hands together.

"Haven't got any," we said.

"Well, then you're doing something wrong," he said without hesitation. "Let's see how you're rigged."

I reeled up and showed him the lightly hooked, very lively chub.

"For Gawd's sakes," he crowed. "It's alive! You can't catch 'em on *live* chubs; it's gotta be dead ones!"

"I don't remember you saying that," I stammered.

"Well, I thought you knew that much," he snorted.

With that he unhooked the chub, rapped it over the head, and then scuffed it on the rocks, rubbing off scales and making the bait look extremely dead. Then he hooked it back on to my original equipment and chucked it out.

The bait sunk about halfway down, and suddenly the line started going out.

"There, you see?" he said. "Now let it run out until he stops. When he starts moving again, tighten up on him, and when you feel him pulling, sock it to him."

That was a seven-pounder. When the old man geared up and made his first cast, he took one that went 10. The fish ran that size for three more days.

The next year I went up there again on the same dates, sure that I could pull a repeat.

When I got to the campsite, however, two other fishermen were already there. They were the most sodden, fly-bitten, frustrated people I'd ever seen.

"Been fishin' here three days and haven't had a strike," they said. "Some damn fool outdoor writer wrote about catching lake trout in a place that sounded just like this. We thought we had it knocked, but he probably just made the whole thing up."

"You using chubs?" I inquired.

"Yep."

"Dead or alive?" I queried, sure of what the answer would be and beginning to sense the delight I would feel when I showed them their error. I'd catch a fish, then tell them who wrote the story.

"Dead ones," one of them replied. "We've tried them live, too, of course."

"Dead ones didn't work?" I questioned, beginning to get a sinking feeling.

"Nope," the guys said. "There're no fish here."

I rigged up and started fishing exactly the way we had done the year before on the same date in precisely the same place, but nothing happened. Not a bite.

That night we fed the bedraggled fishermen some spaghetti from our pot and gave them some El Diablo Azul 151 proof rum, but I didn't divulge my name and swore my companion to secrecy.

I imagine that 90 percent of the landlocked salmon taken in Maine each year are caught by trolling, but that is simply an indication of the most popular fishing method, not necessarily the best way to take salmon. Flyfishing for salmon with nymphs in the rivers and streams that feed or drain salmon lakes, for example, is almost entirely overlooked.

One spring a bunch of us were canoeing and fishing the Rangeley Lakes. During a midmorning cloudburst we pulled in at the mouth of Rangeley Stream to wait out the downpour. Sitting there hunched in our ponchos, we noticed that raindrops weren't the only things making circles on the water.

"Trout or chubs, I wonder," Al muttered. "I'm going to find out."

He rigged a flyrod and tied on a big fuzzy green nymph. Then he waded out in the rain. I can still see the water pouring off him and the lightning splitting the clouds. But those were the days of bamboo rods, not graphite, so he wasn't the walking lightning rod he would be today.

The fish were rising on the far side of the stream, against a bank of overhanging alder bushes, and it was impossible to estimate their size because the driving rain pounded the fish rings flat the instant they were made.

Al dropped his nymph close to the alder and kept a tight line as the drift began. We all saw the swirl and the way the line jumped and straightened out. Al tightened up and gave a methodical twitch, the way you do when you think you are hooking a chub and don't care whether you hook him or not, and then all hell broke loose. The fish went straight into the air, shimmering silver, hit the water with a splash, jumped again, and then ran for the lake.

"Aiyiyi!" Al cried, his reel singing that high staccato we all love so.

"It's a salmon!" somebody yelled.

"Ya, ya. Salmon iss right," our Swiss friend chortled. Al was still smoking then, and fighting the salmon with one hand, he started digging in his pocket for a cigarette. I can still see him standing there in the pouring rain, somehow lighting the cigarette and then playing the fish in the downpour with his head wreathed in smoke, like some sort of demon.

We all got in the act then and found that ranks of salmon were lying in the current and taking nymphs that were hatching in the streambed. That morning got me started nymphing for salmon, and it's been a successful method ever since—and a lot more fun than trolling.

We were all starting to give up smoking in those days, but never sure whether we were quitting for good or just temporarily. I remember one spring trip when Al and I had each taken vows not to smoke as long as the other one didn't—but we didn't trust each other not to sneak one when the other wasn't looking.

We were up on the Penobscot nymphing for salmon, and the fishing was good. I knew that the one time Al always had to have a smoke was when he had a big fish on, so when I fished down around a bend and spied him up ahead with his rod plunging to the beat of a big fish, I was not surprised to see smoke drifting away from him on the breeze.

"That son of a gun," I muttered, mentally registering that his breach of faith licensed me to break my own vow. I started down toward him, ostensibly to marvel at his fish but secretly wondering if I should bum a smoke, when I saw Al start pounding at his neck.

At first it was just his left hand doing the smacking while his right still fought the fish, but then he jammed the plunging rod under his arm and started slapping his neck with *both* hands and wading for shore in a frenzy, clouds of smoke pouring from him.

On shore he flung down his rod and started yanking his shirt and flyvest off over his head. Needless to say I hurried down to help kill his attacker, but when I got there I found my friend dunking his shirt.

"What in hell's going on?" I asked.

"This damn thing set my collar on fire," he snapped. "Burnt me like hell."

Then he showed me. He had one of those little magnifying glasses pinned to his hat so he could see when he tied on tiny flies, and the sun beating down through the glass had ignited his collar.

"It could kill you, that thing," he said.

"What about the fish?" I questioned.

"Got off," he said.

"I thought you were sneaking a smoke," I told him.

"Wisht I had," he said. "You got one?"

"Nope."

"Me neither."

So we had quit after all.

Those spring trips are fun. Each year we have more to remember of times past and waters waded and paddled. There have been some good fish along the way, and we recatch them around the campfire. And there is always new water someone has heard good things about that we plan to try. Rarely do we get stuck on any one place. Ours is a traveling circus, and new places draw us with magnetism.

Those two old men up on Seboomook had it right about the memories, though. It doesn't matter so much just how good the fishing is at any precise moment because we have all those earlier trips and other fish to recall and talk about. Sometimes it seems to be enough just to be there fishing in a beautiful spot, and to hell with whether or not they're biting.

50

THE BOW RIVER EXPERIENCE

Gerald Almy

This Alberta stream hasn't been stocked in decades so the trout are wonderfully wild and full of fight, reports this SPORTS AFIELD fishing master. (May 1986)

WHAT STRIKES one first about the Bow River—aside from its beauty as it twists its way eastward in lazy serpentine bends—is the sheer ferocity and unfettered spirit of its fish. These are no hatchery patsies. The Bow hasn't been stocked for decades, and the fish inhabiting it are incredibly strong, full of the spunk only wild, stream-spawned trout can display. The initial fish you hook will probably sprint off on a line-stealing dash, then shatter the river's surface with three or four arching leaps. When you work it in, you'll be amazed that the trout isn't twice the size it turns out to be.

After soaking in the grandeur of the river and marveling at the strength of these silvery rainbows and saffron-flanked browns, your focus shifts to the sheer abundance of the quarry. Maybe three or four casts after you release your first Bow River trout, another smashes into your fly.

By the time you float and strip streamers through a half mile of river or wade and drop dry flies over 100 yards of rise-dimpled flat, a final major impression asserts itself: These are *all* large fish. That 15-incher you started off with was no fluke. Indeed, if anything, it's a trifle small for the average you take over the course of the day's fishing. Sixteen to 17 inches is the norm. Many reach the 19- to 21-inch class.

A gorgeous river, laden with large, wild trout. Those, in a nutshell, are the impressions that dominate when one finally makes his first long-anticipated pilgrimage to this river that flows east from the Canadian Rockies through the shimmering wheatfields of the Alberta prairie.

For years I had heard rumors about this fabulous fishery. When the jet thumped down onto the Calgary runway, and I realized I had finally arrived, I tried to prepare myself for a letdown. My hopes were built so high there was no way the river could satisfy my great longings. But it did—even under the most inauspicious conditions.

Eric Grinnell, wildlife biologist and owner of Silvertip Outfitters, shoves the beamy johnboat into the sparkling Bow five miles above Carseland Weir, as cattle mill around us in the shade of cottonwoods. A searing sun bears down relentlessly. It's midafternoon on the hottest July 10 in Alberta's history—93°F.

Not propitious conditions for fishing. Eric is still confident, however, we'll enjoy good sport in spite of the scorching heat and bright midday sun.

Rowing hard across current, the guide flings the anchor overboard and leaps out, directing me to the edge of a gurgling riffle where it drops off into a deep green pocket. Casting a Size 2 marabou leech to the head of the dark lie, I mend line and strip the offering in with sharp, animated tugs. Three pulls and the rod tip lurches downward.

"Just a little one," Eric needles as the 15-inch rainbow slices across stream, leaps twice, then powers downstream in a drag-burning run that reaches the backing.

A little one? Maybe so. The next fish, on the third cast of the trip, goes 17 inches. The fifth cast produces a 16-incher. Two more trout strike short before we hop in and continue the float. With five miles of river to probe before dark, there's no use dallying in one spot long.

The fishing slacks off somewhat from that torrid beginning pace as we drift downstream, slapping jumbo streamers into eddies, beaver huts and logjams. Still, every fifth or sixth cast draws either a solid hookup or a flash of color as a trout lunges at the fluttering leech fly and misses. Most are rainbows; a few are browns.

By 7:00 p.m. we drift into Eric's favorite dry-fly water. Trout are already beginning to dimple the surface of the long, slick glide. Pulling the johnboat up on shore, we rig up lighter 5-weight outfits and begin chipping away at the risers. Small olive-brown *Baetis* mayflies are hatching, and a few Pale Morning Duns and spinners are floating on the water. But it's the rusty-hued caddis that the trout are busily slurping from the surface. We cast No. 16 dries above the riseforms and spend the next four hours fighting scrappy rainbows.

I lost count of the number of trout fought that afternoon on the Bow. Streamers hooked at least 30 while Eric handled the oars. Probably 20 of those made it to the boat to be released. Dries accounted for a similar number of trout as a cool, soothing dusk settled over the Alberta prairie. All of the dry-fly-caught fish ran 14 to 19 inches, except one gorgeous rainbow that taped 21. Considering that we hadn't hit the river until 4:00 p.m., it was a phenomenal day's sport.

It was nearly 11:00 p.m. when darkness finally fell. We reeled in and continued floating as squadrons of beavers splashed water in minidetonations and mallards powered east against the darkening blue sky. A short way downstream we pulled in and set up the tent, then built a fire. As we dined on steaks, potato salad and wine and watched the campfire burn down, Eric spoke of the Bow.

A few locals, he said, and a handful of visiting anglers had known about the Bow's quality sport for years. It was Russell Thornberry, however, who got the ball rolling toward establishing the river as a world-renowned fishery when he started a guiding business on the Bow in the late 1970s. For the first time, traveling sportsmen who didn't want to bring boats, trailers and shuttle vehicles could simply fly or drive to Calgary and floatfish the river hassle-free. Once those logistics were taken care of by the availability of a guide service, the Bow quickly became recognized as perhaps the finest accessible flyfishing river in North America for mixed browns and rainbows of exceptional sizes.

Born in the Columbia Icefield in Banff Park, the Bow slices eastward across Alberta for 325 miles to the Oldman River, where it becomes the Saskatchewan and drains into Hudson Bay. Until it nears Calgary, the Bow has the makeup of a typical steep-gradient, infertile freestone stream. As it approaches this city of 620,000, however, several dams dampen its fluctuations and spare the stream from destructive spring scouring. Nutrient input (phosphates and nitrogen from treated sewage) also flow in here, enriching the stream's chemistry. This combination of factors transforms the Bow into a fecund river that has all the characteristics of a giant spring creek—heavy weed growth, bountiful populations of insects, and large, abundant trout. Growth rates and population densities of fish in the Bow downstream from where the nutrients flow in are astounding, matching those of the most fertile fisheries in North America.

Despite all the nutrients, the river is sparkling and attractive. Although it flows through a major city, there is little access and virtually no development along its banks. The valley the Bow slices through outside of town is a secluded patchwork of grazing prairie, steep gray cliffs and wooded islands. Tall cottonwoods and black poplars line the banks. Islands are dotted with willows and sweet-smelling spruce. The pungent aroma of sage wafts on prairie winds. Mule deer roam the rough breaks and cactus-spattered coulees along shore. Whitetails thrive on the untouched islands. Swallows and gulls feed on the river's ubiquitous insects. Great blue herons, mergansers, cormorants and pelicans are sighted often as you drift in the flow.

The majority of fishing on the Bow takes place from 10 miles above Calgary, where the first of two doses of nutrients flows in, downstream for 50 miles to the Carseland Weir. Formerly this river was managed with a 20-trout limit, and baitfishing was permitted. Now that the world-class quality of the fishery has been recognized, regulations have been upgraded. From Calgary downstream to Carseland the limit is currently two fish, *maximum* size 16 inches. Only artificial lures are allowed.

Eric Grinnell is one of the few people who have probed the stretch of water below Carseland, and he's the only outfitter currently offering trips in this section. He believes the sport should be good for 40 miles below the weir. So far he's tried the first 20. This is all near-virgin territory for flyfishermen. For the most part, the browns and 'bows in this stretch have only seen a few spoons cast on spin gear by the Blackfoot Indians, through whose reservation the lower river flows.

Eric and I floated the first 10 miles of this lower water on the second day. We were joined by Calgary chiropractor Peter Korebisch. We cast huge white Marabou Muddlers, leech flies and Zonkers into back currents and sweepers along shore, stopping often to wade riffles where the trout hung in the deep green pockets. We took plenty of trout, but four pounds was the heftiest our streamers could pry from the river.

Toward evening, as we neared the takeout point, we traded our 7-weight outfits for 5-weight wands, and found receptive risers in a side slough off the main flow. In the final hour of daylight I put an Elk Hair

Caddis over a dozen risers. All 12 rose up and softly sipped in the fly. Two broke off; two pulled free; eight were fought in and released. Across the channel, Peter found a similar number of obliging surface feeders. Between us, we wrapped up the day with nearly 60 trout brought to hand, an equal number pricked and lost. It had been a long, delightful float, and at 10:30 p.m. we pulled off the stream and headed for Calgary for a hot shower and a midnight meal.

Eric was booked to guide Curt Gowdy, an avid Bow River fan, on my third day in Alberta. But Jim McLennan, who runs the Orvis Country Pleasures fishing shop in Calgary with co-owners Don Cahoon and Neil Jennings, agreed to fill in and take me to some of his favorite dry-fly haunts on the upper river. Jim was one of the first guides to work the Bow back in the 1970s, and he knows the river intimately. "Fish seem to rise better on the water closer to the city," he said as we finished omelets and pastry and piled into his pickup. "We should find trout surface feeding all day long where we're going today."

Some of the fish would be rising in the main river current. But much of the best dry-fly sport on the Bow, Jim said, takes place in quiet backwaters, side sloughs and narrow channels off the main river. At just such a location, we planned to launch Jim's boat in order to reach a prime wading area on the opposite shore. But to clear a path, I first had to catch a rainbow that was in our way, gently sipping caddisflies and Pale Morning Dun spinners from the surface. After all, we couldn't just launch the boat right on top of a rising trout. Dropping a No. 16 Elk Hair Caddis in the direction the trout was cruising, I waited patiently and was soon rewarded with the slurping rise of a 21-inch rainbow. *Now* we could launch the boat, cross the river, and hike up to the water Jim intended us to fish.

Well, almost. Trouble was, more fish kept getting in the way! The spot McLennan had in mind was a mile upstream. But every time we trekked 50 or 60 yards, we'd spot another trout rising. We took turns trying for the large ones—which meant virtually every fish we saw boil—and each trout obligingly drifted up and sipped in our offerings.

In contrast to the lower water I had fished with Eric, where nine out of 10 fish were rainbows, about 50 percent of the fish we caught in this area were browns.

After landing close to a dozen trout, we finally reached the glide Jim had planned to fish all morning. It was nearly noon. I saw quickly why he was so captivated with this spot. Broad-shouldered trout were lined up in pods of three and four, all 16- to 22-inchers, as far as you could see upstream. We fished over them—catching some, being spurned by others—until 2:30, when we took a lunch break.

After a leisurely meal, we had six more hours of fishing light remaining, due to the long summer days. This evening Jim picked a five-mile stretch to float, from the provincial park in Calgary downstream.

As we drifted we saw a few Pale Morning Duns on the water, but the bulk of the hatch had petered out earlier than usual this year, due to hot weather. Normally, these elegant mayflies offer the best dry-fly fishing of the year on the Bow. They can provide steady surface action from mid-June through July, with rising activity lasting from midmorning well into the afternoon. The *Baetis*, or Blue-winged Olive, is another important fly on the river, offering good angling periodically from August into October.

The third major mayfly on the Bow is the *Tricorythodes*, a tiny white-winged, black-bodied insect imitated with Size 20 to Size 24 hooks. Spinnerfalls of this mayfly on August and September mornings can literally blanket the water, drawing hordes of fish topside. The fishing, however, is quite difficult. With so many naturals on the surface and the fish gulping up to half a dozen flies at a time, the odds of them taking your tiny imitation are slight.

The caddis is the final aquatic insect of importance to dry-fly anglers on this river. Several species emerge sporadically during the day and come off in heavy clouds just before dark. Patterns such as the Elk Hair Caddis (Sizes 12 to 18, in rust brown or olive) are very effective during these hatches. These are also good workhorse searching flies to use during the day, when few naturals are present.

Besides these aquatic hatches, the Bow provides spectacular grasshopper fishing from late July through September. Some anglers wade and fish hopper patterns from Sizes 4 to 10, but the most fun comes when you float downstream, tossing the big dries to lies along the bank as you drift. Patterns such as Joe's Hopper, Dave's Hopper and the Letort Hopper all score well.

The most useful dry during my visit was the caddis, Sizes 14 and 16. Jim and I didn't even rig streamer rods this final evening, but instead just drifted along looking for dimples near shore. When we saw good risers, Jim would pull the boat in below, and we'd stalk up on foot and try for them.

The fishing was outstanding along the whole stretch we floated, but one tiny side riffle proved particularly intriguing. The water was barely six inches deep, yet we could make out a few tiny riseforms breaking the surface. I cast the buoyant caddisfly over them, and every one turned out to be a large trout. Before we left the spot, I had hooked three browns in the 18- to 20-inch class. It was fabulous dry-fly fishing.

Yet in spite of this incredible angling and the easy access Calgary provides, the Bow is still lightly fished. On busy weekends, McLennan says, a dozen guide boats and a few private craft will work the first 40 miles of water below Calgary. On a big river, such pressure is negligible.

The day was waning fast now. I could feel a sadness that my time on the river was drawing to a close. As the sun set, clouds of caddis began hatching. The tent-winged insects covered our clothing and made it difficult to breathe without inhaling them as they swarmed around our faces. The trout, which had been feeding well all day long, now went into a frenzy of rising. Wrapped up in the excitement of the scene, I shotgunned my casts, hooking a trout here, a trout there, of mixed sizes. Jim, accustomed to this frenetic display of surfacing fish, took a more studied approach and worked strictly over large trout, landing several beauties and losing a big one. Finally, it grew too dark to see our flies or the riseforms of the trout. Reluctantly, we reeled in and floated down to the takeout point by starlight, soaking in the sounds and smells of the night.

51

TROUT IN WINTER

John Gierach

If cabin fever has you down, try tailwater fishing.
(January 1987)

ALL SPORTSMEN get cabin fever now and then, but the most susceptible seem to be trout fishermen. They make it through the fall in good shape (some of the best fishing is in the fall), and some even manage to stay amused through the holidays, but at some point every winter the dreaded shack nasties move in and settle like pack ice. Relatives, coworkers and friends of trout anglers will testify to this, though it's probably best not to ask the fishermen themselves about it until spring.

There are some who have found a cure, however. In many parts of the country, dedicated trout fishermen with a sense of adventure solve the problem in the most obvious way: They go trout fishing anyway.

In most trout fishing areas, the streams and rivers remain largely unfishable through the coldest winter months. Slower-moving streams often freeze bank to bank. Faster ones with steeper gradients may stay open, but they'll still be too cold for the fish to be active.

A welcome exception to this situation is the tailwater fishery. A tailwater is a stretch of stream immediately below a bottom-release dam, a piece of water usually at least a few miles long where the water stays relatively warm (by trout standards) and that remains open and fishable through winter.

According to Robin Knox, a fisheries biologist with the Colorado Division of Wildlife, the 39°F water in a reservoir is the densest. It sinks to the bottom and comes out of the dam into the stream below, making it roughly 7°F warmer than what it would normally be. Now 39°F water isn't what I'd call bathtub-warm, but then I'm not a trout. At 39°F, the water will stay open and will be warm *enough* to keep the fish feeding on something like a regular basis.

They'll usually have plenty to feed on, too, because reservoirs act as nutrient sinks. Knox said that the mechanics of this are complex, but the upshot is that the water below the dam is noticeably richer in nutrients than the water in the streams above the reservoir. Higher nutrient levels grow more aquatic vegetation, which breeds large numbers of aquatic insects, which, in turn, produce fat, healthy trout.

The nearly year-round growing season doesn't hurt, either. In fact, a good tailwater stream is like an artificial spring creek.

Dams are a ticklish and emotional subject with trout anglers, and rightly so. Still, without making any other comments on the construction of impoundments on otherwise free-flowing trout streams, it's worth noting that tailwaters can be excellent places to fish, and in many parts of the country they're the only places where you can catch trout in winter without drilling through ice.

Winter trout fishing in tailwater streams usually means nymphing. The water will be warm enough for the trout to be awake and hungry, but it's still cool, even for the cold-blooded. The fish will be less likely to expend energy rising to a dry fly or going much out of their way to chase down a streamer, spinner or plug.

Are there exceptions? Of course. This is trout fishing we're talking about, the sport where exceptions have been known to prove the rule. In my years of fishing tailwaters in winter, I've seen trout caught on slowly retrieved spinners, have caught a few myself on streamers, and have encountered rises to good hatches of midges and tiny mayflies during which trout could sometimes be persuaded to take a dry fly. Finding trout rising to mayflies in January or February can renew your faith in the overall goodness of life, but it's certainly not something that you can count on.

On most winter days, tailwater trout will be found in the deepest, slowest water, where they will feed somewhat lazily on whatever aquatic nymphs the current brings them. The ideal spot to look for is a deep, slow run directly downstream from a good riffle. Riffles serve as both water aerators and insect factories in trout streams, and a deep hole below one will have the oxygenated water, slow current and nymph supply that trout want in winter.

Fishing nymphs on or near bottom in flowing water can be done with either a spinning or a fly rod. Tie the fly onto the end of a light monofilament line or leader, then add some weight about a foot to 18 inches up the line. Reusable split-shot is popular with many anglers, while others prefer products such as Twistons (match-shaped lead strips) or Shape-a-Wate (a kind of lead putty). Whatever is used, it should be easy to put on and take off, as you'll no doubt be changing the amount of weight to account for different depths and current speeds.

Remember that the currents near the bottom of a stream are slower than those at the surface. Use enough weight to get down where the fish are. If you don't hang up on the bottom periodically, you're probably not fishing deep enough. Losing flies is an unavoidable part of the deal.

Once you're rigged up with a nymph pattern and a weighted leader, make a quartering upstream cast, allow the fly to sink down to bottom, and let it drift past you in the current. Leave a little slack in the line so that no action is imparted to the fly. What you're trying to imitate is a natural insect that has been washed loose from the bottom and is now drifting helplessly.

Many experienced nymph fishermen prefer unweighted flies for this operation. After all, they say, all the weight you need is on the leader, and an unweighted fly drifts more realistically in the subtle, sub-surface currents.

The strike to a deep-drifted nymph is often soft and difficult to detect. The fish are generally too lazy to really slash at the fly (or to move very far for it, either), and signs of the take are deadened by the weight on the line. Sometimes all you'll see is the flash of a fish or a momentary hesitation in the line as it moves downstream.

There are also times when you won't see anything. Even experts at this method admit that they get more strikes than they're aware of. Good nymph fishers set the hook at any indication of a strike, and the best of them connect about 50 percent of the time.

One thing that will help improve your odds is a strike indicator. The tip of a floating flyline will work, as will a small, brightly colored cork float. Even then, it's not always easy to tell what's going on down on the bottom of the river.

In recent years, dead-drift or "shortline" nymphing has been touted as a hot flyfishing technique. It's actually quite similar to a standard method used by baitfishermen who work running water. Some split the difference by using a long flyrod for extra reach and drift control, fitted with either a light spinning reel or a flyreel loaded with 4-pound monofilament.

The right fly pattern also makes a difference in winter nymphing situations. Trout have a reputation for selectivity anyway, and cold winter water seems to further chill their sense of curiosity. If your fly doesn't resemble insects they're used to seeing, they'll probably ignore it.

You can get an idea of the size and color of the predominant insects in a stream by turning over a few rocks in a riffle to see what's there. Most good tailwaters are well known, at least on a regional basis, and you can usually get some recommendations on fly patterns before you arrive on the water by contacting flyshops or guide services in the area. Favored local flies, especially those with a seasonal flavor, should never be ignored, even if they don't seem to make sense or fall outside your personal theories about trout fishing.

Because tailwaters often produce exceptional fisheries, many of them are now protected by special regulations. There also may be some tackle restrictions (bait is often prohibited), and many have reduced bag limits, slot limits or even a catch-and-release rule. Naturally, you should always check the current laws before fishing a tailwater.

The best times to fish for trout in the summer are usually the cool evenings and mornings, while in winter you'll often find better action from midday through late afternoon or through the "heat of the day," if that's not too relative a term.

The best days for winter fishing are often those with low, gray skies and perhaps even some light sleet or snow. Trout seem to be much less skittish under overcast skies than they are on bright days. Many anglers also believe that a falling barometer will make the fish feed more enthusiastically.

The best day of winter fishing I've ever had was in some of the worst weather I've experienced in the field, and that includes duck hunting. My friend A.K. Best and I drove the 2½ hours to a local tailwater on a February day that, by all predictions, would be perfect for fishing. It was supposed to be overcast but calm, with highs in the 40s and a falling barometer. The storm was supposed to arrive from the western slope of the Rockies the following morning.

The problem was that in this part of Colorado, as in other mountainous areas, the weather isn't so much predicted as it is *narrated*. The storm, coming a full day early, caught us at the trailhead; by the time we reached the river, a steady snow was falling at a steep angle pushed by a stiff breeze. The air temperature was about 30°F, and one can only guess the windchill factor.

How cold was it? Well, when we arrived at the place appropriately named the Ice Box Pool, we found at least 50 trout rising to mayflies, and the first thing we did was start a campfire and put on a pot of coffee. That's cold.

A.K. and I still argue over whether it was the most miserable or the most glorious day of winter fishing either of us has had. We put on every stitch of clothing we'd carried in, including fingerless wool gloves, and covered it all with rain slickers to break the wind. We wore heavy chest waders over longjohns and wool socks and tried to stay out of the water as much as possible. We were both cold before we'd even wet a line.

Once the lines *were* wet, they constantly froze to the guides on our rods. Our reel spools froze to the frames. Monofilament leaders made brittle by the cold snapped, leaving flies in fish. A trout caught and released meant wet fingers that stung for a few seconds before going numb. All of the above required a trip to the fire and a splash of hot coffee in a tin cup. You know how your fingers feel after they've been frozen and thawed too quickly a dozen times? It was awful, but on the other hand, we lost count of the trout we caught.

Winter fishing is, or should be, a considerable production, and most of that has to do with staying warm. Proper clothing is a must, and you'll have to dress more warmly for fishing than for, say, hiking. Fishing just doesn't involve the kind of exercise that keeps you warm.

Most experienced winter fishermen dress in the layered style with wool shirts, sweaters, down vests, jackets and shells that can be added, taken off, or vented as conditions dictate. A big, heavy coat might look cozy, but most of the time it will be either too much or not enough.

Remember that you lose a good deal of body heat through your head and hands. Quality gloves and a warm hat are essential. It's also a good idea to carry some sort of hooded rain shell or slicker. And it probably goes without saying, but make sure your waders don't leak.

Other items to take, preferably in a medium-sized day pack, include lunch (eating well helps keep you warm) and either a coffee pot or a thermos filled with coffee, hot chocolate or soup. I prefer the coffee pot because there's something hopelessly nostalgic about brewing coffee around a campfire on the banks of a trout stream in the dead of winter. In keeping with this, also take the wherewithal to build that fire quickly and efficiently. Even if you pride yourself on your fire-building skills, back yourself up with some dry matches, kindling and newspaper sealed in an airtight plastic bag.

The advantages of winter fishing? One is that you can have miles of the best trout streams all to yourself, streams that often suffer from too much fishing pressure in summer. Another is the satisfaction that comes from being out on the water catching trout when most of your colleagues are sitting home, waiting for spring.

Winter trout fishing takes a little extra effort, a slightly heavier pack than in summer and perhaps some research to find the right places. Beyond that, it's pretty much what you're used to. If you're careful and persistent, you'll probably catch fish, though there will be days when you don't. After all, it's just trout fishing—and that's the whole point.

OF SALAMI & NO. 32s

Michael Kimmel

Housatonic trout have seen it all—and the river's
dedicated anglers love it that way.
(September 1987)

FOUR FLYFISHERMEN in a cold mizzle at Sand Hole, four middle-aged men hanging tough. They'd poke around on their wading staffs, waft tiny flies across the channel under the west bank. Sand Hole's popular among Housatonic regulars, with relatively easy wading, and Sunday drivers often park on the shoulders of Route 7 to watch the flycasters there. Many are that good with the long wands; they have to be. Goof up a cast with 7X tippet, you lose the fly.

"Keep it simple," Ed Eveleth advised me in his Wilderness Shop. "If the fly isn't working, use a smaller size."

In mid-October, northwest Connecticut's uplands are all earth colors, leaf sugars, and the Blue-Winged Olives were pullulating, the year's final hatch. Twenty feet away from me in Monument Pool, good brown trout were sipping at the largess—what looked like a lot of skimming dots in the murky light. The drift was the thing, but you had to be able to see the No. 24, too. You need a long, unfettered drift that will make your morsel indistinguishable from the dust storm of real things around it. Then you and the trout have to find it. That initial session, I got one hit, I think, a *blip* off to my right. Then the rocks in front of me started vanishing, and I retreated to shore. 203/824-7861 is the number to know, the Northeast Utilities recording at Great Falls Dam, which tells you when the 135-year-old gates will open that week. The schedule varies widely, and the Housey rises fast, frequently leaving anglers on the wrong sides of channels. Generally, though, the river rises around noon, putting the trout down in the process, and recedes by late afternoon, in time for an evening hatch, as if with the trout fishermen in mind, which, indeed, is the idea. Northeast Utilities, the Connecticut Department of Environmental Protection (DEP) and the anglers have been getting along swimmingly of late.

Briefly, the Housatonic had gone the way of most eastern trout streams—lost its brookies to civilization and then subsisted on imported browns and rainbows until pollution became an issue. In 1980 the DEP suspended stocking in the river. The Housatonic Fly Fishermen's Association (HFFA), established in 1961, suggested that a no-kill policy be instituted, a catch-and-release program. The state said no, and the HFFA petitioned, then sued in superior court and won! In 1981 nine miles of the Housatonic became a Trout Management Area (TMA). And since polychlorinated biphenyls no longer enter the river and in this case seem to be degrading quicker than was originally calculated, toxic levels have receded dramatically, as much as 79 percent in the managed nine miles. Forget pristine; you've got to have a perspective. The Housatonic Valley is a painterly delight, spectacular, and in shooting distance of everyone between Boston and Philly. And the river is wide, rocky, tantalizing and prolific.

"These new biologists use terms like 'quality experience,' " Ed Kluck marvels. Kluck, 62, was the president of the HFFA when the organization went to court. A furrier in Hamden, he's currently chairman of a citizens' advisory council on conservation, claims his secret tactic has always been "never to go after them [the bureaucrats and politicians] with a baseball bat."

"There is a place in the world for 7X tippets" is actually the way Bob Orciari, the state's biologist on the Housatonic, puts it. "And, of course, the Housey's a logical one; it's that rich."

It is. Twilight, the river low again, I must have cast 50 times at a dozen 14- to 16-inch browns gorging themselves on *ephemeras* in a pool in Spring Hole, a couple hundred yards above the Housatonic Meadows Campground. All my life I'd been making "puddle casts," except now, when

I needed one. Now I was laying out rockets that resulted in two-foot drifts, and when I finally did sucker a fish into hitting, I nearly broke its jaw. It ain't easy, and I was rapidly decimating Eveleth's Olives, along with my tippet. When closing a knot of 2-pound or less, don't pull as you would on 2X. By then I was snarling. Not easy at all. Mercifully, soon I couldn't see the infinitesimal fly anyway, much less worry whether my turle knot was around its neck.

On my way back to the campground, a pair of anglers in Pine Pool, tight lines arabesques above them, a distinctively "eastern" scene, not so much because the leaves were red and yellow, or the Housey so full of Latin names. But because, I think, the hills are round in this part of the country.

Thank you, Lord, for Woolly Buggers on sinking tips. It's a relief to know what you're doing. Spring Hole was low and sunny at 8:00 a.m., and I was the only angler in it. And soon as I realized I'd hooked that first brown on the bright side of the river, and turned back around, I hooked another, this one solidly. The fish surfaced bucking, good looking, and zipped around the pool against my trusty 2X, 9 pounds, thank you. It was a 14-incher with a clipped right pectoral fin, which marked it a Bitteroot strain. The fish was bull necked, plump. The brown caddises start hatching around the middle of May and are followed by green caddises and Light Cahills, all of these fairly delicate, Nos. 14 to 18. Next come the whopping Brown and Green Drakes, No. 10s, and then the March Browns and Alderflies and the rest of the species, including some flurries of very tiny ants, all the way down to No. 26, what you call humility in a hurry. And the trout are eating all of these one item at a time and become very choosy, unless nothing happens to be hatching. Then they'll settle for Zonkers and Spruce Flies and Muddlers, Woollies and Buggers, Nos. 4 to 8, black or brown. Weighted flies are legal, split-shot are not. I used neither, because the sinking tip felt deadly. What I sensed that morning and am now convinced of is that the Housatonic is a surprisingly *exciting* river, with plenty of unpressured stretches within the TMA, which is by far the best trout habitat on the river. Many dry-fly fans ignore many miles of rocks and riffles. Fishing big wets three mornings in a row, I had steady action until around 11 o'clock, when the Olives would appear.

One of the reasons some holes are less popular than others: I hooked a really big brown later that first morning and, trying to stay with it, stepped off a boulder and fell in. It is a mother, that bottom, hellacious, impossible. Everyone advises everyone to bring a wading stick, yet every year guys break rods and nearly drown. Felt soles are another must (Kluck studs his with the *tips* of nails before the soles are attached to the uppers), as are polarized sunglasses. And, of course, you've got to watch every step.

The Meadows are comfortable, 451 wooded acres in the middle of the TMA and free that time of year. My neighbors were anglers and hunters up for the opening days of the pheasant season, a stocked hunt in the Housatonic State Forest, which explained the mound of shells in the Torrington K mart, which I drove to through blazing hills, passing innumerable stone walls and fences, towns founded in 1740, 1760, with names like Cornwall, Kent, Cordelia. What a difference a state makes. You can walk the entire TMA if you've a mind to, but even if you're in and out of it, when you're in it you're in a rough, jagged river, rather than some mere "mecca."

Push 'Em Up is the top of the TMA, a wide stretch with deep channels along both banks, riffles at its head. Bill Blotney, 39, the HFFA's new president and a student of Ed Kluck, is an assemblyman at Sikorski Helicopter and ties approximately 3000 flies a year professionally, a couple dozen of which he'd brought along just in case. They're parachute patterns, for their visibility and because they can pass for emergers; more minute Olives and a few Tricos.

"This river is a big part of my life," Blotney tells me while I'm ogling his handiwork. He says he's constantly on the phone with Kluck or Orciari. Holdover rates are rising, adult browns (11 inches) up to 50 percent, fingerlings around 35 percent (the Bitteroot youngsters lack adequate anti-smallmouth bass instinct); and the trout are surviving the dog days by stacking up in the mouths of feeder streams. This recently compelled the DEP to bar anglers from within 100 feet of these cool spots during stress periods.

"I can't understand some people," Blotney, a brawny, likable guy, says. "We've got something special here, the only catch-and-release program in the state, something we fought hard for. Twice as many trout are caught per fishing hour in these nine miles than in any put-and-take river in the state. I never expected to be president of any 361-member organization. But we matter. We helped create this. It's sort of precious to us."

He'll walk the banks, drive over from Milford for the day just for a visit, sometimes not even bothering to rig a rod. You could do a doctorate on caddises right here, or on trout genetics. This river could turn you on to Darwin, Mendel.

Blotney used a 7½-foot 5-weight bamboo that day. Eveleth uses a nine-foot 4-weight graphite. But the Housey can funnel a lot of wind, and neither rod would have been efficient with the chunky steamers I had been twitching all morning. Determined to fish one rod both ways, I stayed with an eight-foot 6-weight Cortland graphite that is more forgiving than my other rods.

Like Eveleth, Blotney believes in yard-long tippets. His second cast at the channel under the west bank—and the rod, a Duracane, wasn't slow at all—produced a nice fish. And while I absorbed the lesson, Blotney played the trout for several minutes, then removed the hook with a hemostat. Browns have good recovery rates when handled properly, like via hemostats or cotton nets, and barbless hooks are popular on the Housatonic. Paradoxically, though, so are treble hooks and bait in the upper two-thirds of the TMA, where they're legal, thanks to local pressure.

"As professionals, we felt bait was inappropriate in a catch-and-release area," Orciari responded, straight-out. "It's definitely unique, strange. . . . I think I've heard of one other instance, in Missouri. . . . Fortunately, most of the baitfishing's done in the spring, when the trout are least vulnerable to abuse. . . ."

I found a two-inch surface plug at Corner Hole; it had six fine-wire hooks. Have you ever seen one of those plugs maul an adolescent bass, a much tougher, hardier fish? Crazy.

Contrast that to the sanity of Blotney's parachute models, which dried fast and stayed dry. A drop of goop saturated them. Mine got so slick, however, it was like Peggy Fleming out there. And besides, the browns had all read Bachman and so knew better than to waste calories chasing fewer calories.

Inexplicably, then, I finally nailed a good fish. It bolted; I decided I'd better fight from the reel. Slowly. I was terrified. *Lightly. Lightly.* Pray. Easy . . . Ha! What good's Bachman gonna do you now? And what did these guys do before the invention of high-tech tippet material?

Blotney watched me release the fish and gave me a victory sign and motioned me toward shore, the river rising again.

Some addicts jump into their cars and speed downriver on Route 7 to gain a few extra moments of surface action. Others relax, stand around picnic tables tying blood knots. Chest flyboxes, those Plano 777RNs of the trout world, are not uncommon. Blotney's buddy Sam D'Ambruoso, a media consultant and HFFA member, told me he once fished No. 32s in vain. I told him I once struck out on salami after throwing everything else I had at a pod of humongous rainbows in a deep pool.

"What kind of salami?" he asked.

"A No. 32?"